Water Law & Policy

Water Law & Policy

Governance Without Frontiers

Elli Louka

OXFORD
UNIVERSITY PRESS

OXFORD
UNIVERSITY PRESS

Oxford University Press, Inc., publishes works that further Oxford University's objective of excellence in research, scholarship, and education.

Oxford New York
Auckland Cape Town Dar es Salaam Hong Kong Karachi Kuala Lumpur Madrid Melbourne
Mexico City Nairobi New Delhi Shanghai Taipei Toronto

With offices in
Argentina Austria Brazil Chile Czech Republic France Greece Guatemala Hungary Italy
Japan Poland Portugal Singapore South Korea Switzerland Thailand Turkey Ukraine
Vietnam

Published by Oxford University Press, Inc.
198 Madison Avenue, New York, New York 10016

Oxford is a registered trademark of Oxford University Press
Oxford University Press is a registered trademark of Oxford University Press, Inc.

Library of Congress Cataloging-in-Publication Data

Louka, Elli.
Water law & policy : governance without frontiers / Elli Louka.
p. cm.
Includes bibliographical references and index.
ISBN 978-0-19-537413-1
1. Water resources development—Law and legislation—European Union countries. 2. Water-supply—European Union countries—Management. 3. Water-supply—Law and legislation—European Union countries. 4. International rivers—European Union countries. I. Title.
KJE6094.L68 2008
346.2404'691—dc22

2008019071

Note to Readers
This publication is designed to provide accurate and authoritative information in regard to the subject matter covered. It is based upon sources believed to be accurate and reliable and is intended to be current as of the time it was written. It is sold with the understanding that the publisher is not engaged in rendering legal, accounting, or other professional services. If legal advice or other expert assistance is required, the services of a competent professional person should be sought. Also, to confirm that the information has not been affected or changed by recent developments, traditional legal research techniques should be used, including checking primary sources where appropriate.

(Based on the Declaration of Principles jointly adopted by a Committee of the American Bar Association and a Committee of Publishers and Associations.)

Contents

Preface

Water Law and Policy focuses on the first years of the implementation of the water framework directive (WFD), the legislation with the ambition to change the course of water management in Europe. The book is an outgrowth of a Marie Curie Fellowship granted by the European Commission of the European Union (EU).

The most fascinating part of this study was the fieldwork that involved interviews with a number of policymakers who are in charge of the implementation of the EU policy in water management. Interviews were conducted with the water directors of the countries examined in this study to determine the potential and impediments in the designation of a European integrated water management policy.

One of the challenges of any interview process is to elicit meaningful answers rather than prepared responses to formal questions. Policymakers in general are predisposed to present a favorable image of their organization. Most of the water directors who were interviewed were not only happy to note the successes of water management but also candidly acknowledged the challenges that still await us.

Further insights were gained through interviews with international commissions focusing on the transboundary management of waters (the International Commission for the Protection of Danube River and the International Scheldt Commission), and the various nongovernmental organizations and members of the European Commission. The bulk of the fieldwork for this study took place in 2006, although the secondary sources were updated throughout 2007 and 2008.

The study culminated to an International Conference that took place in May 2006. The proceedings of the conference were published at the end of 2007 by the Directorate General (DG) Environment of the European Commission, "*Implementing the EU Water Framework Directive: Towards Integrated Water Management in Europe.*" I would like to thank the conference participants for their contributions. Without these contributions, it would have been extremely difficult to complete this study.

Many special thanks to: Pavel Punčochář, Deputy Minister for Forestry and Water Management, Ministry of Agriculture, Czech Republic; Gyula Holló, Head of Department River Basin Management, EU Water Director, Ministry of Environment and Water, Hungary; Kálmán Papp, International Coordinator, Water Center, Ministry of Environment and Water, Hungary; Aurora Vasiu, Head of Management Plans Office, National Administration Romanian Waters, Romania; Lubka Katchakova, Deputy Minister, Ministry of Environment and Water, Bulgaria; Vladimir Dontchev, Water Directorate, Ministry of Environment and Water, Bulgaria; Elena Fatulová, Deputy Water Director, Ministry of Environment, Slovakia; Daniel Bond, Ribble Pilot Technical Advisor, United Kingdom Environment Agency; Maria Ghini, Ministry of Development, Greece; Willem Mak, Ministry of Transport, Public Works and Water Management, the Netherlands; Helena Matoz, Undersecretary, Ministry of the Environment and Spatial Planning, Slovenia; Željko Ostojić, Head of International Cooperation Department, State Water Directorate, Croatia; Ioannis Sibetheros, Special Secretary and Head, Central Water Agency, Ministry for the Environment, Physical Planning and Public Works, Greece; Gabrijela Grčar, State Undersecretary for Water, Slovenia; Bob Dekker, Ministry of Transport, Public Works and Water Management, the Netherlands; Dr. Erik Mostert, the Delft University of Technology, the Netherlands; Reolof Kruize, CEO of Waternet, the Netherlands and Ovidiu Gabor, Deputy Manager, National Administration "Romanian Waters."

Arnould Lefébure, Secretary General of the International Scheldt Commission, was very generous with his time during my visit to the commission, and Philip Weller, Executive Secretary, International Commission for the Protection of the Danube River (ICPDR), made sure than I got the most out of my visit there. My thanks also to Jasmine Bachmann, Technical Expert on Public Participation of the ICPDR; Gerhard Skoff, President, Danube Tourist Commission; Petur Farkas, Regional Environmental Center (REC) Country Office, Hungary; Leticia Hernando, Legal Advisor, European Landowners' Organization (ELO), Brussels; Rob Uijterlinde, Association of Water boards (UVW), the Netherlands; Vladimír Hudek,

Director, REC, Slovakia; Monika Kováčová, Danube Environmental Forum (DEF); Peter Whalley, Environmental Specialist with the Danube Regional Project (UNEP/GEF); Ursula Deutch, Secretary General, Danube Tourist Commission; Sergey Moroz, WWF Global Freshwater Programme-Europe; Dolf van Wijk, Euro Chlor; Frédéric De Hemptine, EUREAU; and Maria Karamanof of the Hellenic Council of State. I would like to thank Helmut Bloech, Deputy Head of Unit, Protection of Water & Marine Environment, DG Environment, the European Commission, who conveyed the nuances of the role of the commission in the implementation process.

I am very grateful and honored to have been a Marie Curie Fellow. My many thanks to Raffaele Liberali, Director of "The Human Factor, Mobility and Marie Curie Activities," during the duration of the fellowship, for his support; Alessandra Luchetti, Deputy Head of Unit, Marie Curie Actions Fellowships; and Dr. Pavlos Mouratidis. George Kremlis, Head of Unit, Cohesion Policy & Environmental Impact Assessment, DG Environment, European Commission, provided pointed remarks during the Marie Curie Conference in Athens.

Although the interview process provided many insights and stimulation for the completion of this study, none of the views presented in this book should be attributed to any particular interview and all potential errors and omissions are exclusively mine.

Elli Louka
January 2008

List of Acronyms

A

ARGE-ELBE, Consortium for the Prevention of Pollution of the Elbe

B

BSSAP, Black Sea Strategic Action Plan

C

CCNR, Central Commission for Navigation on the Rhine
CF, Cohesion Fund
CHR, International Commission for the Hydrology of the Rhine Basin
CIPMS, International Commissions for the Protection of the Moselle and Sarre against Pollution
COP, Conference of the Parties

D

DABLAS, Danube Black Sea task force
DCP, Danube Cooperation Process
DEF, Danube Environmental Forum
DGs, Directorates General (of the European Commission)
DRPC, Danube River Protection Convention

E

EAFRD, European Agricultural Fund for Rural Development
EC, European Community
ECMT, European Conference of Ministers of Transport
EEB, European Environmental Bureau

EEC, European Economic Community
EFTA, European Free Trade Association
EIA, Environmental Impact Assessment
EU, European Union
EUREAU, European Union of National Associations of Water Suppliers

F

FGG-Elbe, River Basin Consortium Elbe

G

GEF, Global Environment Facility

I

ICPBS, International Commission for the Protection of the Black Sea
ICPDR, International Commission for the Protection of the Danube River
ICPE, International Commission for the Protection of the Elbe
ICPR, International Commission for the Protection of the Rhine
IGKB, International Commission for the Protection of Lake Constance
INE, Inland Navigation Europe
IPPC, Integrated Pollution Prevention and Control Directive
IRBMPs, International river basin management plans
ISKB, International Navigation Commission for the Lake Constance
IWRM, Integrated water resources management

N

NAIADES, Navigation and Inland Waterway Action Development in Europe

P

PPCC, Prespa Park Coordinating Committee
PRTR, Pollutant Release and Transfer Register

R

RBMPs, River basin management plans
REC, Regional Environmental Center

T

TEN-T, Trans–European Transport Networks

U

UN, United Nations
UNDP, United Nations Development Program
UNECE, United Nations Economic Commission for Europe

W

WFD, Water Framework Directive 2000
WMO, World Meteorological Organization
WSSD, World Summit on Sustainable Development
WTO, World Trade Organization

Introduction

Can a natural resource, like water, that knows no national borders, be managed based on such borders? This book deals with the paradox of managing waters based on artificial and administrative boundaries and the damage done to a notion of coherent water policy by a number of activities and rules that have treated water as an exclusive national and local resource. Watercourses and lakes are often shared among states and regions, and the actions of states that are upstream of a river can have detrimental effects downstream. Conflict often erupts when a state, taking advantage of its position on a watercourse, restricts the water quantity released downstream or intentionally affects the water quality supplied. The fragmentation of water governance is at the root of the mismanagement of water resources. If fragmentation is the problem, integration must be the answer and integrated water resources management (IWRM) has been transformed from a managerial device into a political slogan deemed central for the future of global water management.

The book analyzes the efforts of the European Union (EU) to address water management in an integrated fashion, ensuring that states take into account the environmental externalities of their actions on water resources mandating that land uses (industry and agriculture) incorporate into their management the maintenance of sustainability of water resources. Using the European experience, as an example, the book attempts to answer the question: Is water governance without frontiers possible, and, if so, can practices used in Europe provide some insights for water management for other regions or countries of the world?

The book is an outgrowth of the Marie Curie study sponsored by the European Commission (the Commission) of the EU that involved a number of EU countries and international water commissions. In addition to secondary research, fieldwork in terms of interviewing officials of the countries involved in the implementation of the EU water policy were executed during the course of the study. A number of interviews were conducted with water directors of member states, members of the Commission, members of industry associations and civil society groups, and secretaries-general of international water commissions. The study is the amalgam of insights gained through research and fieldwork undertaken during the Marie Curie study and further work executed in understanding the European experience within the global context.

Part one examines the basic elements of water management policy and the fundamentals of EU organization and establishes why an integrated water management policy became essential for the furtherance of goals of the EU. Before the adoption of integrated water management, the EU water policy was fragmented with a number of institutional devices that addressed water management sector by sector (energy, agriculture, and transportation) or issue by issue (pollution by nutrients, pollution by hazardous substances, and drinkable water). The large number of international river basin districts in Europe, that generate upstream and downstream externalities, induced a gradual understanding that integrated water management is a must if serious efforts are to be undertaken to maintain some of the quality of water resources and to restore some of the damaged ecosystems. Part one analyzes the specifics of integrated water management and the difficulties involved in the application of the concept in Europe. The institutional development of the EU is examined with an emphasis on the development and evolution of integrated water management policy that was adopted in 2000 through the water framework directive (WFD). The EU has developed further strategies so that implementation is executed as much as possible uniformly all across Europe. Part one looks in depth into the EU implementation strategy, the issues it is facing, while it is evolving, as well as the coordination of various EU policies with the water policy (including regional policy, navigation policy, agricultural policy, and industrial policy).

Part two examines the structures that have been put in place in specific EU countries for the implementation of integrated water management policy. Part two examines the parameters of effective organization and policy issues states are confronted with when managing waters at the river basin scale. Integrated river basin management, as mandated by the EU policy, requires the management of waters at the river basin independent of administrative frontiers (regions, districts, and counties) that states have established. This presents problems as new river basin organizations may face institutional competition from other organizations that are functioning at the administrative level, generating, thus, a number of institutional veto players to the implementation of integrated water management policy. Part two proposes a framework for understanding policies adopted by states based on the number of institutional veto players that exist in a polity, and the establishment of river basin authorities. The existence of multiple institutional veto players necessitates the coordination of policies both at the horizontal level (ministry to ministry, and agency to agency) and at the vertical level (EU, international, national, and subnational). Part two examines in detail the coordination policies as they have been established in various states. Coordination policies are necessary especially in the absence of strong river basin institutions and the existence of multiple institutional players that wish to have a say in the congested administrative space.

A key to effective water governance is the provision of information, consultation with, and participation of stakeholders and the public in water management. Part three examines the right to information as the cornerstone of democratic ideal in today's societies. Today, the right of water users to be consulted on water management has been established in many states as a means to induce compliance under the following rationale: If those who use water are able to participate in making decisions on water use, they are likely to comply better with these decisions and to reduce, thus, enforcement costs. Part three examines the use of participation mechanisms as a realistic means of effective rulemaking. It further explores the participation of the larger public, the citizen, as a mechanism for the furtherance of democracy in many states.

Part four examines the institutional structures put in place at the international level to implement water management policy. Integrated water management mandates the management of water at the river basin, independent of national frontiers, so that water can be managed as the unity nature intended it to be and not through partitions established due to politics. In practice, if states share a water resource (river and lake), they need to cooperate in the management of the resource so that management by one state does not generate adverse externalities for other states. Cooperation, seemingly a rational proposition, is not always followed thereby leading to conflicts with regard to the management of water resources. In Europe, many water resources are managed cooperatively but there are still issues that need to be resolved in terms of upstream and downstream use and the priority granted to various uses. Cooperative arrangements for the management of resources have been established in the form international commissions created through international treaties. A number of such commissions have been established in Europe such as the commission for the protection of the Danube River and the commission for the protection of the Rhine River. These commissions have functioned more or less independent from each other and their authority has been parallel rather than subordinate to the authority of the EU. With the adoption of integrated water management policy, one begins to detect the transformation of international water commissions into water agencies of the EU. This is a remarkable development that is to foster integrated water management policy. Having said that, the number of international commissions that address various aspects of water management and bilateral arrangements–not always in sync with multilateral development–point out that integrated water management is still an aspiration rather than a reality and further efforts at integration need to be pursued as water policy is maturing.

Part five examines the right to participation of civil society in the work of international water commissions. While the right of participation of the public in the affairs of the state is increasingly propagated under ideals of direct democracy—elaborated as associative or functional democracy—the right of civil society to participate in international institutions is not that self-evident. This is because international commissions are examples of delegated models of authority. States, based on the constitutions of their establishment, have the power to delegate some of their authority to international institutions. Therefore, international institutions are primarily accountable to the states that have established them and not to the public of those states. Despite the delegated mode of authority of international institutions, civil society groups are increasingly involved in the work of international organizations and the functioning of international commissions. Part five examines the modes of consultation adopted by various international water commissions that seem to converge into a single standard and the reasons why further participation arrangements have yet to be explored. Part five analyzes the role of secretariats in the evolution of international water commissions. The role of secretariats in the manipulation of dynamics in an era of institutional evolution in Europe could be central in achieving the goals of water management.

Part six juxtaposes the EU experience and the Australian experience in an attempt to derive insights that will contribute to the success of the European experiment. Part six examines the various facets of the European policy as applied by member states—including the emphasis on centralization, multilevel parallel coordination, participation as a mechanism of decentralization—to derive the guiding parameters for the initiation of integrated water management policy in Europe and potentially in other international and local arenas.

Part One

The Making of Water Policy

Chapter 1

Water Governance

Life makes sense not when reason tells you that everything is as it should be. Life makes sense when some imponderable and apparently random event confirms your most irrational prejudices about the world.[1]

According to the United Nations (UN) Secretary-General Ban Ki-Moon, the civil war in the Sudan region of Darfur, the cause of thousands of deaths and atrocities in the last decade, was not a totally unpredictable and, thus, an unpreventable event.

> Almost invariably, we discuss Darfur in a convenient military and political shorthand—an ethnic conflict pitting Arab militias against black rebels and farmers. Look at its roots, though, and you discover a complex dynamic . . . Two decades ago, the rains in Sudan began to fail. According to UN statistics, average precipitation has declined 40 percent since the early 1980s. It is no accident that the violence in Darfur erupted during the drought.[2]

1 Michael Kimmelman, *The Accidental Masterpiece: On the Art of Life and Vice Versa* 85 (2005).
2 Ban Ki Moon, *A Climate Culprit in Darfur*, Washington Post, June 16, 2007, at A15.

Before the drought, according to the secretary-general, farmers and herders got along well, and black farmers welcomed herders as they crossed their land and shared the wells. After the rains stopped, the farmers fenced their land and wells because they feared their water supply would be depleted by the herders. As a result, conflict erupted that evolved into a full-fledged civil war in 2003.[3]

Sharing natural resources has been often a cause of conflict in Sudan. How to distribute revenues from the exploitation of oil resources, and apportion the waters of the Nile River and land property have been often the source of acrimony. Resource conflicts have been exacerbated by ethnic tensions, the militarization of the youth, and social inequities. The civil war in the Sudan is not simply the escalation of a rebellion of the black African South against the Northern Arab elite. How an oppressive regime decided to squash that rebellion has generated the catastrophe that Sudan is today. Thus, although the scramble over water resources may be at the root of the conflict, such a conflict does not deterministically have to ignite civil war. In Sudan, the social and economic conditions of the country and the political regime itself incite conflict.[4]

Water is everywhere. Water determines food security because we need water to irrigate agricultural fields. Water propels industrial growth. Clean water suitable for drinking is essential for healthy livelihoods. Water makes for the open space and environmental sustainability that is a prerequisite for the quality of human life and the survival of many ecosystems.

Today, many think that a water crisis can be defined as the failure of the supply of water to meet the demand arising from population growth and pressures imposed by the various industrial and agricultural uses of water resources. In 1995, the world withdrew 3,906 cubic kilometers of water for various purposes. By 2025, water withdrawal for most uses (domestic, livestock, and industrial) is projected to grow by 50 percent.[5] Where will this water come from?

The water crisis is not a crisis of water availability. It is a crisis of the mismanagement of the resource and the inadequacy of the institutions

---

3 *Id.*

4 *See Climate Change–Only a Cause among Many for Darfur Conflict*, UN Integrated Regional Information, June 28, 2007.

5 Mark W. Rosegrant *et al., Global Water Outlook to 2025: Averting an Impending Crisis* 2 (International Food Policy Research Institute and International Water Management Institute, Sept. 2002).

and governance structures that can ensure that every drop of water is used wisely to cover human needs and increase environmental sustainability. There is sufficient water for human needs. The problem is how to share water in an equitable manner to ensure both the service of human needs and the sustainability of natural ecosystems. This goal has yet to be achieved in many regions of the world.

Status of World Water Resources

Today, there are 1.1 billion of people without access to a water supply and 2.4 billion people without access to any sort of improved sanitation facility.[6] Most of these people live in developing regions, namely, Africa and Asia. Africa has the lowest total water supply coverage of any region, with only 62 percent of the population having access to improved water supply. The situation is even more precarious in rural areas where there is only 47 percent coverage compared with 85 percent coverage in urban areas.[7] Sanitation coverage in Africa is also poor, with only 60 percent of the population having access to adequate sanitation.[8]

Water coverage in Asia is the second lowest in the world after Africa at 81 percent. Access to sanitation coverage is the lowest of any region in the world at 48 percent.[9] Because of the large population size of countries like India and China, Asia is a region where the vast majority of people do not have access to an adequate water supply and sanitation. Eighty percent of the global population without access to improved sanitation and two-thirds without access to adequate water supply are located in Asia.[10]

In Latin America, the situation is better; water supply coverage at about 85 percent of the population and the sanitation coverage at about 78 percent.[11] However, there are large disparities between urban and rural areas. In Europe, the situation is even brighter, with 96 of population having access to an adequate water supply and 92 percent of population having access to improved sanitation coverage, again with some discrepancies

6 World Health Organization, *Global Water Supply and Sanitation Assessment 2000 Report*, at 7 (2000).
7 *Id.* at 41.
8 *Id.*
9 *Id.* at 47.
10 *Id.*
11 *Id.* at 55.

between the rural and the urban population.[12] In North America, 99.9 percent of population has access both to adequate water supply and improved sanitation, the highest of any region in the world.[13]

Despite an optimistic picture for water supply and sanitation, Europe and North America have their own share of problems about how to clean heavily polluted waters as a result of years of spiraling and negligent industrialization and infrastructure building that have heavily polluted and altered many water ecosystems and undermined the environmental sustainability of many watercourses, lakes, and coastal areas.

Most water abstracted in Europe is used for hydropower and industrial cooling (38 percent), while the rest is used for agriculture (30 percent), the public water supply (18 percent), and industry (14 percent excluding cooling water).[14] Because water is used intensively in Europe for industry and agriculture, there are several problems with the concentrations of various pollutants including phosphorous, nitrates, and ammonia in many water bodies. Although the concentrations of phosphorus have been reduced in the 1990s, it has been more difficult to tackle the pollution produced by nitrates and the ammonia that comes from sewage effluents, or as runoff from fields spread with animal manure.[15] Nitrates come mostly from agricultural fertilizers and affect not only surface waters but also the groundwater.[16] Discharging nutrients into the waterways (nitrates from agriculture and sewage from municipal plants) is the main cause of the slow death of rivers and lakes, which is called *eutrophication*. As nitrogen and phosphorous enter the waterways, they contribute to the excessive growth of plants. These plants, as they decay, deplete water oxygen levels, making waters inhospitable to life. The acidification of lakes, due to eutrophication and atmospheric pollution, continues to persist, despite some improvement in recent years.[17] Chlorinated hydrocarbons, hydrocarbons, and heavy metals are contributing to the deterioration of freshwaters in many countries in Europe and often are the source of local pollution.[18]

---

12 *Id.* at 65.

13 *Id.* at 71.

14 S. C. Nixon *et al.*, *Sustainable Use of Europe's Water? State, Prospects and Issues, Environmental Assessment Series No 7*, at 10 (European Environment Agency, 2000) [hereinafter *EEA paper*].

15 *Id.* at 16.

16 *Id.* at 19.

17 *Id.* at 22.

18 *Id.*

Many of Europe's waters are recording consistent improvements in recent years, but the general water quality is considered poor.[19] Although addressing the pollution from point sources (industrial plants) is manageable, coping with the diffuse sources of pollution (runoff from agricultural fields and urban areas and pollution from waste disposal) is a challenge for the future.[20]

The management of water resources in Asia and the Pacific presents various challenges that have to do with the uneven water distribution and the host of environmental problems arising from the increasing industrialization of the region. Precipitation is abundant in the southern slopes of the Himalayas, in western India, Indo-China, and Indonesia that receive rainfall of 1,500 mm to 3,000 mm annually. On the other hand, most of the northwestern part of the region is dry with an annual precipitation of less than 200 mm.[21] An idiosyncratic climatic condition in the region is the cyclical monsoon rainfall with distinctive wet and dry seasons. The uneven distribution of water all through the year and among countries and localities of the region has spurred the development of water infrastructure. There are 800 major reservoirs for irrigation, flood control, and the production of hydropower with a total capacity of 2,000 cubic kilometers and there are thousands of small reservoirs in China, India, Sri Lanka, and Russia.[22] Because of the increasing population in the region, the per capita allocation of water is expected to diminish, which may increase water stress in some areas.[23]

Agriculture is the main use of water in the region (84 percent), industrial use claims 10 percent of water, while domestic use is 6 percent of the overall water use.[24] Hydropower generation accounts for 50 percent of the electricity generated in some countries (50 percent of electricity generated in Bhutan and Nepal is by hydropower). Only 10 percent of the sewage released in the waters is treated, thus contributing to the transmission of water-related diseases. In China, during the mid 1990s, the Huaihe River received seven million tons of untreated sewage.[25] In the industrialized

---

19 *Id.* at 19.
20 *Id.* at 25.
21 *State of the Environment in Asia and the Pacific* 76 (UN Economic and Social Commission for Asia and the Pacific and Asian Development Bank, 2000).
22 *Id.* at 77.
23 *Id.* at 78–79.
24 *Id.* at 79.
25 *Id.* at 84.

regions of Asia, water bodies are being polluted by high concentrations of metals and toxic chemicals that often exceed national standards.[26] The siltation of water bodies as a result of increasing deforestation and soil erosion is acute in a number of countries. For instance, in the Ganges, Brahmaputra, and Yellow River basins, erosion is responsible for an annual yield of over 1,000 tons of sediment per square kilometer of land.[27] Another problem in the region is the increasing salinity of waters as a result of the excessive irrigation, mining, and deforestation that mobilizes salts and deposits them in high concentrations in surface waters and groundwater bodies. Asia and the Pacific region have the world's greatest concentration of soils affected by salt.[28]

Latin America and the Caribbean are rich in water resources. Although Latin America claims 15 percent of the world's land and 8.4 percent of the population, it receives 29 percent of total precipitation and it is the home of one third of world's renewable water resources. Disparities in the distribution of water across the region, however, could generate conflicts. The Gulf of Mexico, the South Brazilian Atlantic, and the Paraná-Uruguay-La Plata Basins carry 40 percent of the region's population and occupy 25 percent of the territory but have access to only 10 percent of water resources of the region.[29] Agriculture accounts for about 73 percent of total water use and domestic consumption accounts for 18 percent of water use while industry uses 9 percent of water resources.[30] Because agriculture is the main water use, it is also the main source of pollution. Untreated sewage and wastewater contribute to the deterioration of waters in Latin America and the Caribbean.[31] In Peru, high doses of agrochemicals used to grow coca crops are discharged into the rivers exacerbating pollution.[32]

The distribution of water resources is uneven in Africa where many countries are experiencing water scarcity while others are endowed with plentiful water resources.[33] Most freshwater resources are located in western

26 *Id.* at 85.
27 *Id.*
28 *Id.*
29 United Nations Environment Program (UNEP), *Global Environmental Outlook: Latin America and the Caribbean* 78 (2003).
30 *Id.* at 83.
31 *Id.* at 84.
32 *Id.*
33 Economic Commission for Africa, *State of the Environment in Africa, ECA/FSSDD/01/06*, at 55 (2001)[hereinafter *State of Africa*].

and central Africa. Northern Africa, the Horn of Africa, and southern Africa are experiencing water scarcity. Africa is home to the world's longest river, the Nile River; the second largest river, in terms of flow and basin, is the Congo River. The central and southwestern African countries produce 95 percent of Africa's total water flow while the arid and semiarid zones produce only 5 percent. Africa has seventeen rivers with catchment areas greater than 100,000 square kilometers and 160 lakes, most of which are transboundary.[34] Groundwater makes 15 percent of Africa's water resources but, in some countries, it is more than 75 percent of drinking water supply.[35] This is the case for the North African countries of Libya, Tunisia, Algeria, and Morocco.[36] Some countries, including Algeria, Egypt, Libya, Mauritius, Morocco, Tunisia, and South Africa, use desalinated water to meet water needs.[37] The spatial rainfall distribution is varied with most rainfall occurring in central African countries.[38]

Water scarcity in Africa cannot only be attributed to the population growth of 3 percent annually; it has also to do with the governance of water resources. The region uses only 3.8 percent of its renewable resources for agriculture, industry, and human consumption.[39] It is estimated that the lack of safe drinking water and sanitation is responsible for the deaths of about three million Africans per year.[40] African countries are estimated to have developed less than 20 percent of their irrigation potential and, unfortunately, much of water used is wasted: Unaccounted water amounts to about 50 percent in urban areas.[41] Some river basins in Africa have been used for electricity production but most of the hydroelectricity potential of the continent remains under-used.[42] Climate change is expected to reduce the water volumes of rivers and lakes, jeopardizing energy supply, agriculture, and fisheries production.[43]

Industrial and agricultural pollution has affected the water quality of many rivers and lakes in Africa. The intrusion of salt into the groundwater

---

34 *Id.* at 55.
35 *Id.*
36 *Id.*
37 UNEP, *Africa Environment Outlook: Past, Present and Future Perspectives* (2002).
38 *State of Africa, supra* note 33, at 55.
39 *Id.* at 56.
40 *Id.* at 57.
41 *Id.*
42 *See infra* note 57.
43 *State of Africa, supra* note 33, at 58.

resources presents a challenge for the countries bordering the Mediterranean.[44] Overgrazing and deforestation have resulted in soil loss and sedimentation of water bodies. In western Africa, some of the reservoirs of the Niger River have lost half of their capacity due to siltation over the last fifteen years.[45]

Uneven water distribution, pollution, salinization, droughts, and floods are typical problems in many countries of the world. A number of these problems are becoming increasingly acute in industrializing countries. It is somewhat unfortunate that the same issues are repeating themselves in country after country as states are going through the process of industrialization. One would have hoped, instead, that history would have provided some lessons, for this is its purpose, in lieu of repeating itself time after time.

In most countries, environmental standards have been established, but not always rigorously applied. To abate pollution, environmental impact assessments are now executed before proceeding with large infrastructure projects, such as hydroelectric dams, flood protection devices or reservoirs. However, problems persist that have to do with institution building and the governance of water resources.

Understanding Water Governance

Governance[46] is understood here to mean the government organizations, agencies, and ministries that are put in place to manage waters, which is government. Governance is inclusive also of the societal formal and informal organizations and groupings that address or are concerned about water management encompassing the networks of interaction among them and their linkages with formal government structures. Such formal and informal organizations and groupings include informal water rights systems as they are established in some societies, water user associations, private entities that have a stake in water management, environmental nongovernmental organizations, and the citizen that has an interest in the availability of affordable water of drinkable quality.

---

44 *Id.* at 59.

45 *Id.* at 60.

46 For the concept of governance, *see generally Governance without Government: Order and Change in World Politics* (James N. Rosenau and Ernst-Otto Czempiel, eds., 1992).

Some of the governance issues that pertain to water management include:

- How to ensure that countries sharing a watercourse do so in an equitable way without causing harm to each other.[47]
- How to foster cooperation among countries sharing a river so that industrial discharges are controlled and that pollutants discharged upstream of a river do not have adverse repercussions downstream.
- How to abate pollution from the many small and large agricultural fields maintained with pesticides and fertilizer, pollutants discharged into water ecosystems increasing environmental damage through eutrophication.
- How to tap into financing and increase investment so that cities do not discharge wastewater and sewage untreated into waterways.

These issues are not only central to water management. They have to do with how a society plans its future development. For instance, abating pollution caused by agriculture may be managed better by reducing agricultural subsidies. For most countries, though, this would be a politically untenable solution.

Uneven Water Distribution

Uneven water distribution, the fact that some areas are water-rich while others are water-poor, has preoccupied policymakers in many states. The uneven distribution of water presents challenges and certain countries, such as India, South Africa, and Spain, have initiated water transfers from water-abundant regions to water-deficient regions. Although in the past, such projects were almost unobstructed, today there is often insurmountable opposition from environmental groups and increasing levels of scrutiny by international lending institutions. Instead of constructing large infrastructure projects, it has been proposed that more attention should be placed on new technologies, such as water reuse and water desalination.

---

47 There are more than 3,800 unilateral, bilateral, or multilateral instruments on water. There are 286 international treaties, with 61 covering 200 transboundary river basins, *see* http://www.unesco.org/water/wwap/wwdr2/facts_figures/index.shtml.

Rainwater harvesting is another method to increase the availability of water resources.[48]

There are many methods to balance water demand and water availability that have either to do with increasing water supply or controlling water demand:

- The water supply can be increased by building reservoirs and transferring water from water-rich to water-deficient areas.
- The water supply can be augmented by reusing water (using treated wastewater for certain irrigation needs or using desalinated water).
- Water availability can be increased by repairing water infrastructure and reducing the leakage of various water distribution systems.
- Water demand can be controlled by putting a price on water and encouraging water metering, so that consumers become mindful about how much water they consume, and by other methods that instill awareness about the scarcity of the resource.[49]

Water Demand Management

Water demand management means that, in order to secure water supply for multiple uses, one must control demand through pricing. Placing the right price on water should ensure that users are careful about how much water they use and maximize water use efficiency. Managing water by controlling demand can be achieved by charging consumers the full cost of water production (including water service and infrastructure costs), making farmers pay for irrigation and the polluting externalities of agricultural activities, and charging industry for its water use and the externalities of hazardous discharges.

An understanding of water as an economic good, however, conflicts with a view of water as a public good or even as a human right. Everybody should be entitled to water of adequate quality and sufficient quantity, at least, for survival.[50] Thus, although some countries have pursued full water pricing, others have been more reluctant to do so. Countries subsidize

[48] *Water, a Shared Responsibility: The Second United Nations World Water Development Report*, at 14 (2006) [hereinafter *WWDR2*] available on line http://www.unesco.org/water/wwap/.

[49] *EEA paper, supra* note 14, at 26.

[50] Peter H. Gleick, *The Human Right to Water*, 1(5) Water Policy 487, at 496 (1999).

water use when full cost recovery is likely to undermine the poorest in their societies.

Industry

As industry is the main contributor to gross domestic product (GDP) in industrializing countries,[51] the control of pollution from industrial discharges is becoming all the more important for developing economies. It is often argued that the developing world should be allowed to repeat some of the mistakes of the developed world for the sake of growth. Still, the polluted watercourses and degraded coasts of Europe leave one with regret that developed states have not followed a more cautious approach to development. Although the introduction of the best available technology may not be a feasible option for many developing countries, in principle, wastes should not be released to water streams without some form of treatment, and wastewater treatment investment should increase.

Agriculture

Agriculture has been isolated for its detrimental effects on the environment because of the use of fertilizers and pesticides and the wasteful use of water. The current food crisis is to intensify the use of fertilizers and pesticides in the agricultural sector.[52] The future of agriculture and its effects on ecosystems will not only be decided by environmental policies but mostly by global agricultural policies as they may be shaped by the Doha round of negotiations of the World Trade Organization (WTO). The Doha round of negotiations is focusing on the reduction of agricultural subsidies and this will certainly to have an impact on the further development of agriculture in the developed and the developing world and, consequently, on the distribution and use patterns of water resources.

Urbanization

Increasing urbanization presents many challenges for water governance. Many people in Africa and Asia are migrating from rural to urban settlements. Because infrastructure in urban areas cannot meet demand, about 900 million urban dwellers (roughly one-third of all urban dwellers) in the

51 *WWDR2, supra* note 48, at 24. On the other hand, the production of manufactured goods is making only 29 percent of the GDP of developed countries and services are increasingly making the bulk of the economy in these countries.

52 *Id.* at 23. On the food crisis, *see* Paul Krugman, *Grains Gone Wild*, New York Times, Apr. 7, 2008.

world are living in slums. A slum dweller has 5 to 10 liters of water per day at his or her disposal while a middle income household in the same city can use from 50 to 150 liters of water per day.[53] Lack of water infrastructure in rural and urban areas remains one of the leading causes of disease in the developing world. Diarrhea is the main cause of death from water-related diseases. In developing countries, diarrhea accounts for 21 percent of deaths in children under the age of five. Malaria, another water-related disease, causes illness in about 400 million people per year.[54] Many water-related diseases can be controlled by providing access to adequate water supply and sanitation.[55]

Water for Energy

Water for energy production through the use of hydropower has been controversial. Hydropower has been blamed for many environmental problems presented in river ecosystems. These include river fragmentation and the disruption of the migratory patterns of species that leads to species demise and decreasing biodiversity. The production of hydropower has been associated with adverse social impacts such as the displacement of local populations from areas where hydroelectric dams are to be built. Two billion people in developing countries have no access to reliable electricity and, in Africa alone, 526 million people do not have access to electricity, yet the hydropower potential of the continent has not been exploited.[56] Although Europe uses 75 percent of its hydropower, Africa has developed only 7 percent of its hydropower. Despite this apparent discrepancy, there is still a debate over whether hydropower should be classified as a renewable source of energy suitable for investment in developing countries.[57] Water professionals have deplored the politics that surround hydropower production and have underlined that the construction of dams (big or small) is not a bad or good *per se* but that, instead, the focus should be on:

> how best we can plan, design and construct them [dams] where they are needed so that their performances in economic, social

[53] http://www.unesco.org/water/wwap/wwdr2/facts_figures/index.shtml.
[54] *WWDR2, supra* note 48, at 18.
[55] *Id.* at 19.
[56] *Id.* at 27.
[57] *Id.*

> and environmental terms can be maximized and their adverse impacts can be minimized; and how we can simultaneously ensure that those who may have to pay the costs of their implementation are explicitly made their beneficiaries.[58]

The importance of hydropower production may become increasingly relevant as a result of climate change and the need to reduce the emissions of greenhouse gases in the atmosphere. One the other hand, some countries, especially countries in Africa, will experience increasing temperatures and decreases in water supply that will affect their potential for hydropower production.

Climate Change

Water is at the center of the climate change debate. As glaciers are expected to melt in many areas of the world, the potential of flooding followed by subsequent drought is increasing.[59] Climate change may fuel extreme weather phenomena. It has been noted that 90 percent of natural disasters in the last decade have been water-related events, including tsunamis, floods, droughts, and polluting accidents.[60] Systems will be needed to manage such disasters, such as easy-to-use geographic information systems (GIS), coordination mechanisms for the transmission of information in case of a disaster, and risk management programs. Such systems are often lacking in both developed[61] and developing countries, even while natural disasters take an increasing toll on many peoples in the world.

Corruption

Systematic corruption is the result of failed states. Systematic corruption is distinguished from the occasional corruption that takes place in most government and governance functions. Corruption becomes systematic

---

58 Asit K. Biswas, *Dams: Cornucopia or Disaster?* 20(1) Water Resources Development 3, at 14 (Mar. 2004).

59 *Melting Himalayan Glaciers Poses Security Risk, UNEP Says*, Reuters, Apr. 17, 2007; *see also Germany is Losing Battle to Save Last Glacier*, Reuters, Apr. 30, 2007.

60 *WWDR2, supra* note 48, at 30.

61 *See* James P. Kahan *et al.*, *From Flood Control to Integrated Water Resource Management: Lessons for the Gulf Coast from Flooding in other Places in the Last Sixty Years*, RAND Occasional Paper (RAND Gulf States Policy Institute, 2006). Hurricane Katrina hit the United States coastal region in the summer of 2005. Failures at multiple levels brought unprecedented destruction and deaths all over a 90,000-square-mile area.

when it is perceived as the normal way of business practice among government agencies, citizens, and the private sector.[62] Corruption costs the water sector millions of dollars per year. Although many conventions, guidelines, and other instruments have been adopted against corruption,[63] it seems that it is still endemic in many societies of the developing world. How to break the cycle of corruption engrained in certain societies has yet to be resolved by policymakers and undermines the institutions of water governance in many societies.

62 *WWDR2, supra* note 48, at 9.

63 *See,* e.g., *United Nations Convention against Corruption,* Oct. 31, 2003 (entry into force Dec. 14, 2005). *OECD Convention on Combating Bribery of Foreign Public Officials in International Business Transactions,* Nov. 21, 1997 (entry into force Feb. 15, 1999); *OECD Guidelines for Multinational Enterprises,* June 27, 2000; *African Union Convention on Preventing and Combating Corruption* (July 11, 2003).

Chapter 2

Principles of Water Management

Basics of Integrated Water Resources Management

Ideas are not real things. They are conjectures in minds that hope for change. What is interesting about ideas is that they are as fugitive as they are concrete. Volumes and volumes have been written about the meaning of justice, and still the concept escapes universal definition. Those at the margins of societies, however, have a succinct understanding of what justice means. Justice is at the center of debate on the equitable use of natural resources including water resources.

When one first ponders it, water management sounds like an oxymoron. The question is how to manage a resource that is fleeting, crosses national boundaries, and evaporates into the air. Water makes up the oceans and seas and navigable waterways, but also the ephemeral streams[64] and groundwater bodies. How to share water and protect it from environmental threats is a persistent source of concern for policymakers worldwide. An amalgam of policies has addressed water in a fragmented manner, and consistent policies for water management have been the exception rather than the rule.

64 These are the streams with a flow of less than 120 days per year.

Water has been conceived as a public good available to serve society's various needs. Too little water could become the cause of food scarcity and poverty. Too much water could flood agricultural fields and cities and cause destruction. With industrialization, and the increasing use of waters as convenient medium for the disposal of various pollutants, protecting water quality has become as salient as sharing water quantity. Water of the wrong quality—infused with chemicals, salt, or nutrients—can cause health ailments and damage established ecosystems. Because quantity and quality are inseparable in water management and because policies of addressing water based on national boundaries are not successful, integrated water resources management (IWRM) has been proposed as a means to redefine water management. Integrated water management is, today, the answer to the fragmentation that has characterized water management for ages.

IWRM means that a policymaker cannot make decisions about the quantity of water to be allocated to various uses without incorporating into those decisions environmental concerns, including the purification and restoration of degraded water resources. Integrated water management means that water cannot be managed *per se*, but for meaningful management to occur, one has to consider land use planning and management, since water pollution is caused often by activities that occur on land. IWRM is an idea that has been touted by various international organizations since the mid 1970s[65] and eventually took root as a staple of international discourse.

Popularizing Integrated Water Resources Management: International Arenas

The principles adopted by the International Conference on Water and the Environment, in 1992, the so-called Dublin principles, are frequently

65 *See* Muhammad Mizanur Rahaman and Olli Varis, *Integrated Water Resources Management: Evolution, Prospects and Future Challenges, Sustainability: Science, Practice, & Policy* (Spring 2005) available on line http://ejournal.nbii.org/archives/vol1iss1/0407-03.rahaman.pdf. (The authors trace the development of the concept of IWRM from the United Nations Conference that took place in Mar del Plata, Argentina, in 1977, through the Dublin International Conference on Water and Environment that took place in 1992, the Second World Water Forum, [2000], the Bonn International Conference [2001], the 2002 World Summit on Sustainable Development and the Third World Water Forum in Kyoto [2003]).

cited as the principles that should guide IWRM.[66] IWRM has been defined:

> as a process which promotes the coordinated development and management of water, land and related resources, in order to maximize the resultant economic and social welfare in an equitable manner without compromising the sustainability of vital ecosystems.[67]

This is not a straightforward definition that can be put immediately into use. What constitutes a coordinated process for water management and the maximization of welfare in an equitable manner is not easy to translate into practical recommendations. The 1992 United Nations Conference on Environment and Development (the Earth Summit), held in Rio,[68] and the 2002 World Summit on Sustainable Development (the WSSD), held in Johannesburg,[69] both intergovernmental environmental conferences, attempted to exemplify further the components of (IWRM).

One of the documents produced during the Earth Summit was Agenda 21, a voluminous document that addresses various cross-cutting issues of environment and development.[70] According to Chapter 18 of

66 The Dublin Conference was not an intergovernmental conference. It was a conference that took place among experts in water management. The Dublin Conference was quite influential in the evolution of the concept of IWRM. *See International Conference on Water and the Environment (ICWE)*, Dublin, Ireland, Jan. 26–31, 1992.
The principles of water management articulated in the conference include:

- Fresh water is a finite and vulnerable resource, essential to sustain life, development and environment.
- Water resources management should be based on the participatory approach involving users, planners and policymakers at all levels.
- Women play a central role in the provision and management of water.
- Policymaking for water management must take place at the most appropriate level.
- Water has an economic value in all its competing uses and should be recognized as an economic good.

67 Global Water Partnership (GWP), *Integrated Water Resources Management*, Technical Committee, TEC Paper 4, 2000.

68 United Nations Conference on Environment and Development (Earth Summit), Rio de Janeiro, Brazil, June 3–14, 1992.

69 World Summit on Sustainable Development (the WSSD), Johannesburg, South Africa, Aug. 26-Sept. 4, 2002.

70 *Agenda 21*, June 5, 1992 available online http://www.un.org/esa/sustdev/documents/agenda21 (Division for Sustainable Development, United Nations Department for Economic and Social Affairs).

Agenda 21, entitled "Protection of the quality and supply of freshwater resources: Application of integrated approaches to the development, management and use of water resources:"

> The widespread scarcity, gradual destruction and aggravated pollution of freshwater resources in many world regions, along with the progressive encroachment of incompatible activities, demand integrated water resources planning and management. Such integration must cover all types of interrelated freshwater bodies, including both surface water and groundwater, and duly consider water quantity and quality aspects.[71]

Agenda 21 proposed program sectors for water management, namely:

1. Integrated water resources development and management;
2. Water resources assessment;
3. Protection of water resources, water quality and aquatic ecosystems;
4. Drinking water supply and sanitation;
5. Water and sustainable urban development;
6. Water for sustainable food production and rural development; and
7. Impacts of climate change on water resources.[72]

According to Agenda 21, IWRM must take place at the level of catchment basin or subbasin and must follow four objectives, including a multisectoral approach to water management, public participation in decision-making, and the strengthening of institutional, legal, and financial mechanisms.[73] At the international level, furthermore, states must cooperate in line with existing agreements and arrangements, taking into account the interests of all riparian states.[74]

Other themes of water resources management mentioned in Agenda 21 include the formulation of "costed and targeted national action plans and investment programs,"[75] the development of interactive databases for water management and planning, demand management through

71 Para. 18.3, *id.*
72 Para. 18.5, *id.*
73 Para. 18.9, *id.*
74 Para. 18.4, *id.*
75 Para. 18.12(a), *id.*

appropriate pricing, the development of new and alternative sources of water supply, and the establishment of public participatory techniques.[76] Furthermore, Agenda 21 addresses the issue of decisionmaking in water management, at the lowest appropriate level.[77]

The theme of IWRM was picked up by the Johannesburg Plan of Implementation adopted during the 2002 WSSD.[78] According to the plan of implementation, countries need to develop integrated water resources management and efficiency plans by 2005 including:

- Strategies, plans, and programs with regard to the integrated river basin;
- Efficient water allocation among competing uses that gives priority to the satisfaction of basic human needs;
- Mitigation of extreme water-related events;
- Diffusion of technology through capacity building and technology transfers to developing countries; and
- Facilitation of public-private partnerships, within stable and transparent national regulatory frameworks, while respecting local conditions and involving all concerned stakeholders.[79]

As the notion of integrated water resources management matured into the acronym IWRM, attempts were made to define the components of such management. One such component has to do with the fluid nature of water that does not conform to national and administrative boundaries. National and administrative frontiers have been put in place through politics, wars, or simply to simplify the administration of nation-state. The fact that water does not respect national and administrative frontiers challenges the notion of a state single-handedly addressing water management.

A classic example involves a state that is upstream of a watercourse and could discharge pollutants in that watercourse that detrimentally affect water life downstream. Or, alternatively, an upstream state could try to keep as much water for its own use through various technological devices. Unless the downstream state can, by might or right, convince the upstream

[76] Para. 18.12, *id.*

[77] *Id.*

[78] Sept. 4, 2002 available online http://www.un.org/esa/sustdev/documents/WSSD_POI_PD/English/POIToc.htm.

[79] Para. 26, *id.*

state to modify its behavior, it would have to accept the polluting externality, absorb the costs of remedial action, and make do with the quantity and quality of water released upstream.[80]

IWRM is an attempt to address water management based on hydrographic boundaries and organize such management around the river basin district as the coordinating unit regardless the national and administrative borders that may be on the way. This means, in practical terms, that upstream states and downstream states have to cooperate to treat a watercourse as the unity nature intended it to be—not piece-by-piece based on artificial boundaries created by states.

Components for successful integrated water resources management include:

- Investment in water resources management;
- National/ transnational water legislation;
- Water legislation based on integrated water resources management;
- Water legislation that provides for river basin organizations;
- Water legislation defining the authorities of central governmental and the regional authorities (national/transnational) involved in water management;
- Water law that supports the role of municipalities and inter-municipal associations in water management;
- Clear roles for institutions involved in water management and clear apportionment of responsibility;
- Good organization of all relevant stakeholders;
- Definition and administration of difficult tasks, such as disaster and pollution control.[81]

States have established international commissions to address the allocation of water resources and then address water quality in terms of transnational upstream-downstream use. Chapters 16 to 21 provide an extensive analysis of international water commissions established in Europe to address primarily issues of water quality. In the domestic sphere, certain

80 A downstream state can also have the upper hand in water management as it is the case in the Nile River basin, *see* Elli Louka, *International Environmental Law: Fairness, Effectiveness and World Order* 193–99 (2006) [hereinafter *Louka(1)*].

81 Alex Dourojeanni, *The Status of Integrated Water Management in Latin America and the Caribbean* 14 (2006) (UNESCO Contract 1061.5).

states have established river basin authorities to address water management at the river basin scale including land-use planning. The Tennessee Valley Authority (TVA)[82] in the United States and the Murray-Darling Basin Commission in Australia[83] are frequently cited as examples of integrated river basin management. The TVA is particularly interesting as it was established with the goal not only to manage waters but also to reduce poverty in the Tennessee Valley area. During the 1970s, some European countries experimented with the adoption of integrated watershed plans that include many components of what today could be characterized as IWRM plans. One such example is Finland that established a national board dedicated to water management charged with the implementation of watershed management plans.[84] In Valencia, Spain, water tribunals have operated since the tenth century, and Spain was one of the first countries to organize water management based on the river basin through a system of confederaciones hidrográficas established in 1926.[85]

Attempts at integrated river basin management have been undertaken in developing states. A number of countries in Asia have adopted national water plans that attempt to apply the concept of water management at the river basin and to integrate land use and water management. In India, the national water policy mentions that water resources planning must take place at the level of hydrological unit, such as the drainage basin or subbasin.[86] One of the cornerstones of IWRM is an initial comprehensive assessment of water resources. Such assessment will be problematic in Asia as monitoring networks range from quite comprehensive (Japan) to scattered monitoring attempts in China and the Pacific.[87] However, countries are engaging in efforts to monitor their water resources, use

82 *See Comprehensive River Basin Development: The Tennessee Valley Authority*, World Bank Technical Paper No. 416 (Barbara A. Miller & Richard B. Reidinger, eds., 1998). For a comprehensive analysis of the attempts at integrated water management in the United States, *see* Robert W. Adler, *Addressing Barriers to Watershed Protection*, 25 Environmental Law 973 (1995) providing an insightful analysis of the problems encountered and conditions that must be fulfilled for effectively implementing integrated water management.

83 *See* William A. Blomquist *et al.*, *Institutional and Policy Analysis of River Basin Management: The Murray-Darling River Basin*, Australia, World Bank Policy Research Working Paper No. 3527, Feb. 2005, available online Social Science Research Network (SSRN), http://ssrn.com/abstract=673519.

84 Rahaman and Varis, *supra* note 65, at 20.

85 *Id.* at 15.

86 *State of the Environment in Asia and the Pacific* 88 (UN Economic and Social Commission for Asia and the Pacific and Asian Development Bank, 2000).

87 *Id.* at 89.

irrigation water more efficiently,[88] and promote demand management.[89] Institutional fragmentation is one of the major obstacles to IWRM in the region because many institutions and agencies are involved in the management of water resources. In a number of countries, fragmentation has been addressed by establishing interagency coordinating committees and groups comprised of high-ranking representatives of various agencies and ministries.[90] In Philippines, for instance, the National Water Resource Board has been coordinating the activities of eleven government agencies. In India, the Central Water Commission is coordinating surface water management.[91]

Latin America countries have experimented with various facets of IWRM. Countries have established national water authorities and have transferred partially water management from the centralized public sector to decentralized public bodies or to private operators including community associations. The Inter-American Development Bank issued a strategy for IWRM in 1998.[92] In Mexico, Colombia, Cuba, and Ecuador, decentralization efforts have been undertaken. However, without technical support and regulation, decentralization has been less than optimal in most cases.[93] The privatization of water services and water pricing has been quite controversial[94] in a region that still experiences great levels of poverty, unequal distribution of wealth, and increasing urbanization, evident in the large number of slums that are changing the face of cities. Privatization in most countries has been equated with increases in water rates, cutoffs of service to customers who cannot pay, and the bribery of government officials. When Bechtel established a subsidiary in Bolivia and took over the water sector, it effectuated a 200 percent increase in water rates. This caused public uproar, and the privatization program was put aside.

88 *Id.* at 91.
89 *Id.*
90 *Id.* at 92.
91 *Id.*
92 Inter-American Development Bank, *Strategy for Integrated Water Resources Management*, No ENV-125 (1998). *See also Integrated Water Resources Management in Latin America and the Caribbean, Technical Study*, No. ENV-123, Dec. 1998.
93 United Nations Environment Program, *Global Environment Outlook: Latin America and the Caribbean* 86, 88 (2003) [hereinafter *Latin America Global Outlook*].
94 *Id.* at 87.

The idea of managing water based on the hydrographic basin has been gaining ground in Latin America, and there have been subregional efforts at transboundary water management. The La Plata Water Basin System established in 1969 by Argentina, Brazil, Bolivia, Paraguay, and Uruguay is an attempt to address the La Plata basin in an integrated way. A fund of $350 million has been used to promote various development projects in the region.[95] The Guaraní Aquifer System shared by Argentina, Brazil, Paraguay, and Uruguay has been the focus of transnational activity. In 2002, the governments of the four countries, with the support of international donors, began to prepare a joint management framework for the system based on the principles of environmental sustainability and public participation putting special emphasis on the geothermic potential of the system.[96] On a broader scale, the Amazon Cooperation Treaty does not only address water resources management but also encompasses the overall development of the Amazon region.[97] Countries have established bilateral water commissions to deal with management of transboundary rivers (i.e., Guatemala and El Salvador).[98]

Despite significant improvements in the region in terms of water management and a general acceptance of the approach of IWRM,[99] water management in Latin America and the Caribbean is still fragmented: water management for the various uses (i.e., hydroelectricity, drinking water, and sanitation) is taken care of by different agencies that do not necessarily coordinate with each other. Water resources management that coherently integrates the various uses of water, including environmental use, rarely captures consistent attention.[100] The approach to water management

95 *Id.* at 88. In 1967, the countries of the region established the Intergovernmental Coordinating Committee of the Countries of La Plata Basin (CIC). In 1969, a treaty was adopted that addressed various issues including navigation, fishing, and pollution. The La Plata initiative is funded by the GEF, the UNDP, and the Organization of American States.

96 *Id.* at 88.

97 *Treaty for Amazonian Cooperation*, July 3, 1978, reprinted in 17 ILM 1045 (1978). State parties to the treaty are Bolivia, Brazil, Colombia, Ecuador, Guyana, Peru, Surname, and Venezuela. For more details on the treaty, *see Louka(1), supra* note 17, at 333–34.

98 *See*, e.g., *Treaty for the Delimitation of the Boundary between Guatemala and El Salvador*, Apr. 9, 1938 available online http://ocid.nacse.org/cgi-bin/qml/tfdd/treaties.qml.

99 Nine countries have ongoing or proposed river basin organizations, namely, Brazil, Colombia, Costa Rica, El Salvador, and Mexico. These countries have laws that promote the river basin as the unit for water management. *See* Peter Rogers, *Water Governance in Latin America and the Caribbean*, at 19 (paper presented at the Inter-American Development Bank's Annual Meeting in Brazil, Mar. 7, 2002).

100 *Latin America Global Outlook, supra* note 30, at 88.

has lacked stability and uniformity, and the growth and change in management systems have been irregular.[101]

Attempts at integrated water management have been initiated in Africa. The SADC Protocol on Shared Watercourses[102] incorporates some principles of IWRM and river basin organizations have been established for the Niger,[103] Senegal,[104] and Gambia Rivers[105] as well as for Lake Chad.[106] However, hardly any of these regional organizations function to their full potential because of weaknesses in national institution structures that lead, inevitably, to feeble international arrangements.

Almost invariably, successful integrated water management has more to do to with the general level of development of a nation. Some of the predictors of success of IWRM include:

- The level of economic development of a nation;
- The level of economic development of a river basin district;
- Local experience in self-government (i.e., in spatial planning);
- Strong commitment of central government to IWRM;
- Financial autonomy at the river basin district level; and
- A water rights system that is quantified.[107]

---

101 Alex Dourojeanni, *The Status of Integrated Water Resources Management in Latin America and the Caribbean*, at 6, 2006 (UNESCO Contract 1061.5).

102 *See Protocol on Shared Watercourse Systems in the Southern African Development Community (SADC)*, Aug. 28, 1995, reprinted in 34 ILM 854 (1995). For more details on the protocol, *see Louka(1), supra* note 80, at 201.

103 *Convention creating the Niger Basin Authority*, Nov. 21, 1980 available online http://ocid.nacse.org/cgi-bin/qml/tfdd/treaties.qml. For more details, *see Louka (1), supra* note 17, at 207.

104 *See* Organisation pour la mise en valeur du fleuve Sénégal (OMVS), Mar. 11, 1972. The aim of the organization is to improve food security and preserve the ecosystems of the river. For more details on the organization, *see* http://www.omvs.org.

105 *See Convention Relating to the Creation of the Gambia River Basin Development Organization*, June 30, 1978 (state parties: Senegal, Gambia, Guinea, and Guinea-Bissau). The Gambia River Basin Development Organization (OMVG) has recently launched a study to explore the hydroelectric potential of the region.

106 Lake Chad located at the end of the Sahara desert is a source of water for many communities. It is one of Africa's largest lakes but has shrunk significantly over the last forty years. The Lake Chad Basin Commission was established in May 22, 1964, by Chad, Niger, Nigeria, and Cameroon. In 1994, the Central African Republic was admitted to the commission and, in 2000, Sudan was also admitted. The goals of the commission are to regulate water use, initiate development projects and facilitate the settlement of disputes. *See* Eric O. Odada *et al.*, *Lake Chad: Experience and Lessons Learned Brief*, International Waters Learning Exchange and Resource Network (IW: LEARN/GEF, 2005) available online http://www.iwlearn.net/publications/ll/lakechad_2005.pdf/view.

107 William A. Blomquist *et al.*, *Comparison of Institutional Arrangements for River Basin Management in Eight Countries*, World Bank Policy Research Working Paper 3636, June 2005, available online Social Science Research Network (SSRN), http://ssrn.com/abstract=757225.

River basin management cannot be established when there are:

- Extreme asymmetries in resource endowments among various stakeholders;
- Cultural and social inequities among users;
- Stakeholders with minimal access to river basin authorities.[108]

River basin management cannot be established overnight. It often takes years to develop successful river basin institutions[109] and it requires commitment, after these institutions are established, to continue to be creative and devise new arrangements and methodologies to address the multifaceted issues of water management.

Making and Applying Decisions in Water Management

The central focus of IWRM is to minimize the misuse of water resources and prevent water deprivation for some uses and overendowment for others. Setting the correct price for water is believed to achieve the desired water efficiency. Water may be freely available but not suitable for consumption in its natural condition. Water has to be purified to be drinkable. Water works and irrigation schemes have to be put in place to make water available for agricultural fields. Given that water has to be "produced" according to certain specifications[110] so that it can be consumed, the question is: Who is to pay for the costs of water production? Water infrastructure maintenance and development is usually undertaken by the state because water is considered a public good. The typical misallocation of water resources is that users use far more water than they need. This has led to the conviction that users will be willing to conserve and protect water only if they are made aware of the costs of water production. To achieve this, states should refrain from subsidizing the costs of water production. Therefore, the misallocation of water resources resulting from state subsidies has generated demands to make users pay.

The dichotomy between "water as an economic good" and "water as a public good" forces the question of who should be making decisions on

108 *Id.*
109 *Id.*
110 Such specifications differ for water that is suitable for drinking versus water that is used for irrigation or cleaning.

water management. The state, through its presumed disinterested public agencies, should be making decisions on water management in the pursuit of public interest. Or, water users and public interest advocates should bargain among themselves and decide on water management and use. Or, the general public (citizens) should vote on issues of water allocation and preservation. IWRM requires the involvement of water users and the public in decisionmaking that affects water management. The involvement of water users and the public is viewed as a means to guarantee better decisions (since all interests are taken into account and are balanced against each other) and better implementation of decisions, given that all concerned participate in the making of decisions. Interest participation is one of the most difficult components of IWRM to apply in practice in terms of including all people and groups with a stake in water management and ensuring that the participation of the interested public does not subvert the welfare of the general public.

IWRM incorporates many claims about the proper management of water resources. These claims are not always consistent with each other. Putting the right price tag on water may mean high water prices that would make water unaffordable for poor communities, challenging ingrained beliefs that water is a public good and access to water is a human right.[111] Advocating the management of water at the river basin district would involve the creation of large institutions which may not be amenable to the participation of local stakeholders in water management.

In addition to these apparent inconsistencies, many countries do not strictly practice the management of water at the river basin district level because they engage in extensive interbasin water transfers. South Africa and India engage in interbasin water transfers in order to bring water from surplus areas to deficit areas.[112] When interbasin transfers take place, the appropriate concept to use seems to be that of interbasin integration rather than of integration within a river basin. Commentators, therefore, distinguish the concept of integrated river basin management

---

111 *See*, e.g., Salman M. A. Salman and Siobhán McInerney-Lankford, *Human Right to Water: Legal and Policy Dimensions*, World Bank (2004).

112 Interbasin transfers are not widely practiced, however, and only few countries are engaging in such transfers—United States and Canada in the Americas, China and India in Asia and Russia in Europe. In Africa and Oceania, there are a small number of interbasin water transfers. *See Experiences with Inter Basin Water Transfers for Irrigation, Drainage and Flood Management*, Revised Draft Report of the International Commission on Irrigation and Drainage (ICID) on Inter Basin Water Transfers (Aug. 2006).

(IRBM) from the concept of IWRM and point out that the river basin may not be the appropriate unit for the management of waters.[113] It must be clarified, though, that interbasin water transfers *per se* do not militate against river basin planning. Interbasin transfers should not in principle happen without, first, assessing how the water transfer is to affect the donor basin. In other words, the donor basin is the primary unit of assessment before planning for water transfers to other basins or regions.[114]

Another issue that makes IWRM difficult to apply in practice is the integration of land use and water management that is essential for ensuring water quality. As mentioned, water quality depends on activities on land including agriculture, industry, and town management. Water quality is compromised because of the amounts of industrial discharges, nutrients, and sewage, often untreated, that are disposed of in rivers or coastal waters. To ensure IWRM, all activities on land have to be controlled and standards must be established so that wastes do not go untreated into the waters, if they need to go there at all. The question, therefore, becomes how all these different activities and industrial sectors are to be managed to achieve the goals of water quality as integrated water management mandates. Although water professionals see water as a consolidated sector, other government departments tend to perceive water as a component of their sectoral jurisdiction. Ministries of agriculture, for instance, see water as part of the irrigation scheme. Health ministries are anxious to achieve clean drinking water. Transport ministries view water as the means for navigation. How is it possible to integrate all these different perspectives on water into a single vision encapsulated under the concept of IWRM, especially, taking into account the amount of institutional rivalry that exists among various government departments?

The difficulties involved in realizing the desirable integration have created doubts about whether IWRM can be operationalized in practice in a coherent fashion.[115] Actually, few institutions have applied all components

113 A.D. Mohile, *Integration in Bits and Parts: A Case Study for India* 39, at 57, in Integrated Water Resources Management in South and South-East Asia (Asit K. Biswas, Olli Varis and Cecilia Tortajada, eds., 2005).

114 *See also* C.D. Thatte, *Sabarmati River Basin (India): Problems and Prospects for Integrated Water Resources Management* 66, at 72, in Integrated Water Resources Management in South and South-East Asia, *id.*

115 *See* Asit K. Biswas, *Integrated Water Resources Management: A Reassessment*, 29(2) Water International 248, June 2004.

of integrated water resources management both at the international and domestic spheres.[116]

Still, it is probably harsh to dismiss the idea of IWRM as lacking operative value or as a fad that needs to run its course. The power of ideas that often find expression in popular concepts lies exactly in their indeterminate contours, and their ability to command public attention and reinvolve policymaking. As mentioned in the beginning of the Chapter, definitions of justice are usually vague as the concept becomes determinable based on the circumstances of each individual case.[117] Lack of clairvoyance into the potential applications of the concept justice, though, do not generally lead to concept dismissal.

Unquestionably the concept of IWRM, as it has evolved to encompass many claims and meanings, may seem unworkable. Possibly, in a few years, the concept will be eclipsed, and replaced in the international vocabulary by other concepts, such as adaptive management.[118] It is maintained here, however, that the concept of *integration* in water management should have some staying power despite the flippancy of fashionable jargon. In the majority of cases, the idea of integrating water management at the river basin district for waters shared across borders should endure because the separation of a river based on national frontiers does not make sense.[119] An issue that has motivated the adoption of the principle of IWRM has to do with the unfairness of shifting environmental externalities among coriparians. The externalities of upstream and downstream use require elucidation in terms of coherent and equitable solutions. Given the increasing transparency in the international space, it is becoming difficult to transfer, with impunity, environmental externalities from medium to medium or from state to state.[120]

---

116 *Louka(1), supra* note 80, at 182–85.

117 *Id.* at 68.

118 C.S. Holling, *Adaptive Environmental Assessment and Management* (2005).

119 *See* the exception of the Indus River shared between India and Pakistan, *Louka(1), supra* note 80, at 212–13. In some cases, countries unable to reach cooperative arrangements regarding a whole river basin have, instead, concluded agreements encompassing frontier waters. *See, e.g.*, Itay Fischhendler and Eran Feitelson, *The Formation and Viability of Non-Basin Water Management: The U.S.-Canada Case*, 36 Geoforum 792, Nov.2005. The authors demonstrate how frontier water agreements, through a number of flexible arrangements, have been used to address problems that affect the whole river basin.

120 A dispute has erupted between Argentina and Uruguay on the construction of paper mill factories on River Uruguay. The construction of the mills in Uruguay caused uproar in Argentina where residents and activists protested against the project. The dispute demonstrates that public opposition can have crippling effects on projects that are to have transboundary impacts. For a commentary on the case brought before the International Court of

Furthermore, water management, in order to even claim the appearance of coherence, cannot be separated from future societal trends of increasing urbanization, changes in the agricultural sector, the anticipated population increase, as well as further advances in technology.[121] This is especially so because infrastructure water projects undertaken now are usually completed in fifteen to twenty years and need to be relevant at the time of their fruition.[122]

The concept of IWRM deserves credit for bringing to the fore the idea of the integration of upstream and downstream uses and of land-use planning and water resources management. Integration may not always be fully achieved simply because of the magnitude of sectors that need to be integrated. It is essential, nevertheless, for any meaningful water management to take place, to establish strong coordinating linkages between upstream and downstream uses and between land-use planning and water resources management.

What is most useful in the concept of IWRM is that provides decisionmaking processes for the management of waters. This is what the European Union (EU) has attempted to do through the adoption of the water framework directive (WFD),[123] the first instrument that attempts to establish integrated water management in a consistent fashion on an international scale.

As mentioned in the beginning of the chapter, the puzzle of ideas is that they can simultaneously be beyond the grasp of our imaginations but also suddenly very relevant to situations that call for their application. For academics, IWRM may seem like an abstract principle since the tasks of integrating land-use management and water management, let alone of including stakeholders and the public in decisionmaking, seem

---

Justice, *see* Pieter H.F. Bekker, *Argentina-Uruguay Environmental Border Dispute Before the World Court*, ASIL Insight, Volume 10, Issue 2, May 16, 2006.

For the decision of the International Court of Justice, see *Case Concerning Pulp Mills on the River Uruguay*, (*Argentina v. Uruguay*), Provisional Measures, Jan. 23, 2007, available online http://www.icj-cij.org/docket/files/135/13615.pdf.

121 For an eloquent argument about how future societal trends are to influence water management, *see* Asit K. Biswas, *Water Management in the 21st Century for the Developing World*, First Lecture under Distinguished Speaker Series Phnom Penh Plan for Development Management Greater Mekong Subregion, Phnom Pehn, Cambodia, Oct. 18, 2006.

122 *Id.*

123 *Directive 2000/60/EC* of the European Parliament and of the Council of 23 October 2000 establishing a framework for Community Action in the field of water policy, OJ L 327/1, 22.12.2000 [hereinafter *WFD*].

complex in their idealism. For a water director, who receives conflicting requests from various ministers and deputy ministers and who has held consultations with various constituencies that have presented her with ever-conflicting demands, the need to streamline the whole process of decisionmaking in water management and coherently integrate a very inchoate reality are urgently pertinent. For a water director, IWRM is not an abstraction. It is a do or die matter; as a water director put it: "Water is everywhere. One cannot stop thinking about it."[124]

[124] Interview, Gabrijela Grčar, State Undersecretary for Water, Ministry of the Environment and Spatial Planning, Slovenia, June 2005.

Chapter 3

The Making of the European Union

Establishment and Evolution of the European Union

The process of European integration started with the rationale that if Europe is to avoid future wars and develop economically, it has to establish, first and foremost, free trade among European states. The European Economic Community (EEC), also identifiable as simply the European Community (EC) or the European Union (EU), was first an attempt to establish free trade among the member states under a belief that close cooperation in economic matters will spill over and generate cooperation in other matters.[125] The spillover effect seems to be working. The EC has expanded through the years to regulate not only economic matters but also a host of various other matters, such as consumer protection, environmental protection[126] and social policy. The EU is even contemplating the development of a common security and defense policy and the introduction of a European military force.

---

125 *See generally* E.B. Haas, *The Uniting of Europe* (1958).

126 For more information and in-depth analysis on the shaping of EU environmental law, *see* Jan H. Jans, *European Environmental Law* (2000); Ludwig Kramer, *EC Environmental Law* (2003).

Integration among member states of the EC was brought about through a series of international treaties. The Treaty Establishing the European Economic Community was adopted in 1957 and was followed by the Single European Act (adopted in 1986 and ratified in 1987); the Maastricht Treaty (Treaty on the European Union, adopted in 1992 and ratified in 1993), the Amsterdam Treaty (signed in 1997 and ratified in 1999) and the Treaty of Nice (signed in 2001 and ratified in 2003).[127] The Treaty of Lisbon was adopted on December 13, 2007 and is expected to be ratified in January 2009.

The Single European Act was the treaty that gave a new impetus to the Community after the stalemate of the 1970s. The Treaty on the European Union established what have been called the second and third pillars of the communities. The first pillar is economic integration based on the first EEC treaty. The second pillar has to do with the common foreign and security policy and the third pillar focuses on enforcement and cooperation in criminal matters.

The Amsterdam Treaty put in motion the social protocol, emphasized the strengthening of public health and consumer protection policies and allowed for the introduction of more openness. The Nice Treaty prepared the EC for its first big enlargement that took place in 2004 and included ten new member states that have imbued the EC with new ideas and perspectives including Cyprus, the Czech Republic, Estonia, Hungary, Latvia, Lithuania, Malta, Poland, Slovakia, and Slovenia. The Treaty of Lisbon was adopted in 2007 and is expected to be ratified in the beginning of 2009. The treaty was adopted after failed attempts to ratify a constitution for Europe. The treaty increases the powers of the parliament and national parliaments are granted more opportunities to get involved in the work of the EU. Qualified majority voting in the EC is extended to new areas while the rights of citizens are further guaranteed under a Charter of Fundamental Rights. Furthermore, the EU is hoping to speak with one voice in external affairs by creating a new position for a High Representative for the Union in Foreign Affairs and Security Policy.

The integration achieved at the EU scale through a number of basic international treaties has intrigued many commentators who view the European organization as a *sui generis* phenomenon difficult to replicate

---

[127] A consolidated version of *The Treaty on European Union* is available online http://europa.eu.int/eur-lex/lex/en/treaties/index.htm.

For summaries and the text of the various treaties, *see* http://europa.eu/abc/treaties/index_en.htm.

in other regions. Optimists in the early 2000s started to become vocal about the possibilities of adoption of a European constitution (or rather a treaty establishing a constitution for Europe). The proposition for a constitution was defeated after the Dutch and French referenda that rejected the constitution. The French and Dutch rejections generated questions on whether the elite of decisionmakers in the EU are, indeed, in tune with the wishes of the European public. Nevertheless, the debate on the adoption of a constitution continues; it seems unavoidable not to, at least, strive for coherence among the different international treaties that today make up the EU. A constitution for Europe is probably inevitable. Nevertheless, the nature of the constitution and the type of federation that it will promote are yet to be determined. Furthermore, as constitutional practice has demonstrated, the in-the-making reality of societies constantly reinterprets and reshapes the orderliness of constitutions.

The level of integration achieved today in the EU has been often credited to its institutions whose mandate is to promote European integration and whose officials are urged to shed their national affiliations and exhibit independence in the pursuit of their duties as officers. Europe, a continent without definite geographical frontiers, is an idea[128] and European integration cannot materialize without a certain sort of institutional europhilia.

Legislative and Executive Organs

Commission

The European Commission (the Commission), along with the European Parliament (the Parliament) and the Council of Ministers (the Council), governs the EU. The primary role of the Commission is to propose legislation to the Council and to the Parliament, what is called the right to initiative.[129] The Commission is also the guardian of the treaties. It must ensure the smooth functioning of the Common Market and the compliance of

---

[128] *See generally The Idea of Europe: From Antiquity to the European Union* (Anthony Pagden, ed., 2002).

[129] Art. 211, *Treaty Establishing the European Community, see Consolidated Versions of the Treaty on European Union and of the Treaty Establishing the European Community*, OJ C 321 E/1, 29.12.2006 [hereinafter *EC Treaty*] available online http://europa.eu.int/eur-lex/lex/en/treaties/index.htm.

member states with the legislation enacted. If member states do not comply with the measures issued by the European Community, the Commission has the power to bring them before the Court of Justice.[130]

The Commission is headed by a president who is assisted by two vice-presidents.[131] The president of the Commission is nominated by member states. The members of the Commission are appointed by member states in agreement with the president of the Commission. Commissioners are appointed for a renewable term of five years[132] and they are supposed to be independent in the performance of their duties and not accept instructions from their national governments.[133]

If one sees the EU as a federation of states, then the Commission is a sort of government and the commissioners are the ministers that make the cabinet.[134] Each commissioner is responsible for one or multiple departments of the Commission called Directorates General (DGs). The commission is today divided into 27 directorates general (DGs) and nine services. DGs cover internal matters such as the Directorate-General for Information Society and Media or external policies such as the Directorate-General for External Relations.

Because the Commission is conceived as the government of the EU the fact that it is appointed by member states rather than elected by the general public has generated concerns about the *democratic deficit* of the EC. Since commissioners are not accountable to the public and are even instructed to shed their national allegiances, the Commission is often viewed as a faceless nonelected executive bureaucracy. As analyzed below, the Commission has engaged in extensive efforts to alleviate its image as a hard-core bureaucracy by initiating consultations with a vast variety of stakeholders before proposing legislation. It is unclear, however, whether such efforts have improved the image of the Commission in the eyes of the public.

---

130 Art. 211, *id.*

131 Arts. 214(2) and 217, *id.*

132 Art. 214(1), *id.*

133 Art. 213(2), *id.* "Members of the Commission shall, in the general interest of the Community, be completely independent in the performance of their duties. In the performance of these duties, they shall neither seek nor take instructions from any government or from any other body . . . Each Member State undertakes to respect this principle and not to seek to influence the Members of the Commission in the performance of their tasks."

134 *See also* John McCormick, *The European Union: Politics and Policies* 102 (1999).

Council of Ministers

The Council together with the Parliament is the legislative organ of the EC. It is composed of twenty-seven national ministers (one per state),[135] who act as ambassadors of states to the EC. *Council of Ministers* is not the best name for an institution that is actually a number of councils; a general and foreign affairs council (comprised of foreign ministries), a health council, an agricultural council, and other such councils. The Council is conceived to be superior to the Parliament because it only has to consult with the Parliament. However, with the introduction of the codecision procedure, the Parliament's legislative role has increased.[136]

The function of the presidency of the Council is rotated every six months among member states so that all states of the EU have the opportunity to preside over the Council. In effect, in order to preserve continuity, a troika, consisting of the previous, current, and next presidents, runs the presidency of the Council. The presidency sets the agenda of the Council and moves forward the work of the Council.[137]

Parliament

The European Parliament is the only organ of the EU directly elected by the population.[138] The Parliament represents about 496 million citizens of the EU. Members of the Parliament are elected every five years by universal suffrage. Since January 1, 2007, there are 785 members of the Parliament. The role of the Parliament has evolved from that of consultative body to that of colegislator on EU matters.

The Parliament, unlike other parliaments in the world, does not have the power to initiate legislation; that function belongs to the Commission. The Parliament does not appoint the Commission, the way national

---

135 Art. 203, *EC Treaty, supra* note 129.

136 Codecision is one of the legislative procedures used in the EU. The procedure gives the parliament and the council equal power to amend or to reject legislation. Other procedures, for instance, the cooperation procedure (the council can by unanimous voting overrule the parliament) are still used in the EU. There are matters decided by unanimous voting of the council in which the role of the parliament is purely consultative. Such matters include matters of fiscal nature, town and country planning, land use planning with the exception of waste management, the quantitative management of water resources and measures affecting the choice between energy sources and the general structure of energy supply. For more details on the decisionmaking procedures used in the EU, *see* Elli Louka, *Conflicting Integration: The Environmental Law of the European Union* 41–48 (2004) [hereinafter *Louka(2)*].

137 For more information on the Council, *see Louka(2), id.* at 30.

138 Arts. 189 and 190, *EC Treaty, supra* note 129.

parliaments appoint the executive, but it can influence the appointment of the Commission. It has some supervisory powers over the Commission since it can file a motion of censure against the activities of the Commission. If the motion of censure is carried through by a two-thirds majority of votes cast by the parliament, the Commission must resign as a body.[139] Because the censure procedure is quite drastic, it is rarely used by the Parliament.

The Commission must submit reports to the Parliament and must answer questions from its members. Furthermore, a legal person or a citizen of the EU can petition the Parliament on a community matter that affects them directly.[140]

The Parliament is governed by its president. Most of the work of the Parliament happens in different committees. Members of the Commission appear before these committees to explain proposed legislation. The committees prepare in response the opinions of the Parliament on the proposals of the Commission. They prepare also amendments to the common position of the Council and execute all the technical work of the Parliament.

European Council

The European Council is the name for the EU summit that takes place every six months and is comprised of heads of states and presided over by the head of state that holds the presidency. The summit meetings are major media events and it is in interest of all EC organs to ensure that the summit meetings are a success. The purpose of summit meetings is to provide impetus for moving forward the EC policies, establish guidelines for foreign policy, and start cooperation in new areas. The European Council looks at the strategic dilemmas facing the EU while the rest of the EC institutions are in charge of implementing that strategy.

Court of Justice

The purpose of the Court of Justice, now assisted by the Court of First Instance, is to apply and interpret EC law. The Court of Justice has consistently interpreted EU law in a way that furthers integration. The most important principles of the EU law, such as the principle of supremacy of EC law, the principle of direct effects, and respect for human rights, have been launched by the Court of Justice.

---

139 Art. 201, *id.*

140 Art. 194, *id.*

From the initial stages of EC development, two principles have been established with certainty: the principle of the supremacy of EC law over member states' law and the principle of the direct effects of EC law. The principle of direct effects means that EC law does not apply only to member states and their institutions but also creates direct rights and duties for the citizens of member states that make the EU.[141] These rights and duties are actionable before courts.[142]

Comparing the Court of Justice with national courts, one could say that the Court of Justice is the constitutional court of the EU. Both the Court of Justice and the Court of First Instance are comprised of one judge per state.[143] Judges are supposed to be independent and must possess the qualifications to be appointed to the judicial offices of their country.[144] They are appointed by a common accord of governments of member states for a renewable term of six years but every three years there is a partial replacement of judges.[145]

Other Institutions

Other institutions of the EC include the European Economic and Social Committee, the Committee of the Regions, the European Court of Auditors, the European Central Bank and the European Environment Agency. As the EU grows and integration deepens the functions of these institutions increase in complexity and jurisdictional reach.

What Type of Union?

The EC is an entity that has sprung out of a number of international treaties that, with minute detail, have designed an institutional development that resembles more or less the institutional structure of a federal state. Member states have remained sovereign but, given the prerogative of their sovereignty, have surrendered many policymaking functions to the EU. Although foreign and defense policies are still in the hands of member states, monetary policy is handled now by the European Central Bank. A host of other policies, including environmental policy, are decided at the level of the EU.

---

141 *Van Duyn v. Home Office*, case 41/74, 1974 ECR 1337.

142 For the principles of Community law, *see Louka(2), supra* note 136, at 9–26.

143 Arts. 221 and 224, *EC Treaty, supra* note 129.

144 Art. 223, *id.*

145 *Id.*

The EU is, doubtless, a powerful institution that claims to represent the interests of citizens who make the EU. The lack of a direct representational link between those citizens and the organs of the EU has created some disaffection that has been epitomized in the phrase *democratic deficit*. The Commission, the most powerful of governments, the argument goes, is not elected. The Council is comprised of ministers who are accountable to national governments and, therefore, to the citizenry of their country in very indirect way. The Parliament is not elected on a European agenda but on a national agenda and it is not perceived as a powerful organ since it does not elect the Commission. It is unfortunate that the Parliament has not succeeded in projecting itself as the connecting link between European citizens and their EU as it is the only organ of the EC elected directly by the population. For European citizens the Parliament is a remote institution that plays hardly any role in the evolving national reality. Serving on the Parliament is not the best way for a politician to keep in touch with the national electorate. The turnout for the European parliamentary elections is low and seems to be falling. The Parliament is institutionally wanting for lack of a European *demos* preoccupied with European politics that votes for a Parliament; national allegiances still reign high in all member states.

Despite recurrent misgivings, however, no one can seriously doubt the legitimacy of the EU. The EU has been created by national governments which, based on the constitutions of member states, are entitled to enter into treaties to create international organizations such as the EU. Indeed, the creation of all international institutions is based on the treaty-making power of states that enter into agreements to establish international organizations.

The democratic deficit has not so much to do with the perception of the EU as an international institution but with the understanding that the EU is a nascent federation. If the EC continues to evolve as a federation, the methods of accommodating direct inputs from the electorate will continue to haunt it—because they are haunting today's representative democracy as it is practiced by nation states. As the European idea evolves, the perception of Europe as an elite project has to subside and the EU of the peoples of Europe has to replace it.

The Commission, to its credit, has undertaken initiatives to ensure that the promulgation of legislation does not happen without consultation with relevant stakeholders. There have been efforts to streamline legislation and the production of legislation has declined significantly in the last decade, which strengthens the principle of subsidiarity, namely, that decisions should be made at the lowest level that is appropriate for the nature of the decision made. The Parliament has been playing an increasingly important role in the adoption of legislation and it influences the work of the Commission.

The understanding of Europe as multilevel governance is pertinent here. For those who are involved in EU policymaking, it is obvious that decisions cannot be taken monolithically by one institution and there are significant checks and balances between the supranational and national organs. Furthermore, various other actors exert influence on European policymaking, such as industry associations, environmental nongovernmental organizations (NGOs), the regions, and civil society actors. The EC is exhibiting many of the characteristics of what has been called multilevel governance, in which decisionmaking occurs simultaneously at different levels (intergovernmental, supranational, regional, and local). Decisions cross-pollinate each other to shape and modify the ideas, interests, and expectations of both domestic actors and supranational organs. The adoption and evolution of the water framework directive (WFD) exemplifies a modeling of the EU after the paradigm of multilevel governance.

Chapter 4

Water Management in the European Union

Revolutionizing Water Management in the European Union: Water Framework Directive 2000

Integrated water resources management entered the European Union (EU) agenda through the adoption of the water framework directive (WFD) in 2000.[146] The WFD, like most directives issued by the EU, is a type of legislation that sets the framework of legislative action. Because of the complexity of environmental issues, though, even framework instruments often tend to be quite detailed, technical, and off-putting to the uninitiated. The WFD is a multi-page instrument, with many annexes.[147] The European Commission (the Commission), therefore, has been concerned with ensuring that the directive is applied in a consistent fashion all across member states. The idea behind the WFD is to consolidate into one instrument the many disparate instruments on water that have been issued by the Commission and to establish the basis of a coherent water policy for the EU. Before the

---

146 *Directive 2000/60/EC* of the European Parliament and of the Council of 23 October 2000 establishing a framework for Community action in the field of water policy, OJ L 327/1, 22.12.2000 [hereinafter *WFD*].

147 The WFD is seventy-two pages long including eleven annexes.

adoption of the WFD, on-the-ground implementation of water legislation was seriously lacking in many member states.[148]

The WFD[149] does not endorse explicitly the concept of integrated water resources management (IWRM). However, the term *integration* is encountered regularly in the corpus of the directive[150] and the concept of the IWRM is mentioned frequently in the various guidance documents that have been issued to facilitate the implementation of the directive.[151] The directive endorses three concepts that could be considered the organizing pillars of IWRM in the EU, that is:

- The river basin district as the organizing/planning unit for water management;
- River basin management plans as tools for river basin district planning; and
- Consultation with and participation of water users and the public in river basin management.

The directive could be classified as an instrument the goal of which is the improvement of water quality. According to the language used in the directive:

> The purpose of this Directive is to establish a framework for the protection of inland surface waters, transitional waters, coastal

---

148 Christoph Demmke, *Towards Effective Environmental Regulation: Innovative Approaches in Implementing and Enforcing European Environmental Law and Policy* 8, Jean Monnet Program, New York University School of Law, Jean Monnet Working Paper 5/01 (2001) available online www.jeanmonnetprogram.org/papers/01/010501.rtf.

149 *WFD, supra* note 146.

150 The directive refers to the need to deal with water management in an integrated fashion. The Commission refers to its proposal for an "action programme for integrated protection and management of groundwater" (para. 7, preamble, *id.*), the necessity "to develop an integrated Community policy on water,"(para. 9, preamble, *id.*) and the implementation of "integrated programmes of measures" (para. 26, preamble, *id.*). *See also* para. 34, preamble, *id.*: "For the purposes of environmental protection there is a need for a greater integration of qualitative and quantitative aspects of both surface waters and groundwaters . . . " The Commission further refers to the Integrated Pollution Prevention and Control (IPPC) Directive (art. 10(2), *id.*) the purpose of which is to control pollution in an integrated fashion so that abatement of pollution in one medium does not result in transferring pollution to another medium. Abatement of pollution at sea, for instance, should not lead to increasing pollution on land and vice versa. The IPPC directive demonstrates the willingness of the EU to deal with resources in an integrated fashion and the increasing awareness that sectoral measures taken independent of each other may result in the transfer rather than the reduction of polluting externalities.

151 *See* Chapter 5.

> waters and groundwater which prevents further deterioration and protects and enhances the status of aquatic ecosystems . . .[152]

The directive aspires further to assist in the mitigation of effects of floods and droughts, thus, asserting a linkage between issues of water quantity and water quality.[153] For marine pollution, the directive aims at concentrations in the marine environment of close to zero for manmade substances.[154] The goals of the directive are evident from the timetable set to achieve these goals. States must enhance and restore all bodies of surface water to good ecological status within fifteen years after the directive goes into effect.[155]

Based on its introductory provisions, the directive is viewed as an instrument that targets the improvement of water quality in Europe. In reality, the system established is much more customized to the needs of member states. Even more important, the directive, as much as it is focused on water quality, is mostly preoccupied with the establishment of a system for the management of waters in Europe. It is through the establishment of this system based on three organizing pillars of IWRM that the achievement of good water quality would be guaranteed for the future. The directive is an attempt not only to establish the qualitative goals of water management, as those could be different depending on member states or regions, but also to establish institutional mechanisms that could guarantee the accomplishment of qualitative goals.

The WFD must be conceptualized within the general context of legislative action in the EU. The primary purpose of legislative initiative in the EU is integration. Integration has to do with abolishing trade barriers so that the interaction of member states is not hampered by such barriers. Integration has to do with the enactment of EU legislation that would lead to the approximation of the laws enacted by member states so that similar standards are established among the states. The environmental field has been characterized by legislation, the purpose of which is to establish similar standards among member states for various activities that are the cause of environmental externalities—such as hazardous waste disposal,

152 Art. 1(a), *WFD, supra* note 146.
153 Art. 1(e), *id.*
154 *Id.*
155 *See* art. 4(1)(a)(ii), *id.* With the exception of waters that have been heavily modified that need to reach "good ecological potential." *See also* art. 4(1)(a)(iii), *id.*

the emission of greenhouses gases into the atmosphere, or the release of chemical substances into the waters.

The directive prescribes a new planning unit for the management of waters, the river basin district. The directive provides that member states must identify the river basins located in their territory and must assign them to river basin districts.[156] Small river basin districts can be combined to create larger river basin districts. Coastal waters that do not neatly fall within a river basin district must be identified and assigned to the nearest or most appropriate river basin district or districts.[157] Groundwater must be assigned to the nearest or most appropriate river basin district.[158]

After the identification of river basin districts, member states "shall ensure the appropriate administrative arrangements, including the identification of the appropriate competent authority . . . " for the application of the directive in each river basin district located in their territory.[159] Whether an authority or multiple authorities should be responsible for the implementation of the directive was a source of contention during the drafting of the directive. Member states that have not organized their water management using the river basin as a planning unit were reluctant to establish river basin authorities as new administrative units. Fears arose about the costs related to the creation of new administrative units and the problems of coordination with existing authorities in charge of water management. Eventually, it was decided that states did not have to designate a river basin authority in charge of a river basin district and that, instead, existing institutions could coordinate their action to effectuate management at the river basin district level.[160] This opened the way for the establishment of a coordination approach to the implementation of the directive. For federal states, like Germany, the creation of authorities corresponding to river basin districts would have entailed a diminishing role for the *länder*[161]—a politically unpalpable solution. The coordination of various *länder* that make a river basin district was considered the preferred

[156] Art. 3(1), *id.*

[157] *Id.*

[158] *Id.*

[159] Art. 3(2), *id.*

[160] Art. 3(8), *id.* "Member States provide the Commission with a list of their competent authorities. . . . "

[161] *Länder* are the states of the Federal Republic of Germany. The original term *länder* is preserved here in order to avoid confusion with the terms *member state* and *state* that denote the nation-state.

institutional arrangement. In the Netherlands, every administrative unit—in addition to specialized authorities—addresses water management, creating yet another administrative layer does not seem to be the most resourceful solution. Initially, Denmark decided to structure water management around administrative units.[162]

In addition to national river basin districts, the directive prescribes the establishment of international river basin districts. Member states must ensure that a river basin located in the territory of more than one state is designated as an international river basin district. For the portions of the international river basin located in their territories, member states must designate the appropriate authority that will implement the directive.[163] At the same time, member states must coordinate at the international river basin district level so that the environmental objectives of the directive are met. States may, for the purposes of international cooperation, employ already existing administrative structures provided for in international agreements,[164] such as the international commissions in charge of transboundary water management.

The designation of international river basin districts is not an optional requirement as the directive provides explicitly that "Member States shall ensure that a river basin covering the territory of more than one Member State is assigned to an international river basin district."[165] Given that many river basin districts in Europe are transnational, this is a provision that mandates the deepening of cooperation at the international level in order to execute the objectives of the directive. Since the directive is an expression of integrated river basin management, its application at

[162] Denmark consists of fourteen counties and the Copenhagen Community and by consolidating some of these counties it established twelve river basin districts. The Denmark RBD-borders did not conform with the HELCOM (Commission for the Protection of Baltic Sea) sub-regions and Denmark has been encouraged to review the number of its river basin districts. *See* Lars M. Svendsen, *Danish River Basin District Borders compared with Baltic Sea Sub-regions*, HELCOM (Pollution Load Compilation) PLC 1/2004, Document 3/1, Helsinki Commission, PLC Seminar, First Meeting, Helsinki, Finland, Feb. 25-27, 2004. In June 2004, an agreement was reached between the Danish government and Danish People's Party to dissolve the counties and establish five elected regions. *See* website of Danish Regions, http://www.arf.dk/English/Frontpage.htm.

See also Jesper Dørge & Jørgen Windolf, *Implementation of the Water Framework Directive – can we use models as a tool in integrated river basin management?* 1(2) International Journal of River Basin Management 165 (2003).

[163] Art. 3(3), *WFD, supra* note 146.

[164] Art. 3(4), *id.*

[165] Art. 3(3), *id.*

transnational river basin district level essentially means the realization of IWRM at the international scale. The demands placed by the directive on states require a new level of international cooperation if countries not only share goals but also need to align their methodologies and means of achieving these goals. The demand to create a coherent and integrated river basin management system based on shared goals and methodologies has tested the cooperating endurance of member states.

What is even more interesting, and exhibits the desire of the EC to have an impact on areas beyond its current jurisdictional control, but within the ambit of its political influence, is the provision that requests member states to coordinate with nonmember states in water management. The directive explicitly provides that when a river basin extends beyond the territory of the EC member states must attempt to establish coordination with nonmember states with the ultimate goal to achieve the objectives of the directive throughout the river basin.[166]

The WFD is a planning instrument. The focus of the directive is not so much on the accomplishment of specific, quantitative goals but on the establishment of an institutional structure and process that facilitates integrated water management. The directive is process-oriented legislation. The directive focuses on planning mechanisms as the means for the achievement of water quality. Process legislation provides states with some discretion on the specific goals to be achieved, allowing, thus, for some goal customization. The customization of goals is not untrammeled, though, and states have to explain why they have opted for certain goals or why they are entitled to exceptions from the general legislative norms that apply to the rest of member states.[167]

That the directive is a process instrument is evident from the tools that are necessary for implementation. River basin management plans are the tools that are to guide the future of water management. Member states have to produce river basin management plans (RBMPs) for the river basin districts located in their territory.[168] If a river basin district is shared by other member states, member states "shall ensure coordination" with the other member states in order to produce an international river basin

[166] If coordination with non-member states cannot be achieved, member states must apply the directive for the portion of the river basin that falls within their territory. *See* art. 3(5), *id.*

[167] On the concept of controlled customization of legislation to fit the needs of states, *see Louka(2), supra* note 136, at 72–74.

[168] Art. 13(1), *WFD, supra* note 146.

management plan (IRBMP).[169] If a river basin district is shared with non-member states, member states "shall endeavour to produce a single river basin management plan."[170]

The Planning Process Guidance document that was generated during the implementation process[171] provides a glimpse into the intricacies and difficulties of planning under the WFD. Integration[172] is established as the key idea around which the WFD is to evolve. Based on this idea the planning process is described primarily as a top down-bottom up process that involves:

- Scenario assessment (assessment of current water status, and analysis and identification of preliminary gaps);
- Target setting (gap analysis between the current status of waters and what needs to be achieved to meet environmental objectives); and
- The adoption of river basin management plans and program of measures.

In addition to this top down-bottom up process, various parallel processes are to take place including consultation with stakeholders and the public,

169 Art. 13(2), *id.*

170 Art. 13(3), *id.* If the completion of an IRBMP is not possible, member states are to, at least, produce a river basin management plan for the portion of the river basin district that falls within their territory.

171 Guidance Document No. 11, *Planning Process, Common Implementation Strategy for the Water Framework Directive* (2000/60/EC) (European Communities, 2003) [hereinafter Planning Guidance Document].

172 Integration of:

- Environmental objectives;
- All water resources;
- All water uses, functions, and values;
- Disciplines, analyses, and expertise;
- All water legislation into a common and coherent framework;
- All significant management and ecological aspects;
- A wide range of measures, including pricing and economic and financial instruments, in a common management approach;
- Stakeholders and the civil society in the decisionmaking;
- Different decisionmaking levels that influence water resources and water status (local, regional, national);
- Water management from different member states (for river basins shared by several countries). *Id.* at 5–6.

monitoring and evaluation of the process, and feedback for the potential future amendment of the process.[173]

The Planning Process Guidance document generates many questions about water management and general land-use and spatial planning without, however, resolving them including:

- Should land-use planning take into account river basin planning or whether river basin planning should happen within the constraints of land-use planning?[174] (Water management is central to many activities. Nevertheless, making water management an explicit constraint may create acrimony about why water and not other renewable resources should shape development.)
- Will the management of water based on the spatial unit, the river basin, create conflicts with other policy sectors based on administrative boundaries?[175]
- What could be the role of strategic environmental assessment in water management and land-use planning?[176]

The RBMP is central to river basin planning and countries are to produce their first river basin management plan in 2009 and to update such plans every fifteen years.[177] The RBMPs must include programs of measures—the measures that states adopt for the abatement of pollution[178]—the mapping of waters, a summary of significant pressures and impacts in a river basin, the economic analysis of water use, and a summary of the consultation process with stakeholders and the public.[179] Updates of RBMPs must assess the progress made in achieving environmental objectives, explain the environmental objectives that have yet to be achieved, and assess the measures foreseen but not yet undertaken.[180] Thus, the RBMPs assume the function of a scorecard—an evaluative instrument that derives lessons from the past to guide the future. The fact that RBMPs need to provide an explanation of the potential nonattainment of planned

173 *Id.* at 11.
174 *Id.* at 15, 20.
175 *Id.* at 17.
176 *Id.* at 15.
177 Art. 13(6)–(7), *WFD, supra* note 146.
178 Art. 11, *id.*
179 Art. 13(4) and *Annex VII, id.*
180 *Annex VII(B), id.*

environmental objectives transforms them from planning instruments into accountability instruments. The accountability mechanisms included in RBMPs facilitate the process of provision of information to the public and consultation with stakeholders.

The directive methodically provides for a series of deadlines that must be achieved to ensure implementation. By 2003, states had to transpose the directive and establish the river basin districts and authorities.[181] By 2004, states had to produce what is called the article 5 report.[182] The article 5 report provides an analysis of pressures and impacts in a river basin district and a characterization of waters. By 2006, states had to establish their monitoring network.[183] These two deadlines, for the provision of the article 5 report and the monitoring network, were a source of concern since the establishment of a well-functioning monitoring network is a prerequisite for a complete analysis of pressures and impacts on waters. It seems that the directive should have required the establishment of monitoring networks as a precondition for conducting the pressure and impact analysis. Most of the article 5 reports concluded by member states have been considered rudimentary and are replete with qualitative rather than quantitative information. The problem has been particularly acute in the reports on international river basins, in which most of the available data had been compiled in past years by member states, each using a different methodology. The harmonization of available data was not realistically feasible within the short time span of four years after the adoption of the WFD, no matter the amount of resources devoted to the task and the number of negotiating rounds that took place in a number of international river basin districts.

Other deadlines to which states have to comply include the presentation of a draft river basin management plan to the public and interested stakeholders by 2008.[184] In 2009, member states must have a river basin management plan ready, including a program of measures.[185] By 2012, states must make operational their program of measures[186] and, by 2015,

---

181 *See* art. 24(1), *id.*
182 *See* art. 5(1), *id.*
183 *See* art. 8, *id.*
184 Art. 14(1)(c), *id.*
185 Art. 13(6), *id.*
186 Art. 11(7), *id.*

they must meet environmental objectives.[187] By 2021, the second river basin management cycle is expected to be finalized.

As mentioned above, the directive provides for some amount of constrained flexibility with regard to how states are to achieve environmental objectives. The fact that the directive allows for flexibility is evident from the latitude provided in characterizing waters. In identifying water bodies, the directive takes into account the natural and climatic conditions as they vary across the EC.[188] Since such conditions are not the same across the EC, good water status cannot mean the same thing for all states and regions. Thus, from the initial stage of water characterization, the directive promotes customization rather than uniformity. After the initial water characterization, waters need to be further characterized based on what, in the directive, is termed *their ecological status*. Based on their ecological status, waters are classified as high, good, moderate, poor, or bad status.[189] For the classification of waters based on their ecological status, a number of criteria are used, such as the biological, hydromorphological, chemical, and physiochemical characteristics of water.[190] An intercalibration exercise is to take place that would consistently determine the boundaries between the different classifications of water among member states.[191]

The directive focuses on surface waters, and states must take measures to prevent the deterioration of status of waters (for instance, waters of moderate status must not become waters of bad status). States must strive to ensure that all their waters achieve a good status by 2015 and implement the provisions necessary to reduce pollution by priority hazardous substances.[192] Although these seem like stringent objectives, significant

---

187 Art. 4(1)(a)(ii), *id.*

188 *See Annex II, id.* For a more detailed analysis of the classification of waters under the directive, *see Louka(2), supra* note 136, at 184–87.

189 *See Annex V, WFD, supra* note 146.

190 *Id.*

191 The purpose of the intercalibration exercise is to establish consistency all across the EC in distinguishing between water of:

- High status and good status;
- Good status and moderate status;
- Moderate status and poor status; and
- Poor status and bad status.

Establishing the borderline between these categories in a consistent manner all across the various water bodies in Europe is not the easiest undertaking. For the intercalibration exercise, *see* para. 1.4.1., *Annex V, id.*

192 Art. 4(1)(a), *id.*

latitude is provided. Article 4(3)(a) gives the states room for maneuver by allowing them to characterize their waters as heavily modified. This provision is ambiguous enough to allow for various interpretations. It is provided that states may identify certain waters as heavily modified if the changes in the characteristics of water that would be necessary for achieving good status would have adverse effects on the wider environment; navigation, including port facilities; drinking water supply; irrigation; power generation; water regulation; flood protection; land drainage; and other equally important sustainable development activities.[193] The number of sectors that this exception covers, including the provision of "other equally important sustainable human development activities," make the characterization of waters as artificial or heavily modified a convenient means of evading the environmental objectives set by the directive.

Furthermore, technical feasibility and economic costs could be used as a justification for keeping waters in the artificial or heavily modified category and not pursuing efforts to restore them. According to the directive, states can designate waters as heavily modified if the beneficial objectives served by the artificial or modified characteristics of water cannot be achieved reasonably, for reasons of technical feasibility or disproportionate costs, by other means that are a significantly better environmental option.[194] Furthermore, in cases of *force majeure*, for instance, floods and droughts, states are exempt from applying the directive but also must take all practical steps to avoid compromising the objectives of the directive. These *force majeure* exceptional circumstances must be reviewed annually, and all steps must be undertaken to restore water to the status it had before the occurrence of an exceptional circumstance.[195]

More exceptions are provided for waters so affected by human activity that the achievement of good status would be infeasible or disproportionately expensive. In order to use this exception, states must ensure that the environmental and socioeconomic needs served by a human activity cannot be achieved by other means, which would be a significantly better environmental option not entailing excessive costs. States must further ensure that waters that are so affected by human activity reach the

193 Art. 4(3)(a), *id.*
194 Art. 4(3)(b), *id.*
195 Art. 4(6), *id.*

highest ecological and chemical status given the impacts that cannot be avoided.[196]

As mentioned before, the directive provides the goal of nondeterioration of status of waters.[197] The least states can do after the directive is adopted is to ensure that their waters do not become worse than what they were before the adoption of the directive. This nondeterioration goal has been promoted as an important element in the application of the directive. Nevertheless, this seemingly uncompromising goal is not a steadfast rule, and exceptions are allowed. Waters of high status could deteriorate to waters of good status for the purposes of undertaking a new sustainable development activity.[198] This exception was promoted by the southern European states since some of their waters enjoy high status conditions, but future development may very well compromise such conditions. Not allowing, thus, for the deterioration of waters of high status would have left no further room for development. In order to allow for the application of such an exception, states must perform a cost/benefit analysis that weighs the preservation of high water status against the benefits to be derived from sustainable development. States must also provide evidence that the benefits served by the deterioration of water status cannot, for reasons of technical feasibility or disproportionate costs, be achieved by any other means that would be a significantly better environmental option.[199]

Other exceptions that states can ask for have to do with the attainment of deadlines. States do not have to meet the deadline of 2015, a deadline by which all waters are to reach good status, provided that they can demonstrate that meeting the deadline is not possible for reasons of technical feasibility, or because of the high costs involved, or because natural conditions do not allow for the timely improvement of the status of a water body.[200]

The breathing room that the exceptions allow for[201] comes with strings attached. The constraints emanate from processes established in

---

[196] Art. 4(5), *id.*

[197] Art. 1(a), *id.*

[198] Art. 4(7), *id.*

[199] *Id.*

[200] Art. 4(4)(a), *id.*

[201] States seem willing to take advantage of the breathing room, *see EU Water Policy, Making the Water Framework Directive Work: The Quality of National Transposition and Implementation – Snapshot* –, at 13 (Results of an NGO Questionnaire, European Environmental Bureau (EEB),

the directive, especially the methodological compilation of RBMPs. Member states are expected to prepare RBMPs based on scientific data and knowledge derived from monitoring the state of waters. Because RBMPs are expected to be thorough and are conceived as operative instruments, the exceptions that states request have to be mentioned in the RBMPs, including the reasons why the exceptions are necessary.[202] This allows for public scrutiny through the consultation and public participation process provided for in the directive. The quality of the public participation process should prevent some member states from asking for too many unsubstantiated exceptions.

If the public participation process functions well,[203] states are likely to exhibit restraint in proposing river basin management plans in which most waters are classified as heavily modified. If the public participation process works well, states cannot always claim that disproportionate costs and technical feasibility constitute the reasons for lack of action. Furthermore, states are to provide the European Commission with the time limit for exceptions, after which the states are to conform to the general requirements of the directive.[204] If a member state applies for exceptions it must ensure that its application does not permanently exclude or compromise the achievement of objectives of the directive in other bodies of water within the same river basin district.[205] Applying for exceptions must be consistent also with the implementation of other EC environmental legislation.[206] Steps must be taken so that the application for exceptions guarantees the same level of protection already provided by existing EC legislation.[207] The strings attached to exceptions and the quality of implementation expected, as demonstrated by the guidance documents,[208] curbs the latitude granted to states.

The adoption of policies for water demand management, the latest by 2010, is to challenge the administrative capacity of some states.[209]

May 2004) available online http://www.eeb.org/activities/water/11-WFD-implementation-quality-a-snapshot-EEB-May2004.pdf.

202 Art. 4(3)–(7), *WFD, supra* note 146.

203 This means that all interests are represented and are able to engage in an informed discourse on the content of river basin management plans.

204 *See also* art. 15, *WFD, supra* note 146, on reporting to the European Commission.

205 Art. 4(8), *id.*

206 Art. 4(8), *id.*

207 Art. 4(9), *id.*

208 *See* Chapter 5.

209 Art. 9, *WFD, supra* note 146.

The application of the cost-recovery principle is likely to create acrimony in many states and raise opposition from sectors that view water provision as their undisputed entitlement. Cost-recovery will also raise issues of fairness.

The provisions dedicated to groundwater are not as extensive as the provisions for surface waters. In 2001, the Commission established an Expert Advisory Forum that was to come up with a proposal for a daughter directive on groundwater.[210] Groundwater suffers from two ills. First, over-abstraction occurs if groundwater is used for drinking water supplies and too much abstraction leads to depletion. Second, pollution results if hazardous substances disposed of on land seep into the groundwater. The goals for groundwater management are the following:

- Implement the measures necessary to prevent or limit the input of pollutants into the groundwater in order to avert the deterioration of status of groundwater.
- Protect, enhance, and restore all bodies of groundwater, and ensure the balance between abstraction and the recharge of groundwater with the aim to achieve good groundwater status by 2015.
- Take the necessary measures to reverse any significant and sustained upward trend in the concentration of any pollutant in the groundwater resulting from the impact of human activity in order to reduce gradually the pollution of groundwater.[211]

Soon after the adoption of the directive, the commission adopted a list of thirty-three priority hazardous substances, the concentration of which in waters must eventually be eliminated.[212]

Instituting Public Participation in Water Management

The goals, planning processes, and multiple detailed annexes of the directive cultivate the impression that water management is a technical issue, better left to experts skilled in its application. It could come as a surprise,

[210] The groundwater directive was adopted in 2006. *See Directive 2006/118/EC* of the European Parliament and of the Council of 12 December 2006 on the protection of groundwater against pollution and deterioration, OJ L 372/19, 27.12.2006.

[211] Art. 4(1)(b), *WFD, supra* note 146.

[212] *See Decision No 2455/2001/EC* of the European Parliament and of the Council of 20 November 2001, establishing the list of priority substances in the field of water policy and amending Directive 2000/60/EC, OJ L 331/1, 15.12.2001.

therefore, that this directive provides for the participation of water users (stakeholders) and the public in water management. The directive distinguishes between stakeholders and the public. Stakeholders are those who have an interest (a stake) in decisions made on water management; the public at large does not have a specifically defined interest but is affected by water management decisions and is presumed to be concerned with water resources management and the affordability of water.

The involvement of stakeholders and the public in the decision-making process is an important element of IWRM. The prevailing rationale for the necessity of stakeholder involvement is based on an assumption that if those who are interested in water use can be involved in decision-making that affects such use, they are likely to contribute to the making of superior decisions. Even better, as they are now codecisionmakers, stakeholders are likely to be willing to implement their own decisions, thus, avoiding the costs of third-party enforcement. The validity of these assumptions is discussed in Chapter 13, while the remainder of this section analyzes the provisions of the WFD on public participation.

The directive provides that member states "shall ensure" that, for each river basin district, they publish and make available for comments to the public, including water users, the timetable and work program for the production of the RBMP, including a statement of consultation measures to be undertaken at least three years prior to the adoption of the river basin management plan.[213] An interim overview of significant issues presented in a river basin district must be available for comment to water users and the public at least two years before the adoption of the RBMP.[214] Draft copies of the river basin management plan must be available for comments to the public and water users at least one year before the beginning of the planning period to which the plan refers.[215] Access to the background documentation used for preparing a river basin management plan should also be provided upon request.[216] Member states must allow at least six months so that stakeholders and the public can comment on a draft river basin management plan, and this consultation process is to recur with every update of river basin management plans.[217]

213 Art. 14(1)(a), *WFD, supra* note 146. Before the end of 2006 for the first planning period.
214 Art. 14(1)(b), *id.* Before the end of 2007 for the first planning period.
215 Art. 14(1)(c), *id.* Before the end of 2008 for the first planning period.
216 Art. 14(1), *id.*
217 Art. 14(2)–(3), *id.*

In addition to this mandatory consultation process[218] that has to do with the preparation of draft river basin management plan and its submission to water users and the public for comments, the directive opens the door for more direct public involvement. The directive states that

> Member states shall encourage the active involvement of all interested parties in the implementation of this Directive, in particular in the production, review and updating of the river basin management plans.[219]

Thus, even though the consultation process is a mandatory requirement under the directive, the active involvement of interested parties shall merely be encouraged.

There are different gradients of public participation in environmental decisionmaking.

- The mere provision information, under which the public and water users receive information on water management but have no involvement in decisionmaking;
- Consultation, whereby river basin management plans are prepared by expert public officials and the public is consulted after a first draft of a RBMP is already in place; and
- Active involvement, in which the public and water users are actively involved with public authorities in the preparation of river basin management plan.

The provision of information is the first step since, unless information is openly provided, the possibilities of participation are severely hampered. Today, many developed countries have adopted Freedom of Information Acts, and the provision of information to the public is guaranteed in several international environmental instruments.[220]

Consultation and participation processes have been sought by civil society groups and have been adopted in developed countries in accordance with national legislation and international requirements. What distinguishes

---

[218] Art. 14(1), *id.* "Member states *shall ensure* that, for each river basin district, they publish and make available for comments to the public, including users . . . " [*emphasis added*].

[219] Art. 14(1), *id.*

[220] *See* Chapter 12.

consultation processes from the traditional lobbying performed by interest groups is the formality of the consultation process. Lobbying involves various interest groups approaching decisionmakers and presenting their views on different legislative acts or rules before their adoption. Lobbying is initiated by groups that wish to influence the policymaking process and is often done informally. The consultation process consists of a formal invitation by a regulating agency to all interested parties to provide their opinions on a proposed rule or, in this case, the RBMP drafted by a river basin authority. Often, the results of a consultation process are published, and it is considered best practice for a public institution that initiates a consultation process to provide feedback on the comments it receives from the public and how these comments are taken into account in the decisionmaking process. The formality of the consultation process reduces the chances that a public organization can be co-oped, since it has to appear evenhanded and grant similar rights to all groups in the consultation process.

The active involvement of stakeholders in the decisionmaking process is rare in domestic and international practice. To bolster river basin management planning, as analyzed in Chapter 15, a number of countries have developed stakeholder fora. Such fora have been closely involved in decisionmaking and developing a vision and a plan for a river basin. Active involvement, however, has not been widely practiced either because stakeholders are not ready to be actively involved or because the state apparatus is not ready to accept stakeholders as co-decisionmakers. Again, the possibilities of undue influence on a public organization by groups actively involved in the decisionmaking process should not be underestimated; it must be transparent which groups are involved in which matters.

The active involvement of general public, and not simply stakeholders, rarely materializes because the public seems amorphous. One has to wonder what states could or should do, in addition to publicizing river basin management plans, to enlist active public involvement. The public participates in policymaking through the system of representative democracy that is the norm among EU member states. The question then is why the public needs to be additionally involved in water management and, if such involvement is desirable, how it can be secured. Encouraging public involvement may be less about securing efficiency in decisionmaking and more about cultivating the development of participatory democratic norms in a specific economic sector. Representative democracy, today, is often viewed as wanting and in need of strengthening with more direct participation mechanisms.[221] For years to come, policymakers will need to be concerned about methods that involve those who "have no choice" but to live with the decisions made by others in water management.

Making Water Policy Matter

The WFD has been perceived as legislation that focuses on water quality. Southern European states have charged that the directive addresses the environmental issues of northern Europe without addressing the water management issues of the south. In the south, issues of water quantity are more acute than those of water quality because southern states have to address prolonged drought spells or uneven spatial water distribution.

Issues of water quantity are becoming salient in central and northern Europe. Floods are now a big concern for many northern and central European states. Between 1998 and 2002, Europe experienced over a hundred major floods, including catastrophic floods in the Danube and the Elbe River basins.[222] Since 1998, floods have caused deaths, the displacement of about half a million people and insured economic losses totaling at least twenty-five billion euros.[223] Flooding is not the central focus of the WFD[224] as much as the maintenance of water quality. The directive is a framework directive for the management of water; addressing specific climatic phenomena, such as floods, droughts, and ice hazards, is beyond its scope. Climatic conditions could be addressed and planned for, though, in the river basin management plans provided for in the directive.

States that have developed an administrative structure for protection against floods have opted for arrangements that do not necessarily coincide with the institutions put in place for river basin planning.[225]

---

221 *See* Chapter 14.

222 *Making the Structural and Cohesion Funds Water-Positive, Document by the European Network of Environmental Authorities (ENEA)*, Feb. 2006 available online http://fi.kvvm.hu/bm/kohezios_alap/kezikonyv/final_handbook.pdf/

223 *Id.* at 9.

224 The issue of floods is mentioned in the article that establishes the purposes of the directive, *see* article 1(e) where it is provided that "The purpose of this Directive is to establish a framework for the protection of inland surface waters, transnational waters, coastal waters and groundwater which . . . contributes to mitigating the effects of floods and droughts . . . " Other articles refer to floods as *force majeure* circumstances that states can use to obtain exceptions from achieving environmental standards. *See*, e.g., art. 4(6), art. 11(3)(l), and art. 11(5), *WFD*, *supra* note 1.

225 *See generally* Chapter 11.

This seems counterintuitive since river basin planning should provide for flood protection and flood defense measures if it is to be comprehensive planning. One would expect also that the directorates and agencies devoted to river basin planning would be the appropriate authorities to be involved in emergency planning addressing the control of floods. Most states, though, view flood defense as an emergency planning issue that calls for the involvement of traditional administrative institutions (districts, regions, and municipalities). River basin directorates, as a norm, do not play a central role in flood management and planning. Flood protection in most states necessitates the involvement of top central authorities (at the level of the ministry in charge or even the prime minister's office), as a whole state or a region may be designated a disaster area, and the employment of local authorities who must take measures to reach the affected populations that fall within their jurisdictions.

In 2007, a new flood directive was adopted by the EU. In addition to the real issue of flooding that needs to be addressed, the flood directive is motivated by concerns that a strict interpretation of the WFD may prevent infrastructure projects that are likely to alter the hydromorphology of a river but, nevertheless, are deemed necessary to prevent flooding. A flood directive could then provide a counterbalance to a strict interpretation of the WFD. Environmental groups have sensed correctly that addressing the issue of floods in a separate directive may mean the allowance of construction works on river basins that may prevent flooding but also adversely affect the hydromorphology of a watercourse. Infrastructure projects for the prevention of flooding may conflict with the goal of non-deterioration of current water status.

The flood directive,[226] as it currently stands, provides many linkages between flood planning and river basin management planning. The Commission's goal is to completely align the institutional arrangements and timing between the two directives. Timetables have been aligned so that the consultation process with stakeholders and the public is coordinated under both directives. Reporting to the European Commission itself

---

226 *Directive 2007/60/EC* of the European Parliament and of the Council of 23 October 2007 on the assessment and management of food risks, OJ L 288/27, 6.11.2007. *See also Proposal for a Directive of the European Parliament and of the Council on the Assessment and the Management of Floods*, COM(2006)15 final, 18.01.2006.

is to be fully synchronized under both directives. Flood risk management plans are to be fully integrated into river basin management plans.

The urge to adopt a flood directive was fueled by a view of the WFD as an environmental directive. Perceiving the directive solely as an environmental directive does not do justice to the efforts that have been undertaken to create a cohesive framework for water management in Europe. The directive is, above all, a planning directive. The directive is concerned with the achievement of environmental objectives and with the orientation of new or existing institutional structures toward water management at the river basin district. All member states have interpreted the directive to require the management of waters based on hydrographic borders rather than administrative frontiers.

States have emphasized the development of institutions oriented toward river basin management. Bulgaria has established river basin directorates as a new administrative structure.[227] Other countries, including Hungary, are grounding their planning on the international river basin district in the creation of subbasins (or working areas) around which domestic coordination is organized.[228] Other states are aware of the need to further decentralize water management and grant more authority to river basin institutions.[229] Some states, for which privatization has not been a fruitful experience, are cautious and would like to ensure that the river basin institutions are able to handle the increasing responsibilities handed to them. Existing institutional arrangements for transnational watercourses had to reorganize their administrative structure to become coordinating platforms for the implementation of the WFD.[230]

A central issue in the implementation of the directive, as demonstrated in Chapter 9, has to do with the impossibility of isolating water management from land use planning and the future direction of development in a state. Therefore, the institutional structure put together for river basin management cannot be isolated from the rest of the administrative structure of a state. Establishing river basin authorities, based on hydrographic boundaries, may seem like a sensible solution for water management but could create a host of other coordination inconsistencies. This is because other administrative authorities, for instance, agriculture or

227 *See* Chapter 11.
228 *Id.*
229 *Id.*
230 *See* Chapters 17–20.

land-use institutions, are organized based on administrative boundaries rather than hydrographic boundaries. Commentators have wondered whether the zeal to organize water management based on hydrographic borders may jeopardize the interaction between river basin institutions and the remainder of authorities based on administrative subdivisions.[231] In other words, the question is whether the WFD, by correcting the "spatial fit"[232] through the creation of institutions with jurisdiction over the entire river basin district, creates a "collaboration misfit" because institutions that fit hydrographic borders may have difficulty collaborating with institutions based on administrative borders.

The fit between the mission and the jurisdiction of an organization is an important ingredient for organizational effectiveness.[233] Aligning the mission with the jurisdiction of an organization may create problems of interchange among organizations. As organizations broaden their jurisdiction to fit their mission, they may step on boundaries of other institutions. In most states, river basin authorities are created as an additional institutional layer on top of an already existing administrative structure. In most cases, river basin authorities are not elected democratically, and this creates problems with their legitimacy in making decisions that affect a whole river basin district. The traditional administrative authorities, such as regions (and regional governors) and prefectures are often vying for the extensive powers granted to river basin authorities. Often, various municipalities administered by democratically elected mayors may refuse to coordinate with appointed water directors. As should be expected, some rivalry between existing authorities and newly developed river basin authorities is unavoidable.

The issue of institutional rivalry may be particularly acute in central and eastern European countries. In addition to a rushed privatization, after the fall of communism, central and eastern European countries have been faced with demands to overhaul their administrative structure, to decentralize and adopt the basic elements of democratic governance. Such an overhaul has involved the creation of municipal self-government. Now, in most central and eastern European countries, mayors and municipal

231 Timothy Moss, *The Governance of Land Use in River Basins: prospects for overcoming problems of institutional interplay with the EU Water Framework Directive*, 21(1) Land Use Policy 85, Jan. 2004.

232 *Id.*

233 James Q. Wilson, *Bureaucracy: What Government Agencies Do and Why They Do It* 187–88 (1989).

councils are directly elected by the population. The structural funding provided by the EU and aimed at correcting imbalances among the regions of member states requires the reorganization of the domestic administrative structures based on regions. Although regions were initially created as planning units for the disbursement of EC funding, there is some expectation that they would evolve into more or less semiautonomous administrative structures.

Many member states have been tinkering with their administrative arrangements before the adoption of the WFD. Given the mishaps of privatization that most central and eastern European countries have experienced, there has been a resistance to an inerudite decentralization that could potentially take place without sufficient thought to the modes and tools that facilitate devolution of authority. Because devolution is not advisable without a thorough examination of possible ramifications, the adoption of the WFD has not often led to the adoption of new administrative structures, and most countries have opted to engage existing authorities in the implementation of the WFD.

Furthermore, because existing local authorities often lack expertise in river basin management, there is resistance to the decentralization of such management and, at present, central institutions are the focal point in river basin management. Thus, although the implementation of the WFD has been taken seriously and most states agree that river basin management is the way to the future, there has been some reticence to create brand-new authorities and to proceed with bold steps toward decentralization. This is probably a wise approach for the time being as it is important to comprehend the WFD within the political and administrative context of a state that attempts to apply it–not in a vacuum. As mentioned above, the success of the WFD does not depend on the creation of specific structures or the adoption of specific measures but rather on the establishment of an operative, coordinated, and organized system of water management around the river basin district, as that district is realized through international, national, and local layers.

Chapter 5

Implementing Water Management

Legislating and Facilitating: The Role of the European Commission

The European Commission (the Commission) plays an important role in the everyday affairs of the European Union (EU). This is because it has the right to initiate legislative proposals that the European Parliament (the Parliament) and the Council of Ministers (the Council) may adopt and because it is the enforcer of the treaties that make the European Union (the EU). The fact that the Commission is an appointed and not an elected body has created some misgivings about the legitimacy of a legislative process that is initiated by a bureaucracy located in Brussels and, to most Europeans, far too removed from local problems and concerns. The fact that the main legislative body of the EU is not elected has exacerbated the angst about the so-called *democratic deficit*. In order to abate concerns about its democratic legitimacy, the Commission has developed a practice to consult with the constituencies affected by laws it initiates. Because the consultation process that the commission initiates is often said to be lacking in transparency about who should be consulted and why and how they are to be consulted, the Commission has issued two documents to demystify the consultation process.

The Commission, in its European governance paper,[234] underlines the importance of transparency in the consultation process. The Commission has emphasized the principles all community institutions are to adhere to, namely, openness, participation, accountability, effectiveness, and coherence, while reinforcing the principles of subsidiarity[235] and proportionality.[236] According to the Commission, creating "a culture of consultation and dialogue" means creating a code of conduct that sets the minimum standards on what to consult on, when, whom, and how to consult.[237] Establishing such a code of conduct should decrease the risk of a number of groups acquiring a privileged role in the consultation process creating the likelihood that policymakers listen to only one side of the argument. The Commission further exemplified the consultation process by providing the minimum standards that should apply to such a process.[238] One such clear minimum standard that the Commission has adopted mandates that contributions to the participatory process must be acknowledged, and the results of the consultation process must be displayed on websites linked to a single access point on the internet.[239]

The governance paper and the minimum standards document proposed by the Commission are remarkable in demonstrating the commitment of the Commission to an open and accountable consultation process.[240] The fact that these documents exist and could be used as

---

234 *European Governance: A White Paper*, COM(2001) 428 final, 25.7.2001 [hereinafter *Governance Paper*].

235 For the principle of subsidiarity, *see* art. 5, *EC Treaty, supra* note 129. The principle of subsidiarity is based on the idea that the central government should have a subsidiary function, performing only those tasks that cannot be performed effectively at a more immediate or local level. *See Oxford English Dictionary* (1989). In the context of the EC, subsidiarity means that decisions must be made as close as possible to the citizens and that action at the EC level is justified when the objectives of the action cannot be achieved by member states, regional, or local governments.

236 *Governance Paper, supra* note 234, at 10.

237 *Id.* at 17.

238 *Communication from the Commission: Towards a reinforced culture of consultation and dialogue—General principles and minimum standards for consultation of interested parties by the Commission*, COM(2002)704 final, 11.12.2002.

239 *Id.* at 20–21.

240 In addition, the Aarhus Convention has established the right to information and the right to participation in decisionmaking in environmental matters. The convention is now applicable at the level of EU institutions, *see Regulation (EC) No 1367/2006* of the European Parliament and of the Council of 6 September 2006 on the application of the provisions of the Aarhus Convention on Access to Information, Public Participation in Decision-making and Access

reference points could help shape the culture of the Commission in being more open and democratic. As a general rule, though, the adoption of documents does not fundamentally alter the culture of an organization. The mandate to adopt open and transparent consultation procedures has changed the formal organization but the ingrained institutional culture has not necessarily dashed to adapt to change. As a result, a number of Directorates General (DGs) are more open to a wide variety of stakeholders than others that limit themselves to listening primarily to traditional interests they perceive they need to advance or protect. Few of the Commission's officials are convinced in their role as shapers and makers of the EU law and are not always receptive to inquiries into the decisionmaking of the Commission.

In the case of the WFD, the Commission held extensive consultations with the constituencies that will be affected by the implementation of the WFD, such as the chemical industry, the water industry, and the environmental nongovernmental organizations (NGOs). The groups that participated in the consultation process were those that have a stake in the legislative outcome and the ability to organize at the EU level. Participating in the consultations held by the Commission is not for the uninitiated. The groups that are effective in the consultation process are those able to amass resources and expertise to present a coherent position to the Commission. This generates recriminations that only resource-rich NGOs can successfully participate in the consultations held by the Commission.

The Commission issued an open call for the participation of all interested parties in the drafting of the WFD. An open call for participation could be translated as an invitation for all to participate. In addition to issuing the open call, the Commission invited certain groups and organizations to participate. These organizations, to the credit of the Commission, cover the full gamut of sectors affected by water legislation—the water sector, the chemical industry, the fertilizer industry, private water suppliers, and farmers unions. Furthermore, the Commission considered inputs from stakeholders who intervened in the consultation process on their own initiative, such as local authorities, landowners' organizations, statutory agencies, and consumers.[241]

to Justice in Environmental Matters to Community institutions and bodies, OJ L 264/13, 25.09.2006. For more details on the Aarhus Convention, *see* Chapter 12.

241 Maria Kaika, *The Water Framework Directive: a New Directive for a Changing Social, Political and Economic European Framework*, 11(3) European Planning Studies 303 (2003).

The consultation process, while in principle open to everyone, ended up favoring large associations that keep a Brussels office. The European Environmental Bureau (EEB), the European Union of National Associations of Water Suppliers (EUREAU), the European Crop Protection Association (ECPA), and the European Fertilizer Manufacturers Association (EFMA) had an advantage by their mere location in Brussels. For a number of associations, this was a double advantage because their member associations could lobby national governments while they could participate in the consultation process launched by the Commission.[242]

The water industry was, in principle, supportive of the directive. This is because the directive focuses on the reduction of pollution at the source, minimizing the costs of water purification later. The chemical industry, on the other hand, was displeased with a directive that sets a goal of zero concentrations for "man-made synthetic substances in the marine environment."[243] The organized lobbies of farmers resisted provisions that provided for full cost recovery. Farming consumes large quantities of water especially in the southern European states. The use of pesticides and fertilizers in agriculture contributes to water pollution. Pollution by nitrates discharged from agricultural fields is one of the least tractable sources of pollution. Farmers have claimed that regulation is not the way to change agricultural practices and that education on best agricultural practices is the preferable way to address a sector that has been notoriously resistant to change.

The directive touched the nerves of other institutions. Socialist members of the Parliament opposed full cost pricing for water use. Since water is a public good, it was argued, everyone should be entitled to clean and drinkable water whether she can afford it or not. Full cost pricing could place an unacceptable burden on the European consumer. It was argued that full cost pricing assumes that water is an economic good, to which market principles apply, meaning the costs for provision of water services must be recovered. This analysis conflicts with the traditional understanding of water as a public good.

Local authorities viewed the WFD with some suspicion. The creation of new river basin authorities was alarming since the establishment of such authorities would certainly mean the diminution of duties, and

242 *Id.*

243 Art. 1(e), *WFD, supra* note 146.

thus, the authoritative influence of existing regional and local authorities. At the same time, not all local authorities were attuned to the possible implications of implementation of the WFD. Local authorities did not lobby the Commission directly and, instead, relied on central governments to enunciate their perspective.[244]

Implementation Strategy

The water directive is a framework directive. Because it is a framework directive, it does not provide the specifics of implementation that are to be ironed out through subsequent "daughter directives." The directive has an extensive reach as it regulates almost every inch of the EU's territory and affects multiple sectors of the economy. The directive, beyond its framework character, is a planning instrument for water management in Europe. Because of the wide reach of the directive and a framework that allows for diverging interpretations, the Commission was compelled to initiate a common implementation strategy.

The directive provides states with significant latitude in terms of the institutions they could put in place and how these institutions should apply the directive. These provisions could create the problem of a too-customized, thus, overdiversified implementation. One way to curb over-diversification is to plan and monitor the implementation through the establishment of a common implementation process that would, at least, set the floor of implementation. An implementation process, the Commission considered, should curb the costs of enforcement. The Commission has resolved that the antagonistic process of bringing infringement proceedings against states that are not in compliance has not been that productive;[245] instead, more effort should be expended on facilitating implementation by providing guidance and advice and a forum for the exchange of insights, concerns, and ideas.

As iterated by the Commission itself, the implementation of the WFD presents challenges that are shared among member states. A common implementation strategy (CIS) has been established in recognition that an integrated approach to river basin management is crucial

[244] Kaika, *supra* note 241.

[245] Ben Page and Maria Kaika, *The EU Water Framework Directive: Part 2. Policy Innovation and the Shifting Choreography of Governance*, 13 European Environment (2003).

for the implementation of the directive.[246] The CIS was put into effect through a strategic document that was issued in May 2001. The purpose of CIS is to:

- Develop a mmon understanding of and approach to the WFD all through the EU;
- Elaborate informal technical guidance; and
- Share experiences among states in order to avoid duplication of effort and to limit the risk of poor application of requirements of the directive.[247]

Some of the achievements of the CIS from its beginnings all through 2005 include:

- Development of fourteen guidance documents and various other reports on different articles of the directive;
- Development of a Water Information System for Europe (WISE);
- Electronic newsletters providing updates on the implementation all through the EU;
- Execution of pilots through pilot river basins in which many of the provisions of the directive were tested and validated.[248]

The CIS has progressed through a number of work programs that are being developed every two years. The purpose of a new work program is to evaluate the implementation that occurred during prior work programs and to build on lessons learnt for the future. Up to 2006, three work programs had been adopted covering the periods 2001 to 2002, 2003 to 2004, and 2005 to 2006.

The CIS strategic document[249] underlines the demanding timetable for the execution of different aspects of the WFD, the complexity of the text, and the diversity of possible solutions to the scientific, technical, and

---

246 *Overview of the Common Implementation Strategy* (CIS, CD – ROM 2005) [hereinafter *Overview of CIS*].
247 *Id.*
248 *Id.*
249 *Common Implementation Strategy for the Water Framework Directive* (2000/60/EC), Strategic Document as Agreed by the Water Directors under Swedish Presidency, May 2, 2001 [hereinafter *CIS 2001*].

practical questions raised by the directive. A number of issues presented in the WFD need further elaboration and substantiation to facilitate the transition from principle to implementation.[250] The water directors of member states who contributed to the compilation of the CIS strategic document agree to concentrate on a number of activities including information sharing, developing guidance on technical issues, information and data management and testing, and the validation of guidance documents issued for the implementation of the directive. In parallel with these activities the Commission has established multistakeholder fora comprised of participants from member states, stakeholders, NGOs, outside experts, and the Parliament. The purpose of these consultative fora is to provide advice on the "daughter directives" adopted to exemplify the application of the WFD.[251]

The overall organization of the CIS process is provided in Figure 5.1. Schematically, it could be said that the water directors are the ultimate decisionmaking authority and their purpose is to provide strategic guidance for the unfolding of implementation process. The strategic coordination group reports to the water directors and their purpose is to coordinate and evaluate the work of various working groups that have been established to offer guidance on various aspects of implementation. The strategic coordination group is comprised of the Commission and member states. Various stakeholders could be invited as observers to the meetings of the group.[252] The working groups[253] work on the specific policy areas in

[250] *Id.* at 1.

[251] The following expert consultative fora were established: the Expert Advisory Forum on Priority Substances and Pollution Control, the Expert Advisory Forum on Groundwater and the Expert Advisory Forum on Reporting, *see id.* at 6–9.

[252] *Id.* at 12.

[253] The working groups that were established were to develop guidance on:

- The analysis of pressures and impacts;
- Designation of heavily modified bodies of water;
- Classification of inland surface water status and the identification of reference conditions;
- Development of typology and classification systems of transitional and coastal waters;
- Establishing the intercalibration network and the intercalibration exercise;
- Economic analysis;
- Monitoring;
- Tools for the assessment and classification of groundwater;
- Best practices in river basin planning;
- A shared Geographical Information System. *Id.* at 13–14.

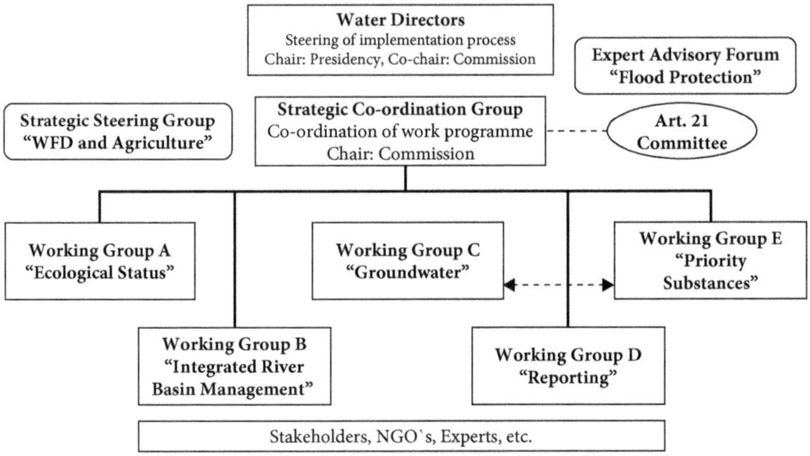

Figure 5.1 EU Organization Common Implementation Strategy 2005–2006

order to clarify certain aspects of the implementation of the WFD and report directly to the strategic coordination group.

The involvement of NGOs in the strategic coordination group and the working groups is decided on a case-by-case basis.[254] The topic of a working group and the kind of involvement needed helps to define who is to participate in the activities of a working group. Overall, the involvement of NGOs is based "on the principles of openness and transparency encouraging creative participation of interested parties."[255] The CIS document itself does not specify prerequisites for the engagement of non-governmental organizations in the working groups or in the strategic coordination group. The strategic coordination group attracted many participants rendering the logistics of managing such a group more complex.[256] Overall, the whole CIS process was well attended,[257] and this demonstrated a strong interest in the implementation of the WFD. On the other hand, the sheer number of participants may have compromised the effectiveness of the process.

---

254 *Id.* at 14.

255 *Id.*

256 By the beginning of 2006, the Strategic Coordination Group was comprised of more than sixty participants. There were proposals to streamline the strategic coordination group so that each interest is represented by one representative.

257 In the whole CIS process, it is estimated that more than 1,000 participants were actively involved (including member states, Norway, Iceland, Switzerland, Industry NGOs—EUREAU, CEFIC, ECPA—irrigators associations, landowners, environmental NGOs). *See* Patrick Murphy, *The EU Water Framework Directive*, INBO Conference, Sept. 29, 2005.

As the CIS process progressed more fine-tuning became necessary to ensure that the process produces desirable outcomes. Several issues identified as problematic during the 2001–2002 work program were addressed in the 2003–2004 work program[258] including:

- The coordination of working groups, given that there was no mechanism to address the cross-cutting issues faced by working groups until the meeting of the strategic coordination group;[259]
- The lack of integration between the work executed by the working groups and the work accomplished by the expert advisory fora;[260]
- Issues of data collection, that proved to be more time-consuming than anticipated, and language barriers that seemed more potent than prognosticated.[261]

Because of these various stumbling blocks, some of the guidance documents issued were too vague to become directly operational. Because the decisionmaking process was consensual, some member states adopted the tactic of vetoing the final guidance documents.[262] Some understood the CIS process to be a process that was to promote a best practices approach to the implementation of the WFD that went beyond the legal requirements of the directive. This approach displeased member states that were already struggling to comply with the requirements of the directive, let alone apply best practices.

Because of the high number of participants, and the number and complexity of issues, the CIS process had become too difficult to manage by the end of 2003. Although the basic structure of the process remained (water directors, strategic coordination group, working groups) the number of working groups was significantly reduced from ten to four.[263]

[258] *Common Implementation Strategy for the Water Framework Directive* (2000/60/EC), Carrying forward the Common Implementation Strategy for the Water Framework Directive—Progress and Work Programme for 2003 and 2004 as agreed by the Water Directors, June 17, 2003 [hereinafter *CIS 2003*].

[259] *Id.* at 6.

[260] *Id.*

[261] *Id.* at 7.

[262] *Id.*

[263] *Id.* at 9. The four working groups are on:

- Ecological Status;

Working groups could be broken down into drafting teams, that is, groups mandated to draft the issue paper for the whole working group. It was specified, though, that drafting groups were not to become working groups in their own right and that they should be dismantled after their mandate expires.[264]

The third cycle of review of the CIS process[265] touched on the real issues of implementation that had not gone as planned despite the number of guidance documents and the role of the Commission as the driving force behind the CIS process. The concern had to do primarily with the results of the first analysis of waters in various member states. This analysis executed by member states revealed that, in many cases, waters at risk of not meeting environmental objectives were exceeding 50 percent and, in some cases, 98 percent of all water bodies in a river basin district.[266] The Commission concluded that the methodology of the first analysis of waters probably overestimated the water bodies that were at risk of not meeting the objectives of the directive.[267] The third cycle of review also stressed the importance of interlinking the EU environmental policy with the regional and cohesion policy, the transport policy (navigation) and the renewable energy policy (hydropower) since navigation, hydropower, and flood protection can severely affect the hydromorphology of river basins.[268] The impact of agriculture on water quality was further emphasized. The Commission seemed concerned that the problems of national implementation are not always obvious in the reports of states and that efforts have to be undertaken to address the challenges of implementation.[269]

- Integrated River Basin Management;
- Groundwater;
- Reporting.

With regard to the Expert Advisory Fora (EAF), it was decided that the Expert Advisory Forum on Priority Substances will continue to work. The EAF on groundwater will continue until the finalization of a proposal for a groundwater directive. The EAF on reporting was transformed into a working group. *Id.* at 11.

264 *Id.* at 10.

265 *Common Implementation Strategy for the Water Framework Directive* (2000/60/EC), Moving to the next stage in Common Implementation Strategy for the Water Framework Directive–Progress and work programme for 2005 and 2006 as agreed by the water directors, Dec 23. 2004 [hereinafter *CIS 2004*].

266 *Id.* at 1.

267 *Id.*

268 *Id.* at 8.

269 The Commission, in this context, referred to a report issued by the EEB, *see Tips and Tricks for the WFD Implementation*, issued by the EEB in 2004, CIS 2004, at 2. For the Tips and Tricks report, *see infra* note 283.

The corpus of the CIS process is provided in the guidance documents the purpose of which is to help states avoid duplication of effort and minimize the risk of poor application of the directive. Guidance documents were intended to be informal, nonbinding documents on a number of issues that need to be addressed for the implementation of the WFD.[270]

In addition to the guidance documents, a number of other documents had to be produced on the synthesis of the results of pilot testing on the economic analysis of water use and groundwater.

One can fathom, from the sheer number and content of guidance documents, the technical consistency that is necessary for the uniform implementation of the WFD. Despite the differentiation encouraged by the directive, a consistent and harmonized methodology of implementing the directive is necessary for avoiding à la carte implementation.

An annual survey of EC law[271] has demonstrated that, in general with regard to the implementation of EU environmental legislation, the practice of preparation of guidance documents[272] and the establishment of

---

270 Guidance documents issued include:

(1) Guidance Document No. 1 on the Economics and the Environment (2003)
(2) Guidance Document No. 2 Identification of Water Bodies (2003)
(3) Guidance Document No. 3 Analysis of Pressures and Impacts (2003) (analysis of the pressures and impacts of activities that affect water quality in a river basin)
(4) Guidance Document No. 4 Identification and Designation of Heavily Modified and Artificial Water Bodies (2003)
(5) Guidance Document No. 5 Transitional and Coastal Waters—Typology, Reference Conditions and Classifications Systems (2003)
(6) Guidance Document No. 6 Towards Guidance on Establishment of the Intercalibration Network and the Process on the Intercalibration Exercise (2003)
(7) Guidance Document No. 7 Monitoring under the Water Framework Directive (2003)
(8) Guidance Document No. 8 Public Participation in Relation to the Water Framework Directive (2003)
(9) Guidance Document No. 9 Implementing the Geographical Information System Elements (GIS) of the Water Framework Directive (2003)
(10) Guidance Document No. 10 Rivers and Lakes—Typology, Reference Conditions and Classification Systems (2003)
(11) Guidance Document No. 11 Planning Processes (2003)
(12) Guidance Document No. 12 The Role of the Wetlands in the Water Framework Directive (2003)
(13) Guidance Document No. 13 Overall Approach to the Classification of Ecological Status and Ecological Potential (2005)
(14) Guidance Document No. 14 Guidance on the Intercalibration Process 2004–2006 (2005)

271 *See Seventh Annual Survey on the implementation and enforcement of Community Environmental Law 2005*, SEC(2006) 1143 [hereinafter *2006 Survey*].

272 Guidance documents were issued in the waste sector, the air sector, for the implementation of the directive on environmental impact assessment and for species protection. *Id.* at 8.

formal and informal networks among policymakers and experts[273] has improved implementation in member states. The pilots were undertaken to test the implementation of guidance documents and to provide additional insights into the advantages and disadvantages of guided modes of implementation.

Testing the Implementation Strategy

Various national and transnational river basin districts were proposed as pilots to test the implementation of the WFD and the practicability of guidance documents. A number of those responsible for implementation in the pilot basins found the guidance documents too general and, thus, of limited operational value. A number of administrators stated that they would have preferred shorter focus reports or fact sheets rather than the laborious guidance documents. This is because a number of guidance documents were general in character and did not provide details on methodologies for data collection in order to ensure consistency. The lack of a consistent methodology for data collection became acute in international river basins. For instance, in the Scheldt River basin, three countries are involved in the water management of the basin and the related regions. Each used the guidance documents and came up with a different methodology and different final results.[274]

The compilation of data necessary for the production of the report on pressures and impacts (article 5 report), became a painstaking exercise for some states and regions for various reasons:

- Monitoring programs were supposed to be put in place in 2006. Therefore, most analysis executed before that date was considered provisional.
- In order to compile information on international river basins, the same type of data had to be produced by all states and regions at the same scale, with the same level of detail, and in the same format.

273 Such a network in the WFD context has been the semiannual meeting of water directors. *See also id.* at 9 (referring to meetings between experts, seminars, and workshops).

274 *Pilot River Basin Outcome Report: Testing the WFD Guidance Documents*, at 28 (Joint Research Centre and the Directorate-General Environment of the European Commission, 2005) [hereinafter *Pilot Basins*].

This, in most cases, was not possible.[275] It was decided, therefore, that the comparability of data was more important than the complete harmonization of methodologies for obtaining the data.[276]

- A number of states believed themselves to be overwhelmed with amount of information that they had to collect because of the large number of water bodies in a number of river basin districts. An analysis of all pressures and impacts for all water bodies requires the accumulation of huge amounts of data that are not always available.[277]
- Language was an issue in certain international river basins. A number of international commissions, such as that of the Moselle-Saar River Basin, decided to translate all documents in all official languages. In other basins, English was used as the official language; for example, the Somes River Basin shared by Romania and Hungary.[278]

Public participation, as it enveloped in different pilots, demonstrated that most administrators viewed the initial stages of implementation as a technical matter and, therefore, did not engage in substantive efforts to include stakeholders and engage the public.[279] In some cases, the lack of stakeholder involvement was viewed as an advantage because there was some apprehension that stakeholder participation could compromise the authenticity of the scientific exercise.[280] A number of international river basin districts conceived the participation of the public as a concern of the national state and not an issue of international salience. Most international river basin districts developed modes for consultation with stakeholders (by granting them observer status) and focused on the provision of information through websites, newsletters, brochures, and information events.[281] None of the river basin districts, during the pilot phase, had developed a method for providing stakeholders with access to background documents.[282]

---

275 *Id.* at 36.
276 *Id.* at 22.
277 *Id.* at 75.
278 *Id.* at 21.
279 *Id.* at 25.
280 *Id.* at 34.
281 *Id.* at 37.
282 *Id.* at 86.

Evaluating the Implementation Strategy

The implementation process has not always attracted positive commentary. Although most involved in the process have claimed that the process added value (in lieu of the alternative of no process at all), many shortcomings have been pointed out.

Environmental groups have claimed that the voluminous nature of guidance documents produced did not really add much to already overburdened decisionmaking.[283] The sheer length of these documents, indeed, gave the impression that the implementation process was attuned to large bureaucracies and that it was overwhelming for smaller states that were under constant pressure to play catch up with the process. Some water directors were overwrought by a process that made so many demands on limited expert and administrative personnel. The fact that the guidance documents were not translated into national languages added to concerns that they would not be used by domestic actors and administrators.

To some, the EU implementation seemed to be driven by member states considered leaders in environmental EU matters. Many member states followed the CIS process faithfully, but did not really contribute much to it. For states that remained observers, the whole process (until at least the end of 2006) seemed like a virtual exercise. The initial article 5 reports that were produced by some states were considered of doubtful quality and raised concerns about the usefulness of guidance documents. During the strategic coordination group meeting of February 22, 2006, the Commission provided its first analysis of article 5 reports submitted by member states and expressed doubts about the quality of the reports. Some industry and environmental groups, therefore, questioned the added value of the whole CIS process.

Overall, the European Commission has supported the CIS process and frequently has claimed that implementation would have been much worse had the process not been in place. The Commission is the driving force behind the process and it hopes to use the process to reduce implementation

---

283 Environmental groups have charged that the guidance documents are "difficult to read because of their length and lack of clarity." Furthermore, guidance documents are based on consensus compromises, which means that they often reflect the "lowest common denominator." *See Tips and Tricks for Water Framework Directive Implementation: A resource document for environmental NGOs on the EU guidance for the implementation of the Water Framework Directive*, at 11 (World Wide Fund for Nature and European Environmental Bureau, Mar. 2004) available online http://assets.panda.org/downloads/wfdtipstricksmarch2004.pdf.

costs in terms having to bring states before the Court of Justice. The Commission can bring states before the Court of Justice for bad implementation or nonimplementation of the EU legislation and the Commission eventually did bring some states in front of the Court of Justice for lack of implementation of the WFD.[284]

But the Commission was internally divided by its dual role. The CIS process is a consensual process that requires a facilitator. The purpose of a facilitator in the context of the CIS is to get the buy in from states and to virtually pave the way for states through the implementation process. In its role an enforcer of the treaties, the Commission can adopt a legalistic and an antagonistic style towards member state noncompliance. At the same time, in its role as a facilitator, the Commission has to maintain a low-key stance and demonstrate more understanding and awareness of problems of domestic compliance because issues that are urgent in Brussels are rarely viewed the same way domestically. The role of the Commission as enforcer of the treaties, though, could not lend much credibility to the Commission's role as a facilitator. Member states knew that behind claims about facilitating implementation, their failure to comply would have legal repercussions. The question, therefore, is whether an institution whose primary role is that of an enforcer could simultaneously develop a function as a facilitator. Though the Commission drove the CIS process with a firm hand, it did not hesitate to evoke court proceedings as a sword of Damocles.

A facilitator's role further assumes that states are willing to comply but they do not know how to do so or that they need to synchronize and harmonize their activities of implementation. If so, a facilitator can show states how to proceed with implementation and can stage discussions and exchanges among states. The lack-of-know-how postulation may be correct for some states but it cannot by itself explain the mien of states that have developed a reputation as foot-draggers in the implementation of EU legislation. The problem in some of these states rests on domestic institutions driven by officials for whom compliance with the EU environmental law is not a matter of urgency, as sanctions that may be imposed often do not affect personal career advancement. In a number of these states, inaction at

[284] *See Action brought on 17 October 2006—Commission of the European Communities v. Hellenic Republic*, Case C-426/06; *See also Action brought on 15 February 2007–Commission of the European Communities v. Italian Republic* Case C-85/07. The cases of the Court of Justice can be found online, *see* www.curia.europa.eu/en/transitpage.htm.

the top is presented not for what it is, that is lack of leadership, but as a result of ineffective civil service.

The WFD, furthermore, requires the cooperation of a number of domestic institutions. This cooperation cannot be taken for granted in situations in which institutional rivalry acquires pathological dimensions as various institutions try to capture the leading role in the management of water policies. These are not problems that can be solved by the European Commission in its role as facilitator of the WFD implementation process. These are endemic domestic problems and what the EU could hope for, with its constant nudging, is to inspire domestic agents of change in these states to pursue and effectuate reform policies.

The Commission has allowed an array of interests to participate in the implementation process in order to ensure buy-in and, hopefully, compliance of these interests. Environmental NGOs that had played a leading role in the adoption of the WFD believed, by the end of 2006, that they had lost some control over the process. Because of the overwhelming representation of NGOs representing economic interests, environmental NGOs often found themselves on the defensive and their focus moved on preserving some of the gains emanating from a strict interpretation of the directive. By 2006, environmental groups were somewhat disappointed as they had accepted that the achievement of environmental goals by 2015 might not be attainable. Instead of concentrating on the achievement of long-term objectives, they rightly decided to focus their efforts on maintaining a robust process in place. Environment groups, to their credit, put a lot of emphasis on the production of quality article 5 reports and on the economic analysis of water use. Environmental groups commented favorably on the openness and transparency of the CIS process that allayed fears that some associations may achieve advantages behind closed doors.

The fact that environmental NGOs had assumed a more tempered positioning during the CIS process was echoed by industry as well. NGOs that represent industry and economic interests were content that some of their colleagues in the environmental field scaled back their demands and started to realize the constraints involved in the WFD implementation. Industry NGOs believed that, because environmental NGOs had lost some of their influence, the outcomes of the CIS process would be more evenhanded. Most of the criticism of industry NGOs concentrated on the effectiveness of expert advisory fora (EAF). The role EAF was weakened as the CIS process unfolded.

One of the first appraisals of on-the-ground implementation of the WFD was conducted by environmental NGOs.[285] The appraisal is not based on the facts of on-the-ground implementation provided by official sources but rather on a survey of environmental groups that operate in member states. The survey requires environmental groups to report their experience with implementation in member states. The value of the study rests on the assumption that if states were serious about the WFD implementation, they would, at least, ensure that their NGOs receive information and that they stay in touch with the process of implementation.

Domestic NGOs who responded to the study were disappointed with the deficiencies of some of the transposition laws and the fact that only a minority of states opted for the establishment of competent river basin authorities with control over a river basin district. Environmental NGOs are also concerned that, although public participation is addressed in the laws of most countries, there is still a long way to go before one could say that NGOs are involved in the decisionmaking process.[286] Environmental NGOs suggest that water managers should be trained in the social aspects of WFD implementation and that, in states in which civil society organizations are not strong, the state must provide funding for the further development of environmental NGOs.[287] This latter suggestion goes to the heart of public participation debate that has to do with whether public participation should be engineered from the top or spring spontaneously from the bottom.

The implementation strategy that was adopted for 2007–2009 took into account a number of the concerns and criticism expressed about the implementation process as it had progressed from its inception all through the end of 2006.[288] According to the strategy:

> [T]here is an increasing awareness (sometime criticism) that the work intensive process may put additional pressure on

[285] *EU Water Policy: Making the Water Framework Directive Work—The Quality of National Transposition and Implementation of the Water Framework Directive at the end of 2004 (A second "Snapshot" Report—Assessment of results from an environmental NGO questionnaire by the EEB and WWF)*, Feb. 2005 [hereinafter *Snapshot*] available online http://www.eeb.org/activities/water/making-WFD-work-February05.pdf.

[286] *Id.* at 23.

[287] *Id.* at 6.

[288] *Common Implementation Strategy for the Water Framework Directive* (2000/60/EC), Improving the comparability and quality of the Water Framework Directive implementation, Progress and Work Programme for 2007–2009 as Agreed by the Water Directors (Nov. 30/Dec. 1, 2006) [hereinafter *CIS 2007*].

> national authorities which are faced with a high work load of national and river basin tasks in the implementation process. This situation will certainly become even more relevant in the preparation of the river basin management plans.[289]

According to the strategy, it is important to demonstrate that the CIS process "is a model to follow and not just another 'meeting machinery created by the Brussels bureaucracy.'"[290] The benefits of the CIS process came increasingly under doubt, according to the strategy, because "there are several findings that suggest that there was only limited or no use made of the CIS guidance documents which, of course, would question the added value of all the past efforts on the CIS."[291] Overall, the strategy concludes that the CIS process works but more efforts are needed to achieve results on the ground by producing less paperwork and engaging, instead, in information exchange.[292]

The CIS process was reorganized by the end of 2006 to include, *inter alia*, a drafting group on environmental objectives and exemptions, a working group on floods (what was previously an expert advisory forum on floods), and a drafting group on environmental objectives and exemptions. Interestingly, the working group on integrated river basin management was disbanded and its activities have been undertaken by the other groups or by *ad hoc* workshops and various information exchange activities.[293] (See Figure 5.2, Organization of Common Implementation Strategy 2007–2009).

The Commission provided its first assessment of the implementation of the WFD in 2007.[294] The assessment evaluates both the establishment of the institutional framework in member states for the implementation of the WFD and the preparation of article 5 report that includes the pressures and impacts on waters all across the EU.

---

289 *Id.* at 1.

290 *Id.*

291 *Id.* at 2.

292 *Id.* at 5.

293 *Id.* at 8.

294 *See* Commission Staff Working Document, *Accompanying Document to the Communication from the Commission to the European Parliament and the Council 'Toward Sustainable Water Management in the European Union,' First Stage in the Implementation of the Water Framework Directive* 2000/60/EC, SEC(2007) 362, 22.3.3.2007 [hereinafter *2007 Assessment*] available online http://ec.europa.eu/environment/water/water-framework/implrep2007/pdf/sec_2007_0362_en.pdf.

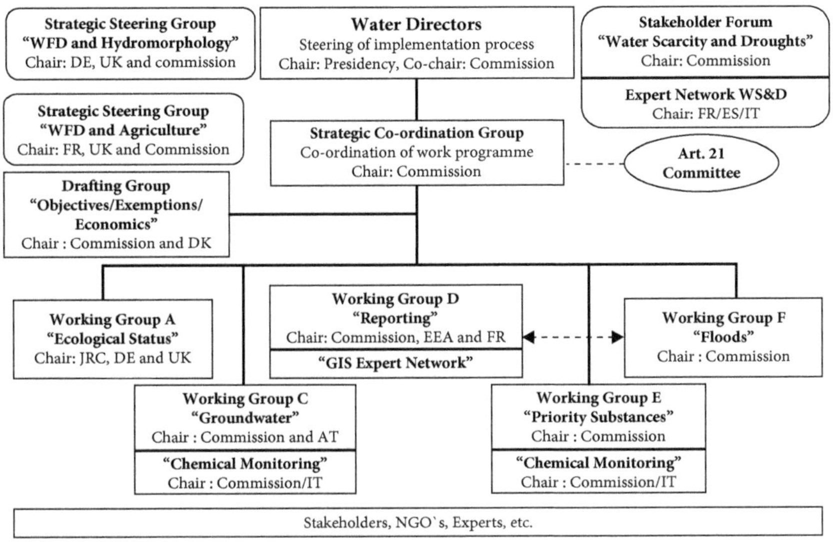

Figure 5.2 EU Organization Common Implementation Strategy 2007–2009

The Commission finds many deficiencies in the implementation of the WFD especially with regard to the transposition of article 4 that has to do with environmental objectives, article 9 on cost recovery, and article 14 that focuses on public participation.[295] With regard to the administrative arrangements put in place for the implementation of the directive, the Commission noticed that 110 river basin districts[296] have been established all over the EU and that states have differed significantly in the administrative arrangements they have put in place for the management of river basin districts since:

- Some states have established one competent authority per river basin district.
- Other states have established one competent authority for several river basin districts.
- Still other states have established several competent authorities for one river basin district.[297]

[295] *Id.* at 11.
[296] *Id.* at 15.
[297] *Id.* at 16.

The Commission notes that the reason behind the divergence in national approaches to river basin district administration has to do with the differences in the administrative structure of states and with existing institutional frameworks of water management. The Commission, however, remarks that new member states that entered the EU in 2004 designated competent authorities "in a more appropriate way" than old member states.[298] The commission is satisfied that the designation of river basin districts has taken place based on hydrographic boundaries and that the grouping of smaller river basin districts into a larger river basin district has happened, in most cases, in a meaningful fashion. In the case of the United Kingdom, many small catchments that drain directly into the sea have been combined into a river basin district. In Greece, many small islands have been grouped together in a single river basin district.[299]

The Commission, however, seems less clear about the coordination arrangements concocted by states to execute river basin management in river basin districts. The Commission is well aware that a number of authorities are involved in the WFD implementation in different member states. The Commission has some doubts about whether the often complex coordinating arrangements put in place by states would achieve the goals of the directive in a cost-effective way.[300] With regard to the international administrative arrangements, the Commission notes that there are differences in the ambition, approach, and mechanisms used by international commissions. The Commission seems satisfied that there is an information exchange mechanism in place for communication among international commissions that helps them share their experiences and learn from each other.[301] However, the Commission is far less satisfied with the quality of bilateral arrangements that are now only partially oriented towards the WFD implementation.[302]

With regard to environmental objectives, the Commission notes that some member states have designated a large proportion of their waters as heavily modified or artificial. The classification of waters as heavily modified or artificial is relevant since waters designated, as such, do not have to meet environmental objectives. Four member states have classified more

---

298 *Id.* at 17.
299 *Id.* at 18.
300 *Id.* at 19.
301 *Id.*
302 *Id.* at 20.

than 50 percent of their waters as artificial or heavily modified. Such states include the Netherlands, Belgium, Slovakia, the Czech Republic, parts of Estonia, and the United Kingdom. The Netherlands, in particular, has identified only five percent of its waters as natural water bodies. The remaining member states have identified about 16 percent of their water as heavily modified and artificial. Ireland and Latvia are the outliers; they have identified less than two percent of their waters as heavily modified.[303]

For waters unlikely to meet environmental objectives, the preliminary assessment has revealed that about 40 percent of surface water bodies are at risk of not meeting environmental objectives, and 30 percent are not at risk of meeting environmental objectives. For about the remaining 30 percent of water bodies, the results of risk assessment are not conclusive because of lack of data.[304] Similar concerns are paramount about groundwater bodies. Although 30 percent of groundwater bodies have been identified to be at risk of not meeting environmental objectives, 25 percent have been classified as not being at risk while, for a large percent of groundwater bodies (45 percent), the data are inconclusive.[305] The economic analysis of water use is one of the weakest elements of reports submitted by states, especially when addressing the cost recovery of water services.[306]

The Commission further attempts to examine the overall costs and benefits of the implementation of the WFD. The question is whether the administrative costs for the implementation of the WFD are warranted, given benefits achieved from implementation in terms of attainment of water quality and coherence in water management. An assessment of costs and benefits of the WFD implementation, before such implementation is finalized, is bound to remain inconclusive, especially because the river basin management plans are still under preparation. Furthermore, one should not underestimate the methodological difficulties involved in isolating the costs and benefits of the application of a single directive—since the success of implementation depends simultaneously on other pieces of related environmental legislation.[307]

303 *Id.* at 26.
304 *Id.* at 28.
305 *Id.* at 29.
306 *Id.* at 39.
307 *Id.* at 47.

The WFD has put in place a whole machinery for the management of waters in Europe. Improvement of water quality is one metric that could be used to assess the value added by this machinery. The other, more preliminary metric has to do with the establishment of institutions that can work in a cooperative and transparent way to achieve coherent management of water resources. As long as coordinating structures are in place, the opportunities for achieving the environmental objectives are amplified. The Commission has pledged to look more carefully into the coordinating structures that states have put together for the implementation of the directive in case there is a consistent failure to meet environmental objectives.[308] Chapter 11 of this study assesses the coordinating structures that have been put in place for the implementation of the WFD in member states and concludes that some structures are still at a nascent stage. It is hoped that the momentum created by the implementation of the WFD will eventually trickle down and spur stronger coordinating linkages in member states.

In addition to providing a first overview of the implementation process, the Commission further underlines its efforts to promote sound water management through the adoption of the Groundwater Daughter Directive,[309] the decision on the thirty-three priority substances,[310] and various other efforts to reduce pollution by dangerous substances. These are, for instance, the Integrated Pollution Prevention and Control Directive (IPPC),[311] the thematic strategy on pesticides,[312] and the Registration, Evaluation, Authorization and Restriction of Chemicals (REACH) regulation that has to do with the formulation of an EU policy on chemical substances.[313]

---

308 *Id.* at 20.

309 *See supra* note 210.

310 *See* OJ L 331/1, 15.12.2001, *supra* note 212. On July 17, 2006, the Commission adopted a proposal for a Daughter Directive on environmental quality standards for priority substances. *See Proposal for a Directive of the European Parliament and of the Council on environmental quality standards in the field of water policy and amending Directive 2000/60/EC*, COM(2006)397 final, 17.7.2006.

311 *Council Directive 96/61/EC* of 24 September 1996 concerning integrated pollution prevention and control, OJ L 257/26, 10.10.1996.

312 *Communication from the Commission to the Council, the European Parliament, the European Economic and Social Committee and the Committee of the Regions: A Thematic Strategy on the Sustainable Use of Pesticides*, COM(2006)372 final, 12.7.2006.

313 *Regulation EC No 1907/2006* of the European Parliament and of the Council of 18 December 2006 concerning the Registration, Evaluation, Authorization and Restriction of Chemicals (REACH), establishing a European Chemical Agency, amending Directive 1999/45/EC and repealing Council Regulation (EEC) No 793/93 and Commission Regulation (EC) No 1488/94

Furthermore, the flood directive was adopted in 2007.[314] The Parliament adopted in 2007 a Marine Strategy Directive that would be based on European marine regions that are to be established based on geographical and environmental criteria. Such regions have already been established through the regional agreements that regulate sea pollution, such as the Convention for the Protection of the Baltic Sea (HELCOM Convention), the Black Sea Convention, the Convention for the Protection of the North-East Atlantic (OSPAR Convention), and the Convention for the Protection of Mediterranean Sea (Barcelona Convention).[315] According to the marine strategy directive, each member state is to work with other member states and third states to develop marine strategies. The idea is to adopt a Marine Framework Directive that works in tandem with the WFD.[316] The Commission, moreover, has emphasized the importance of addressing water scarcity and droughts that affect mostly the southern European member states.[317]

as well as Council Directive 76/769/EEC and Commission Directives 91/155/EEC, 93/67/EEC, 93/105/EC and 2002/21/EC, OJ L 396/1, 30.12.2006.

314 *Common Position (EC) No 33/2006 adopted by the Council on 23 November 2006 with a view to adopting Directive of the European Parliament and of the Council on the assessment and management of flood risks, C 311E/10, 19.12.2006.* On April 24, 2007 the European Parliament and the Council adopted a compromise package which means that the directive has been agreed upon and what remains is the formal adoption later in 2007. The directive was finally adopted on October 23, 2007. *See Directive 2007/60/EC* of the European Parliament and of the Council of 23 October 2007 on the assessment and management of flood risks, OJ L 288/27, 6.11.2007.

315 *See also EU Marine Strategy: The Story Behind the Strategy* (European Commission, 2006).

316 *Proposal for a Directive of the European Parliament and of the Council establishing a Framework for Community Action in the field of Marine Environmental Policy* (Marine Strategy Directive) COM(2005)505 final, 24.10.2005.

317 *2007 Assessment, supra* note 294, at 9.

Chapter 6

Coordination Policies and Politics

The European Commission (the Commission) as the initiator of legislation in the European Union (the EU) addresses all aspects of EU policy including competition, environmental protection, transportation, and regional policy. One, then, could question how these policies are to be coordinated so that if there is overlap, the Commission does not appear to self-contradict itself. In that vein, the Cardiff process, adopted in 1998, addressed the issue of the integration of environmental concerns into other policy areas, since environmental issues cut across many sectors of the economy.[318]

It is unclear whether the coordination process of various EU policies is optimal today as there are contradictory reports about the effectiveness of intra-EU coordination. One could state that, rhetorically, the various Directorates General (DGs) of the European Commission seem to be quite aware of the benefits of coordinating their policies and that most DGs seem to have espoused the importance of integrating environmental

[318] The Cardiff process was launched by European heads of state—the European Council—at their summit meeting in Cardiff, in June 1998, requiring the council of ministers to integrate environmental considerations into the various policy sectors.

concerns into their agendas.[319] In practice, most DGs have established formal or informal groups whose purpose is to coordinate with other DGs. When a cross-sector issue reaches the Commission, it establishes cross-sector teams to address the issue. These are, however, *ad hoc* processes that are put into action as the Commission is pressed to address various issues. Because they are *ad hoc* procedures, they often lack the transparency required of established procedures. For instance, there are no procedural rules for the selection of the external consultants who serve on these *ad hoc* cross-sector teams, the evaluation of Strategic Environmental Assessments (SEAs) produced by states, and the resolution of differences of opinion among various expert positions.[320]

The coordination among the DGs of the Commission has further to do with the coordination of the actors that participate in the legislative process. Member states, though often projected as unitary entities, have their own problems of coordination, and the ministries in charge of various EU policies are rarely models of good coordination. Ministries of environment are active in shaping environmental policies, ministries of agriculture are responsible for agricultural policies. Ministries of transport deal with transportation policies and ministries of finance are involved in regional policy development and funding. As long as these ministries fail to coordinate domestically, they are unlikely to allow for the production of coherent EU policies.[321]

Usually, DGs are open to the interests that they need to protect or advance. For instance, major farmers' unions have a traceable influence over DG Agriculture and other interest groups do not always enjoy easy access to this DG. The representation of diverse stakeholders seems to be more evident in DG Environment, especially since the adoption of the WFD. In the formulation of regional policy, member states are at the helm because they determine how to use the resources that the EU distributes to

---

319 For instance, the WFD states in the preamble (para. 16, preamble, *WFD, supra* note 146) that further integration of water management into other EC areas such as energy, transport, agriculture, fisheries, regional policy, and tourism is needed. Furthermore, the directive mentions (para. 12, preamble, *WFD, id.*) that the economic and social development of the EC as a whole and the balanced development of its regions must be taken into account in preparing a policy for the environment.

320 Giorgos Kallis *et al.*, *Integration of EU Water and Development Policies: A Plausible Expectation?* 195, in Policy Integration for Complex Environmental Problems: The Example of Mediterranean Desertification (Helen Briassoulis, ed., 2005).

321 *Id.*

their national budgets. Still, environmental NGOs often air their concerns about large regional projects sponsored by EU funding likely to have adverse effects on the environment.[322]

Making Regional Policy Work for Water Policy

The EU regional policy is an exemplification of what has been called multilevel governance. Multilevel governance in the context of the EU means that, in addition to cooperation among member states, there are other levels of coordination among actors at the subnational level such as regions, municipalities, and various economic and professional actors and associations.

With respect to the regions, the EU has already developed a Committee of the Regions for the purpose of representing local concerns at the EU level. The Commission has been concerned about how to develop a meaningful discourse with regions and localities for the making of EU policy. The white paper produced by the Commission is very telling about the importance that the Commission places on the development of a dialogue with regions. According to the Commission, "the way in which the Union currently works does not allow for adequate interaction in a multilevel partnership; a partnership in which national governments involve their regions and cities fully in European policy-making. Regions and cities often feel that, in spite of their increased responsibility for implementing EU policies, their role as an elected and representative channel interacting with the public on EU policy is not exploited."[323] The Commission has proposed the adoption of tripartite contracts. The parties to such contracts are to be the Commission, the regions and localities of member states, and the member states themselves. The central government would prepare the contract and would be the ultimate party responsible for implementation. The contract will specify the designated subnational authority responsible for the implementation of EU primary legislation. The contract would include mechanisms for monitoring. Environmental policy is singled out as the ideal for the adoption of such

322 *Id. See also Handbook on Environmental Assessment of Regional Development Plans and EU Structural Funds Programmes* (2005) (The handbook has been prepared under the initiative of DG Environment with the active cooperation and assistance of DG Regional Development and Cohesion Policy, and DG Agriculture).

323 *Governance Paper, supra* note 234, at 12.

tripartite contracts as environmental policies are often adopted at the EU level, are transposed by the member states but are applied on the ground locally.[324]

The purpose of the regional and cohesion policy is to provide funding to less advantaged regions of the EU so that development among regions becomes more balanced. Development in the EU, therefore, is not from the point of view of states, since, within most member states, some regions are more affluent while others lag behind. Development in the EU is understood as regional development. Regional policy targets social and economic cohesion by reducing the disparities among regions that belong to member states of the EU. Support is provided to less developed regions so that they can catch up with more developed regions. This regional policy is realized through a number of funds dispensed by the EU to the member states. Member states, in turn, must channel such funds to disadvantaged regions. Such funds include the:

- European Regional Development Fund (ERDF);
- European Social Fund (ESF); and
- Cohesion Fund (CF).[325]

For member states to receive funding they have to regionalize, that is, to develop regions as planning units for the disbursement of funding. Member states that have not identified regions according to the EU standards are required to establish such regions for the purposes of receiving EU funding. Regions begin as planning units but could evolve into self-administrative structures—a development that is encouraged because of the funding targeted at them.

This top-down regionalization is taking place today in central and eastern European countries that, in order to receive funding, had to establish regions. These regions often parallel the existing administrative authorities, such as districts and counties. Regional development may appear

---

324 *Id.* at 13.

325 Although the ERDF and the ESF are addressed directly to regions, the CF is directed to member states and provides support to states that would like to advance some of their sectors further (for instance, the transportation sector). The ESF includes a number of initiatives such as the INTERREG and the LEADER that target cross-border cooperation and rural development initiatives. By being involved in regional development and providing financing for such development, the DG Regions has been a driving force in motivating states to review their administrative arrangements.

antagonistic to municipal development as municipalities have become self-governing units in most member states. Municipalities often lament that increases in their authority in multiple areas is not necessarily matched by adequate resources. At the same time, they are not particularly enamored of the continuing trend of regional emancipation.

The water framework directive (WFD) is a first attempt to reconsider administrative arrangements from the point of view of environmental planning and the application of the concept of integrated water resources management (IWRM). The decision to establish the river basin district as the organizing unit of water management has affected coordination among various subnational authorities, spurred the creation of new authorities, and modified and strengthened already existing coordinating structures at the international level.

The interplay between regional planning and river basin planning has acquired renewed attention because states that are preparing to submit proposals for structural funding must provide operational plans that explain why the funds are needed and how they will be disbursed. Operational plans designated to obtain regional funding could be used for financing water infrastructure projects oriented toward the implementation of the WFD.[326] As the EU regional policy is attuned to spatial planning, the integration of spatial planning initiatives and river basin management planning needs to be further investigated, including the delineation of sphere of responsibility among administrative authorities of member states.[327]

Furthermore, the implementation of the WFD is bound to become a factor in the EU's external policies as it is clearly provided in the directive that member states need to work with nonmember states for the establishment of international river basin districts. Cooperation with

[326] *See also Making the Structural and Cohesion Funds Water Positive*, Document by the European Network of Environmental Authorities (ENEA), Feb. 2006.

[327] *See also* Mette Fosgaard Kragh, *New Danish Regional Development Plans – An Effort of Combining Economy and Spatial Aspects for Urban and Rural Areas* (International Federation of Surveyors, 2005). Although spatial planning is not a formal responsibility of the EC, the EC published in the late 1980s a compendium of spatial planning systems and policies in the EU. Furthermore, the European Spatial Development Perspective (ESDP) was adopted at the Potsdam Council in May 1999. The Commission has developed the EPSON (European Spatial Planning Observatory Network), the purpose of which is to improve the European overview of spatial planning, assist in the European Spatial Development Perspective (ESDP), and support the coordination among different regional levels of decisionmaking, as well as the dissemination of regional and land use studies. The ESPD has inspired a regional reconfiguration in Denmark in terms of the reduction of number of regions and municipalities and the further clarification of their responsibilities.

Russia on the cross-border management of common water basins is an important feature of the exchange that is taking place in defining the EU/Russia Common Economic Space.[328]

Environmental Policy and Industrial Competitiveness

Industry has often complained about the multitude of regulations issued at the EU level and has charged that an increasing regulatory burden is making European industry less competitive. Many of these regulations are environmental regulations that place limits on industry discharges[329] and establish schemes for the ecomanagement of enterprises.[330] The Commission has tried to address the concerns of the industry by undertaking a "better regulation initiative."[331] Under this initiative, the Commission resolves to produce more quality legislation through a more rigorous public consultation process and to engage in the codification of EU legislation. Impact assessments that were adopted in 2003[332] have the goal to improve the quality of legislative proposals of the Commission. The assessments focus on evaluating the positive and negative impacts of proposed regulations in terms of their environmental and social effects and their alignment with the Community Sustainable Development Strategy.[333] Impact assessments are now to be evaluated by an independent Impact Assessment Board (IAB) that is to function under the president of the Commission. This board is to evaluate draft impact assessments and provide feedback to various DGs on improvements that are necessary.[334] It would be interesting to see how such assessments will work in practice and whether they will have any meaningful influence on the quantity and

328 *2007 Assessment, supra* note 294, at 55.

329 For a detailed account of legislation that has contributed to the reduction of polluting substances into the waters, *see Louka(2), supra* note 136, at 166–75.

330 *See Regulation (EC) No 761/2001* of the European Parliament and of the Council of 19 March 2001, allowing voluntary participation by organizations in a Community ecomanagement and audit scheme (EMAS), OJ L 114/1, 24.04.2001.

331 *See Annex to the Communication on Better Regulation for Growth and Jobs in the European Union, Minimising administrative costs imposed by legislation*, SEC(2005)175, 16.3.2005.

332 Impact Assessments that were adopted in 2003 replaced the Business Impact Assessments. *See Communication from the Commission on Impact Assessment*, COM(2002)276 final, 5.6.2002.

333 *Communication from the Commission: A Sustainable Europe for a Better World: A European Union Strategy for Sustainable Development*, COM(2001)264 final, 15.5.2001.

334 For more information on the Impact Assessment Board, *see* http://ec.europa.eu/governance/impact/iab_en.htm.

quality of the legislation produced. The streamlining of legislation is evident in the environmental field, where an effort has been undertaken to rationalize a number of legislative instruments under a framework approach so that linkages and references between similar regulatory instruments become obvious and the regulatory burden on the industry is alleviated.[335]

A High Level Group (HLG) on Competitiveness, Energy and the Environment has been functioning under the auspices of the DG Enterprise and Industry since 2006.[336] The group is a cross-functional advisory platform that consists of commissioners of various DGs,[337] members of the European Parliament, industry and environmental NGOs, consumers, trade unions, and representatives of the various regulatory bodies. The mandate of the group has to do with the functioning of energy markets, climate change, the use of renewable energy, waste recycling, and the development and dissemination of innovative technologies. The group addresses water management only in the context of renewable energy (that is, hydropower).

The establishment of the group is important not only because of the breadth of the subjects addressed but because of its method of operation seems to be open and transparent. The agenda of the group, the planning of meetings, and the minutes of meetings are published on the DG's website. Who participates in the group is also public information available on the DG Enterprise website. The members of the group are appointed *ad personam*, and no further clarification is provided to explain why these members rather than others have been selected.

The fact that the minutes and the agenda of the group are published on the DG Enterprise website demonstrates a certain sort of openness. In contrast, the minutes of the meetings of the Strategic Coordination Group, established as part of the implementation of the WFD, were not published for a wider audience. Publication of those minutes might have helped demystify somewhat the WFD implementation process for the interested public.

335 For the efforts to organize the EU legislation under a framework approach, *see Louka(2)*, *supra* note 136, at 144.

336 More information on this group is available online http://ec.europa.eu/enterprise/environment/hlg/hlg_en.htm.

337 DG Enterprise and Industry, DG Competition, DG Energy, and DG Environment.

Transportation and Energy Policy and Sustainability of Water Resources

The pan-European waterway network consists of 28,000 kilometers of internationally classified waterways available for inland navigation. The potential of inland navigation is not the same for all European countries. Most of the inland waterway traffic is taking place in the Rhine River basin that accounts for 80 percent of navigation, while only 9 percent is realized in the Danube and the Rhine-Maine-Danube connection. Inland waterway networks exist in Russia and Ukraine, but these networks are disconnected from the pan-European networks.[338]

The Trans-European Transport Networks (TEN-T) have been the focus of EU policy since the early 1990s. The purpose of transport networks is to provide connection and easy access from one area of the EC to another. In 2001, the TEN-T guidelines were extended to port infrastructure including seaports, inland ports, and intermodal terminals. A number of EC regulations have been issued on the elimination of barriers to inland navigation.[339]

Inland transportation has become an issue in river basin management due to its potential environmental implications. The NAIADES (*N*avigation *A*nd *I*nland Waterway *A*ction *D*evelopment in *E*urope), a communication of the Commission on the Promotion of Inland Waterway and Transport[340] has advanced inland navigation as a means to bolster competitiveness and to achieve environmental objectives. The Commission alludes to the delays, congestion, and capacity issues affecting Europe's freight transport undermining competitiveness and environmental protection. Inland navigation is viewed, therefore, as a shift to less

338 Economic Commission for Europe (UNECE), Inland Transport Committee, Working Party on Inland Water Transport (Special session, Mar. 15–16, 2006, agenda item 4), ECE/TRANS/SC.3/2006/3, Feb. 1, 2006.

339 Including certificates needed in order to exercise the occupation of boatmaster, on technical requirements for ships and on the development of River Information Services (RIS).

340 *Communication from the Commission on the promotion of inland waterway transport (NAIADES) — An Integrated European Action Programme for Inland Waterway Transport* COM(2006)6 final, 17.1.2006 [hereinafter *NAIADES*]. Furthermore, in 2001, the Commission released the White Paper *European Transport Policy for 2010: Time to Decide.*

In 2006, the Bucharest Declaration was adopted during the Pan-European Conference on Inland Waterway Transport, Sept. 13–14, 2006. The declaration recognized the need for harmonization and integration of the regulatory framework, the imperative for the coordinated development of inland waterway transport, and the need for infrastructure development and the protection of the environment.

energy-intensive and cleaner transportation modes.[341] The development of inland navigation, however, has been facing a number of challenges including:

- Fragmentation of the market structure, which creates conditions for cut-throat competition and limited investment;
- Failure of integration of inland navigation into regional planning;
- Lack of supportive infrastructure and outdated ship construction;[342] and
- Fragmentation of the administrative institutions that address inland navigation.

The Commission refers to several bottlenecks that hamper inland navigation, including limited draught, bridge clearance, and lock dimensions.[343] Institutional fragmentation is a major concern since a shipper, in addition to national regulations and those issued at the EU level, has to operate under the regulations issued by the Central Commission for Navigation on the Rhine (CCNR) and the recommendations of Danube Commission. This multilevel regulation of the inland navigation sector generates, according to the European Commission, substantial inefficiencies. The Commission is attempting to obtain membership in the CCNR and in the Danube Commission and addresses issues of collaboration with these commissions through Memoranda of Understanding.[344] At present, there are, at least five institutions that address issues of inland navigation in Europe, namely, the Inland Transport Committee of the Economic Commission for Europe (UNECE), the European Conference of Ministers of Transport (ECMT), the Central Commission for Navigation on the Rhine (CCNR), the Danube (Navigation) Commission, and the European Community through its various institutions. The Commission is further promoting the development of an intergovernmental Pan-European Inland Navigation

341 *NAIADES*, *id.* at 2.

342 The problem is quite acute in the Danube and central and eastern European countries, given the undercapitalization of the private companies in the region combined with years of insufficient investment and neglected maintenance. *See* ECE/TRANS/SC.3/2006/3, *supra* note 338.

343 *NAIADES*, *supra* note 340, at 9.

344 Recommendation of 1 August 2003 from the Commission to the Council in order to authorise the Commission to open and conduct negotiations on the conditions and arrangements for the European Community's membership of the CCNR and of the Danube Commission, SEC(2003) 897.

Organization based on a new international convention that would involve all European countries and various organizations that have an interest in inland waterway transport. The promotion of inland navigation is supported at the nongovernmental level by the Inland Navigation Europe (INE). The INE was created in 2000 with the support of the EU to actively promote inland navigation.[345] Various national and transnational bodies as well as port authorities of states are members of the INE.

The environmental benefits of increasing inland navigation,[346] have not blinded the Commission to the environmental externalities of inland navigation. Such externalities include the use of carbon fuels and the often necessary adaptation of rivers to the requirements of ship navigation.[347] Some rivers or portions of a river may be shallow hampering, thus, the seamless navigation of ships. The artificial deepening of a river so as to reach a desirable depth for all seasons takes place to facilitate inland navigation. This artificial deepening has environmental repercussions and is often admonished by environmental groups. Other problems related to inland navigation have to do with air, water, and noise pollution.[348]

Taking as an example the Danube River, the Commission is dissatisfied that only ten percent of the capacity of the Danube is used for navigation.[349] The further development of the Danube as the link in Corridor VII that would connect the North Sea to the Black Sea has been frequently mentioned.[350] In order to transform Danube into Corridor VII, several bottlenecks have to be removed requiring the artificial deepening of the river. This has caused consternation in environmental circles that claim that hydromorphological changes in the river would adversely affect protected areas. Other projects that may be executed and are likely to produce environmental externalities include the Danube-Oder-Elbe Canal Plan the purpose of which is to connect the three seas—the Baltic Sea, the North Sea, and the Black Sea.[351]

---

345 More information about INE is available online http://www.inlandnavigation.org.

346 *NAIADES, supra* note 340, at 4. It is mentioned characteristically that if inland navigation cargoes were to be carried by road, polluting emissions would increase by 10 percent.

347 *Id.* at 7.

348 *See* Michael Baltzer, *Inland Navigation in the New EU–Looking Ahead: Corridor VII or Blue Danube?, Presentation for Green Week's "Die schöne blaue Donau"*, June 4, 2004 available online http://assets.panda.org/downloads/wwfgreenweekdanubenavigationpaperfinal.pdf.

349 *NAIADES, supra* note 340, at 3.

350 This is the TENs-T Rhine-Main-Danube inland waterway axis project.

351 Baltzer, *supra* note 348.

Energy generation through the use of hydropower could alter the hydromorphology of a river. Despite the potential of hydropower to replace fossil fuels, its accelerated development has been stalled due to a number of "complex administrative processes and almost systematic regulatory barriers."[352] The lack of enthusiasm for hydropower in Europe has certainly to do with the associated environmental impacts. Large hydropower projects have caused the fragmentation of rivers, disrupting species migration, and the displacement of populations.[353] Although hydropower *per se* does not have to be unsustainable,[354] it remains to be seen whether hydropower will be used more extensively in Europe.

The European Union has emphasized the production of clean energy through the adoption of the renewable energy directive that promotes the development of all types of renewable energy including wind, solar, geothermal, wave, tidal, hydropower, biomass, landfill gas, sewage treatment plans, gas, and biogases.[355] In addition, the EC has adopted a directive on energy efficiency that includes specific goals for achieving such efficiency.[356]

---

352 *See* http://ec.europa.eu/energy/res/sectors/small_hydro_en.htm. The European Small Hydropower Association (ESHA) was founded in 1989 as an initiative of the European Commission. The ESHA is the founding member of the European Renewable Energy Council which groups together all main European renewable energy industry and research associations. The main activities of the ESHA are to inform and lobby local authorities, national governments and the European Commission about the issues that hydropower faces. More information on small hydropower is available online http://ec.europa.eu/energy/res/sectors/small_hydro_en.htm. For more information about ESHA, *see* http://www.esha.be.

353 Patrick McCully and Susanne Wong, *Powering a Sustainable Future: The Role of Large Hydropower in Sustainable Development, Prepared for the UN Symposium on Hydropower and Sustainable Development*, Beijing, China, Oct. 27–29, 2004.

354 *See* World Commission on Dams (WCD), *Dams and Development: a New Framework for Decision-making* (2000). *See also Sustainability Guidelines adopted by the International Hydropower Association*, Feb. 2004 available online http://www.hydropower.org/sustainable_hydropower/sustainability_guidelines.html. Sustainability in hydropower is not based on how big or how small hydropower is. As Dr. Klaus Toepfer, Executive Director of UNEP has stated: "We are not interested in the large or the small [hydropower], but the well planned and the well managed."

355 *See Directive 2001/77/EC* of the European Parliament and of the Council on the promotion of electricity produced from renewable energy sources in the internal electricity market, OJ L 283/33, 27.10.2001.

356 *See Directive 2006/32/EC* of the European Parliament and of the Council of 5 April 2006 on energy end-use efficiency and energy services and repealing Council Directive 93/76/EC, OJ L 114/64, 27.4.2006.

Greening Agricultural Policy

Agriculture, a diffuse source of pollution, severely undermines water quality all over Europe.[357] Agriculture consumes large quantities of water accounting for 30 percent of total water use in Europe with significant variations all across Europe. In southern Europe irrigation accounts for about 60 percent of all water use while in northern Europe agriculture accounts from zero to 30 percent of water use.[358] The Common Agricultural Policy of the EU is one of the most prominent policies, at least, in terms of expenditure. Agriculture was 55 percent of the EU budget in 1998 and 46 percent of the EU budget in 2006.[359] Although traditionally agriculture has been oblivious to environmental concerns, there has been a significant change in rhetoric and various agricultural programs claim to be supportive of sustainable development, for instance the European Agricultural Fund for Rural Development (EAFRD)[360] that encourages farmers to employ methods of land use compatible with the need to preserve the natural environment and landscape and to protect natural resources. The fund provides assistance for rural development programs which are investments in agriculture, without commercial returns, compliant with environmental commitments.

Agricultural policy has evolved and now it is more mindful of the impacts of farming on the environment, especially through the development of instruments that link payments to farmers with the application of environmental standards, what has been called cross-compliance.[361]

[357] The Commission adopted the nitrates directive to reduce pollution caused by agriculture, *see Council Directive 91/676/EEC* of 12 December 1991 concerning the protection of waters against pollution caused by nitrates from agricultural sources, OJ L 375/1, 31.12.1991.

[358] Website DG Agriculture, http://ec.europa.eu/agriculture/envir/index_en.htm#water.

[359] *Id.*

[360] *Council Regulation (EC) No 1698/2005* of 20 September 2005 on support for rural development by the European Agricultural Fund for Rural Development (EAFRD), OJ L 277/1, 21.10.2005. The aim of the regulation is to improve the competitiveness of the agricultural sector and forestry sector, to improve the environment and the countryside and to enhance the quality of life in rural areas including the diversification of rural economy. In addition to environmental protection that is a must in order to receive agri-environmental payments, the regulation supports diversification of farmers towards nonagricultural activities, including microbusiness, the promotion of tourism, and the renovation and development of villages.

[361] *See* Nadine Herbke *et al., WFD and Agriculture Linkages at the EU Level, Analysis of the Policy and Legal Linkages between CAP and WFD*, Background Paper, Final Version, Feb. 13, 2006 (cofunded project with the European Commission within the Sixth Framework Program by Ecologic and Warsaw Agricultural University) available online http://www.ecologic.de/download/projekte/1950-1999/1966/1966_deliverable_2-1.pdf.

Farmers who decide to go beyond the minimum environmental standards and apply best agricultural practices are eligible for agri-environment payments. Programs that are funded by agri-environmental measures include integrated farm management, organic agriculture, the preservation of historical and landscape features, and the protection of biodiversity. The cofinancing of the EU in these types of agri-environment measures could be up to 85 percent of the total budget.[362]

An issue that goes to the heart of implementation of the WFD has to do with the synchronization of the rural development plans (RDPs) with the river basin management plans (RBMPs). The EC has developed a funding mechanism for the advancement of sustainable farming through a series of regulations that support, *inter alia*, agri-environmental measures that have positive effects on water and soil quality, village renewal, and the conservation of local heritage. In order to benefit from the funds dedicated to rural development, states have to prepare rural development plans. Some of the funding provided for the execution of rural development plans that states prepare could be dedicated to the protection of water resources.

The WFD is based on the river basin management approach while the RDPs draw on a regional approach.[363] The RDPs are to be implemented by regional authorities, while the RBMPs are to be implemented by river basin authorities. In order to allow for cross-fertilization between river basin planning and rural development, the authorities responsible for each type of planning must be willing to cooperate with each other. In practical terms, this means that authorities in charge of RDPs must be represented when decisions are made on river basin planning, and river basin authorities must be consulted when RDPs are conceived and executed. The incorporation of programs of measures into RDPs, as these plans are to undergo a midterm review in 2008, should be further explored.[364] Furthermore, since river basin catchments are usually larger than the administrative regions used for rural development planning, one should expected a river basin authority to seek to provide input in many rural development plans and that many rural regional authorities will be involved as stakeholders in a river basin district.[365] As the second cycle of

362 *See Council Regulation 1698/2005*, *supra* note 360.
363 Herbke, *supra* note 361, at 19.
364 *Id.*
365 *Id.*

the RDPs is taking place, one of the questions that preoccupies policy-makers is the alignment of the timetable of these plans with that of the WFD.[366]

The implementation of IWRM in the European Union has put in motion an elaborate coordinating structure. Water directors of the different member states and the participation of a vast array of well-organized and well-funded NGOs and associations provide the foundational network for this structure. Although this coordinating apparatus has been criticized for not producing the optimal results, one wonders how the implementation of the WFD would have evolved if states had been left to their own devices.

366 *Id.* at 16.

Part Two

National Institutions for Water Management

Chapter 7

Designing Effective Organizations

Managers of organizations wish that a blueprint existed that, if mimicked, could provide a guarantee of institutional effectiveness. Such a blueprint is hard to find no matter what the efforts to decode institutional success. Similar organizations, arising similarly in comparable settings, do not necessarily follow the same trajectory. Good leadership, the nature of formal and informal networks built within an organization, and the rapport between an organization and its clientele make for some institutional success. Nevertheless, the specifics of leadership, networks, and rapport that generate institutional success remain difficult to translate from theory to practice. Organizational theories often do not produce, when applied, the organizational success they prognosticate. Since there is no organizational *tabula rasa*, and many scripts have been written and been rewritten, what is welcomed are the already ingrained, new opportunities circumvented with a sense of *déjà vu*.

Given the institutional reorganization necessitated by the water framework directive (WFD) in many countries, the issue of institutional effectiveness is very pertinent. The WFD prescribes that a river basin district must be managed by a competent authority. Certain states have interpreted this provision as a requirement to establish river basin districts that would be governed by river basin institutions. Other countries have adopted more of a coordinating outlook to implementation, according to which multiple national, regional, and local authorities are to work together to prepare a river basin management plan. The preoccupation of both new and existing institutions of river basin management is how to ensure a high degree of effectiveness in water management.

Some percepts of effective organization—specialization as a means to efficiency (the logic of the assembly line)[1] and hierarchy as the emblem of effectiveness (bureaucracy) have been around for too long to be challenged and have worked out in most of cases.[2] Today, specialization is prevalent. Masters of all trades are not in high demand in a world defined by an overwhelming amount of information and knowledge based on the *modus vivendi* of "divide and conquer." Bureaucracy—an organization with established channels of communication and command—is tautological to organization. It is frequently argued that if the right hierarchy is established and the appropriate controls are in place, organizations wondrously flourish.[3] On the other hand, too much emphasis on formal organization does not take into account the informal organizational-making that arises from a number of unofficial norms and custom networks.[4]

Organizations are made of formal and informal elements including inputs, processes, outputs, and feedback loops.[5] Formal elements are encapsulated in the organizational structure, the rules of procedure, the mission, and the goals of an organization. The informal organization, another term for *organizational culture*, is "the way things are really done in an organization," and involves the informal networks cultivated among those who work for an organization that shape the outlook of an organization. Organizations can also be deconstructed into their constituent components, including customers, employees, and various other stakeholders.[6]

1 *See* Frederick Winslow Taylor, *The Principles of Scientific Management* (1998 edition).

2 *See also From Max Weber: Essays in Sociology* (H.H. Gerth and C. Wright Mills, eds., 1973), reprinted in *Classics of Organization Theory* 81(Jay M. Shafritz and J. Steven Ott, eds., 1992) [hereinafter *Classics*].

3 *Id.* at 201.

4 Peter M. Blau and W. Richard Scott, *Formal Organizations: A Comparative Approach* 2–8, reprinted in *Classics, supra* note 2, at 212.

5 *See generally* James D. Thompson, *Organizations in Action: Social Sciences Bases of Administrative Theory* (2003 edition).

6 Ian I. Mitroff, *Stakeholders of the Organizational Mind* 32–47 (1983), reprinted in *Classics, supra* note 2, at 370. Organizations have multiple choices with regard to their stakeholders. They could ignore them, appease them by giving in to some of their demands, identify with stakeholders or coopt stakeholders to accept the organizational goal.

This way, an organization is viewed as the center point of multiple interactions among constituencies with changing interests and a shifting balance of power. Understanding organizations as no more than the sum of their constituting parts reveals why conflict is part of organizational life and why bargaining among different stakeholders is necessary for the functioning of organizations.[7] Given that the informal organization coexists with the formal organization, the success of a formal organization has to do with whether it is able, through its formal structures of authority and command, to constrain the informal organization so that the way things are really done does not grossly deviate from the way things ought to get done.[8]

Although the informal nature of organization guides everyday action, the formal structure of an organization matters equally because it establishes boundaries that prevent disorganization. Domestic laws and international treaties that set the mission, structure, and rules of procedure of organizations are instrumental in preventing organizations from spinning out of control and disintegrating. Boundaries prevent organizations from becoming a tool in the hands of constituencies that attempt to capture organizations to serve their own interests. But strictly enforced boundaries also can hamper the evolution of an organization. Thus, a balance must be struck between the formal and informal structures of an organization. It is important for organizations to have some latitude in the pursuit of their mission but equally important to ensure that an organization does not develop codependence on a set of constituencies that are using the organization to achieve their own goals.

Organizations function within the limits of what has been called *bounded rationality*.[9] It is often claimed that for organizations to function effectively they need to:

- Establish goals;
- List alternative strategies to achieve those goals;

---

7 Jeffrey Pfeffer, *Power in Organizations* 1–32 (1981), reprinted in *Classics*, *supra* note 2, at 404.

8 *See* Chester I. Barnard, *The Functions of the Executive* 180 (1976 edition). Barnard underlines the importance of formal organization arguing that an informal organization will quickly disintegrate if the formal line of authority is broken. This is the case, for instance, when an organization is rife with politics. *See also* Herbert A. Simon, *Administrative Behavior* 198 (1997 edition).

9 Simon, *id.* at 122.

- Determine the consequences that follow from the pursuit of alternative strategies;
- Perform a comparative evaluation of all consequences.[10]

Although this is a good theory of how organizations are supposed to work, the reality is that organizations rarely function this way.[11] Administrators usually make decisions under conditions of bounded rationality, which means that they are rarely able to formulate all possible alternatives and list all the possible consequences of each alternative, let alone comparatively evaluate such alternatives. These alternatives are not preexisting and ready to be considered, but rather must be designed by an administrator,[12] with the result that administrators are often content with solutions that appear satisfactory, and rarely attempt to concoct the optimal solution of all possible designed alternatives.[13] This may have to do with lack of time because administrators are constantly under pressure to produce quick results. It may also have to do with the lack of human foresight and the inability to predict how future events will unfold, which prevents meaningful planning. No matter the cause, bounded rationality explains why it is difficult to develop coherent policies and why a step-by-step approach is often preferable to administrative overhaul. In the environmental field, bounded rationality explains why it is difficult to prepare meaningful environmental impact assessments and to complete those sections of assessments if an evaluator must list all possible alternatives to a proposed project.

The organizations examined in this study are public organizations. Because of their public nature, they function within the constraints of such organizations. Such constrains in democratic states may involve requirements such as:

- Giving notice of a proposed rule;
- Submitting proposed legislation for final adoption (or rejection);
- Responding to comments about a rule brought up by various constituencies;

---

10 *Id.* at 93–94.

11 *See also* Charles E. Lindblom, *The Science of "Muddling Through,"* XIX Public Administration Review 79 (1959).

12 Simon, *supra* note 8, at 122–27.

13 *Id.* at 122.

- Ensuring formal or informal consultation with various stakeholders; and
- Being accountable for organizational activity so as to ensure funding for the organizational mission.

It is not enough for public organizations to achieve their goals because these goals may be defined, for instance, as better environmental quality, better transportation infrastructure, or the improvement of public heath. In meeting these goals, public organizations must be able to prove that they have satisfied provisions of procedural fairness, have not displeased a vocal portion of the electorate, and are accountable for all their actions. In other words, public organizations have to deal with "politics" in order to make policy to an extent that private organizations can rarely fathom.[14] The constraints, imposed by politics, must be taken into account when judging the effectiveness of public organizations.

This section includes an analysis of formal structure of organizations involved in the implementation of the WFD. This formal analysis of organizations, in combination with some early indications of implementation of the WFD, should shed some light on the effectiveness of institutions entrusted with water management and should provide some useful predictions about future performance. The organizations examined in Chapter 11, are not evaluated according to some abstract idea of effectiveness. Instead, obstacles to organizational performance, as they are dictated by bounded rationality and the constraints that are inherent in the life of public organizations, are taken into account. An effective institution is not a "perfect" institution that can invent responses to all problems of river basin management. It is an institution that is able to question itself, recognize its defaults, and learn from its mistakes.

14 James Q. Wilson, *Bureaucracy: What Government Agencies Do and Why They Do It* 196 (1989).

Chapter 8

Centralization/Decentralization Dilemmas

The requirement of the WFD to develop river basin districts managed by a competent authority or authorities could be viewed as a requirement for decentralization. The directive, thus, could be perceived as an instrument that mandates the de-concentration of water management at the river basin level. This is true to some extent, but the mandate to manage water at the river basin scale is not only a call for decentralization. It is more appropriate to envision the mandate for river basin district management through the various levels of the "river basin scale," namely, the international, the national, and the local. International river basin district management is necessary because there are many international river basin districts in Europe; it makes sense to manage them as international districts in order to effectively address the externalities of upstream-downstream use. International river basin district management, though, involves the centralization rather than the decentralization of river basin activities.

National river basin management is an organizational necessity emanating from the reality that the world is still defined by state boundaries. River basin management at the state level involves the development or strengthening of regional authorities to manage water at the river basin district. This is, equally, a decentralization move and a centralization task.

It is a decentralization move since the central government in many states would have to divest some strategic authority by delegating to river basin administrators. At the same time, it is centralization task if there are many local and regional authorities addressing water management in a disparate and fragmented manner and for which a river basin authority can provide structure and guidance. At the local level, subdistricts make sense in order to further organize various local interests that wish to assert their voice in river basin management.

For most member states of the European Union (EU), therefore, the mandate to manage water at the river basin involves an intricate balance between decentralization and centralization because some of the operational tasks delegated to local authorities would need to be coordinated better and some river basin planning would have to devolve to river basin institutions. River basin management involves the devolution of planning authority from the central level to the river basin level. River basin management encompasses, simultaneously, the systematization of tasks, loosely performed by various local authorities, at the river basin level. The need to concentrate and coordinate various activities that have been performed in a fragmented manner at the local or regional level is as important for the execution of the WFD as the need to deconcentrate some of the central authority by assigning responsibilities to the basin district. Centralization at the river basin district is sometimes viewed as cumbersome and river basin authorities are perceived as inflexible and overambitious. On the other hand, unstructured decentralization is often responsible for the increase in transaction costs because many agencies with overlapping activities are simultaneously engaged and various water users are too disorganized to assume their role in water management.[15] Viewing water management through a multilevel river basin scale, rather than as exclusively a centralization issue or a decentralization agenda, could assist in managing the dynamics of centralization and decentralization by recognizing the necessity of coordination at the top and the desirability of innovation at the bottom, and by forging top-down and bottom-up coordinating linkages.

Centralization is more evident in the case of international river basin districts in which states comanage water resources through international commissions that are acquiring a pivotal role in international and, thus, in

[15] Jyothsna Mody, *Literature Review: Management of River Basin Systems through Decentralization*, Report prepared for the World Bank, Washington DC, 2001 (unpublished).

national water management. The creation of international river basin districts and their management by international commissions is an attempt to centralize water management at the international level. The notion of "integrated" water resources management, after all, evokes images of centralization rather than decentralization because economies of scale are achieved by integrating and, thus, concentrating water management at the river basin district.[16]

The debate about whether states need to centralize or decentralize is as old as the existence of the state. In our era, this debate reached its apotheosis in the years after the collapse of the Soviet Union when the central state and central planning were blamed for the ills and malfunctioning of communist states. Nevertheless, neoliberalism, with its calls for decentralization and privatization, did not provide a miracle remedy because public enterprises that were privatized often fell in the hands of interests in pursuit of personal enrichment rather than the public good. The problems with privatization that were related closely to calls for decentralization led inevitably to some retrenchment and questioning about whether the central state is the inevitable villain and whether it makes sense to inquire into the method of decentralization and the type of privatization that would produce the desirable results for specific states.

The debate over centralization and decentralization remains potent today. Decentralization, understood as the transfer of decisionmaking power from the center to the periphery,[17] is still praised for its many advantages, such as the downward transfer of decisionmaking that is thought to allow organizations to be more responsive to local circumstances and concerns. Decentralization evokes positive connotations that are associated with democracy and participation.[18] However, one must be careful in drawing conclusions based on the stereotype that "centralization is always bad—decentralization is unfailingly good." Rather, the focus must be on what sort of centralization or decentralization makes sense and for which institutions and processes.[19] Unless there are satisfactory answers to these questions, decentralization has to stay.

---

16 *Id.*

17 Simon, *supra* note 8, at 44. Decentralization does not have to do with the number of branch offices an organization has. It has to do with the devolution of authority to these branches.

18 Francis Fukuyama, *State Building: Governance and the World Order in the Twenty-First Century* 91–94, 98 (2005).

19 Simon, *supra* note 8, at 42.

In certain instances, decentralization is ill-advised. This occurs when the central state has to assume accountability for the potential missteps of the decentralized unit. In this case, decentralization will involve a high level of risk for the central authority and would be resisted.[20] Decentralization may be opposed by constituencies in less than homogenous states in which the deconcentration of power presents a threat to the unitary state. Decentralization often means that policymakers are willing to accept a lower level of consistency in government performance. In a federal state, states that make a federal union may not apply federal laws uniformly and some states may actually lag behind other states.[21] Decentralization is not successful if there are high levels of corruption in a state. If corruption is endemic, decentralization empowers local elites and strengthens their role *vis-à-vis* an impotent public, allowing elites to use the state for personal gain.[22]

Ideally, the process of decentralization should be staggered. Delegating authority to many newly created institutions is bound to generate a certain dissonance. This is particularly pertinent for the new EU members for which top-down regionalization has been a prerequisite to the receipt of EU cohesion funding.[23] Empowered and self-governed municipalities backed by the Council of Europe are now a reality for many central and eastern European countries.[24] The addition of river basin authorities to these newly created institutions generates questions about the proper delegation of authority, the linkages between regional planning and river basin planning, and the relationship between democratically empowered institutions (municipal councils) and appointed regional or river basin administrators. All these institutions are vying for spots in the administrative space, where some of

---

20 Fukuyama, *supra* note 18, at 91–94.

21 *Id.*

22 This holds under the assumption that some of the central organization is serious about fighting corruption.

23 *See* Chapter 6, on the regional policy of the EU. The top-down regionalization takes place at the EU in order to allow for the disbursement of funding to disadvantaged regions. The final aim of this policy is to achieve the cohesion of all regions and to eliminate regional disparities and inequalities.

24 Autonomous local self-government has been supported by the Council of Europe though the Charter of Local Self-government that mandates an autonomous character for local authorities. Accordingly, local authorities should be voted into office instead of being appointed and must develop independence in their decisionmaking. *See European Charter of Local Self-Government*, Oct. 15, 1985 available online http://conventions.coe.int/treaty/en/Treaties/Html/122.htm.

the old structures still pertain, rendering the configuration of institutional boundaries and responsibilities quite perplexing.

Decentralization is often expressed as regionalization. There are various types of regionalization. The difference between a federation and regionalization is that the federal state has come into being as a result of a bottom-up process involving a number of states that have agreed to form a federation. On the other hand, decentralization, which may take the form of regionalization, is a top-down initiative. One form of regionalization has been called *political regionalization*.[25] This is when a central government has agreed to grant some autonomy to regions. This has been the case in France and Spain.[26] Other types of regionalization involve the creation of regions for the purposes of spatial planning. Regionalization does not have to do with the creation of new institutions but simply with the reorientation of existing institutions to perform regional planning. The regionalization imposed top-down by the EU involves regional denomination for the implementation of cohesion policies. Regional institutions often have purely organizational tasks and are deprived of formal authority over municipalities or local bodies.[27] Municipalities zealous of their institutional independence usually resist receiving orders from regional authorities.

Another potentially complicating factor with decentralization at the river basin level has to do with the prescription of authorities that function at the hydrographic level but have to cofunction with authorities that perform at the administrative level. This, in practice, would often necessitate communication between a river basin administrator and multiple administrative authorities. The legitimacy of a river basin authority necessarily depends on whether it can invoke the allegiance of already established administrative authorities. Because of the complexities of delegation of authority to the hydrographic level, many member states have decided to bypass the creation of river basin authorities and have opted, instead, for the coordination of already established administrative authorities to perform functions at the river basin level.

---

25 Claudia Pamfil, *Evolving Intergovernmental Relations for Effective Development in the Context of Regionalization* 27–29 (Open Society Institute and Local Government Public Service Reform Initiative, 2003).

26 *Id.*

27 *Id.* at 30.

Chapter 9

How to Predict Success in Water Management

The Role of National Water Institutions

The transposition of the water framework directive (WFD) into the domestic legislative culture is the first step in the implementation process. Subsequently, member states have to establish the institutions that will carry forward the implementation of the directive. The WFD imposes a model for water management based on the river basin district. Given that the majority of states do not manage their water sector based on the river basin district, the directive constitutes a top-down imposition of a model for water management. This top-down imposition of norms that have to be applied by all states in order to create some level of harmonization of administrative space in the European Union (EU) has been called Europeanization. More specifically, Europeanization is a process of construction, diffusion, and institutionalization of formal and informal rules, procedures, policy paradigms and styles, shared beliefs, and norms first defined at the EU policy level and then incorporated into the domestic institutional structure of member states.[28] Europeanization could be seen in the larger context of internationalization[29] or globalization. Many commentators have attested to the processes of convergence of administrative structures of states as facilitated by the information age.[30]

The harmonization of environmental policies of member states has been called *positive integration*.[31] Through the transposition of environmental policies, states have to incorporate into their legislation substantive requirements and procedures as dictated by various directives and regulations. In the context of the WFD, some of the requirements have to do with the establishment of river basin districts and authorities, the adoption of river basin management plans, and monitoring mechanisms. The question, from an Europeanization perspective, therefore, is whether member states will smoothly implement EU legislation and what obstacles may exist that would prevent on-the-ground implementation.

Commentators have maintained that the ease with which an environmental directive is adopted depends on the "institutional fit" between the prescriptions of the directive and the institutional structure that is already in place in a member state.[32] In the case of the WFD, this means that, if member states, before the adoption of the directive, had in place river basin districts and authorities they would likely to implement the directive swiftly and smoothly. On other hand, states that have not organized

---

28 Simon J. Bulmer and Claudio M. Radaelli, *The Europeanisation of National Policy?* Queen's Papers on Europeanisation No 1/2004. *See also* Alec Stone Sweet, *Integration and the Europeanisation of the Law*, Queen's Papers on Europeanisation No 2/2002; Gerda Falkner, *Comparing Europeanisation Effects: From Metaphor to Operationalisation*, Paper for the ECPR General Conference, Marburg, Sept. 18–21, 2003; Johan P.Olsen, *Towards a European Administrative Space?* 10(4) Journal of European Public Policy 506 (2003); Brigid Laffan, *The European Union: A Distinctive Model of Internationalization*, 5(2) Journal of European Public Policy 235 (1998).

29 Jacques Fournier, *The Internationalisation of Policy Making* 11, in The Internationalisation of Policy-Making: Institutional and Organizational Options to Integrate Domestic and International Aspects of Policy Making (Organization for Economic Co-operation and Development, Sigma Papers No. 6, 1996).

30 *Id.*

31 In other cases, member states do not have to incorporate regulations but instead need to dismantle existing barriers to trade, as it is the case with road haulage. This has been called negative integration.

In still other cases, the EU may attempt to change the belief systems of certain state actors in order to effectuate change. *See generally* Christoph Knill and Dirk Lehmkuhl, *The National Impact of EU Regulatory Policy: Three Europeanization Mechanisms*, 41(2) European Journal of Political Research 255 (2002).

32 *See generally* Christoph Knill, *The Europeanisation of National Administrations: Patterns of Institutional Change and Persistence* (2001).

their water management sector around river basin districts and authorities, are likely to face obstacles in the implementation phase.

This prediction is true with respect to the implementation of the WFD. The United Kingdom (UK) has been a champion of the WFD as a result of a high institutional fit between the United Kingdom water management system and the WFD. Similarly, because of an institutional culture that has been based on planning, the fit between the WFD and domestic institutions is high in central and eastern European countries.[33] The river basin model established in most northern European countries is not tailored to Greece, however, a country characterized by fragmented water resources that do not neatly fit under the definition of a large river basin district. Under these circumstances, the decision to assign water management to existing administrative bodies should be considered positive, assuming there is coordination among such bodies so that there is coherence in domestic management and in the partnerships established with third states. The Netherlands can be characterized as a case of misfit, given that there are no river basin authorities designated based on hydrographic borders. The Netherlands has decided not to change its established institutional structure for water management by creating river basin authorities. It resolved, instead, to coordinate established institutions for the purposes of realizing river basin management. In the Netherlands, the commitment to apply the river basin principle through well-organized coordinating structures seems to be strong because the Netherlands is a downstream state likely to be affected by the environmental externalities created upstream.

Veto Players as Inhibitors of Effective Water Management

In addition to the institutional fit, factors that affect implementation have to do with:

- Administrative capacity (financial resources, the level of corruption, and policy coordination); and

[33] For the role of Europeanization in the EU accession process, *see* Heather Grabbe, *Europeanization Goes East: Power and Uncertainty in the EU Accession Process* 303, in The Politics of Europeanization (Kevin Featherstone and Claudio M. Radaelli, eds., 2003).

- Political capacity (the number of veto players, the legitimacy of EU institutions, and the awareness of environmental issues).[34]

The issue of administrative and political capacity is quite salient for the countries studied here. Most central and eastern European countries do not have many financial resources to devote to the environmental and water sector. Some have been singled out for corruption, though, often, corruption levels are no higher than those of countries with a long-established EU presence.[35] Assuming that financial resources will be forthcoming because of high growth rates and EU funding, and assuming that institutional accountability is strengthened through EU membership, the foreseeable obstacles to implementation would have to do with the coordination of water policy and the number of veto players willing to sabotage the WFD implementation.[36]

Political veto players consist of a number of constituencies that perceive the implementation of WFD as a threat to their interests. These political veto players are primarily water users who are concerned about forfeiting perceived entitlements to water use. Other veto players are institutional—already established institutions could view with suspicion new authorities entrusted with water management or existing authorities vested with new powers. Given that the WFD is, in essence, an exercise in coordination that has to happen horizontally (i.e., among the ministries of environment, transport, and agriculture) and vertically (i.e., at the international, national, regional, and local levels), the danger of obstruction of implementation through institutional roadblocks is quite real.

34 *See* Tanja A. Börzel, *Shaping and Taking EU Policies: Member State Responses to Europeanization, Queen's Papers on Europeanisation*, No. 2/2003. *See also* Oliver Treib, *EU Governance, Misfit and the Partisan Logic of Domestic Adaptation: An Actor-Centered Perspective on the Transposition of EU Directives*, paper presented at the (European Union Studies Association) EUSA 8th Biennial Conference, Nashville, Tennessee, Mar. 27–29, 2003; Gerda Falkner *et al.*, *Worlds of Compliance: Why Leading Approaches to the Implementation of EU Legislation are Only "Sometimes-True Theories"?* Paper presented at the UACES 36th Annual Conference, Limerick, Ireland, Aug. 31-Sept. 2, 2006.

35 *See generally* Merek Hessel and Ken Murphy, *Stealing the State, and Everything Else: A Survey of Corruption in the Postcommunist World, Working Paper, Transparency International*, (Oct. 22, 2004). *See also Global Corruption Report*, Transparency International, 2003.

36 For the role of veto players in the implementation of EU policies, *see also* Markus Haverland, *The Impact of the European Union on Environmental Policies* 203, in The Politics of Europeanization (Kevin Featherstone and Claudio M. Radaelli, eds., 2003).

Because veto players are bound to play a pivotal role in whether the directive will be implemented smoothly, transparency in the process of implementation is important. Transparency may help attenuate the vigor of particularistic positions expressed by veto players. Such players may resolve to assume a more conciliatory tone as their positions are exposed in public. Particularistic interests are more potent when they act informally and covertly attempt to influence an organization. Rent-seeking interests are less potent when transparent processes are in place that force them to expose and explain their positions in public.[37]

[37] *See* Philip Selznick, *TVA and the Grass Roots: A Study in the Sociology of Formal Organization* 260–63 (1966).

Chapter 10

Models of Water Policy

Institutional Leadership in Water Management

The question of which authority should be entrusted with the water framework directive (WFD) implementation is not as simple as it seems. For a directive that promotes water quality, the institution that should be responsible for implementation at the central level seems to be a ministry of environment. This is, indeed, what has happened in many central and eastern European member states that have assigned the implementation of the WFD to their ministries of environment. Assigning the WFD to ministries of environment is in accordance with the precept that an organization's mission should match its jurisdiction.[38] The mission of ministries of environment is to improve environmental quality; thus, their jurisdiction should cover all matters of environmental quality including water quality.

Giving ministries of environment a central role in implementation is based on an evaluation of the directive as an environmental directive. As mentioned in Chapter 4, the WFD is more than an environmental directive.

---

[38] Wilson, *supra* note 14, at 187–88.

It is a planning directive that attempts to establish a system for the harmonious management of waters all across Europe. The implementation of the directive presupposes the establishment of coordinating mechanisms at the international, national, and subnational level—both horizontally and vertically—among various institutions and organizations. Ministries of environment are relatively new institutions in most central and eastern European states and, in some cases, the question is whether environmental ministries can amass the institutional will to initiate and maintain the level of coordination required for the implementation of the WFD. On the other hand, putting environmental ministries in charge of the WFD certainly strengthens the role of such ministries since water regulation affects many sectors of the economy.

Not all states have assigned the implementation of the WFD to environmental ministries. In the Czech Republic, the Ministry of Agriculture, Forests and Food is primarily responsible for implementation, under a cocompetence arrangement with the Ministry of Environment. In the Netherlands, water management is still under the auspices of Ministry of Transport, Public Works and Water Management that has had a long history of addressing water management. In Greece, water management has been assigned to the Ministry of Environment and Public Works that has been, until now, mostly a ministry of public works.

To address cross-sector coordination, most countries have established interministerial committees comprised of ministries that have to work together to effectuate implementation. Ministries of the environment often have to coordinate with the ministries of agriculture and industrial development for the adoption of measures against pollution. Whether interministerial coordinating committees will become the fora for the resolution of contentious issues remains to be seen, though the experience with interministerial bodies has not been that encouraging. What is certain is that for coordination to become successful, it has to reach deeper than the interministerial level and draw in the many regional and local institutions involved in everyday water management.

Four Models of Implementation

The hydrological model, the administrative model, and the collaboration model constitute potential paradigms for the management of water resources.[39] The hydrological model requires a fit between the organization that manages water and the hydrological unit—the establishment of a river basin authority in charge of a river basin district. In the administrative model, water management is entrusted to administrative authorities within the jurisdiction in which it happens to fall. The collaboration model implies that the various authorities that have jurisdiction over the same river basin district collaborate to effectuate water management.[40]

The administrative model is no longer applicable within the European Union because the WFD explicitly establishes the river basin district as the organizing unit of water management. The directive is flexible, though, in that it does not mandate the establishment of a river basin authority per river basin district and it leaves it to the states to decide how they will coordinate already-existing and new administrative structures to enable the management of the river basin level. Many states have opted for collaboration for the implementation of the WFD among national institutions and with neighboring states and authorities. The danger inherent in a collaboration model is that it may lapse into an administrative model if collaboration becomes ineffectual. Whether collaboration becomes ineffectual depends on the number of veto players, including institutional veto players, that may sabotage implementation. If the authority designated as a competent authority for the WFD implementation lacks legitimacy, other institutional players may vie for its position. Too many institutional rivalries can lead to the collapse of the collaboration model into an administrative model.

Figure 10.1 classifies states based on the number and clout of potential institutional veto players and the establishment of river basin district authorities within their territory. Since the administrative model is not an option anymore, states could establish a river basin authority per river basin district—what is called here the *river basin model*—or could designate a number of authorities to coordinate for the management of waters in a district—what is called here the *collaboration model*. For both these models to take roots, intense coordination will be needed. Coordination could be viewed as a top-down function requiring centralization. It could

39 *See also* Erik Mostert, *et al.*, *River basin management and planning*, in River Basin management: Proceedings of the International Workshop, The Hague, Oct. 27–29 1999 (IHP-V. Technical documents in Hydrology. Erik Mostert *et al.*, eds., 2000).

40 *See also id.*

also be viewed as a horizontal networking function in which each actor undertakes the responsibility to consult with its counterparts before adopting a policy. This means, for instance, that ministries must communicate and consult with other ministries before formulating their policies.[41] If consensus among ministries is not possible, arbitration and conciliation procedures must be made available through central processes that establish institutional boundaries and set government priorities. Coordination, not an easy task for central governments, is even harder for regional and local authorities because, in order to implement the WFD, coordinating mechanisms must be established all through various governance levels including the international and local levels.

The quality of coordination at the national and international level depends on the number and strength of institutional veto players. Too many institutional veto players could create bottlenecks in developing policymaking processes.[42] Institutional veto players could be ministries reluctant to cooperate with the ministry that is in charge of the WFD implementation. Ministries can raise roadblocks in efforts to protect certain constituencies or in the hope of usurping the competence of the WFD implementation and capturing all the prestige and benefits associated with a directive designed to change the course of water management in Europe.

Institutional bottlenecks could be created when the mayor of a municipality, taking advantage of his or her popularity, adopts policies of low consistency with river basin planning claiming local empowerment as a means of confronting faceless bureaucracies. Players with institutional vetoes may be newly created regions, zealous of their autonomy, and reluctant to cooperate with river basin boards for the promulgation of river basin management plans unless they are highly consistent with regional development plans. Although it is debatable whether the role of institutional

---

41 Les Metcalfe, *National Preparation for International Policymaking: Capacities for Managing National Policy Coordination in the Context of European Integration* 29, at 40, in The Internationalisation of Policy-Making: Institutional and Organizational Options to Integrate Domestic and International Aspects of Policy Making (Organisation for Economic Co-operation and Development, SIGMA Papers: No. 6, 1996).

42 For an example from France, *see* Matthieu Glachant, *Water Agencies in France: A Case of Conflict between Common and State Institutions,* CERNA, Ecoles des Mines de Paris, France, July 1999 available online http://www.isnie.org/ISNIE99/Papers/glachant.pdf (website of international society for new institutional economics).

players is paramount in consensual cultures,[43] the power of their veto can be scathing in administrative environments in which many new institutions are simultaneously developing and seeking autonomy, while existing players continue to compete, and all are struggling for congested administrative space.

A high-level coordination (the horizontal axis, see Figure 10.1) implies a low number of institutional veto players anticipated to create bottlenecks in river basin management. The emphasis is placed on institutional veto players as the number and intensity of conflicts among political veto players (e.g., water users) is bound to be played out at the institutional level as various water users and other interests will attempt to exert their influence on the decisionmaking process through the institutions perceived to be more sympathetic to their views.[44]

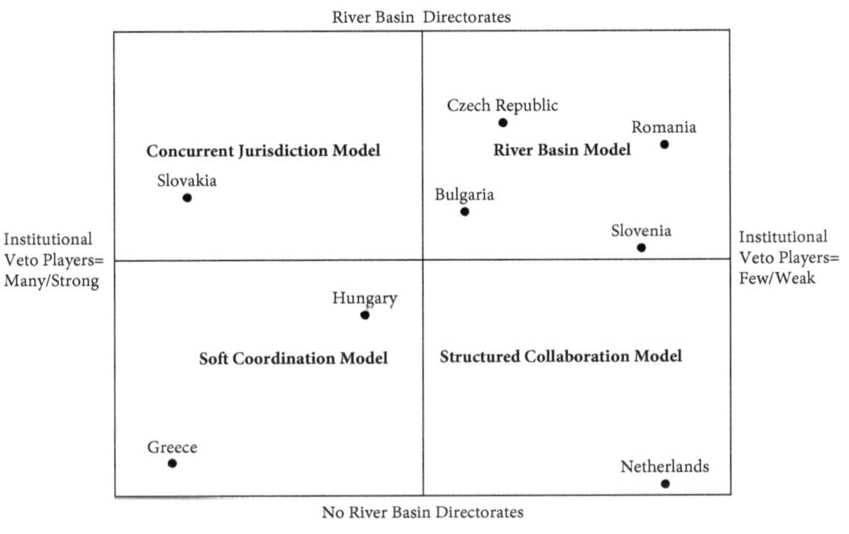

Figure 10.1 Models of WFD Implementation

43 Attempts to achieve consensus at all costs may lead to sidelining of contentious issues that are to re-surface later more potent. A consensual culture may equally lead to the adoption of the lowest common denominator.

44 The more dispersed and fragmented the institutions concerned with water management are, the more likely for various water users and other interests to attempt to locate "institutional pockets" to exert their influence.

Whether countries have established river basin directorates per basin district (the vertical axis, see Figure 10.1) is the other parameter used to classify countries. Not all countries have established river basin directorates per river basin district at the national level and a number of countries have opted for the coordination of existing administrative authorities to produce river basin management plans.

Centralization/decentralization in river basin management has not been used here to classify counties for the simple reason that a quest into the tendency to centralize would place all countries under the centralization quadrant. Centralization in water management in terms of regulatory initiative is quite high in all countries examined here for a number of reasons:

- The WFD is a new legislation and the central government has to straighten out how to implement the directive before it delegates such authority to its sub-units;
- A potential delegation of authority has to be accompanied with the concomitant granting of resources and training. If such resources and training are not forthcoming it is better not to delegate;
- It seems unlikely that most local or regional authorities, given their current structure and expertise, will be able to deal successfully with the complexities of the WFD implementation; and
- It is hard to simultaneously have a good grip on implementation (for purposes of EU reporting and international coordination) while decentralizing and delegating.

For all these reasons, centralization in water management is still prevalent in all countries examined here. Because of centralization, the requirements of a river basin model—in terms of a river basin directorate having real authority over a river basin district—have not been fulfilled. Having said that, some countries have put in place a regional unitary administrative structure based on hydrographic boundaries rather than administrative borders. The water boards (provodi) of the Czech Republic are such a case. The same holds true with the directorates that are branches of Apele Romane (the Central Water Agency in Romania) that are regional unitary structures based on hydrographic borders. Another such structure consists of the new river basin directorates in Bulgaria. Although these river basin "directorates" cannot be called "authorities," at present, they could qualify to become such authorities if the grip of the central state loosens a bit in the future and some decisionmaking is delegated to them.

In other countries, administrative structures do not coincide with the river basin districts. Such countries are Hungary and the Netherlands. In the Netherlands, regional or local authorities involved in water management have not been designed based on the hydrographic unit. On the contrary, various authorities based on administrative boundaries are to work together for the management of a river basin district. In Hungary, water directorates and water inspectorates have been established at the catchment level but how they are to coordinate at the level of subdistricts and districts is yet determinable. Greece falls under the coordination model since existing regional authorities have been entrusted with water management under the direction of a recently created central water agency. The difference among these three countries is the level of coordination achieved or anticipated. In the Netherlands, coordinated structures have been explicitly established at the national and regional levels. In Hungary, coordination is evident mostly at the interministerial or intraministerial level. In Greece, how the regional authorities are to coordinate with the central water agency and among themselves still needs to be ironed out.

The success of both the river basin model and collaboration model (See Figure 10.1) depends on the number of institutional veto players and whether some cooperation could indeed be established among the various institutions that address water management. In the case of the river basin model, coordination is necessary because the river basin district directorates (or boards) do not currently have the authority to dictate water management policies for other subnational actors. Instead, they are dependent on central institutions and codependent on other bodies. The central institutions that supervise river basin directorates are also codependent on other central institutions. Based on the degree of dependence and codependence, water management plans could become the plans that constrain national and regional planning or vice versa: national and regional development plans would set the boundaries for the river basin management plans. In some ways the WFD, at least as initially conceived, is a bet designed to ensure that the pursuit of water quality becomes a constraint on regional development. From a pragmatic point of view, the WFD should, at least, give leverage to water managers to negotiate with other authorities from a position of strength.

The Czech Republic, Romania, and Bulgaria could be considered examples of the river basin model since river basin directorates have been established in each of these countries. In both the Czech Republic and Romania, the model of the river basin directorate is part of a long institutional tradition in water management. In Bulgaria, river basin directorates have been established for the purpose of implementing the WFD. Because of the recent establishment of these directorates, the number of veto players that may wish to undermine their future empowerment may be high. Such veto players are unlikely to emerge in the Czech Republic and in Romania simply because the mandate of river basin bodies in river basin management has been old and largely uncontested. However, the development of regions and municipalities and their role in river basin management and regional planning may contribute to diffuse the authority entrusted to water boards. In the Czech Republic, regions are involved in river basin management since they have to approve the river basin management plans. In Romania, it seems that the central water agency (Apele Romane) still holds firmly the strings of water management. The new water act adopted in Bulgaria in 2006 delineates specifically the role of each and every authority in water management. As such, it may assist in thwarting some institutional rivalry.

The case of Slovakia and Slovenia is more difficult to typify. Both the countries in their legislation have identified river basin districts. The competent authorities at the central level are the Ministries of Environment.[45] River basin management will be delegated to the environmental agency of Slovenia and will initially be performed through its regional offices designated in the future to become decentralized units of water management. To make decentralization possible, though, the environmental agency must be supported and possibly revamped. The branches of the environmental agency must be strengthened and human resources must be retrained to address the challenge of river basin planning. The role of the environmental agency, though, as a future central river basin authority is not seriously contested.

In the case of Slovakia, there seem to be a number of contenders for the possible role that could be played in the future by the regional branches of the ministry of environment. One of them is the Slovak Water Management Enterprise that has been playing a predominant role in water management. Slovakia falls under the concurrent jurisdiction model

45 In Slovenia, it is the Ministry of Environment and Spatial Planning.

because many authorities may end up having parallel jurisdiction in river basin management and a number of other institutional players vie for the role of the ministry of environment as a competent authority for the WFD implementation. Countries that are placed under the river basin model could lapse into the concurrent jurisdiction model if the river basin directorates fail to solidify into river basin authorities and other institutional rivals may wish to safeguard a primary role in river basin management (i.e., newly created regions). Structured coordination may face challenges in the Netherlands especially because of the number of authorities that have to be coordinated. Because of the number of authorities that need to be coordinated, water management in the Netherlands remains centralized. In Hungary and Greece, the use of the current administrative structure was probably the correct choice because both countries are still trying to define the administrative space between newly established authorities and already existing administrative bodies. The coordination linkages that have been put in place, however, are still soft, in both countries, and need to be strengthened to ensure the implementation of the WFD.

Chapter 11

Case Studies

Czech Republic

Selected Sources

August 2002 Catastrophic Flood in the Czech Republic, T.G. Masaryk Water Research Institute & Ministry of Environment of the Czech Republic (2004);
"Conception of Water Management Policy of the Ministry of Agriculture of the Czech Republic, for the Period after European Union (EU) Accession (2004–2010)" (2004);
Cuatrecasas, Llibert and Michel Guegan, *Report on Local and Regional Democracy in the Czech Republic–CG(7) rev Part II*, Congress of Local and Regional Authorities of Europe (CLRAE), Council of Europe, May 2000;
Drinking Water Supply, Sewage Systems (Ministry of Agriculture, 2003);
Implementation of the EU Water Framework Directive in the Czech Republic, Ministry of the Environment of the Czech Republic (2004);
Punčochář, Pavel, *The Institutional Framework for the Implementation of the Water Framework Directive in the Czech Republic* 10, in Proceedings of International Conference "Implementing the European Union Water Framework Directive: Towards Integrated Water Management in Europe,"

May 12, 2006, Athens (DG Environment, European Commission, Technical Report-2007-021, Elli Louka, ed., 2007);
Punčochář, Pavel, *Institutional Framework, Water Management in Czech Republic* available online http://www.aquamedia.at/templates/index.cfm/id/3945;
Punčochář, Pavel, *Water Management in the Czech Republic after the Accession to the European Union* (no date);
Report on the State of Water Management in the Czech Republic (Ministry of Agriculture, Ministry of the Environment, 2003);
Report on the State of Water Management in the Czech Republic (Ministry of Agriculture, Ministry of Environment, 2004);
Report on the State of Water Management in the Czech Republic (Ministry of Agriculture, Ministry of Environment, 2005);
Water Act (2004).

Websites

Ministry of Agriculture:[46] www.mze.cz
Water Management Information Portal: www.voda.mze.cz
Ministry of Environment: www.env.cz
Czech Hydrometeorological Institute: www.chmi.cz
Forests of the Czech Republic: www.lesycr.cz
Agricultural Water Management Authority: www.zvhs.cz
Ministry for Regional Development: www.mmr.cz

Water management has a long tradition in the Czech Republic considered one of the leading states in the adoption of environmental policies after the fall of the communist regime.[47] Master water management plans were prepared right after World War II under a centralized system of water management. Because planning has been enshrined in the Czech water management system, one could predict a good institutional fit between river basin planning mandated by the water framework directive (WFD) and the Czech water management.[48] Water management takes place under

[46] The website of the Ministry of Agriculture provides a wealth of information on water management in the Czech Republic in English.

[47] Joann Carmin and Stacy D. Vandeveer, *Enlarging EU Environments: Central and Eastern Europe from Transition to Accession,* 13(1) Environmental Politics 3 (2004).

[48] Water management in the Czech Republic is administered under a number of legislative acts: Act No. 20/2004 transposed the WFD in the Czech Republic [hereinafter *Water Act*].

a "shared competencies" arrangement. The central authorities that share responsibility for water management include the:

(1) Ministry of Agriculture that has the role of central water authority;[49]
(2) Ministry of Environment that has specific functions related to issues of water protection, international cooperation and flood management.[50]

Other ministries involved in water management include the Ministry of Transportation, the Ministry of Health, and the Ministry of Defense. The protection against floods falls under the Ministry of Environment, though, preventive measures against flooding are to be taken by the Ministry of Agriculture.[51]

The designation of the Ministry of Agriculture as the lead authority in river basin management is an interesting choice since most countries studied here have assigned water management to the Ministry of Environment. The Ministry of Agriculture has retained its authority in water management probably because of the infrastructural and economic issues that are at the heart of such management.[52] It is unclear whether the

In addition to this act, a number of other acts have been adopted.
Act No. 258/2000 Col., on public heath and amendments of other acts;
Act No. 254/2001 Col., on water and amendments of some other acts;
Act No. 274/2001 Col., on public water supply and sewage systems and amendments of some other acts (Water Supply and Sewage Act). *See* Pavel Punčochář, *Water Management in the Czech Republic after the Accession into the European Union* (no date).
Further government decrees were adopted to operationalize the directive:

- Ordinance No. 142/2005 Coll., on Water Planning;
- Ordinance of Ministry of Agriculture No. 292/2002 Coll., on River Basin Districts as last amended by Ordinance No. 390/2004 Coll.;
- Decree No. 333/2003 Coll., Amended decree No. 470/2001 Coll. The decree designated some previously defined small watercourses as significant watercourses and, thus, transferred their management to the water boards. Some other watercourses previously defined significant watercourses were re-defined as small and were transferred from the water boards to the Agricultural Management Authority.
- Decree of the Ministry of Agriculture No. 139/2003 Coll. Concerning Records about the State of Surface and Groundwater and Concerning the Methods for Putting Information into the Public Administration Information System.

49 Section 108(1), Water Act, *id.*
50 Section 108 (2), *id.*
51 Section 108 (3)–(5), *id.*
52 The waters of the Czech Republic, like the waters of most industrialized countries, have been heavily impacted by various uses. Water quality is improving due to the construction of wastewater

designation of shared competencies between the Ministry of Agriculture and the Ministry of Environment has worked smoothly in practice. Commentators have underlined the need for more cooperation between the Ministry of Agriculture and the Ministry of Environment.[53] It seems that the Ministry of Environment has yet to amass the expertise needed in water management. In terms of implementation of water management, the Ministry of Agriculture has a cogent conception of the future of water management in the Czech Republic.

River boards (*provodi*) have been established since 1966 in the Czech Republic. River boards are the regional authorities in charge of river basin management. In 1999, the river boards were transformed from joint stock companies to state enterprises having as a founding authority the Ministry of Agriculture.[54] River boards are responsible for water management in five river basins.[55] The role of river boards is being strengthened, as they are the authorities responsible for river basin management and for the preparation of river basin management plans.[56]

The five river boards are:

- Elbe River Board;
- Vltava River Board;
- Morava (Danube) River Board;
- Odra River Board; and
- Ohre River Board.

treatment plants, but still more investment is needed to improve water quality. *See Report on the State of Water Management in the Czech Republic*, at 10 (Ministry of Agriculture and Ministry of Environment, 2003) [hereinafter *Czech Republic Report 2003*]. Small rivers close to heavily industrialized areas experience high levels of pollution and a vast majority of rivers, with the exception of reservoirs, are considered unsuitable for swimming, *see id.* at 13. Navigation is expected to have an increasing impact on water. According to the "European Agreement on Main Inland Waterways of International Significance" (AGN) the Elbe is referred to as the main European waterway E 20, and the Vltava is referred to as E 20-06. The 2002 floods caused damage to the infrastructure of waterways that had to be rectified in 2003. *Id.* at 32–33.

53 *Baseline Assessment of the Elbe Basin* (NeWater Report Series No. 17, Valentina Krysanova *et al.*, eds., Nov. 2005). The baseline assessment was prepared through the collaboration of the Potsdam Institute for Climate Impact Research (Germany), the T.G. Masaryk Water Research Institute (Czech Republic), and the Institute of Hydrodynamics (Czech Republic).

54 *Conception of Water Management Policy of the Ministry of Agriculture of the Czech Republic, for the Period after EU Accession (2004–2010)*, at 7 (Ministry of Agriculture, 2004) [hereinafter *Conception*].

55 The River Boards were established by the River Boards Act, Act No. 305/2000 Coll., and the State Enterprise, Act No. 77/1997 Coll.

56 Pavel Punčochář, *Institutional Framework, Water Management in the Czech Republic* available online http://www.aquamedia.at/templates/index.cfm/id/3945.

The Ministry of Agriculture supervises the river boards.[57] It is expected that with the increasing deconcentration of the state, the river boards would gradually acquire the function of river basin authorities. The territory of the Czech Republic is further divided into eight catchment areas that could be called *districts*, using the terminology of the WFD.[58]

The boards are not the only authorities that address water management. The Agricultural Water Management Administration (AWMA) is charged with the management of minor watercourses in agricultural areas under the supervision of the Ministry of Agriculture. Since 2001, the AWMA operates through seven regional offices and its responsibilities are similar to those of river boards in its respective area of competence.[59]

One of the primary roles of AWMA is to ensure protection from flooding and a large percentage of its budget is used for maintenance and repair of water infrastructure.[60] The AWMA addresses the maintenance of drainage facilities including about twelve thousand kilometers of drainage canals.[61] The jurisdictional boundaries between the AWMA and the river boards can be fluid, given that the AWMA has quite extensive authority, and what is a small watercourse and what is a large watercourse is not always a clear-cut distinction.[62] The Forests of the Czech Republic manage water resources located in forests (woodland brooks and torrents) and

---

57 *Czech Republic Report 2003*, *supra* note 52, at 23-24. River boards are further inspected with regard to their handling and operating of waterworks and prices they set for water abstraction. In addition to the Ministry of Agriculture, the Ministry of Transport, the Inland Revenue Offices, and the State Energy Inspectorate have a supervisory role over the river boards. *See Czech Republic Report 2003, id.* at 24. A significant percent of the revenues of river basin boards comes from payments they receive by granting licenses for the abstraction of surface water and from grants coming from the state budget. *See Czech Republic Report 2003, id.* at 25, 27.

58 The river basin districts of the Czech Republic are: 1. Ohre and Lower Elbe; 2. Lower Vltava; 3. Upper and Central Elbe; 4. Odra; 5. Morava (Danube); 6. Dyje; 7. Upper Vltava; and 8. Berounka.

59 *Czech Republic Report 2003, supra* note 52, at 30. The AWMA was established by the Ministry of Agriculture in 2001 to ensure the exercise of the administration of watercourses; care for the main drainage facilities; management of economically specific state assets; and the provision expert activity in the field of water management, land reclamation, monitoring of surface water, protection and landscape creation including information science. The AWMA assumed the responsibilities of the National Melioration Authority which had been operating in the field of water resources management for more than thirty years. *See* website of AWMA, www.zvhs.cz.

60 *Czech Republic Report 2003, id.* at 30.

61 *Id.*

62 *See supra* note 48.

some of their most recent work had to do with the rectification of damage done by flooding.[63] National Park Authorities manage small watercourses in protected areas and nature reserves.

An explicit connection between water management and land use planning is built into the Water Act. The act underlines that the Plan for the Main River Basins of the Czech Republic and the river basin district plans, including the program of measures, are fundamental for the execution of land use planning, regional decisionmaking, and the granting of construction permits.[64] This, in essence, means that regional land use planning has to take into account river basin planning.

River basin management planning is the joint endeavor of river boards and the regions. River basin district plans are drawn by river basin administrators according to their jurisdiction in cooperation with the relevant regional authorities and the central water authorities.[65] River basin management plans (RBMPs) have to be approved and the approval takes the form of a regional decree approved by the regional council.[66] If more than one region make a river basin district, all regions affected by river basin planning have to approve the river basin management plan. The Ministry of Agriculture must issue a decree that specifies the relationship among river basin districts, regions, and municipalities.[67] Further sections of the act delimit the powers of municipalities, regions, and central authorities in water management.[68] Section 107 of the Water Act provides specifically that regional authorities have an obligation to cooperate with the central administration and river basin administrators in the development of river basin district plans and their implementation.[69] The provisions of Water Act establish a close cooperation link between regions and river basin authorities. The buy-in of regions is hoped to be secured through their involvement in river basin planning.

---

63 *Czech Republic Report 2003, supra* note 52, at 31.

64 Section 23(2), *Water Act, supra* note 48.

65 Section 25(2), *id.*

66 Section 25(5), *id.*

67 Section 25(3), *id.*

68 *See* Section 104 *et. seq., id.*

69 In this respect, regional authorities may request the cooperation of professional institutions, associations of citizens in the area of environmental protection, owners and operators of water supply and sewage systems and other bodies "needed for ensuring co-operation" in the development of river basin management plans and their implementation. *See* Section 107(d), *Water Act, supra* note 48.

The fourteen regions (*kraje*) are relatively new administrative units in the Czech Republic[70] and, while they were initially established to facilitate EU structural funding, they are developing into more autonomous self-administrative units.[71] Regions are to play an increasingly important role in the future of the country. The Ministry of Regional Development develops the regional development Strategy of the Czech Republic. Regional coordination committees and regional development agencies work on regional development strategies. Regional development strategies are used in turn to develop the National Development Strategy of the Czech Republic.[72]

Both the Ministry of Agriculture and Ministry of the Environment are engaged in the promulgation of river basin management plans through a structure that has common elements with the EU Common Implementation Strategy:

- A Steering Working Group led by ten representatives of the main competent institutions (including, *inter alia*, the Ministry of Agriculture, Ministry of Environment, Ministry of Health, Ministry of Transportation, and Ministry of Interior).

---

70 The structure of the administration in the Czech Republic involves the:

- Central government;
- Regional level (14 regions, *kraje*);
- District level; and
- Municipal level (6 248 municipalities). *See* website of local and regional democracy library (loreg) of the Council of Europe, http://www.loreg.coe.int/Database/Loreg/czech_republic.htm.

71 The creation of regions should not be viewed as an isolated phenomenon but a component of the overall effort to overhaul the Czech administrative structure. In the late 1990s and early 2000s over twenty legislative acts were adopted including the Municipalities Act, the Regions and Regional Councils Act, the Capital City of Prague Act, the Regional Elections Act, and the Regional Powers Act.

The Regions Act sets the organization and authority of regions including their supervision, relationships with the ministries, and interregional cooperation. Regions have their own assets that they have freedom to manage. The Regional Powers Act specifies ministry by ministry which responsibilities are handed down to the regions. Regions have executive responsibilities and can propose legislation to the Parliament. Regional bodies include the regional assembly and the regional council. The regional assembly is democratically elected. The regional council is the executive body of the region and all council members are elected and dismissed by the assembly. Supervision of the regions by the central government is limited to matters of legality. *See* Rapporteurs Llibert Cuatrecasas and Michel Guegan, *Report on Local and Regional Democracy in the Czech Republic–CG(7) rev Part II, Congress of Local and Regional Authorities of Europe (CLRAE)*, Council of Europe, May 2000 [hereinafter *CLRAE Czech Republic*].

72 *See* the website of the Ministry of Regional Development, Czech Republic, http://www.mmr.cz.

- The Committee for Planning in the Field of Water is made of fifty representatives of all bodies involved in the plan elaboration–that is, representatives of central water authorities, river basin administrators, significant administrators of small watercourses, regional authorities, significant water users, research and scientific institutions, and other nongovernmental organizations (NGOs).[73]
- Working Groups on Elaboration of Water Plans for designated subwatersheds (districts), which are led by representatives of river boards.

The plan of the main river basins of the Czech Republic is under preparation. The plan is a strategic planning document that presents the framework of objectives for the management of waters based on the goals of long-term sustainable use of water, the protection against the adverse effects of water, and the maintenance of ecological stability of the landscape.[74] The plan is drawn by the Ministry of Agriculture in cooperation with the Ministry of Environment as well as the authorities of three main river basin districts, namely, the Elbe River basin, the Morava River basin, and the Oder River basin. It is explicitly provided in the legislation that the plan has to go through an environmental impact assessment and that the draft plan has to be published and be available for public comment.[75]

In addition to the nationwide committee for planning in the field of water, each river board has established similarly composed committees for planning in the field of water. The structure of these committees is adapted to the needs of various water boards. Regional administrators participate in these committees since regional administrators have to approve the river basin plans issued by the river boards.[76]

The Ministry of Agriculture and water boards provide information, though their website, on the process of planning in the field of water. The information that could be provided on the internet includes activities

---

73 *Czech Republic Report 2003, supra* note 52, at 63.

74 Section 24(1), *Water Act, supra* note 48.

75 Section 24(2), *id.*

76 In addition to regional authorities, the committees of river boards are comprised of representatives of the AWMA, the Forests of the Czech Republic, the Nature and Landscape Protection Agency, those in charge of preparing the RBMP, and other governmental and nongovernmental bodies. *See also Czech Republic Report 2003, supra* note 52, at 63.

that are taking place, the minutes of meetings of the committees and working groups, as well as methodological and legislative material.[77]

The timetable adopted by the WFD for the promulgation of river basin management plans is incorporated into the Water Act with requirements for public participation. For instance, the timetable and work program for the drafting of the plans must be published and made accessible to water users and the public at least three years before the plan becomes effective. The RBMP must be made available to the public at least a year prior to the period for which the plan applies.[78] Provisions are further included on the programs of measures.[79]

The administrative structure in place for the protection against flooding is different from that of river basin planning.[80] Flood protection authorities are comprised of central, regional, and municipal authorities under an understanding that floods are emergency situations and the involvement of local authorities is pivotal in their management. River boards contribute to flood defense under the category of "other participants involved in flood protection."[81] River boards are supposed to cooperate with the flood protection authorities, to make suggestions and prepare proposals providing technical, organizational and other professional assistance to flood protection authorities. The Flood Protection Plans are coordinated by the Ministry of Environment and

77 *Czech Republic Report 2003, id.*

78 Section 25(2), *Water Act, supra* note 48

79 Section 26(1), *id.*
The Ministry of Agriculture in cooperation with the Ministry of Environment and the regional authorities must submit to the government every three years a summary report on:

- The fulfillment of programs of measures;
- The status of surface water and groundwater; and
- Water management in individual river basin districts. *See* Section 26(5), *Water Act, id.*

80 Section 77, *Water Act, id.*
The flood protection authorities are, namely:

(1) In periods between floods:
  - Municipal authorities;
  - Regional authorities;
  - The Ministry of Environment;
  - The Ministry of Interior is responsible for ensuring the preparation of rescue activities.

(2) In the period during floods:
  - Municipal flood protection commissions, and in Prague capital, the flood protection commissions as they have been designated for portions of the city;
  - Regional flood protection commissions; and
  - The central flood protection commission, see section 81(2), Water Act, id.

81 Section 82, *Water Act, id.* entitled "Other Participants Involved in Flood Protection."

they are not integrated, at least according to the act, into the RBMPs.[82] However, the flood strategy is being revised and RBMPs will include sections on flood protection integrating, thus, flood management, and river basin management.[83]

The water supply and sewage network and the operation of wastewater treatment plants were privatized in the period between 1993 and 1997. Private bodies have become the operators of water supply and sewage networks, while municipalities or associations of municipalities[84] have remained the owners of assets through joint stock companies in which the municipalities are the primary shareholders. Some of the initial contracts between municipalities and private operators are instructive about the importance of institutional controls when privatization takes place. The Act on Water Supply and Sewage was adopted in 2001 and is currently amended to include an institution that would focus on water pricing. The creation of a water-pricing institute has been resisted by private companies[85] that view such an institute as a reassertion of central control.

Further issues encountered in the water sector have to do with the effective use of information system. Information should be used by river basin administrators to involve the public and water users in the planning process.[86] Such users have been organized through various NGOs, such the agrarian chamber, the agricultural association, the association of private farming, and the association of chemical industry. One of the goals of water management has to do with the establishment of controls so that private enterprises do not misuse their monopoly position and that they

---

82 Section 71, *Water Act, id.*

83 Pavel Punčochář, *Institutional Framework for the Implementation of the Water Framework Directive in the Czech Republic* 10, in Proceedings of International Conference, "Implementing the European Union Water Framework Directive: Towards Integrated Water Management in Europe," May 12, 2006, Athens (DG Environment, European Commission, Technical Report-2007-021, Elli Louka, ed., 2007).

84 The Municipalities Act is a real municipal code that provides in great detail for the organization, powers, and responsibilities of municipalities. The code is in compliance with the subsidiarity principle and the European Charter of self-government. The act delegates to municipalities the power of administration for all matters of municipal concern that are not legally the responsibility of regions. To carry out their duties, municipalities receive funds from the national budget. The act provides for the possibility of municipalities to create associations. The Union of Towns and Municipalities of the Czech Republic (SMOCR) is such an association. *See CLRAE Czech Republic, supra* note 71.

85 The private companies have formed an association called Association of Water Supply and Sewage Services (SOVAK).

86 *Conception, supra* note 54, at 16.

focus on providing reliable services.[87] Communication systems need to be further improved in case of flooding.[88] Another goal is to increase the efficiency of state administration and continuously improve the quality of relevant legislation.[89]

Slovakia

Selected Sources

Administrative Capacity for Implementation and Enforcement of EU Environmental Policy in the 13 Candidate Countries, Final Report to DG Environment by ECOTEC *Research and Consulting*, the Institute of European Environmental Policy and the Finnish Environment Institute (Service Contract B7-8110/2000/159960/MAR/H1) (2000);

Fatulová, Elena, *The Institutional Framework for the Harmonization of the Water Framework Directive in Slovakia* 21, in Proceedings of International Conference "Implementing the European Union Water Framework Directive: Towards Integrated Water Management in Europe," May 12, 2006, Athens (DG Environment, European Commission, Technical Report-2007-021, Elli Louka, ed., 2007);

Knape, Anders & Miljenko Doric, *Report on Local and Regional Democracy in the Slovak Republic–CG(8)5 Part II,* Congress of Local and Regional Authorities of Europe (CLRAE), Council of Europe, Oct. 2, 2000;

Report of the Slovak Republic processed for the European Commission in line with Water Framework Directive, Article 3 and Annex I (developed by the Ministry of Environment of the Slovak Republic, Water Research Institute, Slovak Hydrometeorological Institute, Slovak Environmental Agency, June 2004);

Report on Water Management in the Slovak Republic in 2003 (Ministry of Environment of the Slovak Republic, Sept. 2004);

Slovakia National Report, *Seminar on the Role of Ecosystems as Water Suppliers under the Convention on the Protection and Use of Transboundary Watercourses and International Lakes*, Dec. 13–14, 2004 available online

87 *Id.* at 21, 25.

88 *August 2002 Catastrophic Flood in the Czech Republic,* T.G. Masaryk Water Research Institute & Ministry of Environment of the Czech Republic (2004).

89 *Conception, supra* note 54, at 20.

http://www.unece.org/env/water/meetings/ecosystem/Reports/Slovakia_en.pdf;
Public Management Profiles of Central and Eastern European Countries: Slovakia, (OECD SIGMA papers, Sept. 1999).

Websites

Ministry of Environment: www.enviro.gov.sk
Slovak Hydrometeorological Institute: www.shmu.sk
Water Research Institute: www.vuvh.sk
Slovak Environmental Agency: www.sazp.sk
Ministry of Construction and Regional Development: www.build.gov.sk/mvrrsr

Almost a hundred percent of Slovakia's territory belongs to international river basins (96 percent to the Danube River basin district and four percent to the Vistula River basin district).[90] After the adoption of the 2004 Water Act, the Ministry of Environment is the competent authority for the implementation of the WFD, while in the past the responsibility for water management was shared between the Ministry of Environment and the Ministry of Agriculture. The Ministry of Environment has to coordinate its activities with other ministries such as the Ministry of Agriculture, the Ministry of Health, and the Ministry of Regional Development. The Ministry of Agriculture deals with irrigation, drainage, and fisheries (aquaculture). The Ministry of Health regulates drinking water. The Ministry of Construction and Regional Development deals with land-use planning and matters of regional development. The Ministry of Economy is involved in matters such as investments in hydroelectricity and funding for future development.

The legislation that transposed the WFD in the Slovak Republic is the Water Act[91] that came into force on July 1, 2004.[92] According to the act,

---

90 The Slovak catchment area of Danube includes the tributaries of Danube, Vah, Hron, Bodrog, and Hornad. The catchment of Vistula consists of the Poprad and the Dunajec tributaries. *See Report of the Slovak Republic processed for the European Commission in line with Water Framework Directive*, Article 3 and Annex I, at 2 (developed by the Ministry of Environment of the Slovak Republic, Water Research Institute, Slovak Hydrometeorological Institute, Slovak Environmental Agency, June 2004) [hereinafter *Article 3 Report Slovak Republic*].

91 Act on Waters and on changes of the Act No. 372/1990 Coll. on offenses as later amended and approved by the National Council of the Slovak Republic, Water Law No. 364/2004 Coll.

92 *Article 3 Report Slovak Republic, supra* note 90, at 7.

the Ministry of Environment is responsible for the development of programs of measures, RBMPs, the water plan for Slovakia, and the international cooperation on the Danube River basin and the Vistula River basin.[93] Other authorities involved in water management that need to coordinate their activities include the Slovak Hydrometeorological Institute, the Water Research Institute, the Slovak Water Management Enterprise (Banska Stiavnica, SWME), the Slovak Environment Agency,[94] and the Slovak Inspectorate for Environment.

The SWME operates through its headquarters and branches and supervises the river basin authorities responsible for water management within the subriver basin districts.[95] The SWME is now under the Ministry of Environment but previously, it was under the Ministry of Agriculture. The SWME was established in 1997 through the merger of four river basin enterprises.[96] The SWME has as its main objective the management and protection of surface water and groundwater and its authority extends to the management of water works, flood protection, and the enforcement of obligations that emanate from international agreements.[97]

---

93 *Id.*

94 *See* Elena Fatulová, *The Institutional Framework for the Harmonization of the Water Framework Directive in Slovakia* 21, in Proceedings of International Conference "Implementing the European Union Water Framework Directive: Towards Integrated Water Management in Europe," May 12, 2006, Athens (DG Environment, European Commission, Technical Report-2007-021, Elli Louka, ed., 2007).

95 *Id.*

96 *Administrative Capacity for Implementation and Enforcement of EU Environmental Policy in the 13 Candidate Countries*, at 89, Final Report to DG Environment by ECOTEC Research and Consulting, the Institute of European Environmental Policy and the Finnish Environment Institute (Service Contract B7-8110/2000/159960/MAR/H1) (2000) [hereinafter *Administrative Capacity*].

97 The SWME has extensive authority which includes:

- Meeting the demand for water;
- Administration of watercourses, ensuring their function;
- Water construction management;
- Ensuring the effective protection of water, watercourses, and the water constructions;
- Enforcement of special activities related to the management of transboundary watercourses and follow-up activities resulting from particular agreements concerning boundary watercourses;
- Provision of surface water supply from watercourses and reservoirs including the utilization of electric energy production to the extent defined by the state water administrative bodies;
- Enforcement of precaution measures with regard to flood protection;
- Enforcement of various service works such as river material exploitation, mining, and the production of stone materials;
- Monitoring and assessing water quality;

The Water Research Institute administers the drinking water database, the public water supply, and public sewage database and it operates the National Reference Laboratory for the water sector. The Hydrometeorological Institute assesses monitoring and information gathering both with regard to water quantity and quality. It develops hydroecological plans and programs for the control of dangerous substances discharged into the waters. The Slovak Environment Agency is responsible for assessing the state of environment and for reporting to the EU as well as for the administration and development of information systems. However, the agency does not engage in the collection of information. It is, instead, dependent on different research institutes to provide the information it needs.

Five out of eight Regional[98] Environmental Departments (REDs) supervised by the Ministry of Environment are to have extensive jurisdiction over the management of water resources. The future ambition is to transform such departments into river basin authorities. The departments include:

1. The Trnava Regional Environment Authority is responsible for the Danube River Basin District.
2. The Zilina Regional Environment Authority deals with the water management in the Vah River Basin District.
3. Banska Bystrica Regional Environment Authority is involved in the Hron River Basin District.
4. The Presov Regional Environment Authority is responsible for the Bodrog River Basin District and the Poprad and Dunajec River Basin Districts.
5. The Kosice Regional Environment Authority addresses water management in the Hornad River Basin District.

- Fishery management operation;
- Flood protection;
- Other tasks including the operation of protected water management areas;
- Enforcement of other supporting and associate activities to the extent that it does not interfere with the main objectives and performance. *See Report on Water Management in the Slovak Republic in 2003*, at 5 (Ministry of Environment of the Slovak Republic, Sept. 2004) [hereinafter *Ministry Report*].

98 The departments operate out of the eight regions. Regions are the newly created administrative units that are to become independent authorities with their own resources and funding. The Ministry of Construction and Regional Development is responsible for the further development of regions and drafts the National Development Plan that determines the direction of development and the priorities for the disbursement of structural funds provided by the EU.

The Regional Environmental Authorities of the Ministry of Environment, on matters of WFD implementation, supervise the forty-six District Environmental Departments (DEDs) (that are established per district)[99] and cooperate closely with the:

- Slovak Water Management Enterprise and its six branches that acts both at the national and district level;
- Slovak Environment Inspectorate (SEI), which is an entity specifically supervised by the Ministry of Environment;[100] and
- Municipalities.

The SEI is based in Bratislava but has also four regional offices and is responsible for monitoring and inspections.[101] The DEDs are responsible for the enforcement of environmental policy in all media at the local level. These DEDs deal with all environmental issues and not exclusively with water. It seems that Slovakia has a well-established system of granting permits including permits for water use. Decisions made at the DED level can be appealed at the RED level and then can be referred to the Ministry of Environment, which examines whether administrative procedures have been violated.[102] Revenues collected through the permitting process go directly to the state budget.

---

99 The forty-six districts have many responsibilities that demonstrate the centralized character of state administration. Some of the responsibilities of the districts are to be moved back to the branch offices of the ministries. *See* Rapporteurs Anders Knape & Miljenko Doric, *Report on Local and Regional Democracy in the Slovak Republic–CG(8)5 Part II,* Congress of Local and Regional Authorities of Europe (CLRAE), Council of Europe, Oct. 2, 2000 [hereinafter *CLRAE Slovak Republic*]. *See also Article 3 Report Slovak Republic, supra* note 90, at 15 ("Regional Environment Authorities provide methodical supervision and guidance over District Environment Authorities in their territories").

100 *See* Fatulová, *supra* note 94. *See also Article 3 Report Slovak Republic, supra* note 90, at 15.

101 The Water Protection and Inspection (DWPI) unit of the SEI is responsible for water inspection. In 2003, the DWPI concluded 1,011 inspections that focused on:

- Accident plans and hazardous substances disposal plans;
- Waste and, especially, water discharging and wastewater treatment plants operation and effectiveness.

The SEI has regional offices in Nitra, Zilina, Banska Bystrica, and Kosice.

The DWPI has an investigative role regarding complaints and reports on water pollution. It specifically focuses on monitoring the quantity and quality of discharged wastewater. After the analysis of results, the revision of wastewater discharging permits may be authorized. The DWPI provides the environmental departments of district and regional authorities with expert assistance in matters relating to its capacity. *See Ministry Report, supra* note 97, at 7–8.

102 *Administrative Capacity, supra* note 96, at 144–46.

The coordination effort put in place for the implementation of the WFD is quite extensive and all the bodies involved in the implementation process are having a contribution.[103] Given the number of institutions that are involved in water management, identifying the organization that is responsible for certain activities is not always easy. The delineation of responsibilities among the various actors involved in water management is becoming increasingly important. This is especially so with regard to the responsibilities of five REDs and the Slovak Water Management Enterprise.

The municipalities are responsible for the operation of water and sewage services. In 2003, the process of transformation of water and sewage state enterprises into municipal joint-stock companies was finalized. Before 2003, the bulk of water and sewage services were managed by the state.[104]

Slovakia has already issued a strategy on public participation.[105] Some of the problems that are anticipated include the participation of municipalities. This is because of the sheer number of municipalities and the plurality of municipal associations that they have been formed.[106] Consultations with farmers may present difficulties as farmers have yet to organize effectively to address the WFD requirements.

Slovenia

Selected Sources

Administrative Capacity for Implementation and Enforcement of EU Environmental Policy in the 13 Candidate Countries, Final Report to DG

[103] Fatulová, *supra* note 94.

[104] *Ministry Report, supra* note 97, at 58.

[105] Fatulová, *supra* note 94.

[106] Municipal governments are now self-governing units and mayors and municipal councils are elected by direct universal suffrage. There is a high number of municipal authorities (2,887) that tend to increase since often municipalities split up to form new municipalities. Local authorities have created associations, for instance, the Association of Towns and Communities of Slovakia (ZMOS — www.zmos.sk) and the Union of Town and Cities (UMS — www.unia-miest.sk). The ZMOS includes 96 percent of all towns in Slovakia. Today, ZMOS is regarded as a nonpartisan organization that defends the interests of local authorities and lobbies for further decentralization of the Slovak state. In addition to the ZMOS, a number of towns and villages have created regional associations each having at least one representative at the ZMOS. *See CLRAE Slovak Republic, supra* note 99. For the administrative organization of Slovakia, *see* http://www.loreg.coe.int/Database/Loreg/slovakia.htm.

Environment by ECOTEC Research and Consulting, the Institute of European Environmental Policy and the Finnish Environment Institute (2000) (Service Contract B7-8110/2000/159960/MAR/H1);
Engel, Gerhard and Owen Masters, *Report on Local and Regional Democracy in Slovenia – CG(8) 6 Part II*, Congress of Local and Regional Authorities of Europe (CLRAE), Council of Europe, 2001;
Fink-Hafner, Danica and Damjan Lajh, *Managing Europe from Home: The Europeanisation of the Slovenian Core Executive*, (European Consortium for Political Research) ECPR Conference, Marburg, Sept. 2003;
Matoz, Helena, *Development of Institutions for the Implementation of the Water Framework Directive in Slovenia* 47, in Proceedings of International Conference, "Implementing the European Union Water Framework Directive: Towards Integrated Water Management in Europe," May 12, 2006, Athens (DG Environment, European Commission, Technical Report-2007-021, Elli Louka ed., 2007);
Public Management Profiles of Central and Eastern European Countries: Slovenia (OECD SIGMA papers, Sept. 1999);
Water Act (2002).

Websites

Ministry of the Environment and Spatial Planning: www.mop.gov.si
Environmental Agency: www.arso.gov.si

River basin management planning is engrained in the Slovenian administrative practice since, before independence, a master RBMP was prepared for all Slovenia, without having an environmental component, however. RBMPs were prepared also for the districts that today correspond to the regional offices of the Environmental Agency.

The Ministry of the Environment and Spatial Planning has been designated the competent ministry for the implementation of the WFD.[107] The Environmental Agency that, through its branches, is supposed to undertake the duties of river basin planning is under the supervision of the ministry. The Environmental Agency operates through eight regional

[107] For more information about how the ministry is structured, *see* Helena Matoz, *Development of Institutions for the Implementation of the Water Framework Directive in Slovenia* 47, in Proceedings of International Conference "Implementing the European Union Water Framework Directive: Towards Integrated Water Management in Europe," May 12, 2006, Athens (DG Environment, European Commission, Technical Report-2007-021, Elli Louka, ed., 2007).

offices and is mostly involved in operational tasks and activities, such as construction, issuing of permits, and flood management. Because the agency has not been involved in planning, many of the activities for the implementation of the WFD in Slovenia remain fairly centralized.

Other organizations provide expert advice and research and others execute support activities for the Ministry of Environment such as the Water Institute,[108] the National Institute for Biology (NIB) and the Geological Institute. Other ministries that have duties in water management include the Ministry of Agriculture, Forestry, and Food; and the Ministry of Health. The process of the WFD implementation in Slovenia has been streamlined along the lines of the EU common implementation strategy. Steering groups are driving the process while working groups are providing support for the execution of tasks and activities.[109]

In Slovenia, "two water management areas"—the Danube and the Adriatic—have been identified. The Danube management area is comprised of three basins: the river basins of Sava, Drava, and Mura. The river basin of Soca and the coastal rivers and seas make the Adriatic water management area.[110]

National water management programs are adopted for periods of twelve years and delineate the national water policy in Slovenia.[111] National water management programs are adopted by the National Assembly.[112] The act further refers to the program of measures that must be adopted, which is a direct implementation of the provisions of the WFD.

Article 58 of the Water Act provides for the initiation of public participation. This is one of the most extensive public participation

---

108 Art. 159, Water Act adopted July 22, 2002.

109 *See* Matoz, *supra* note 107.

110 Art. 52, Water Act, *supra* note 108.

111 A national water management program must contain in particular:

1. An assessment of state of affairs in the area of water management;
2. Objectives and guidelines for the protection and sustainable use of waters;
3. Priorities for achieving water management objectives;
4. An assessment of funds required for the implementation of programs and deadlines for the achievement of objectives;
5. Guidelines for the implementation of treaties for water management. *See* art. 54(2), Water Act, *id.*

112 They are adopted for a maximum of 12 years, *see* art. 54(3), Water Act, *id.* Article 55 prescribes the details that must be included in the water management plans for the management areas of the Danube and the Adriatic. The act further refers to the achievement of good condition and good ecological potential of waters and provides for derogations similar to derogations contained in the WFD (*see* art. 56, Water Act, *id.*).

procedures included in a national legislation. In most countries, issues of public participation are addressed in government decrees and not in legislative acts. The ready endorsement of participative water management should probably be attributed to Slovenia's familiarity with participatory institutions. The National Council that assists the National Assembly is comprised of forty members representing functional and local interests.[113]

The Water Act provides for the timeframe of preparation of RBMPs and how public participation is to fit in the process of RBMP preparation. Stakeholders are to receive a report that must outline the extent and method of consideration of comments they provided during the compilation of RBMP.[114] They could receive copies also of the background information that was used for the elaboration of the river basin management plan.[115] The adopted RBMPs must be published and must be publicly accessible.[116] More detailed plans may be adopted and the procedure of notification and consultation for these more detailed plans must be followed also.[117]

Water councils, as envisioned in the Water Act, are comprised of ten representatives of local communities, ten holders of water rights, and five NGOs involved in water management and environmental protection registered with the competent authority located in a river basin.[118] Water councils are entrusted with the following tasks:

1. Monitoring the implementation of water management plans;
2. Participating in the preparation of water management plans.[119]

Members of a water council are to be elected through a water conference[120] convened exclusively for the purposes of election of water council. The right to vote for and to be elected in a water council is vested in all

[113] Danica Fink-Hafner and Damjan Lajh, *Managing Europe from Home: The Europeanisation of the Slovenian Core Executive,* ECPR Conference, Marburg, Sept. 2003.

[114] Art. 58, Water Act, *supra* note 108.

[115] Art. 58(8), *id.*

[116] Art. 59, *id.*

[117] Art. 60, *id.*

[118] Art. 165(1), *id.*

[119] Art. 165(2), *id.*

[120] The first water conference must be called by the government, which shall appoint the election commission. The act calling the first election must prescribe specifically the passive and active water rights for the individual members of the conference, the day of the election and other procedural details.

representatives of local communities, including representatives of municipal councils, water users, and members of NGOs "involved in water management and environmental protection and registered with the competent body" in the area where the conference is held.[121] The candidates who receive the most votes are appointed to the water council. The election is deemed valid if more than half of those entitled to vote cast their votes. If a number of candidates receive the same number of votes, the election must be repeated.[122] The provisions of Water Act on public participation through water councils are quite clear. What is most interesting is that members of water councils are elected and are not appointed.

Water conferences take place in all five water management districts, namely, the Soca, Sava, Drava, Mura, and the Adriatic Sea. The purpose of water conferences is to enable local communities, holders of water rights and NGOs to have an influence in water management. The costs for the operation of the conferences are to be handled by the national budget.[123]

Water management and spatial planning cannot be executed separately and the Water Act already foresees the dynamic relationship that needs to exist between land-use planning and river basin management. The Water Act goes as far as to prescribe how the water management plans will be linked to the spatial planning acts.[124] The fact that the competent authority for the implementation of the WFD is the Ministry of Environment and Spatial Planning cannot but facilitate the much-needed interaction between water management plans and spatial planning policies.

The act contains extensive provisions on the protection against the adverse effects of water including flooding.[125] The control and protection against flooding are left to local communities affected by flooding incidents.[126] The water management plans, however, must provide a

---

121 *See* art. 163, Water Act, *supra* note 108. *See also* art. 168, *id.*

122 *See* art. 172, *id.*

123 Art. 163(3), *id.*

124 Art. 61, *id.*

125 Art. 82, *id.* The act provides specifically that the state and the local communities shall ensure the planning, construction, and management of water infrastructure. *See* art. 90(1), *id.*

126 The responsibility for taking measures against the adverse effects of waters is entrusted to the local community. It is provided, for instance, in article 93(1) that the operation, maintenance, and monitoring of water infrastructure for the protection against the adverse effects of water shall be a compulsory commercial service for the state or the local community. In article 98(1), it is also provided that state and local communities shall ensure the maintenance of water and waterside land as a compulsory commercial public service. *See* Water Act, *supra* note 108.

detailed account of measures to be taken to protect against flooding and other adverse effects of waters.[127]

A challenge Slovenia is faced with, during the initial stages of implementation of the WFD, is the transformation of the Environmental Agency, with its eight regional offices, into the key agency of river basin planning. The agency, though it has regional offices that coincide with the river basin districts, is not an institution that has developed skills in water planning. The function of the agency has concentrated, instead, on operational matters, such as issuing licenses. In order for the agency to become a decisive player in the execution of the WFD, it needs first to develop capacity in river basin planning and further to acquire more independence in the execution of its duties.

The transformation of municipalities into entities that could provide consultation in water management is another issue that could affect water management in Slovenia. It has been claimed that the current number of municipalities (193) is too large for a country of the size of Slovenia. The large number of municipalities leads to fragmentation of municipal governance and the inability of municipalities to play an effective role in local self-government. Overall municipalities have not been able to speak with one voice.[128] Efforts to create regions for the allocation of structural funding have been resisted by municipalities. Municipalities are apprehensive that the creation of regions will encroach on their authority.[129]

Netherlands

Selected Sources

Enserink, Bert, *et al.*, *Public Participation in River Basin Management in the Netherlands: (Not) Everybody's Concern,* HarmoniCOP Project, Dec. 12, 2003.

---

127 *See* art. 90(3), *id.* More specifically, according to article 91(2), *id.*, "The scope of protection against the adverse effects of waters and the necessary measures shall be laid down in water management plans."

128 Rapporteurs Gerhard Engel and Owen Masters, *Report on Local and Regional Democracy in Slovenia–CG(8) 6 Part II*, Congress of Local and Regional Authorities of Europe (CLRAE), Council of Europe, 2001. The Association of Municipalities and Towns of Slovenia (SOS), that seems to represent most municipalities, has been challenged by the Association of Municipalities of Slovenia (ZOS) as not being representative of the interests of smaller municipalities. For the administrative organization of Slovenia, *see* http://www.loreg.coe.int/Database/Loreg/slovenia.htm.

129 Engel, *id.*

The HarmoniCOP project was sponsored by the European Commission. For information about the project *see* http://www.harmonicop.uos.de/index.php;
Huisman, Pieter, *Water Legislation in the Netherlands* (2004);
Huitema, Dave and Hans Bressers, *Scaling Water Governance: the case of the implementation of the European Water Framework Directive in the Netherlands*, paper presented at the Synthesis Conference of the Institutional Dimensions of Global Environmental Change Program, Bali, Indonesia, Dec. 2006;
Mak, Willem, *The Implementation of Water Framework Directive in the Netherlands and Cooperation in the Ems, Meuse, Scheldt and Rhine River Basins* 77, in Proceedings of International Conference, "Implementing the European Union Water Framework Directive: Towards Integrated Water Management in Europe," May 12, 2006, Athens (DG Environment, European Commission, Technical Report-2007-021, Elli Louka, ed., 2007);
Mostert, Erik, *Integrated Water Resources Management in the Netherlands: How Concepts Function*, 135 Journal of Contemporary Water Research and Education 19 (2006);
Uijterlinde, Rob, *The Dutch Polder Model: The Evolution and Current Role of Waterboards* 101, in Proceedings of International Conference "Implementing the EU Water Framework Directive: Towards Integrated Water Management in Europe," May 12, 2006, Athens (DG Environment, European Commission, Technical Report-2007-021, Elli Louka, ed., 2007);
Water in Focus 2003: Annual Report on Water Management in the Netherlands (2003);
A Different Approach to Water, Water Management Policy in the 21st Century (Ministry of Transport, Public Works and Water Management, Dec. 2000);
Water in the Netherlands: Managing Checks and Balances (Netherlands Hydrological Society, 2004);
Wolsink, Maarten, *River Basin Approach and Integrated Water Management: Governance Pitfalls for the Dutch Space-Water-Adjustment Management Principle*, 37(4) Geoforum 473, July 2006.

Websites

Ministry of Transport, Public Works and Water Management:
www.verkeerenwaterstaat.nl

Ministry of Spatial Planning, Housing and the Environment, http://international.vrom.nl
Association of Water Boards: www.uvw.nl
Website of Amsterdam water board (after the merger with the drinking water company): www.waternet.nl

The Netherlands has a reputation as a pace setter in European environmental policy. Pace setters are countries with resources and expertise to devote to EU environmental rule making. The advantage of being a policymaker consists of the avoidance of costs of being a policy taker. Policymakers "upload" their policies to the EU, while the policy takers follow by having to adjust to legislative changes imposed from above. Because pace setters have resources to exert influence, they are often able to have their policies and views endorsed by the European Commission.[130] Dutch policymaking at the level of the EU is focused on developing coherent positions and on speaking with one voice in European politics.

The Netherlands is a unitary, decentralized state with three levels of government, which are national, provincial, and regional or local (the water boards and municipalities).[131] The Netherlands has a well-developed institutional structure and a system of laws that support a coherent framework for water management.[132]

The approach of the Netherlands to the adoption of the WFD has been to accept the river basin principle but resist the paradigm of establishing a river basin authority in charge of a river basin district. The Netherlands resolved not to create new authorities for the application of the directive and to use, instead, existing institutions devoted to water management. The concept of integrated water resources management has been appealing to policymakers in the Netherlands since the early 1980s.[133] Despite such interest, the WFD seems to have been perceived in some circles as an expensive and unnecessary legislative instrument and the implementation of the directive has been met with institutional reluctance.[134]

---

130 Tanja A. Brözel, *Pace-Setting, Foot-Dragging and Fence-Sitting: Member State Responses to Europeanization,* Queen's Papers on Europeanization, No. 4/2001.

131 *Water in the Netherlands: Managing Checks and Balances* 87 (Netherlands Hydrological Society, 2004).

132 *See*, e.g., Pieter Huisman, *Water Legislation in the Netherlands* (2004).

133 Erik Mostert, *Integrated Water Resources Management in the Netherlands: How Concepts Function* 135 Journal of Contemporary Water Research and Education 19 (2006).

134 Dave Huitema and Hans Bressers, *Scaling Water Governance: The Case of the Implementation of the European Water Framework Directive in the Netherlands,* paper presented at the

The competent authority for water management is the Ministry of Transport, Public Works and Water Management. The Ministry, through its Rijkswaterstaat (the Directorate General for Public Works and Water Management), that was established in 1798, exerts significant authority in water management and flood protection.[135] The Ministry of Transport is expected to collaborate closely with the Ministry of Housing, Spatial Planning, and Environment. The Ministry of Housing, Spatial Planning, and Environment is responsible for the general environmental policy, including the promulgation of water quality standards.[136] The Ministry of Agriculture, Nature Management, and Food Quality is involved in water management because of the dependence of agriculture on water resources management.[137]

At the regional level, twelve provinces are in charge of implementing the national water policy. The provinces are administered by a provincial council. The provincial council elects the provincial board and the chairman of the provincial board is the governor of the province. Each province coordinates the policies of various sectors, such as water management, environment, nature conservation, housing, physical planning, transport, economics, and welfare. Provinces can formulate policies of their own, but they must also adhere to the policies issued by the central government. Provinces must ensure that national policies are implemented by the water boards and municipalities.[138]

Besides the provinces, twenty-six water boards are exclusively targeting water management. More than four hundred municipalities execute specific operational tasks with regard to water management.[139] The function of water boards as institutions that are central to water management is guaranteed in the constitution. Water boards were formed spontaneously

---

Synthesis Conference of the Institutional Dimensions of Global Environmental Change Program, Bali, Indonesia, Dec. 2006.

135 *Water in the Netherlands, supra* note 131, at 88.

136 *Id.* at 89.

137 *Id.*

138 *Id.*

139 *Id.* at 90. Municipalities are organized also under the Association of the Netherlands Municipalities (VNG). Municipalities have specific duties in water management, *see* Rob Uijterlinde, *The Dutch Polder Model: The Evolution and Current Role of Waterboards* 101, in Proceedings of International Conference "Implementing the European Union Water Framework Directive: Towards Integrated Water Management in Europe," May 12, 2006, Athens (DG Environment, European Commission, Technical Report-2007-021, Elli Louka, ed., 2007).

by landowners who organized to defend their land from invasive waters. Because of their grass-roots origins, the initial number of water boards was quite high. The high number of water boards fragmented water management, and water boards frequently merged and reorganized to realize economies of scale in water management.[140]

Landowners, owners of houses, renters of buildings, farmers, and inhabitants of an area are the constituencies on which water boards are based. Water boards are founded on the principle that those who have an interest in water management must pay for such management in order to have a say in water management. This interest-pay-say motto endorsed by the water boards is probably one of the oldest articulations of the polluter pays or cost recovery principle, as it clearly states that those who have an interest in water management must pay for such management. Furthermore, those who have an interest and pay for water management must have a say in such management. This is an expression of associative or functional democracy; a restrictive expression, though, because the ability to have a voice in water management is based on the ability to pay (i.e., through taxes or fees). This linkage between participation and taxation excludes a large category of stakeholders that have an interest in water management but are not taxed for such management, namely, the environmental NGOs. The environmental interest has been represented in water boards through the residents' category as many residents who participate in water boards are motivated by their concern about the environment. Today, water boards are government institutions and are no longer associated, at least, in the minds of the public, with fora of citizen participation.[141]

Water management in the Netherlands, thus, involves a process of coordination of activities of various national and subnational authorities involved in water management. The process used to be a clear-cut, top-down planning process. At the strategic level, a national document on spatial planning, a national document on water, and a national environmental

---

[140] *Water in the Netherlands*, *id.* at 90.

[141] Bert Enserink *et al.*, *Public Participation in River Basin Management in the Netherlands: (Not) Everybody's Concern*, at 7, HarmoniCOP Project, Dec. 12, 2003 ("It would not be correct to qualify the water boards, in their present form and in the present Dutch context, as water users associations. They should rather been seen as ordinary government bodies with specific tasks and a special electoral system. In practice only some 25% of the voters show up at the waterboard elections . . . and even people that do show up often do not know exactly what the tasks of water boards are."). The HarmoniCOP project was sponsored by the European Commission. For information about the project *see* http://www.harmonicop.uos.de/index.php.

policy plan were adopted. Taking their cues from the national documents, the provinces used to develop a regional spatial plan, a provincial document on water, and a provincial environment policy plan. Then, the water boards and the municipalities proceeded with local water management and sewage plans.[142]

The implementation of the WFD has altered this top-down planning process. Now, international river basin districts have been established and working areas within the Netherlands have been designated around which coordination efforts must converge. The Netherlands shares with its neighbors four river basins the Rhine, the Meuse, the Scheldt, and the Ems. For three of these river basins, namely, the Rhine, Meuse, and the Scheldt, international commissions have been established that drive cooperation among the neighboring countries. These international commissions are now the platforms for coordinating the WFD planning. Working areas (or subriver basin districts) have been designated within the Netherlands, namely, the Meuse, the Scheldt, Rhine-west, Rhine-middle, Rhine-east and Rhine-north, and the Ems. Given the new dynamics, under which international river basin districts and subdistricts have become the focus of water management, the challenge for the Netherlands has been to fit an already established administrative structure into the river basin model.

Coordination structures have been put in place to enable river basin management. Coordination does not only occur at the interministerial level but also involves the provinces, water boards, and municipalities. In addition to top-down coordination structures, horizontal interlinking mechanisms are in place to ensure lateral coordination, through the River Basin Coordination Bureau.

Some of these coordinating mechanisms were in place before the implementation of the WFD, such as the National Administrative Consultation Water (Landelijk Bestuurlijk Overleg Water (LBOW), a national steering committee comprised of ministers and representatives of regional governments. The preparatory work for the meetings of LBOW is executed by the national coordination group comprised of officials at the nonpolitical level. National working groups facilitate the work of the national coordination group.[143]

---

[142] For a detailed depiction of the process, *see Water in the Netherlands, supra* note 131, at 82.

[143] Willem Mak, *The Implementation of Water Framework Directive in the Netherlands and Cooperation in the Ems, Meuse, Scheldt and Rhine River Basins* 77, in Proceedings of International Conference "Implementing the European Union Water Framework Directive: Towards

While LBOW is a national coordinating structure, the Regionale Bestuurlijke Overleggen (RBO) is a high-level committee comprised of highest level officials from the provinces, the water boards, and some municipalities. RBOs are established in each of the eight subriver basins. The Regionale Ambtelijke Overleggen (RAOs) are the regional coordination groups at the nonpolitical level that prepare the meetings of RBOs. Regional working groups are functioning with stakeholder participation and are supporting the work of the RAO.[144]

The Netherlands River Basin Coordination Bureau coordinates the activities between the national level and the regional level as well as among the eight subriver basins. The river basin coordination bureau has to ensure that regional experiences are not lost at the national policy-making level and that decisions made at the national level are transmitted to the regional level. In other words, the function of the River Basin Coordination Bureau is to ensure that bottom-up and top-down communication is working.[145]

In addition to this coordination structure, the Netherlands aspires to put in place a simultaneous multilevel decision making process.[146] Multilevel decisionmaking is different from sequential decisionmaking. In sequential decisionmaking, the central administrator makes decisions that then have to be adapted at the provincial or water board level and then at the local level. Multilevel decisionmaking means that all levels simultaneously are making decisions so that action, say, at the regional level is not thwarted until final instructions are received from the national level. Multilevel decisionmaking presupposes that all levels have a shared commitment to achieve common goals. For multilevel decisionmaking to function effectively, continuous feedback loops have to be built into it.

It will be interesting to follow how the coordination structure in the Netherlands will function and whether simultaneous multilevel decisionmaking process can become a tangible reality. The complexity of the coordination structure that has been put in place should not be underestimated. How the current administrative structure is to evolve in view of the challenge of the WFD implementation remains to be seen.

Integrated Water Management in Europe," May 12, 2006, Athens (DG Environment, European Commission, Technical Report-2007-021, Elli Louka, ed., 2007).

144 *Id.*

145 *Id.*

146 *Id.*

Water boards have merged from an initial number of 2,500 to twenty six, and their jurisdictional reach has started to overlap with that of provinces. Further mergers are not expected in the near future but should they occur, they will generate further friction over the jurisdictional boundaries between the water boards[147] and the provinces.[148] Some hope that water boards evolve into integrated water management authorities. In this respect, the merger of water boards with the water companies[149] could be encouraged. The first such merger took place between the Amsterdam water board and the local drinking company to form Waternet, "the first company in the Netherlands that combines all water services under one roof."[150]

Given the number and high level of ambition of actors involved in water management in the Netherlands, it would be difficult to marginalize any one actor to favor others. Because of the centrifugal nature of the system, it comes as no surprise that the ministry holds a pivotal role in water management. The complexity of decisionmaking notwithstanding, integrated river basin management has been supported in the Netherlands[151] since an integrated view of the river basin could spur preventive action to thwart pollution coming from upstream states. However, the application of integrated water resources management (IWRM) has not been that easy. All the four river basin districts in the Netherlands (the Scheldt, Meuse, Rhine, and Ems) are international river basin districts. For three out of the four river basin districts, international commissions are now in charge of coordination of river basin management under the auspices of

147 Water boards are also organized under the Association for Water Boards (UVW). Individual water boards as well as the UVW have undertaken a number of international activities not only in Europe but also in other areas of the world.

148 Provinces work together within the Interprovincial Overleg (IPO) (the Association of the Provinces of the Netherlands). Provinces participate in the EU Committee of the Regions.

149 Water companies are in charge of water supply in the Netherlands. Water companies do not differ substantially from private companies. The shareholders of water companies are comprised of local governments and provinces. The VEWIN is the Dutch water works association that is basically an umbrella organization for the water companies. It is expected that mergers among water companies (an initial number of 100 water companies has been reduced to ten water companies) will reduce their number even more. Two to five water companies are considered the optimal number. Further mergers between water boards and water companies cannot be excluded.

150 *See* website of Waternet, www.waternet.nl.

151 *See* Maarten Wolsink, *River Basin Approach and Integrated Water Management: Governance Pitfalls for the Dutch Space-Water-Adjustment Management Principle*, 37(4) Geoforum 473, July 2006.

the WFD. The gestation of these international commissions to authorities in charge of water management would be beneficial for the Netherlands. The river basin district concept is generally beneficial to downstream states as it emphasizes the nature of a river as a single entity and discourages the isolation of upstream actions as they may affect downstream use.

Hungary

Selected Sources

Administrative Capacity for Implementation and Enforcement of EU Environmental Policy in the 13 Candidate Countries, Final Report to DG Environment by ECOTEC Research and Consulting, the Institute of European Environmental Policy and the Finnish Environment Institute (Service Contract B7-8110/2000/159960/MAR/H1) (2000);

Attila Ágh, *Public Administration in Central and Eastern Europe* 536, in Handbook of Public Administration 536 (2003);

Government Order 183/2003, XI.5, effective in 2004;

Holló, Gyula, *Institutional Mechanisms for Water Management in Hungary* 14, in Proceedings of International Conference, "Implementing the European Union Water Framework Directive: Towards Integrated Water Management in Europe," May 12, 2006 Athens (DG Environment, European Commission, Technical Report-2007-021, Elli Louka, ed., 2007);

Hungary National Report, *Seminar on the Role of Ecosystems as Water Suppliers, under the Convention on Protection and Use of Transboundary Watercourses and International Lakes*, Dec. 13–14, 2004 available online http://www.unece.org/env/water/meetings/ecosystem/Reports/Hungary_en.pdf;

Ijjas, Istvan & Krisztina M. Botond, *Towards Win-Win Solutions, Public Participation in River Basin Management in Hungary*, Workpackage 4 (no date), European background (Harmonising Collaborative Planning) HarmoniCOP Project. The HarmoniCOP project was sponsored by the European Commission. For information about the project, *see* http://www.harmonicop.uos.de/index.php;

Kessler, Peter, *Gap Analysis on the Administrative side of the Implementation*, Twinning Project Implementation of Water Framework Directive in Hungary, Activity No. 1, Mar. 2003;

Olbrycht, Jan, *Report on Regional Democracy in Hungary – CPR(9) Part II*, Congress of Local and Regional Authorities of Europe (CLRAE), Council of Europe, 2002;
Papp, Kálmán, Experience with public participation in the field of water management and land use in Hungary, Feb. 25, 2005 (on file with the author);
Péter, Judit, *WaterTime case study—Debrecen Hungary*, Jan. 31, 2005 available online http://www.watertime.net/docs/WP2/D18_Debrecen.doc;
Péter, Judit, *WaterTime case study—Szeged, Hungary*, Jan. 31, 2005 available online http://www.watertime.net/docs/WP2/D39_Szeged.doc;
Public Management Profiles of Central and Eastern European Countries: Hungary (OECD SIGMA papers, Sept. 1999);
Uijterlinde, R.W., *et al.*, *Success Factors in Self Financing Local Water Management: A Contribution to the Third World Water Forum in Japan* (2003);
Water Management in Hungary at the Turn of the Millennium, Ministry for Transport, Communication and Water Management, National Water Authority & Water Resources Research Centre VITUKI Plc, 1998.

Websites

Ministry of Environment and Water: www.kvvm.hu
Hungarian Directorates: www.vizugy.hu
National Directorate for Environment, Nature Protection and Water:[152] www.ovf.hu
Balaton-Uplands National Park: www.bfnpi.hu
Water Framework Directive EU-Twinning Project: www.eu-wfd.info
Ministry of Agriculture and Regional Development: www.gak.hu

The Danube River and its tributary, the Tisza River, define the hydrology of Hungary, a country in which over 95 percent of surface water originates in neighboring countries. Comprehensive flood control measures were launched in the early nineteenth century and continue to these days. Despite extensive works, a large number of people and considerable economic assets are still exposed to flood hazards and further flood management infrastructure may be needed.

Water management in Hungary has three basic functions:

- Protection of population against the hazards of water;
- Meeting water demand in an efficient way;

[152] On January 1, 2006, the National Directorate for Environment, Nature Protection and Water was renamed the Central Bureau of Water and Environment.

- Preservation of water resources, in particular, drinking water resources in order to achieve long-term sustainable use and maintain the necessary level of services and control.[153]

Water management has a long tradition in Hungary. The first water law entered into force in 1885, the second in 1964, and the third in 1996. A permit was required for water management use since 1885. These permits were registered in a water book. The 1885 law put restrictions on water pollution. In 1964, comprehensive legislation was introduced on water pollution.[154] Hungary was one of the first countries to recognize the importance of integrated regional planning in water management and one of the few countries to enact regional water management master plans.[155]

Four working areas[156] have been designated for the purposes of WFD implementation, namely, Duna közvetlen (Danube), Tisza, Dráva, and Balaton.[157] Regional authorities are to coordinate river basin management in these working areas. Hungary considers the international Danube River Basin District to be the river basin district. The purpose of the four working areas, consequently, is to facilitate planning. The regional authorities that need to coordinate their activities in these working areas are the twelve Regional Directorates for Environment, Nature Conservation, and Water (the OKTVF or directorates). The twelve directorates are responsible for the development of RBMPs, the coordination of which occurs at

153 *Water Management in Hungary at the Turn of the Millennium*, at 11 (Ministry for Transport, Communication and Water Management, National Water Authority & Water Resources Research Centre VITUKI Plc, 1998) [hereinafter *Water Management Hungary*].

154 Istvan Ijjas and Krisztina M. Botond, *Towards Win-Win Solutions: Public Participation in River Basin Management in Hungary*, at 4, Workpackage 4, European background HarmoniCOP Project, at 10 (no date) [hereinafter *HarmoniCOP Hungary*]. The HarmoniCOP project was sponsored by the European Commission. For information about the project *see* http://www.harmonicop.uos.de/index.php.

155 *Water Management Hungary*, *supra* note 108, at 30.

156 The WFD was transposed by three legislative decrees:

- Government decree 219/2004 (VII.21.) on the protection of subsurface bodies;
- Government decree 220/2004 (VII.21.) on the regulations pertaining to the protection of surface water bodies;
- Government decree of 221/2004 (VII. 21) on certain regulations pertaining to river basin management, *see Hungary National Report, Seminar on the Role of Ecosystems as Water Suppliers under the Convention on Protection and Use of Transboundary Watercourses and International Lakes, at 8,* Dec. 13–14, 2004 [hereinafter *Hungary National Report*].

157 *Article 3 Report of Hungary to the European Commission on the Implementation of the Water Framework Directive*, June 2004.

the ministerial level. Hungary is a strong supporter of the development of an International River Basin Management Plan for the whole Danube through coordination by the International Commission for the Protection of the Danube River (ICPDR). Hungary supports the idea of a larger delegation of authority for the management of the Danube to the ICPDR.

According to the Hungarian Environmental and Water Structure,[158] water management and nature conservation are under the Ministry of Environment and Water.[159] Other ministries involved in water management include the Ministry of Interior that is responsible for supporting water supply and sewage projects and emergency control activities of local governments. The Ministry of Economy deals with industrial water use. The Ministry of Health is responsible for drinking and bathing water. Soon after the adoption of the WFD, an interministerial committee was put in place to facilitate implementation. The Inter-Ministerial Strategic Committee is mostly a government body and all ministries relevant for the WFD implementation are represented in it. NGOs are represented in the committee and some environmental NGOs, academic institutes, and business organizations have achieved permanent status in the interministerial committee.[160]

The tasks of the Ministry of Environment and Water are performed by the National Directorate for Environment, Nature Conservation, and Water; the National Inspectorate for Environment and Water; and branches of the directorate and the inspectorate that have been established locally. The National Directorate for Environment, Nature Conservation, and Water deals with economic matters, financing, and investment management. The OKTVF, called today Central Bureau of Water and Environment, is the legal successor of the National Water Authority (OVF). The OVF was viewed as overly centralized and was disbanded in the late 1980s. The national inspectorate for environment and water, through its regional inspectorates, grants water permits and acts as a legal office. But because permit requirements often relate to technical matters, the regional inspectorates need to consult with the regional directorates.

The national Directorate for Environment, Nature Conservation, and Water is comprised of twelve directorates. These twelve local directorates are the legal successors of the twelve regional authorities of the

---

158 Government order of 183/2003.(XI.5.) taking effect on Jan. 1, 2004, on Environmental and Water Structure.

159 That responsibility rested before with the Ministry of Transport and Water Management.

160 *Hungary National Report*, *supra* note 156, at 10.

national water authority. The national inspectorate for environment and water functions locally through twelve regional inspectorates. The twelve regional directorates and inspectorates are, in essence, branches of the Ministry of Environment. For every activity or project in which directorates are involved, they receive funding from the ministry. Because of the lack of financial independence, rapid response may be precluded in cases of emergency. The lack of ability to quickly respond to changing circumstances often becomes a source of frustration for the directorates. Sometimes, the ministry bypasses the national directorate and deals directly with the twelve regional directorates.

The regional environment and water directorates[161] are located in the same regions as the regional inspectorates for environment and water and are established based on river catchments.[162] Most directorates include departments for general water management, flood protection, planning, water supply, sewage, and irrigation. The inspectorates operate water quality laboratories that are the backbone of water quality monitoring network. Inspectorates carry out official water analyses, the results of which are used to bring enforcement actions.[163] The inspectorates compile also reports on potential sources of pollution, the major polluters, and the number of licenses issued. Although the twelve inspectorates are responsible for water quality, the directorates are also responsible for hydrological monitoring and some water quality monitoring. Because both inspectorates and directorates perform certain monitoring functions, some duplication of effort is expected.

In principle, in the Hungarian system, the licensing of water use (inspectorates) is separate from water management (directorates). Some have

---

[161] *HarmoniCOP Hungary, supra* note 154, at 14.
The objectives of the directorates are:

- The operation, maintenance, management, and development of state waters and hydraulic structures;
- The performance of flood, drainage, emergency control and water pollution accident control;
- Coordination and supervision of all the activities of state and nonstate actors involved in water management;
- Keeping records on the allocation and protection of water resources; and
- Exercising powers of first instance of water authority (permitting and supervision).

[162] *See Appendix to Government Order 183/2003. (XI.5.), supra* note 158. The directorates and the inspectorates are established based on the subcatchments of the country. Directorates and inspectorates are established in North Transdanubia, West Transdanubia, Mid-Transdanubia, South-Transdanubia, Mid-Danube-Valley, and Lower-Danube-Valley, Upper Tisza, Mid-Tisza, Lower-Tisza, Trans-Tisza, North Hungary, and the Körös Region.

[163] *HarmoniCOP Hungary, supra* note 154, at 16.

claimed that this structure is not workable and that inspectorates and directorates should merge into a single body. The directorates have been separated from inspectorates to avoid the development of clientele relationships between water administration and water users. In the past, when licensing and management were merged under a single authority, clientele relationships developed between the water authority and water users. The separation of licensing from water management has been put in place to discourage rent-seeking behavior.

The ministry of environment and water is comprised of the Deputy Secretary for Water (Water Office), the Deputy Secretary for Environment (Environment Office), and Deputy Secretary for Nature Conservation (Nature Conservation Office).[164] The National Directorate for Environment, Nature Conservation, and Water is under the supervision of all deputy secretaries. Having multiple supervisors can sometimes be confounding, given that the management of water quantity cannot be neatly separated from the management of water quality and the deputy secretary for the environment deals with water quality while the deputy secretary for water addresses water quantity. To enhance coordination, the water office, the environment office, and the nature conservation office have formed a horizontal group that meets regularly for the purposes of WFD implementation.

Flood protection differs from the administration of water management[165] and local governments play an important role in flood defense.[166] The responsibility for managing drinking water and sewage services was transferred to municipalities with the Act on Municipalities in 1990. There are about 3,600 local governments and, as a result, water management at the local level is very fragmented. Municipalities have formed joint venture companies, limited liability companies, or corporations the purpose of which is to provide water services. In some cases, municipalities have collaborated with private companies forming *public-private partnerships.* When public-private partnerships are in place, municipalities retain the ownership of assets while water operations are divided between the

---

164 There is also a Deputy Secretary for Legal Affairs and a Deputy Secretary for Economic Affairs.

165 Gyula Holló, *Institutional Mechanisms for Water Management in Hungary* 14, in Proceedings of International Conference, "Implementing the European Union Water Framework Directive: Towards Integrated Water Management in Europe," May 12, 2006, Athens (DG Environment, European Commission, Technical Report-2007-021, Elli Louka, ed., 2007).

166 *Water Management Hungary, supra* note 153, at 17

municipality and the private company.[167] In other cases, municipalities establish private companies whose shares they own.[168] Requiring consumers to pay the full price for the costs of water has not been pursued aggressively since many consumers cannot afford this cost. The government, as a result, has to subsidize price increases. Although the service costs for the provision of water have been passed onto the consumer, it is difficult to do so with infrastructure costs.[169] Municipalities have to accommodate what could be conflicting functions: the pursuit of public interest and profit maximization. Some municipalities have installed advisory bodies to help them make sense of the bifurcated allegiance necessitated by the pursuit of public good, on one hand, and the running of a profitable enterprise, on the other.[170] The local water service sector has not generated much interest among local NGOs despite the acute equity issues involved. Employees who risk losing their jobs because of privatization are much more active.[171]

A stable administrative structure seems to be in place for water management in Hungary. According to some commentators, "A relatively integrated administrative structure is in place. However, poor coordination at the national and the national/regional level is reported."[172] This probably is due to multiple decisionmaking centers that confound jurisdictional boundaries. The human resources of the Ministry of Environment and of the National Directorate for Environment, Nature Conservation, and Water have been downsized in a period in which a plethora of tasks are emanating from the implementation of environmental legislation.

---

167 Judit Péter *et al.*, *WaterTime case study—Szeged, Hungary*, Jan. 31, 2005 available online http://www.watertime.net/docs/WP2/D39_Szeged.doc [hereinafter *Szeged Study*] (Case study where the assets for water services remained public but the operation was mixed—public and private [Public Private Partnership or PPP]). In this case, the private company filed a lawsuit against the municipality due the latter's refusal to increase prices. Eventually, a compromise was reached according to which how much the consumer pays depends on metered consumption and, as a general rule, prices paid by households and municipal institutions are lower than those paid by other customers. Furthermore, courts have been consistent in abolishing regulations that transfer to consumers costs not related to water service.

168 Judit Péter *et al.*, *WaterTime case study—Debrecen* Hungary, Jan. 31, 2005 available online http://www.watertime.net/docs/WP2/D18_Debrecen.doc [hereinafter *Debrecen Study*].

169 *Szeged Study, supra* note 167.

170 *See Debrecen Study, supra* note 168.

171 *Id.*

172 *Administrative Capacity for Implementation and Enforcement of EU Environmental Policy in the 13 Candidate Countries*, at 248, Final Report to DG Environment by ECOTEC Research and Consulting, the Institute of European Environmental Policy and the Finnish Environment Institute (Service Contract B7-8110/2000/159960/MAR/H1) (2000).

However, the capacity for reform should not be underestimated; Hungary has been characterized a pioneer in developing administrative capacity and exceptional in its efforts at regional re-organization.[173]

The fact that the licensing bodies (inspectorates) are separate from the management bodies (directorates) contributes to administrative complexity. It has been proposed that inspectorates and directorates should merge to create more coherence in water management.[174] Maybe water management in Hungary would have benefited from the existence of a strong central authority modeled after the central water agency in Romania. Ironically, such authority was dismantled as anachronistic and overly centralized.

Regarding decentralization in water management, it does not seem that, up to this point, the directorates and the inspectorates have been designed to become autonomous. Therefore, few jurisdictional conflicts between the directorates and inspectorates, on one hand, and the local authorities or counties, on the other hand, are expected. The lack of conflict, though, does not preclude administrative overlap.

Hungary has opted for a coordination system of water management through the establishment of working areas within the Danube River basin district. The working areas should become the focal points around which the various authorities in charge of water management will function along with the directorates and inspectorates established based on the subcatchment principle. For this coordination model to work well, there must be few veto players. It is not sufficient for the office of water management to operate well. The horizontal group comprised of the offices of water, environment, and nature conservation must be able to accomplish breakthroughs. There must be further coordination between that water office and the national directorate of environment, nature, and water. The national directorate must coordinate the work of the twelve regional directorates, which must, in turn, collaborate with the inspectorates. Furthermore, the whole water management sector must find a position within an administrative structure that is still developing with seven new regions,[175] nineteen

[173] Attila Ágh, *Public Administration in Central and Eastern Europe* 536, 543, in Handbook of Public Administration (2003).

[174] *See* Peter Kessler, *Gap Analysis on the Administrative Side of the Implementation*, Twinning Project Implementation of Water Framework Directive in Hungary, Activity No. 1, Mar. 2003.

[175] The new Development and Planning Regions provide the third level of the Hungarian administrative structure. As it was the case in the Czech Republic and Slovakia, this third level of administrative structure has been put in place for the administration of the EU cohesion funds.

counties,[176] and various municipalities[177] and associations of municipalities[178] that are active in water management. Some commentators have noted that a high number of authorities enmeshed in similar matters may result in weak administrative efficiency and unnecessary bureaucratic duplication for lack of clearly delimited responsibilities.[179]

Water Boards in Regional Directorates

Participation of stakeholders in water management is provided through the water boards that have been established in each regional directorate. Water boards swiftly developed but, subsequently, their activities have slowed down. This may be because those who participate in the water boards do not receive compensation for the services they provide. The directorate to which a water board belongs acts as a secretariat for the water board. Members of water boards are nominated and are comprised of representatives of ministry of environment, national directorate, local assemblies, municipalities,

---

The regions are now evolving into more independent and self-governing units. Seven regions have been created (while there are 12 directorates and inspectorates) and regional development is coordinated by the National Office for Regional Development. Two factors were taken into account in designating regions—the borders of regions should correspond to the borders of counties as much as possible and the distribution of population among regions should be approximately the same. The Regional Development Council is responsible for working out the development concept for each region. It must cooperate closely with the area development councils and the county area development council. *See Rapporteur Jan Olbrycht, Report on Regional Democracy in Hungary–CPR(9) Part II*, Congress of Local and Regional Authorities of Europe (CLRAE), Council of Europe, 2002.

[176] Counties execute a variety of tasks in spatial and environmental planning. Counties historically have played a large role in the Hungarian administrative structure, as they have been functioning for more than a thousand years. But the changes that occurred after 1990 have diminished the importance of counties. There has been some discussion to strengthen the role of counties. Nineteen counties, though, are still too many for a country of the size of Hungary, thus, regrouping counties into larger units has been recommended. *See id.*

[177] Local self-government has acquired a high degree of autonomy and has asserted a wide range of responsibilities in various domains. All local public affairs including water supply, basic education, and health care are under the jurisdiction of local self-government. It seems that municipalities have a wide range of control over the services they perform. The tasks municipalities are not willing to perform remain under the control of counties. *Id.*

[178] The important role that various forms of local self-government play in the management of affairs of the country is demonstrated by the high number of associations of towns and municipalities: Partnership of Associations of Local Communities (KOOSZ), Association of Local Governments of Small Municipalities (KOSZ), Hungarian Village Association (MFSZ), Association of Local Authorities and Hungarian Representatives (MOTZ), Association of Hungarian Cities of County Rank (MJVS), National Association of Hungarian County General Assemblies (MOOSZ), and National Association of Local Authorities (TOOSZ). For the administrative organization of Hungary, *see* http://www.loreg.coe.int/Database/Loreg/hungary.htm.

[179] Olbrycht, *supra* note 175.

water associations, and various NGOs. The main tasks of water boards are the approval and supervision of water-related projects. They are further consulted on the yearly budget of regional water directorate.

Water Associations

Water associations in Hungary, the equivalent of water boards in the Netherlands, have a tradition of more than two hundred years. The first water associations were established in 1810.[180] During the nineteenth century, water associations concentrated mostly on flood prevention and control. In 1870s, most construction of drainage works had already started including the building of canals and pumping stations.

Before World War II, water associations cooperated with the government, but friction was obvious from time to time. After World War II, when the centralized government system was introduced, water associations became a state property tool. In 1957, initiatives were undertaken to reorganize water associations. The new water associations were organized based on the representation principle, and they provided a framework for the exchange of ideas and recommendations for future development. From 1957, until the demise of communism, water associations were involved in drainage, irrigation, and land reclamation. The number of water associations stabilized after several mergers to sixty-seven in the early 1990s.[181] The position of water associations was institutionalized in 1995 with the adoption of Water Act. Since 1998, seventy-five water associations have been functioning under the umbrella of the Ministry of Agriculture.[182]

Water associations are partially self-financed. Water associations represent landowners, basically farmers, and other water users. They are independent associations and their resources consist primarily of membership fees. They are funded also by the ministry of agriculture

---

[180] *Success Factors in Self Financing Local Water Management, A contribution to the Third World Water Forum in Japan 2003*, at 70 (2003) (R.W. Uijterlinde *et al.*, eds., 2003) .

[181] *Id.* at 70.

[182] *Id.* at 71. Some of the main tasks of water associations involve:

- Operation of canal networks (38,000 km) and pumping stations (300 stations);
- Flood control of small rivers and streams;
- Operation of irrigation channels and pumps;
- Construction and operation of small reservoirs;
- Drainage of small settlements;
- Construction and maintenance of drainage canals.

and by local stakeholders, such as farmers, cooperatives, cities, and municipalities.[183] The financial condition of water associations remains suboptimal, partly because the system for property registration has yet to be completed.[184] Water associations established the National Union of Water Management Associations (VTOSZ) in 1992.[185]

In order to achieve better organizational structure water associations must meet two conditions:

- A well-functioning system for property registration that would allow for regular and predictable tax collection; and
- Economies of scale in terms of financing and other services water associations would like to obtain.[186]

Environmental NGOs

Many environmental NGOs are quite active in Hungary, including Club Tisza, which is involved in the Tisza River basin, the Regional Environmental Center (REC), and World Wildlife Fund (WWF) Hungary. The REC in Hungary is involved in river basin planning through the Dutch-Hungarian-Slovakian Hernád/Hornad project.[187] This is one of the rare cases in which an NGO is directly involved in river basin planning. The REC Hungary, with its center in Szentendre, has been quite influential in Hungary and all across central and eastern Europe.

The WWF Hungary is taking part in many water-related programs and events. The WWF Hungary took actively part in the preparation of the National Agri-Environmental Program and has been involved in developing a river basin plan for the Rába River. The Rába River is tributary to the Danube River flowing from Austria into the Hungarian territory.[188]

---

183 *Id.*

184 *Id.*

185 *Id.* at 72.

186 *Id.*

187 Petur Farkas, *Implementation of the Water Framework Directive in a Transboundary Context: Partial River Basin Management Plan for the Hornad/Hernád River* 97, in Proceedings of International Conference, "Implementing the European Union Water Framework Directive: Towards Integrated Water Management in Europe," May 12, 2006, Athens (DG Environment, European Commission, Technical Report-2007-021, Elli Louka, ed., 2007).

188 Kálmán Papp, *Experience with public participation in the field of water management and land use in Hungary*, Feb. 25, 2005. The WWF seems to have played a role in the adoption of Vásárhelyi Plan (VTT plan, the purpose of which was to control flooding in Hungary). During the preparatory phase of the plan over 200 consultations were organized such as committee

Romania

Selected Sources

Frecon, Jean-Claude, Follow-up to the information report on local and regional democracy in Romania, Congress of Local and Regional Authorities of Europe, (CLRAE), Council of Europe, 2003;
Pubic Management Profiles of Central and Eastern European Countries: Romania (OECD SIGMA papers, Aug. 1999);
Romania National Report, *Seminar on the Role of Ecosystems as Water Suppliers under the Convention on Protection and Use of Transboundary Watercourses and International Lakes*, Dec. 13–14, 2004 available online http://www.unece.org/env/water/meetings/ecosystem/Reports/Romania_en.pdf;
Romania's Road to Accession – the Need for an Environmental Focus, Strategic Analysis of the environment-related challenges of Romania (Danish EPA Report, 2003);
Serban, Petru, *Administrative Capacity of National Administration Apele Romane in order to Implement EU Directives*, May 31, 2005 (on file with the author);
Setting up of Inter-Ministerial Coordinating Mechanism for Pollution Control, National Report Romania (UNDP-GEF Danube Regional Project, July 2003);
Vasiu, Aurora R., *The State of the Water Framework Directive Implementation in Romania* 37, in Proceedings of International Conference "Implementing the European Union Water Framework Directive: Towards Integrated Water Management in Europe," May 12, 2006, Athens (DG Environment, European Commission, Technical Report-2007-021, Elli Louka, ed., 2007);
Water Law No. 310/2004 amending Water Law No. 107/1996.

Websites

National Administration Romanian Waters: www.rowater.ro
Ministry of Environment and Water Management: www.mmediu.ro

meetings of the Hungarian houses of parliament; expert and general meetings of county assemblies; meetings of regional water councils; public events and fora; technical and scientific conferences; public hearings.

Upon the initiative of WWF Hungary, with regard to the VTT plan, a Civil Conciliation Committee was established. Furthermore, a local NGO BOKARTISZ prepared a conception plan for an emergency reservoir in Cigánd providing again an example of an NGO involved directly in water management. On the VTT, *see also Hungary National Report, supra* note 156, at 5–6.

Danube Delta National Institute for Research and Development: www.indd.tim.ro

Romania, a country with 98 percent of its territory within the Danube River basin, has a rich tradition in water management. The first river basin management plans of Romania were carried out in the late 1950s.[189]

Some of the provisions of the Water Act, as amended in 2004, demonstrate the precepts of water management in Romania.[190] According to the act, rational and integrated water management activity is organized and carried out at the river basin district. The river basin district is the indivisible geographical entity of quantitative and qualitative water resources management. Water management is based on the principle that surface waters and groundwater constitute a single unit.[191]

The Water Act explicitly provides that water management must be based on the principle of human solidarity and the principle of common interest through the close collaboration among public administration, water users, representatives of local communities and the public in order to obtain the maximum social benefit.[192] The act emphasizes the importance of preparation of an international river basin plan.[193]

The Ministry of Environment and Water Management has the overall supervisory role in water management. The ministry is comprised of three departments: the Department for Water, the Department for the Environment, and the Department for EU Integration. Other ministries involved in water management include the Ministry of Agriculture, the Ministry of Health, and the Ministry of Economy and Trade. Coordination happens through various interministerial mechanisms, such as committees, commissions, or working groups, and various other formal and informal consultations.[194]

---

189 *Romania National Report, Seminar on the Role of Ecosystems as Water Suppliers, under the Convention on the Protection and Use of Transboundary Watercourses and International Lakes*, Dec. 13–14, 2004 [hereinafter *Romania National Report*].

190 Water Law 310/2004 amended and supplemented Water Law 107/1996.

191 Art. 15(1), Water Law, *id.*

192 Art. 15(2), *id.*

193 Art. 15(3), *id.*

194 With regard to formal commissions, there is a Commission and Support Group for applying the Action Plan for water protection against pollution by nitrates from agricultural sources. Furthermore, there is a Working Inter-ministerial Committee for the promotion, coordination, and implementation of the Action Programme for the reduction of the aquatic environment pollution and underground waters caused by the discharge of certain dangerous substances (this Committee is comprised of Ministry of Environment and Water Management,

The Apele Romane (or the National Administration of Romanian Waters) is the central water agency in Romania and it is the competent authority for the implementation of the WFD.[195] The Apele Romane executes water management through its eleven branches,[196] called water directorates, organized according to the river basins of the country. It is expected that in the future, these "branches" are to become independent river basin authorities. The Apele Romane is under the coordinating authority of the Ministry of Environment and Water Management. Apele Romane is established as an institution of national interest that is to be financed from its own income that consists of charges and taxes on water users.[197] The budget of Apele Romane is made up of contributions of water users coming from regular water services, permits, and licenses.[198]

In terms of demarcation of authority between the ministry, the Apele Romane and the branches of the Apele Romane, the Water Act differentiates between strategic management of water resources and operational management of water resources.[199] The elaboration of national water strategy and policy and the coordination in the application of national and international regulations are entrusted to the Ministry of Environment and Water Management.[200] On the other hand, the quantitative and qualitative management of water resources and the operation of water management works as well as the implementation of national policy and strategy

the Ministry of Agriculture, the Ministry of Economy and Trade and the Ministry of Health). The Technical Group that supports this committee is comprised of the National Authority, "Romanian Waters," and the Basin Committees as well as research institutes. Furthermore, there is a National Commission for the Dams and other Hydrotechnical Works Safety and a Central Commission for Flood Control, Dangerous Meteorological Phenomena and Hydrotechnical Constructions Accidents. *See Setting up of Inter-Ministerial Coordinating Mechanism for the pollution control*, National Report, Romania (UNDP-GEF Danube Regional Project, July 2003) .

195 According to the 913/15.10.2001 Order of Ministry of Environment and Water Management, *see* Aurora R. Vasiu, *The State of the Water Framework Directive Implementation in Romania* 37, in Proceedings of International Conference, "Implementing the European Union Water Framework Directive: Towards Integrated Water Management in Europe," May 12, 2006, Athens (DG Environment, European Commission, Technical Report-2007-021, Elli Louka, ed., 2007).

196 The National Administration (Apele Romane) is responsible for the administration of the national water districts, the river basins, *see* art. 15(5), Water Law, *supra* note 190. The national river basin districts include Somes-Tisza, Crisuri, Mures, Banat, Jiu, Olt, Arges-Vedea, Buzau-Ialomita, Siret, Prut-Barlad, and Dobrogea-Litoral. *See id.* art. 15(6), Water Law.

197 Art. 16(1), *id.*

198 Art. 90, *id.*

199 Art. 17, *id.*

200 Art. 17(1), *id.*

are left to the Apele Romane.[201] Thus, although the strategic arm for the implementation of the WFD in Romania is the Ministry of Environment and Water Management, the operational management is executed by the Apele Romane through "its subordinate water directorates."[202]

In practice, the demarcation of authority between the ministry and the Apele Romane may not work as neatly as prescribed in the legislation. The Apele Romane is an institution with a long tradition in Romania. One would expect, therefore, that the Apele Romane, given its long tradition and accumulated expertise, could accomplish more than an operational role as prescribed in formal legislation, and drive water management. The branches of the Apele Romane are just decentralized units of a central agency and have yet to acquire independent authority.

In general, the tasks of the Apele Romane, as prescribed in its own website, are quite extensive. The Apele Romane has to:

- Administer surface and underground waters;
- Protect and restore surface and underground waters and keep them in good condition;
- Modernize, repair, and administer the national water management system;
- Undertake long-term monitoring;
- Establish program of measures for each hydrological unit in order to maintain the good condition of waters;
- Register protected areas;
- Issue authorizations for water use;
- Ensure protection against flooding;
- Maintain permanent technical offices for flood protection;
- Coordinate safety operations to prevent floods;
- Warn the population and intervene in cases of hydrologically dangerous phenomena;
- Draw plans for the protection against floods;
- Intervene in cases of accidental pollution;
- Gradually reduce pollution;
- Create and update the national database for hydrology, hydrogeology and water management;

201 Art. 17(2), *id.*
202 *Id.*

- Draw up water management plans for basins in accordance with EU legislation;
- Impose sanctions according to water management legislation;
- Conduct audits, inspections, and appraisal reviews;
- Create an IT system and a telecommunication system within water management units;
- Follow the provisions of international conventions to which Romania is a party;
- Promote its social and commercial image and inform the public and cooperate with the media with regard to water management;
- Ensure public participation in decisions concerning water management; and
- Administer the water fund.[203]

The Apele Romane administers a system of water quality surveillance that monitors water pollution sources such as wastewater treatment facilities. The Apele Romane imposes fees for wastewater discharged into waterways and administers fines if emission limit values are exceeded. The health inspectorates of the Ministry of Health are responsible for inspection and enforcement when water pollution affects public health.[204]

In the case of Romania, a central water agency has extensive jurisdiction in water management. In other countries, the authority for water management is more diffused and usually exercised primarily by a ministry. There are some advantages in having a central agency devoted to water management. A central ministry is by nature a multitasking institution. Most ministries designated for the implementation of the WFD are not exclusively ministries for water and have to perform various other functions such as environmental management, public works, transportation, or agriculture. Because of their multiple functions, ministries cannot be devoted exclusively to water management the way an independent water agency can.

The Apele Romane has all the advantages of a centralized and focused organization. Decisions made are executed fairly quickly. Some have characterized Apele Romane as a "civil army" or a "strong family." The technical expertise in the organization is quite high and there is pride in being part of

---

203 Available on website of Apele Romane, www.rowater.ro.

204 *Romania's Road to Accession – the Need for an Environmental Focus, Strategic Analysis of the environment-related challenges in Romania*, (Danish EPA Report 2003) [hereinafter *Danish EPA-Romania Report*].

the institution. Because Apele Romane is a strong centralized water agency, it may be less supportive of more decentralized decisionmaking structures and reticent to grant more independence to the directorates.

Other authorities that play more of consultative role in water management include the:

- Central Commission for the Prevention and Control of Floods, Hazardous Phenomena and Hydrotechnical Construction Accidents;
- National Commission for Dam and Hydrotechnical Works Safety;
- Romanian Center for River Restoration; and
- National Committee for the International Hydrological Program.[205]

Planning for river basin management follows the prescriptions of the WFD. Planning is executed through master schemes, an alternative name for RBMPs. Master schemes are to be adopted according to the deadlines provided for in the WFD as they have been transposed into national law.[206] It is provided that programs of measures are to be put in place the latest by December 22, 2009, and all measures must become operational the latest by December 22, 2012. Programs of measures must be reviewed and updated by December 22, 2015, and every six years thereafter.[207] The act provides for the development of local schemes to be included in the master schemes for small basins or subbasins.[208]

Consultation with stakeholders happens through basin committees that have been established in each water directorate and are already functioning.[209] The committees are comprised of fifteen members:

(1) Two representatives of Ministry of Environment and Water Management;
(2) One representative of the central public authority from the Ministry of Health;
(3) Two municipality mayors and one town or commune mayor, elected by the mayors of localities within the relevant river basin;

205 Art. 17(3), Water Law, *supra* note 190.
206 Art. 53, *id.*
207 Art. 53(10), *id.*
208 Art. 55, *id.*
209 Committees were established through a government decision 1115/2002.

(4) One representative of a non-governmental organization having its headquarters in the relevant basin;
(5) One prefect nominated by the Ministry for Public Administration;
(6) One president of the County Council;
(7) Three representatives of water users within the relevant basin;[210]
(8) Two representatives of National Administration Apele Romane; and
(9) One representative of the National Authority for Consumers Protection.[211]

The tasks of river basin committees include the approval of RBMPs, the establishment and revision of standards for the achievement of water quality, and the promotion of public participation.[212]

River basin committees meet monthly and their agreement is necessary before proceeding further with water management. Some view the river basin committees as the "mini-parliaments" for water, which could mean, in certain parliamentary democracy systems, that debate takes place but real decisions are pre-determined by the prevailing majority. Officials, NGOs, and water users who participate in the committees are not compensated financially. This may change in the future as there is a general understanding that river basin committees need to be funded to function effectively. The representation of government officials in the committees is quite high and could overwhelm other stakeholders who may find that they are frequently outvoted by a concert of other interests. The structure of river basin committees based on the representation of various interests demonstrates that most stakeholders would not be able to prevail unless they build and carry through alliances with other stakeholders.

---

210 Art. 57(5), Water Law, *supra* note 190.
211 Art. 57(2), *id.*
212 Art. 57(7), *id.*
Overall the function of a river basin committee is to:
1. Agree on the master schemes and programs of measures;
2. Agree on the accidental pollution prevention and control plans;
3. Approve local schemes and set the technical and financial priorities to integrate them into the master schemes;
4. Review norms and standards especially standards on effluent quality that could be more stringent than the national standards;
5. Establish norms on wastewater discharges;
6. Recommend priorities in terms of water works, installations, and arrangements;
7. Ensure public participation, arranging public hearings and ensuring public access to documents;
8. Agree on a list of protected areas

The river basin committee is an institutional mechanism used at the river basin level to initiate consultation with the wider public. Thus, when a measure is taken, depending on the level at which the measure is adopted, the ministry, the Apele Romane, or the relevant directorate can open consultations with the public. The ministry, the Apele Romane, or its basin directorates, as appropriate, must publish a proposal of the proposed measures in the local newspaper. The same notice shall be sent to water users, residents, or any other person that may be affected. The text of the measure and the appropriate documentation must be available to the public. The act provides for the procedure of receiving written comments and observations on measures taken. A final decision taken by the Ministry of Environment and Water Management or the Apele Romane must include an explanation of why a decision was adopted and must be made available to the public.[213]

Public participation in water management cannot be judged in isolation from the general atmosphere of openness in a society. Public participation as a component of the environmental impact assessment process,[214] for instance, is not enthusiastically adopted in Romania.[215] The question is whether the interest generated by the implementation of the WFD will reverse this trend of noninvolvement. It seems that today more than sixty NGOs are interested in the implementation of the WFD in Romania.[216]

Water management in Romania has many positive attributes. If these attributes were taken advantage of, they could make for a well-regulated and transparent system of water management. The Apele Romane provides a centralized system of water management in a country where such centralization is still needed because too many parochial interests may attempt to influence decisionmaking to their advantage. According to some commentators, the "coordination of sectoral interests and the lack of public participation are both limiting factors in the development of a river-based management plan."[217]

One could characterize Romania as a country with good foundations in water management. Romania has a central agency devoted to water management. Decentralization of water management and the devolution

---

213 Art. 86, *id.*

214 Public participation is part of an environmental impact assessment in the legislation of most countries and in international regulation. *See* Chapter 12.

215 *Danish EPA- Romania Report, supra* note 204.

216 *Romania National Report, supra* note 189.

217 *See* Water Time. WaterTime, is a research project supported by the European Commission, FP5: Energy Environment and Sustainable Development available online http://www.watertime.net/wt_cs_cit_ncr.asp.

of authority down to the directorates are issues that could percolate in the future. Decentralization, though, must not be pursued for the sake of decentralization. Decentralization should be viewed instead within the general context of reform, one of the priorities of which is the fight against corruption and nepotism. Decentralization should be avoided if it results in the strengthening of sectarian interests and the weakening of water sector.

In terms flood management, Apele Romane has retained an important role, but it has to further coordinate with various regional and local authorities. The Central Commission for the Prevention and Control of Floods, Hazardous and Meteorological Phenomena, and Hydrotechnical Construction Accidents is comprised of representatives of ministries and is responsible for the coordination of actions for the prevention and control of floods.[218] In case of a disaster, this Central Commission must cooperate with the Governmental Disaster Control Commission.[219]

County commissions and the Bucharest municipality commission are responsible for flood management at the county level. Apele Romane provides the secretariat functions for these commissions.[220] The prefect of the county where Apele Romane has its headquarters in each river basin has the responsibility of coordinating action in case of floods.[221] The local disaster control commissions that are subordinate to the county commissions have to have a representative of Apele Romane.[222] Overall, the operative coordination and activity for the prevention and control of floods is entrusted to Apele Romane.[223]

The coordination between the water sector and the various regional and local authorities may present a challenge in the future. The multiple levels of local and regional authorities complicate decisionmaking in Romania. In addition to the central government there are:

- 41 counties and the municipality of Bucharest;
- 314 towns (103 of which have the status of municipalities); and
- 2,827 communities (rural administrative units).[224]

---

218 Art. 78(1), Water Law, *supra* note 190.
219 Art. 78(2), *id.*
220 Art. 80(2), *id.*
221 Art. 83(5), *id.*
222 Art. 80(3), *id.*
223 Art. 83(4), *id.*
224 For the administrative organization of Romania, *see* http://www.loreg.coe.int/Database/Loreg/romania.htm.

In addition to these already existing administrative levels, seven regions have been added for the purposes of administration of EU funding. The demarcation of authority among these various administrative structures is not always clear. Associations have been created to represent the interests of various local entities.[225] The independence of the local administrative structures has been a concern for the Council of Europe which, based on a 2003 assessment, viewed unfavorably the control of certain municipal councils by the central government.[226]

Local authorities at the county and municipal level are becoming increasingly responsible for the provision of environmental services. This means putting in place and managing the necessary environmental infrastructure, for example, drinking water supply systems, sewage collection systems, and wastewater treatment works. Local authorities identify and prepare projects for investment. They have also the responsibility of granting environmental permits some of which require an Environmental Impact Assessment (EIA). While some responsibilities have devolved to the local level, such devolution has not been followed with concomitant funding. Local authorities cannot keep undertaking responsibilities without simultaneously receiving the appropriate financial support.[227] Drinking water infrastructure, sewage, and wastewater treatment need substantial investment. This implies long-term financial planning that is not always pursued.[228] The privatization of municipal water management has not always brought the desired results and has been associated often with high costs and poor quality of service.

Bulgaria

Selected Sources

Bulgaria's Road to Accession, (Thematic Report, Danish EPA, 2003);

---

225 Romanian Federation of Local Authorities (RFLA);
Romanian Association of Municipalities (RAM);
Romanian Association of Towns (RAT);
Romanian Association of Communes (ARC);
National Union of the Romanian County Councils (NURCC). *See* http://www.loreg.coe.int/Database/Loreg/romania.htm.

226 Rapporteur Jean-Claude Frecon, *Follow-up to the information report on local and regional democracy in Romania*, Congress of Local and Regional Authorities of Europe (CLRAE), Council of Europe, 2003.

227 *Danish EPA–Romania Report, supra* note 204.

228 *Id.*

De Sabbata, Giorgio and Libert Cuatrecasas, *Report on the situation of local and regional self-government in the Republic of Bulgaria–CG(5) 3 Part II*, Congress of Local and Regional Authorities of Europe (CLRAE), Council of Europe, 1998;

Legislative Gap Analysis between the Bulgarian Water Act and Directive 2000/60/EU, (Danish EPA, July 2004);

Economic Commission for Europe, Committee on Environmental Policy, Environmental Performance Review of Bulgaria discussed and approved by the seventh session of the Committee on Environment Policy, Sept. 2000, available online http://www.unece.org/env/epr/studies/bulgaria/chapter05.pdf;

Katchakova, Lubka and Vladimir Dontchev, *Implementation of the Water Framework Directive in Bulgaria: A Status Report* 29, in Proceedings of International Conference "Implementing the European Union Water Framework Directive: Towards Integrated Water Management in Europe," May 12, 2006, Athens (DG Environment, European Commission, Technical Report-2007-021, Elli Louka, ed., 2007);

Public Management Profiles of Central and Eastern European Countries: Bulgaria (OECD SIGMA papers, Jan. 1999);

Responses to Questionnaires sent to Black Sea Directorate, Danube Directorate, West-Aegean Directorate (on file with the author);

Speck, Stefan, *Financial Aspects of Water Supply and Sanitation in Transboundary Waters of South-Eastern Europe*, A report for the German Federal Ministry for the Environment, Nature Conservation and Nuclear Safety, Oct. 2005 available online http://europeandcis.undp.org/WaterWiki/images/c/c1/Financial_Aspect_of_Water_Investment_SEE.pdf;

Water Act (2002);

Water Act (2006).

Websites

Ministry of Environment and Water: www.moew.government.bg

Executive Environment Agency: http://nfp-bg.eionet.eu.int

Ministry of Regional Development and Planning Works: www.mrrb.government.bg

Bulgaria has decided to organize water management based on four river basin districts by establishing directorates that are to operate in each district. The Ministry of Environment and Water is the competent authority for the implementation of the WFD[229] and, at the river basin district level, the four directorates execute the functions of water management. These directorates include the:

1. Basin Directorate for the Danube Region;[230]
2. Basin Directorate for the Black Sea Region;[231]
3. Basin Directorate for the East Aegean Region;[232] and
4. Basin Directorate for the West Aegean Region.[233]

These river basin directorates are a new administrative structure in a country that consists of six planning regions,[234] twenty-eight districts,[235] 263 municipalities, and 3,840 kmetsva.[236]

---

229 The Department on Water of the Ministry of Environment and Water is divided into two departments: The water use department and the water quality department. The water use department deals with quantity issues, permits and abstractions, dams and reservoirs. The water quality department issues permits for wastewater discharges, prepares water legislation, and engages in international cooperation. Decisions for large infrastructure projects that affect the Danube River and the Black Sea are taken at the ministry level and not at the department level.

230 Based in Pleven–deals with the Danube catchment;

231 Based in Varna–deals with the Black Sea area;

232 Based in Plovdiv–deals with Maritza/Evros, Tundja, and Adra Rivers;

233 Based in Blagoevgrad–deals with Struma/Strymon, Nestos/Mesta River.

234 In order to utilize EU funding, the country was divided into six planning regions as early as in 2000.[189] The Regional Development Plans (RDPs) aim at the regional development and include the priorities provided for in the National Economic Development Plan. Operational Programs for the RDPs have been developed. The basic unit for the implementation for the RDPs is an Economic and Social Cohesion Commission (ESCC) established in each region. These ESCCs include representatives of ministries, the district governors, representatives of the district councils, municipalities, and representatives of trade unions and employment organizations. Each ESCC has thematic working groups such as working groups on SMEs, privatization, foreign investment, human resources, fiscal resources, rural policy, public works, agriculture, development of rural areas, and ecology. These working groups are open to specialists from NGOs, businesses, local authorities, and schools. The ESCC established in each region adopts the criteria for the election of projects to be financed or co-financed by the EU and decides the percentage that should go to each sector. The funds that come from Brussels are centralized and the government decides how these funds are to be distributed per region. Then the ESCC of each region decides how these financial resources are to be allocated per sector. Given this already-established structure that mandates the coordination through the ESCC, the question is what the role would be for the river basin directorates and the function of river basin management plans in the context of regional development plans. On the role of regional planning in Bulgaria, *see* Veselka Ivanova, *Mechanisms of Planning and Monitoring Structures for Co-ordination at Regional and National Level in Bulgaria*, in The INTERREG Model: Practical Experience in Cross Border Co-operation, Friedrich Ebert Stiftung, Zagreb, 2001.

235 Before the establishment of regions for the purposes of EU funding, Bulgaria was already divided into districts; thus, some coordination had to be established between the District Development Councils, the Central Administration, and the Council of Regional Development.

236 *See* http://www.loreg.coe.int/Database/Loreg/bulgaria.htm.

When the Water Act was adopted in 2000,[237] the fifteen regional inspectorates that already existed acted as temporary substitutes for the basin directorates. Since the directorates are a new administrative structure in Bulgaria, preparations were made for their establishment and staffing.[238] The financial and regulatory authority of directorates, as a result, has been limited.[239]

The fifteen Regional Inspectorates of Environment and Water have a significant local presence almost all over the territory.[240] The purpose of the inspectorates is monitoring and enforcement. The Ministry of Environment and Water and the director of each regional inspectorate of environment and water are responsible for issuing permits in accordance with the Integrated Pollution Prevention and Control (IPPC) Directive. Although inspectorates are conceived to execute enforcement and monitoring functions, directorates are to deal with river basin planning and the licensing of water use. In addition to the directorates and the inspectorates, there are also three Park Directorates.[241] There is, further, an Executive Environment Agency. The Executive Environment Agency operates through fifteen branches and focuses on the examination of water status.

Other ministries that have a role in water management are the Ministry of Health, the Ministry of Finance, the Ministry of Transport and Communications. The Ministry of Regional Development and Public Works implements the national policy in the area of territorial planning and public works, including planning for water supply and sewage management. The ministry coordinates the preparation of Local Environmental Action Programs and waste management planning in municipalities.[242] The Ministry of Health deals with the protection of quality of drinking water.

237 The Water Act was adopted in 2000 and amended in 2002. A new Water Act was adopted in 2006.

238 Economic Commission for Europe, Committee on Environmental Policy, Environmental Performance Review of Bulgaria discussed and approved by the seventh session of the Committee on Environment Policy, Sept. 2000, available online http://www.unece.org/env/epr/studies/bulgaria/chapter05.pdf

239 *Id.*

240 There are fifteen Regional Inspectorates of Environment and Water located in Blagoevgrad; Bourgas; Varna; Veliko Tarnovo; Vratza; Montana; Pazardzhik; Pleven; Plovdiv; Rousse; Smolyan; Sofia; Stara Zagora; Haskovo, and Shumen.

241
- Rila National Park Directorate;
- Central Balkan National Park Directorate; and
- Pirin National Park Directorate.

242 *Bulgaria's Road to Accession* (Thematic Report, Danish EPA, 2003) [hereinafter *Danish EPA 2003 Bulgaria*].

The Ministry of Agriculture and Forestry focuses on the protection of agricultural lands and forests, and is directly involved in the implementation of the WFD. The Ministry of Transport and Communication plays an important role in inland navigation. The Ministry of Finance provides the funding for environmental investments and allocates funds to local government budgets. The Water Framework Directive Implementation Monitoring Unit is a coordination body comprised of all ministries involved in the implementation of the WFD.

The National Water Council is set up as the supreme expert water council within the Ministry of Environment and Water. The purpose of the National Water Council is to discuss the draft national river basin management plan, to design national water monitoring networks, and to propose measures to be implemented with regard to transnational water agreements. The National Water Council is comprised of experts of scientific institutions and NGOs. NGO participation in the council is now a reality under the 2006 Water Act.

The four water directorates share similar administrative structures and are comprised of six departments:

- Administration and economy department;
- Planning and water management department;
- Monitoring department;
- Permits department;
- Water and hydroeconomy department; and
- Control, relations with institutions and public information department.

The functions of water directorates include:

- Managing the water district through river basin planning;
- Regulating water use by issuing permits;
- Executing the necessary activities for the functioning of the national water monitoring system at the basin level;
- Collecting fees from granting permits;
- Monitoring the conditions for which permits are granted;
- Delineating the boundaries between water that is state property and other water; and
- Maintaining installations of groundwater which are state property.

Decisions at the directorate level are made by the director. The director is supported in her decisionmaking by the basin council. Basin councils are functioning in all directorates as consultative bodies in river basin management. Basin councils are not only comprised of members of the public and NGOs but also of regional and municipal authorities. More specifically, 30 percent of membership in councils is allocated to water users; 20 percent is allocated to state administration; 30 percent is allocated to municipal administration; and 20 percent is allotted to NGOs and scientific institutions. Because of their composition, the basin councils have been characterized as a combination of a state institution and a public advisory body.

The directorates have a clear vision that they should be involved in the implementation of the WFD through the preparation of RBMPs. The Ministry of Environment plays a central role in the functioning of directorates. The Ministry of Environment and Water nominates the director of the basin directorate. The ministry determines the activities, organization, work, and staff of the directorates. The directorates are new institutions in Bulgaria and, as such, they need more time to develop. Some areas in which management at the directorate level needs to improve include:

- Integrated water management and the fair distribution of water resources;
- Identification of problems in their region and provision of information on the status of such problems;
- Establishment of a unified information system; and
- Coordination with other water management institutions and various stakeholders in the sphere of water management.

Directorates need to acquire trained personnel, funds, and equipment that could help them become more autonomous. The role of river basin management plans *vis-à-vis* national, regional and local plans including land-use plans and urban plans needs to be further clarified. The coordination between the directorates and the municipalities cannot be neglected as municipalities engage in water management at the local level. This coordination could present some challenges because of the number of municipalities and the number of associations of municipalities. Municipalities have formed a plethora of associations based on areas that share some common economic or natural characteristics. Although the creation of municipal associations is positive from the point of view of flourishing local democracy, from the point of view of river basin management, the question is which of these municipal associations should be consulted with in the preparation of the RBMPs. In some cases, this could be easy because municipal associations coincide with a river basin district.[243] However, some municipal associations have been established based on regional planning rather river basin planning[244] or are based on shared geography.[245] Even at the national level, there is more than one national municipal association.[246]

The new Water Act that entered into force in 2006[247] is to rectify some of the problems of prior legislation especially with respect to the delineation of responsibilities of different authorities involved in water management. This in combination with the simplification of a multilayered administrative structure could assist in the development of a more organized water sector. A positive element of water management administration is that the ministry of regional development is also in charge of public works, thus, in charge of drinking water and sewage infrastructure. This should guarantee the integration of development of water infrastructure, the improvement of which is necessary for the future development of Bulgaria, into the regional development plans. The Water Supply and Sewage

[243] The Association of the Danubean Municipalities (DANUBE) was established in 1993. This association brings together municipalities located in the Danube area. The Maritsa Regional Municipal Association (MARITSA) brings together local authorities surrounding the Maritsa River. *See* Giorgio De Sabbata and Libert Cuatrecasas, *Report on the situation of local and regional self-government in the Republic of Bulgaria–CG(5) 3 Part II*, Congress of Local and Regional Authorities of Europe (CLRAE), Council of Europe, 1998.

[244] Such as the Association of Municipalities of the South-Central Region (HEBAR), the South-West Municipalities Association, the Regional Municipal Association of North West Balkans. *See* http://www.loreg.coe.int/Database/Loreg/bulgaria.htm.

[245] Such association is the Association of Rhodopean Municipalities. The association has as its members municipalities from the mountain area that borders Greece. The "Central Stara Planina" Regional Municipal Association brings together the municipalities of the Stara Planina mountains. Other such associations include the Union of Bulgarian Black Sea Local Authorities (UBBSLA), the Trakia Regional Municipal Association (TRAKIA), and the Yantra Regional Municipal Association (YANTRA). *See* http://www.loreg.coe.int/Database/Loreg/bulgaria.htm.

[246] The National Association of Municipalities in the Republic of Bulgaria (NAMRB) was established in 1996 and represents today the majority of municipalities. Other associations at the national level include the National Municipal Secretaries in the Republic of Bulgaria Association, the Foundation for Local Government Reform, the Legal Initiative for Local Self-Governance National Association, and the Municipal Council Chairmen's Association. *See* http://www.loreg.coe.int/Database/Loreg/bulgaria.htm.

[247] *See also Legislative Gap Analysis between the Bulgarian Water Act and Directive 2000/60/EU* (Danish EPA, July 2004).

Implementing Agency and a State Enterprise in Charge with the Water Supply and Sewage Activities are under the supervision of the Ministry of Regional Development and Public works. Both the agency and the enterprise supervise the commercial water supply and sewage companies.[248]

Greece

Selected Sources

Draft Presidential Decree for the implementation of the Water Framework Directive, Nov. 2004;
Kallis, George and Harris Coccossis, *Managing water for Athens: from the hydraulic to the rational growth paradigm*, Department of Planning and Regional Development School of Engineering, University of Thessaly, Oct. 2, 2002 available online http://www.prd.uth.gr/research/DP/2002/uth-prd-dp-2002-11_en.pdf;
Rhodio, Guido and Lambert Van Nistelrooij, *Report on the situation of local and regional democracy in Greece – CG (9) 5 Part II*, Congress of Local and Regional Authorities of Europe (CLRAE), Council of Europe, 2001;
Sibetheros, Ioannis, *The Implementation of the Water Framework Directive: Opportunities and Challenges for Greece* 32, in Proceedings of International Conference "Implementing the European Union Water Framework Directive: Towards Integrated Water Management in Europe," May 12, 2006, Athens (DG Environment, European Commission, Technical Report-2007-021, Elli Louka, ed., 2007);
Spanou, Calliope, *Managing Europe from Home: The Europeanisation of the Greek Core Executive, Organizing for the EU Enlargement Project*, Occasional Paper, Dublin European Institute, University College Dublin, 2002;
Water Law Num. 1739/1987;
Water Law Num. 3199/2003.

Website

Ministry of Environment, Physical Planning and Public Works: www.minenv.gr

[248] As of this writing, thirteen water supply and sewage companies are 100 percent owned by the state. Sixteen water supply and sewage companies are owned 51 percent by the state, and 49 percent by the municipalities. Twenty-one water supply and sewage companies are owned by the municipalities.

In Greece, a decision was made during the transposition process not to establish formal river basin authorities per river basin district, but to use existing regional administrative structures to coordinate management at the river basin level. The decision not to create water authorities per river basin district was based on the fact that water resources are rather fragmented in Greece. Therefore, the practicability of the notion of river basin district as a large hydrological unit is not self-evident. Greece needs further to grapple with a sprawling administrative landscape comprised of regions, provinces,[249] and municipalities.[250] The regions that were previously planning units for the purposes of disbursement of EU funding, are now assuming a more autonomous role. The character of regions started to change in 1994[251] when regions were vested with powers more appropriately reserved for provinces. The regions gained even more leverage in 1997 when they started to have their own budgets allocated by the state and administered by the regional governor.[252] Because of funding committed to regional development, regions are becoming key institutions in the Greek administrative system.

In addition to the management of regional development funds, regions have been involved in a number of activities, such as the preparation of regional plans that are important for receiving EU funding. Regions make proposals to the central government on works necessary for regional development and allocate funds to local authorities. The regional administration is comprised of a general directorate and specialized subdirectorates.

Given the existing and evolving structure of regions, it is not surprising that water management is assigned to them. The problem is that regions do not have experience in water management and that regional water directorates need to acquire expertise in integrated water management. Another issue not addressed in the law is how the regional governor will cooperate with the central water agency, the central institution for water management established within the Ministry of Environment and

249 Provinces have a long history in Greece. They were established as early as in 1833 just after the Greek independence and the governors of provinces (nomarchoi) were appointed officials. Only in 1994 did the provinces acquired self-governance with elected councils and governors.

250 Provinces feel threatened that their authority is diminishing due to the strengthening of the regions and the empowerment of municipalities. *See* Rapporteurs Guido Rhodio and Lambert Van Nistelrooij, *Report on the situation of local and regional democracy in Greece–CG (9) 5 Part II*, Congress of Local and Regional Authorities of Europe (CLRAE), Council of Europe, 2001.

251 *Id.*

252 However, regions still do not have an independent legal personality and still present an administrative layer answerable to the central government.

Public Works. The Central Water Agency does not have formal jurisdictional control over the regions, and its legal nexus with regional water directorates is weak. Furthermore, the regional governors are not answerable to the ministry of environment but to the Ministry of Interior.

The legislation that transposed the WFD in Greece established a Central Water Agency in the Ministry of Environment, Physical Planning and Public Works as the central body charged with water management.[253] The Central Water Agency is responsible for the national programs of protection and management of waters and monitors and coordinates their implementation. It also proposes the general rules for water pricing and the legislation and administration for the protection and management of waters.[254]

The Central Water Agency supervises the operations of regional water directorates and provides them with guidance for the performance of their duties. The regional water directorates are established within the already existing thirteen regions of Greece, as mentioned above.[255] Since regional directorates are not yet equipped to implement the WFD, most of the functions of implementation are still centralized in the ministry and its newly created Central Water Agency. In the future, it is expected that the regional water directorates will become key institutions in regional water management.

The purpose of the National Water Committee is to formulate the policy for the protection and management of waters.[256] The national water committee oversees the implementation of policy and approves, after the proposal of the Ministry of Environment, Physical Planning and Public Works and, after consulting with the National Water Council, the national program for the protection and management of waters.
The National Water Committee is comprised of the:

(1) Ministry for the Environment, Physical Planning and Public Works that presides over the committee;
(2) Ministry of Economy;
(3) Ministry of Interior, Public Administration and Decentralization;
(4) Ministry of Development;

253 Art. 4 of Law Num. 3199, published in the Official Gazette, Dec. 9, 2003 [hereinafter Water Law].
254 Art. 4(1), *id.*
255 *Id.*
256 Art. 3, *id.*

(5) Ministry of Health; and
(6) Ministry of Agriculture.[257]

The national water committee must consult with the National Water Council.[258] The National Water Council is a mechanism of stakeholder participation in the design of national policy for water management.[259]

The law explicitly provides that the protection and management of a river basin belongs to the region within the boundaries of which it is located. The river basins are designated by the National Water Committee. The National Water Committee further designates which region is responsible for the administration of a river. If a river basin extends to more than one region, both the regions could be involved in its management. The National Water Committee may decide to divide the responsibilities of the management of a river basin between the regions that share a basin. The National Water Committee may even designate only one region as the region exclusively responsible for the management of water in a shared river basin.[260]

The water directorates operating in each region have extensive responsibilities, including monitoring, coordination, drafting, and implementing functions.[261] Regional water directorates prepare and implement the RBMPs and program of measures, collect and analyze data on water quality and quantity, and coordinate all actors responsible for the use and protection of waters.[262] To execute these functions, however, directorates need sizeable expertise they do not possess.

---

[257] After the invitation of the president of the national water committee, more ministers may participate in its activities. This is especially so if the committee discusses matters that fall under the jurisdiction of other ministries. The Minister of Foreign Affairs is involved in the works of the committee in matters that affect transboundary waters. *See* art. 3(1), *id.*

[258] Art. 3(1), *id.*

[259] Art. 3(2), *id.*

[260] Art. 5(1)–(3), *id.*

[261] Art. 5(5), *id.* The responsibilities of water directorates include taking measures on:

- prevention of deterioration of surface waters;
- improvement and restoration of water;
- gradual reduction of pollution especially with regard to priority substances;
- sustainable development of water use given the goal of long-term protection of water resources;
- ensuring the balance between the abstraction of water and recharge of water;
- mitigation of impacts from floods and droughts; and
- implementation of goals and standards for protected areas.

[262] Art. 5(5), *id.*

The National Water Council is the body through which stakeholder consultation takes place at the national level.[263] The president of the national water council is the minister for environment, physical planning and public works. The council is comprised of representatives from a variety of institutions including the heads of provinces, municipalities, members of the parliament from various political parties, state enterprises, and various institutional stakeholders.[264]

The National Water Committee has to consult with the council before approving the national programs for the protection and management of water resources.[265] The National Water Committee has to submit to the parliament and to the National Water Council an annual report on the state of water resources, on the implementation of legislation with regard to the protection and the management of waters and their compatibility with the *acquis communautaire*.[266] The council convenes, at least, once per year.[267]

---

263 Art. 3(2), *id.*

264 The National Water Council is comprised of;

- every party that has a sit in the Parliament;
- The Greek Union of Provinces (ENAE);
- The union of urban and rural municipalities;
- The association of municipal enterprises for the provision of drinking water and sewage services;
- Enterprises for the provision of drinking water and sewage services not represented by the municipal association of such enterprises;
- The national association of agricultural co-operatives;
- The association of national industries;
- The public enterprise for the provision of electricity;
- The national association of workers;
- The technical chamber of Greece;
- The geotechnical chamber of Greece;
- The institute of geology and mineral exploration;
- The national center for marine research;
- The national biotope/wetland center;
- Two non-governmental environmental organizations;
- The national center for the environment and sustainable development;
- The general consumers' federation of Greece;
- The national foundation for agricultural research;
- The president of the national committee to combat desertification. (Greece has signed the UN Convention to Combat Desertification. The National Committee to Combat Desertification was established in 2002 and the Greek National Action Plan for Combating Desertification has been developed).

265 Art. 3(1), *id.*

266 Art. 3(3), *id.*

267 Art. 3(4), *id.*

Water directorates within each region have to ensure the participation of the public in the preparation of the RBMPs.[268] More specifically, regional water directorates must provide for comments to the public and, especially, to water users the:

(1) Timetable of the adoption of river basin management plan, at least three years before the period for which such a plan will be designated;
(2) Program of measures; and
(3) Major issues in water management in the two years that have preceded the adoption of the river basin management plan.

Public participation at the regional level is formalized under the regional water council. The regional water council is an organ of social dialogue and consultation on matters of protection and management of waters.[269] Regional water councils are chaired by the regional governor and are comprised of a variety of stakeholders such as:

- The provincial governors of each region;
- A representative of each local union of urban and rural municipalities (TEDKE);
- Various chambers of industry and commerce, such as the technical chamber, the geotechnical chamber; and
- Representatives of civil servants unions, agricultural cooperatives and trade unions.[270]

---

[268] Art. 5(6), *id.*
[269] Art. 6(1), *id.*
[270] In more detail, the regional water council is comprised of:

- The general secretary of the region as its president;
- The head of the regional water directorate;
- A representative of each province that belongs to the region;
- A representative of each local union of urban and rural municipalities of provinces that belong to the region;
- A representative of all municipal enterprises responsible for the provision of drinking water and sewage services;
- A representative of the technical, geotechnical, commercial, industrial chambers;
- A representative of every agricultural cooperative of a region;
- A representative of environmental non-governmental organizations;
- A representative of each general organization for land reclamation (a non-profit association dealing with irrigation); and

The regional council is consulted on the river basin management plan and on every issue that the secretary general of the region proposes for consideration.[271] The regional council is responsible for ensuring that the draft RBMP is available to the public.[272] The regional council convenes at least once per year.[273]

Every region should prepare a RBMP for watercourses belonging to its jurisdiction. For river basin districts for which two regions are responsible, both the regions should be involved in the drafting of a common RBMP[274] unless otherwise provided for by ministerial decision.[275] The RBMP contains all information necessary for the protection and management of waters. The specific content of RBMPs is to be provided in a presidential decree issued in 2007. The RBMP is put together by the regional water directorate and has to be approved by the secretary general of the region after consultations with the regional water council and the concurrent opinion of the central water agency. The first RBMP can be designed by the central water agency.[276] The RBMP is compiled by taking into account the Regional Framework of Planning and Sustainable Development[277] and the content of general and specific development programs including the management of protected areas.

A frequent critique of Greek legislation is that it organizes the management of water according to administrative subdivisions (regions) and not according to hydrological boundaries as implied in the concept of river basin district used in the directive. As a matter of fact, the 2003 law that transposed the WFD replaced a 1987 law, which was based on the hydrological districts,[278] but never became operational. The criticism that

- A representative from every institution concerned with the management of protected areas according to the provisions of the law. *See* art. 6(1), *id.*

271 Art. 6(2), *id.*

272 *Id.*

273 The details of functioning of regional water council and those of public consultation are to be provided in a separate regulation through a common decision of the Ministry for the Environment, Physical Planning and Public Works, and the Ministry of Interior, Public Administration and Decentralization, *see* art. 6(5), *id.*

274 Art. 7(1), *id.*

275 Art. 5(2), *id.*

276 Art. 7(2), *id.*

277 As provided by Law Num. 2742/1999. See art. 7(3), *id.*

278 The law replaced a 1987 law that was based on hydrological districts which were those of: 1.West Peloponnese, 2.North Peloponnese, 3.East Peloponnese, 4.West Sterea Hellas, 5.East Sterea Hellas, 6.West Macedonia, 7.Central Macedonia, 8.East Macedonia, 9.Hpiros, 10.Attiki, 11.Thessalia, 12.Thraki, 13.Crete, 14. Islands of Aegean Sea. *See* Law Num. 1739/87 published in the Official Gazette, Nov. 20, 1987.

hydrological borders have been overlooked in favor of administrative borders is a bit excessive, though. If one looks closely, the thirteen regions on which water management is to be based according to the 2003 law[279] do not differ that much from the fourteen hydrographic districts prescribed under the 1987 law. Furthermore, Greece is not the only country in the EU that decided to forfeit the establishment of a new river basin administrative structure in favor of coordinating the activities of already existing administrative units.

The real issue is not the creation of new river basin authorities, but whether the regions to which water management has been assigned will develop the authority to deal with regional water problems and prepare the river basin plans for subsequent years. Given a history of half-hearted decentralization attempts, it may not be unlikely that the central water agency would remain pivotal in water management. On the other hand, assuming that regional institutional development is something that the government would like to promote, assigning water management to regions may help establish the more autonomous character of regions. Since the central water agency has loose jurisdictional control over the regions, it remains to be seen how the relationship between the regional water directorates, the agency, and the regional governors is to evolve. Good cooperation between the Ministry of Interior and the Ministry of Environment could facilitate matters, but such cooperation cannot be taken for granted.

The Greek system of water management is envisioned as a coordination system. Greece, like the Netherlands, has been reluctant to develop another administrative construct that, in terms of river basin authorities, would superimpose itself on the current administrative structure. However, Greece, unlike the Netherlands, has yet to develop strong coordinating platforms at the national, regional, and municipal levels. The problem with the Greek system is that the interaction between the central level and the regional level, and the collaboration among regions (especially in the case of shared basins) are not clear. The lack of clarity provides fertile ground for the proliferation of institutional veto players, as various actors would try to outsmart each other in obtaining authority in water management.

[279] These thirteen regions include: 1. Peloponnese, 2. Sterea Hellas, 3. West Hellas, 4. North Hellas; 5. West Macedonia, 6. Central Macedonia; 7. East Macedonia and Thraki, 8. Attiki, 9.Thessalia, 10. Hpiros; 11. Ionia Islands; 12. North Aegean, and 13.Crete.

The implementation of the WFD has encountered many problems in Greece. Greece, it is said, is characterized in general by the lack of effective and collective decisionmaking structures. Competition, rivalry, and mutual suspicion is the norm not only among ministries and but also in almost all interactions among public institutions. Greece, in terms of its approach to the EU, could be characterized as a reluctant follower. Reluctant followers are states that do not have the capacity to implement European policies.[280] Their strategy, therefore, is to block such policies unless they receive side payments. Environmental groups do not enjoy high prominence in Greece, and environmental policy does not get much of the attention of the central government.

Greece is typified by a legalistic culture and many rules and procedures are prevalent in the public sector when sometimes one gets the impression that bureaucracy exists for the sake of bureaucracy. For the privileged,[281] informal networks and personal connections often circumvent formal requirements. Since the civil service is considered fragmented and difficult to motivate, political, *ad hoc* appointees handle important matters. Because of the prevalence of personal rule, even minor issues are resolved at the high echelons of government.

On the other hand, what seems, to a third-party observer, like an anarchic polity is simultaneously very humane. Greek society is characterized by a lack of faith in rigid rules and a boundless optimism that the application of discretion and common sense assures that justice can prevail.[282] The lack of reverence for formal rules and the belief that such rules can be constantly subverted resists totalitarianism, discrimination, and other ills resulting from a relentless pursuit of efficiency and the rigid implementation of the rule of law. These attitudes are well worth preserving as globalization is increasingly restricting cultural diversity and one often feels that the real threat is the creation of societies that are mere replicas of each other.

Today, efforts have been made to uproot personalistic influence, dampen the arrogance of civil servants and keep some of the promises of

[280] *See supra* note 34.

[281] This does not necessarily imply an elite class, but simply someone to whom someone else owns a favor. Someone can hand out more favors the higher his or her financial and social standing is.

[282] *See* Sophocles, *Antigone* (translated by Reginald Gibbons and Charles Segal, 2003). In the Greek language, the word δίκαιο (law) and the word δικαιοσύνη (justice) have the same root

decentralization. Some institutions, for instance, the office of the Ombudsman, a relatively young institution, work remarkably well and are doing their share to change the attributes and attitudes of public service. Other actors are devoted to cultivating an environmental conscience through the use of information technology. Such efforts allow for debate and constructive criticism and are free of the personalistic overtones that often thwart collective action.Reforms are often proposed to change the public sector. Reform's handicap, though, has to do with the will of reformers who have to ascend to power to effectuate change—but then it is too late. By the time, they assume public office, reformers have bowed to the same rent-seeking networks that they had previously so fiercely deprecated.

Part Three

Expressions of Democracy

"The story of democracy contains both a celebration of the end of arbitrary rule and paternalistic politics, and anxiety that democracy could mean rule by the rabble."[1]

1 David Held, *Models of Democracy* 231 (2006).

Chapter 12

Information as the Foundation of the Democratic State

The water framework directive (WFD) has institutionalized the participation of the public and stakeholders in water management. This section examines the benefits and costs associated with the right of the public and stakeholders to participate in the decisionmaking process and the soundness of rationale of establishing public and stakeholder consultation in water management. A distinction is maintained all through this discussion between the participation of the general public—that could be conceptualized as the (local) electorate—and the participation of those who have a specific and well-defined stake in the management of water. Since participation is an empty exercise without the provision of information, the right to obtain information is examined first.

On the international level, the Aarhus Convention[2] has established the right of the public to environmental information. The convention, that

---

2 *Convention on Access to Information, Public Participation in Decision-making and Access to Justice in Environmental Matters*, June 25, 1998 [hereinafter *Aarhus Convention*] available online http://www.unece.org/env/pp/treatytext.htm. For an extensive analysis of the convention, *see* Elli Louka, *Conflicting Integration: The Environmental Law of the European Union* 112 (2004).

has become European Union (EU) law,[3] analyzes in great detail the right to information and provides for a number of exceptions that, if interpreted widely, could defeat the right to information that the convention has established. According to the Aarhus Convention, information can be refused if:

(1) The request for information is manifestly unreasonable or has been formulated in too general a manner.
(2) The request for information concerns materials that involve the internal communications of public authorities, taking into account the public interest served by disclosure.
(3) The disclosure of information adversely affects international relations, national defense or public security.
(4) The disclosure of information adversely affects the confidentiality of commercial or industrial information where such confidentiality is protected by law in order to protect a legitimate economic interest.[4]

It does not require legal interpretation to understand that these exceptions could be used in various circumstances to effectively negate the right to access information. Therefore, it is mentioned in the convention that the grounds for the refusal of provision of information "shall be interpreted in a restrictive way, taking into account the public interest served by disclosure and taking into account whether the information relates to emissions into the environment."[5] Furthermore, the refusal to provide information must be stated in writing if the request for information was in writing or the person who asked for information requested an in-writing response. A refusal to provide information must state the reasons for the refusal and must give information on access during a review procedure that is

---

3 *See Directive 2003/4/EC* of the European Parliament and of the Council of 28 January 2003 on public access to environmental information and repealing Council Directive 90/313/EEC, OJ L 041/26, 14.02.2003. *See also Council Directive 90/313/EEC* of 7 June 1990 on the freedom of access to information on the environment, OJ L 158/56, 23.06.1990; *Directive 2003/35/EC* of the European Parliament and of the Council of 26 May 2003 providing for public participation in respect of drawing up certain plans and programmes relating to the environment and amending with regard to public participation and access to justice Council Directives 85/337/EEC and 96/61/EC, OJ L 156/17, 25.06.2003.

4 For these and other exceptions, *see* art. 4(3)–(4), *Aarhus Convention, supra* note 2.

5 Art. 4(4), *id.*

provided for in article 9 of the convention.[6] The refusal to provide information must be articulated within a month after the request for information is made, unless the complexity of information justifies an extension of this period up to two months.[7]

In other words, the Aarhus Convention could be turned on its head by an expansive reading of the exceptions to freedom to access information in states that may wish to protect a developing industry and in states in which laws on freedom of information are a publicity stunt to be subverted by daily restrictive practice. One could presume, however, that democratic states would refrain from a restrictive interpretation of the right to information unless faced with circumstances of national emergency—a presumption that cannot be taken for granted even in democratic societies.

In addition to the right to environmental information, most democratic states have enacted general freedom of information acts that allow for public access to a wide array of previously inaccessible information. Such acts similarly contain exceptions the expansive reading of which could negate the freedom of information that the legislation guarantees. Denying access to information, though, through an expansive reading of exceptions, is unlikely to escape the attention of emancipated civil society institutions.

Freedom of information acts and their implementation are often used to gauge the robustness of democratic institutions and the dynamism of civil society. A number of countries examined here have made strides in providing information and this presumably is conductive to a climate that favors public participation. In 2005, Hungary established an electronic freedom of information system, and an alert civil society defends information openness.[8] In the Czech Republic, the 1999 Law on Free Access to Information was amended in 2006. According to the new law, courts can order public bodies to release information and fees for releasing

6 Article 9 provides that any person who considers that his or her request for information has been ignored, wrongfully refused or inadequately answered must have access to a review procedure before a court of law or another independent and impartial body established by law. *See* art. 9(1), *id.*

7 Art. 4(7), *id.*

8 *See* David Banisar, *Freedom of Information Around the World 2006: A Global Survey of Access to Government Records Laws*, at 55, July 2006, available online http://www.freedominfo.org/documents/global_survey2006.pdf.

information are restricted to direct costs.[9] Furthermore, in the new law, exemptions have been relaxed so that they cannot be used to nullify the right to access information.[10] In Slovenia, the Access to Public Information Act was adopted in 2003 and provides that everyone has the right to information of public character held by public bodies.[11] Although there are exceptions to this general right, the exceptions do not apply if the request for information is based on public interest. Furthermore, there is a right of appeal to the information commissioner and the courts in case the request for information is rejected. The 1993 Environmental Protection Act provides, additionally, that environmental data are public property.[12] In Bulgaria, improvements have been made for the provision of information and awareness about the requirements of the law has increased among public officials.[13]

In Slovakia, although the laws that guarantee access to information rights are similar to those of other European countries, there is still a reluctance to offend special interests, and information included in privatization contracts has been selectively withheld. A new media law to come into force in 2008 is to restrict further the freedom of the press.[14] In Romania, despite improvements noted in the facilitation of access to information, information on sensitive matters is not easily accessible and certain agencies still charge excessive copying fees. Furthermore, a survey by Transparency International has rated Romania as the most corrupt country in the EU.[15] In Greece, although laws on freedom of information have been in force since 1986, there is still a culture that views public information as proprietary. The office of the ombudsman has been mediating between citizens and public authorities on matters of access to information.

In the United Kingdom (UK), the Freedom of Information Act was adopted in 2000 and went into full effect in 2005.[16] Since the act entered into force, the government has been inundated with more than 120,000 requests per year—private citizens accounting for sixty percent of all requests (while journalists and business account for the rest). On December 14, 2006, the Department for Constitutional Affairs proposed a

---

9 *Id.* at 34.
10 *Id.*
11 *Id.* at 108.
12 *Id.* at 110.
13 *Id.* at 25.
14 *Id.* at 107. *See also* The Press in Eastern Europe: Less Free Speech, The Economist, Apr. 24, 2008.
15 *Id.* at 102. *See also* Romania's Rule of Law: Justice for Some, The Economist, Nov. 1, 2007.
16 *Id.* at 129.

reform according to which requests for information will be refused if the costs of supplying information exceed £600.[17] The official explanation given for the reform is that it would cut down on frivolous requests for information. Public interest groups, however, have claimed that the reform is targeting "experienced and serial requesters" namely campaigners and journalists.[18] In the Netherlands, where freedom of information legislation was adopted in 1978,[19] there is a weak demand for information (1,000 requests per year, mostly from newspapers).[20] The lack of interest has been attributed to the consensual character of the Dutch political system. The government announced, in 2005, that it would introduce new legislation that would facilitate access to information.

With regard to the provision of environmental information, implementation, in most countries examined here, though not spotless, is already advanced.[21] By 2004, most countries had appointed information officers at the national level and adopted legislation and procedures for access to information. The information available on the internet is extensive in the majority of countries. In Hungary, more than fifty nongovernmental organizations (NGOs) participate in various committees and boards,[22] and the Czech Republic, with regard to practical application, is implementing the majority of the requirements evaluated under the Aarhus Convention.[23] In Bulgaria, some best practices of public participation have been identified. However, in 2008 there were increasing concerns regarding the high levels of corruption in the country.[24] In Slovenia improvements have been made on the provision of information on the internet.[25] Overall, the most frequently cited problems in all countries are the lack of human and financial resources and the general lack of understanding among public officials about their obligation to provide information.[26] In most

---

17 According to the proposed reform, separate requests for information from the same organization will be treated as one request for the purposes of calculating the cost.

18 *Freedom of Information: Every Expense Spared*, The Economist, Dec. 23, 2006, at 84.

19 Banisar, *supra* note 8, at 84.

20 *Id.* at 85.

21 *Study on the Implementation of the Aarhus Convention in the New Member States, and Bulgaria, Romania and Turkey*, Final Report (European Commission, DG Environment, Aug. 2004) [hereinafter *Aarhus Study*].

22 *Id.* at 34.

23 *Id.* at 50.

24 *Id.* at 34. *See also Bulgaria: Dirty Politics*, The Economist, Apr. 17, 2008.

25 *Id.* at 36.

26 *Id.* at 26.

cases, although a lot of information exists in raw data, it is not presented in a way that would make sense to the public. In the mid-2008, there was an overall concern that, with the EU membership safeguarded, governments in eastern European countries felt free to restrict the freedom of expression.[27]

The implementation of the WFD has been evaluated by environmental NGOs in terms of the provision of information and the opportunities for participation in decisionmaking. It has been noted that, though improvements have been made since the adoption of the directive, information is not readily provided by public authorities and many NGOs do not have the technical knowledge and expertise to get actively involved in the implementation of the directive.[28]

The right to information forms the backbone of a democratic society and it is a prerequisite for meaningful participation. The right to participation can be manipulated by sophisticated public agencies that could use participation to placate and co-opt those who participate. Governments and governing elites are controlled, however, by a self-consciousness that the electorate knows or could obtain information about their actions and performance—and they are often galvanized by a sweeping public opinion.[29]

Information can be manipulated, but this is less likely in the information age in which the sources of information are multiple and cannot always be twisted by official authorities. The challenge in the provision of information has less to do with its manipulation than with how to organize the unwieldy streams of information available from multiple sources in order to cull the information that is vital for one's purposes. This is why the Aarhus Convention emphasizes the organization of information in databases that are easily accessible to the public.[30] The fact that the state

27 *Id. See also The Press in Eastern Europe: Less Free Speech*, The Economist, Apr. 24, 2008 ("this is bad news in a region that used to take pride in its reborn freedom ... [E]x-communist countries show the biggest relative decline in media freedom in the world ... The drop is larger than in Asia, Africa and Latin America.").

28 *EU Water Policy: Making the Water Framework Directive Work: The Quality of National Transposition and Implementation of the Water Framework Directive at the End of 2004, A Second "Snapshot" Report–Assessment of results from an environmental NGO questionnaire by the EEB and WWF*, Feb. 2005.

29 *See also* Bernard Crick, *Democracy: A Very Short Introduction* 119 (2002).

30 *See* art. 5(9), *Aarhus Convention, supra* note 2. *See also Protocol to the Aarhus Convention on Pollutant Release and Transfer Registers*, May 21, 2003 available online http://www.unece.org/env/pp/prtr/docs/prtrtext.htm. The European Community has established the European Pollutant Emission Register (EPER). National governments of member states are required to

plays the role of organizer of information is discomfiting, nonetheless, to those who inherently distrust the good intentions of states.[31]

The problems with the provision of information that confront new member states do not seem more acute than those of old member states. Overall, the right to information is respected more in well-governed societies that enjoy political stability and minimum corruption.[32] The fact that a number of public officials do not always conform to their obligation to provide information reflects that the informal organization is more resistant to change than the formal organization. Thus, although laws and regulations can be amended, the institutional culture is bound to lag behind, at least initially. An educated civil society knowledgeable of the legal twists and turns can push for change in the institutional culture of public authorities.

---

maintain inventories of their emission data from specified industrial sources and to report emissions from individual facilities to the European Commission. The reported data are accessible though the EPER the purpose of which is to provide information on major industrial activities.

31 *See* Elli Louka, *Conflicting Integration: The Environmental Law of the European Union* 115–16 (2004).

32 *See* Daniel Kaufmann *et al.*, *Governance Matters IV (1996-2004): New Data, New Challenges*, May 2005 available online http://www.worldbank.org/wbi/governance/pdf/Synthesis_GovMatters_IV.pdf. The World Bank has identified six parameters of good governance: (1) voice and accountability; (2) political stability and lack of violence; (3) government effectiveness; (4) regulatory quality; (5) rule of law; and (6) the control of corruption, *see* http://go.worldbank.org/ATJXPHZMH0.

Chapter 13

The Participation of the Public: Towards Effective Rules in Water Management?

The water framework directive (WFD) has institutionalized stakeholder consultation and participation of the public in water management through:[33]

- The provision of information to the public;
- The consultation with stakeholders; and
- The active involvement of stakeholders/public in the decision-making process.[34]

---

[33] In this chapter, the terms *consultation* and *participation* are used interchangeably; consultation is considered a less involved form of participation.

[34] The directive on environmental impact assessment and the directive on integrated pollution, prevention and control (IPPC) include the right to information and participation in decision-making. *See Directive 2003/35/EC* of the European Parliament and of the Council of 26 May 2003 providing for public participation in respect of the drawing up of certain plans and programmes relating to the environment and amending with regard to public participation and access to justice Council Directives 85/337/EEC and 96/61/EC, O J L 156/17, 25.06.2003. *See also* art. 15, *Council Directive 96/61/EC* of 24 September 1996 concerning integrated pollution, prevention and control (IPPC), OJ L 257/26, 10.10.1996.

Although stakeholders are identifiable, *the public* is a more amorphous concept and encompasses, in general, the citizens of a state. Most administrative systems, as examined in Chapter 11, focus on the participation of stakeholders in water management; the participation of the general public has yet to be pursued systematically. This probably has to do more with a lack of means rather than a lack of will—as it has been a challenge to engage citizens in matters that they do not view to be their priority. Water quality is taken for granted in most European Union (EU) member states and water management is not an issue that affects election outcomes.

The participation of stakeholders in water management has been touted for the advantages it brings to effective rulemaking. Moreover, the guidance document devoted to public participation[35] urges the participation of stakeholders in the making of public policy because of the benefits that accrue to decisionmaking. Such benefits include:

- Making use of knowledge and experience of various stakeholders;
- Increasing public acceptance of proposed rules; and
- Curtailing the use of litigation and delays in implementation.[36]

Because of these alleged advantages, member states are encouraged to establish a typology of all possible stakeholders. The classification of stakeholders can help states distinguish stakeholders[37] that could facilitate from those that would obstruct the WFD implementation. Overall, member states are encouraged to undertake the following analysis:

- Identification of issues that need to be addressed at each level (international, national, river-basin, water body);
- Determination of stakeholders that could make a contribution at each level; and

35 *Guidance Document No 8, Public Participation in Relation to the Water Framework Directive*, produced by Working Group 2.9—Public Participation, Common Implementation Strategy for the Water Framework Directive (2000/60/EC) (European Communities, 2003) [hereinafter *PP Guidance*].

36 *Id.* at 14. *See also Background Paper on Public Participation in Transboundary Water Cooperation, at 6–7, prepared by the Center for Transboundary Cooperation – Saint Petersburg for the Workshop on information management and public participation in transboundary water cooperation*, St. Petersburg, June 8–10, 2005 [hereinafter *Background Paper*] available online http://unece.org/env/water/cwc/Info-pp/Backdoc_pp_e.pdf.

37 *PP Guidance, supra* note 35, at 15–16.

- Communication of the results of participation both horizontally, among the institutions involved at each level, and vertically, across all international, national, and local levels.[38]

The guidance document provides advice on how to organize participation, manage the whole process, and evaluate the various results.[39] Throughout the document, participation is supported as a learning device (that is, learning from others) and as a way to change perceptions of public officials who need to start viewing stakeholders as co-owners of the decisionmaking process rather than as impediments to sound policymaking. Viewing private interests as an obstacle to rational decisionmaking has strong roots in Europe, where the state is traditionally perceived as an embodiment of the public interest that is above and beyond various individualistic pursuits. This view of the state is usually contrasted with the Lockean tradition in which the state is nothing more than the contractual apposition of private interests.[40]

The concept of the state as an unbiased institution committed to the pursuit of public good fell out of favor when, communism collapsed[41] and fatigue mounted in the face of a number of corrupt and failed states. Public participation in the decisionmaking of state institutions essentially challenges the idea that the state holds a monopoly on the pursuit of public good. The role of state, though, is not totally relegated either. Public institutions have to initiate stakeholder consultation. In order to obtain results from stakeholder participation, they have to assume, at least, the role of arbitrator among the various private interests.[42] Stakeholder participation

38 *Id.* at 20.

39 *Id.* at 49. Some participatory techniques include workshops and hearings, *see id.* at 69–102. Websites, email, newsletters, and toll-free numbers are good devices for the provision of information, *see id.* at 44.

40 *See* John Locke, *Second Treatise on Civil Government*, Chapter VIII (1690). I am indebted to Maria Karamanof for pointing out this difference.

41 And theoretically much before that since the conception of state as an instrument in the hands of an elite class is also a Marxist idea.

42 For the role that public institutions can assume in the process of public participation, *see* Clare M. Ryan, *Leadership in Collaborative Policy-making: An Analysis of Agency Roles in Regulatory Negotiations*, 34 Policy Sciences 221 (2001) (The author examines the roles that the United States Environmental Agency [EPA] can assume in regulatory rulemaking. According to the author, the agency can play the role of technical expert; the role of analyst—the role of analyzing, manipulating, and interpreting data from various sources; the role of stakeholder—the stake of a regulatory agency consists of its mandate to have an effective rule in place and to reduce the costs of litigation; the role of facilitator—in terms of providing

stems from the belief that the negotiation and debate among private interests inevitably leads to the pursuit of public good under the guidance of an honest broker (the state).

Since stakeholder participation has been advanced for its contribution to effective rulemaking, the metrics of such rulemaking have to be established and stakeholder participation must be gauged based on these metrics. Stakeholder participation, from the viewpoint of a decisionmaking institution, will contribute to effective rulemaking if it facilitates implementation and, thus, curbs the costs of enforcement. Whether participation curbs the costs of enforcement is an empirical matter. In order to determine whether public participation has reduced the costs of enforcement, one would need to compare the effectiveness of rulemaking conducted with and without participation—a difficult empirical exercise.

Commentators in the United States, an early adopter of participatory rulemaking, have claimed that prolonged participatory hearings before the adoption of a rule often fail to produce the desired consensus and, thus, reduce litigation costs. Participants in regulatory rulemaking may be apprehensive about raising issues that undermine reaching consensus (groupthink).[43] Subsequently, the same participants who failed to "get their way" with a regulatory agency would not hesitate to challenge the adopted rules in the court system.[44] Furthermore, negotiated rulemaking could end up becoming a process to paper over differences among various constituencies through the use of vague regulatory language. Differences, though, cannot be dissipated forever under the cloak of regulatory terminology and are likely to reemerge during the implementation process.[45]

---

logistical support for meetings and encouraging parties to speak to each other; the role of leader—the agency assumes a leadership role by initiating negotiations, establishing the boundaries for deliberation and by legitimizing and providing credibility for the process. The legitimizing role of a public institution in the participative process is important since certain groups are often overwhelmed by the technical aspects of a regulation and look upon the EPA to help them navigate technical regulations.).

43 With regard to groupthink, *see also* Irving L. Janis, *Groupthink*, Psychology Today 44 (1971). According to Schumpeter, groupthink or what is called crowd psychology is not reserved to rioting groups but every parliament, every committee are suffering from reduced responsibility and influence by nonlogical inferences. *See* Joseph A. Schumpeter, *Capitalism, Socialism and Democracy* 257, 263 (1975 edition).

44 Cary Coglianese, *Assessing the Advocacy of Negotiated Rulemaking: A Response to Philip Harter* 386, at 439–40, 9 New York University Environmental Law Journal (2001). *See also* Philip J. Harter, *Negotiating Regulations: A Cure for Malaise*, 71 Georgetown Law Journal 1 (1982) (Participatory rulemaking is known in the United States as negotiated rulemaking—"reg-neg.").

45 Coglianese, *id.* at 441.

Participatory processes may, instead of bringing the parties together, drive them apart by making their differences more pronounced[46] or, even worse, lead to a search for the lowest common denominator. Many participatory processes, as established by public agencies today, are geared towards the satisfaction of stakeholders. Stakeholder satisfaction, though, is not the proper metric for assessing effective rulemaking. The pursuit of public good[47] is the criterion that should be used, instead, to gauge regulatory effectiveness.[48]

Participative proceedings may fail to produce effective rules because of the possible co-opting of a public agency. Co-opting occurs if an interest group captures a public institution and, thus, uses that institution to serve the group's agenda rather than pursue the public interest.[49] Co-opting may lead to the development of a clientele relationship between a public institution and a constituency. Those who are troubled by participatory processes have in mind experiences in states where too much participation led to the creation of a client state.[50]

Co-opting is a real threat to participatory processes, but the chances of its occurrence are reduced as participatory proceedings become more transparent and formal. If who participates, how they participate, and the results of public participation are a matter of public record, a public institution will be motivated to keep at least the appearance of evenhandedness towards various stakeholders. Cooptation really takes hold if a constituency takes advantage of an informal relationship with an agency

---

46 *Background paper, supra* note 36, at 7.

47 The question here is how to define public good. Negotiated rulemaking rests on the assumption that negotiation among various interests under the watchful eye of an agency will lead to the pursuit of public interest. An alternative way to attempt the pursuit of public interest is through a neutral and expert agency focused on the pursuit of public good.

48 *See* Cary Coglianese, *Is Satisfaction Success? Evaluating Public Participation in Regulatory Policymaking*, Faculty Research Working Papers Series, John F. Kennedy School of Government, Harvard University, Sept. 2002 available online http://papers.ssrn.com/abstract=331420; *See also* William Funk, *Bargaining Toward the New Millennium: Regulatory Negotiation and the Subversion of the Public Interest*, 46 Duke Law Journal 1351 (1997).

49 The concept of coopting has been analyzed extensively in the context of the Tennessee Valley Authority—one of the first river basin authorities. *See* Philip Selznick, *TVA and the Grass Roots* 13 (1966).

50 Antonio Massarutto, *Public Participation in River Basin Management Planning in Italy: An unconventional marriage of top-down planning and corporative politics*, paper prepared for the HarmoniCOP project, Dec. 2003 available online http://www.harmonicop.uni-osnabrueck.de/_files/_down/Italy.pdf. The HarmoniCOP project was sponsored by the European Commission. For information about the project, *see* http://www.harmonicop.uos.de/index.php.

and, thus, influences the agency's policymaking without being exposed.[51] Transparency and openness are indispensable ingredients of participatory processes, and the absence of transparency can corrupt participatory proceedings.

Another question that needs to be examined is why participatory processes are persistently sought in public policy making, even though they may not produce effective results. The answer has to do with the evolving meanings of democracy and the quest to satisfy a jaded electorate.

51 *See also* Selznick, *supra* note 49, at 226, 260–61.

Chapter 14

Public Participation and the Strengthening of the Democratic State

Participative, associative, or functional democracy describes the participation of specific interests, including civil society groups, in the decisionmaking process of states. For some, *participative democracy* is nothing more than another term for lobbying by special interests. Special interests often lobby lawmakers to achieve results advantageous to them. As such, participative democracy could be an affront to representative democracy since the latter is based on the participation of all citizens in the electoral process.[52] For others, participative democracy is an answer to the ills of representative democracy.[53] Representative democracy has been discredited lately. A general disaffection with politics and an inherent belief that the simple citizen cannot really affect global agendas mar today's systems of representative democracy and are exemplified in the absenteeism that characterizes national elections.

---

52 *See generally* John Haskell, *Direct Democracy or Representative Government? Dispelling the Populist Myth* (2001).

53 *See* Benjamin R. Barber, *Strong Democracy: Participatory Politics for a New Age* (2003).

The lure of participative democracy is rooted in nostalgia for the beginnings of democracy, where all citizens[54] contributed to decisions on the future of a *polis*. This form of direct democracy, while not always praised by its contemporaries,[55] is evoked today in town meetings, referenda, and other citizen fora that attempt to replicate the direct participation of citizen in the affairs of the state. Participative democracy, thus, could be seen as a means of infusing representative democracy with elements of direct democracy.

To equate participative democracy with direct democracy requires a leap of faith, though. Participative democracy is effectuated through groups that claim to represent the public interest. Whether these groups can credibly create an accurate version of public interest is debatable. Few of these groups suffer from lack of internal and external accountability.[56] Furthermore, the groups that play a prominent role in the public discourse are a minority of the groups that are able to amass resources and make their voices heard.[57] The confluence of a minority, resource-rich groups in participative proceedings, no matter the sincerity of their intentions, cannot epitomize the democratic principle[58]—unless democracy is perceived as nothing more than the wheeling and dealing of a minority with the acquiescence of a disengaged majority.[59]

---

54 Women, slaves, and foreigners were not considered citizens and were deprived of any sort of political rights, though. *See* Josiah Ober, *Mass and Elite in Democratic Athens: Rhetoric, Ideology, and the Power of the People* 6 (1989).

55 *See* John Dunn, *Setting the People Free: The Story of Democracy* 47–49 (2005). (For Plato democracy [*demokratia*] was far from an ideal political system unless it was to be exercised for the pursuit of public good. Aristotle preferred *politeia* to democracy. *Politeia* had nothing to do with the imposition of the will of majority on others but with a system through which powers and responsibilities are distributed based on the variety of citizens' skills. *Politeia's* legitimacy was not based on the power of majority but on the loyalty generated by a system that has established meritocracy in the institutional organization of power. Aristotle's *politeia* could be considered a model of participatory self-government.)

56 *See* Ruth W. Grant and Robert O. Keohane, *Accountability and Abuses of Power in World Politics*, 99(1) American Political Science Review 1, Feb. 2005.

57 For instance, the lack of capacity of environmental groups to participate in the WFD process was documented in the early stages of WFD implementation, *see NGO Participation in Danube River Basin Management Plans: Information, Analysis and Conclusions on Participation in the Central and Eastern European Implementation of the European Union's Water Framework Directive* (Jeremey M. Alcorn, ed., Regional Environmental Center for Central and Eastern Europe, Slovakia, 2002).

58 For a critique of groups, *see* Cass Sunstein, *Why Societies Need Dissent* (2003); *See also* Bill Cooke, *The Social Psychological Limits of Participation* 102, in Participation: The New Tyranny? (Bill Cooke and Uma Kothari, eds., 2001).

59 A fitting definition for many of today's democratic regimes, *see* John Mueller, *Public Participation and Democracy: Optimal Illusions and Grim Realities, paper prepared for presentation at the Fall Conference of Association for Public Policy and Management*, Washington DC, Nov. 3–5, 2005.

Indeed, the most scathing critique of public participation emanates from concerns that it could be used as an instrument to manipulate and placate the public.[60] According to this view, mass industrialization and the development of the mass public have necessitated new methods of control. States are interested in organizing the undifferentiated public into groups that could be easily accessible and controlled. If these groups participate in the decisionmaking of public institutions, they share the responsibility for the decisions made and are more likely to identify with the purposes of a public institution. Public interest groups, by getting involved in participatory politics, not only add accountability to these processes but also remove accountability from the shoulders of elected or appointed officials.[61] In this manner, public participation becomes, in essence, top-down co-opting.[62]

For participative processes to be called democratic, there must be constraints to prevent powerful and resource-rich groups from running the political process. Transparency is a *sine qua non* in a participatory process so that there is clarity of—who is standing, for what, and why. Public interest, a notion that is used—and often abused in the political sphere—is the yardstick of regulatory policies. At a minimum, the pursuit of public interest entails policymaking that is evenhanded and impartial[63]—the engagement in a conscientious effort to produce objective results taking into account the plurality of presented opinions. *Our common good* does not consist of specific objects, activities, and relations. It consists of practices, arrangements, institutions, and processes that promote the well-being of enough people to make these institutions respected. The essence of the democratic process is a right to disagree with decisions taken and the functioning of institutions that enable the peaceful settlement of disputes.[64]

Effective participation presupposes a democratic process in which:

- All votes are equal when decisions are made.
- There is an enlightened understanding of those who participate (which presupposes the right to be informed).
- Those who participate control at least some of the agenda.[65]

60 Sherry R. Arnstein, *A Ladder of Citizen Participation*, 35(4) Journal of American Institute of Planners 216, July 1969.

61 Haskell, *supra* note 52, at 120.

62 Selznick, *supra* note 49, at 218.

63 *See also* Deborah L. Rhode, *The Profession and the Public Interest*, 54 Stanford Law Review 1501 (2002).

64 Robert A. Dahl, *Democracy and its Critics* 306 (1989).

65 *See also id.* at 109–13.

A further issue is how to involve citizens at large in the participatory process. Most citizens hold values and have concerns that, though often unstructured, inform their decisions. Such concerns may have to do with the resentment of privilege, too apparent in most societies; the lack of meritocracy; and the web of networks that ensure that dissenters remain marginalized. The question for those who really care about democracy is how to organize these unstructured concerns and ensure that the disaffected are given a chance to speak with a coherent voice. The idea behind organizing those not involved in policymaking is not to create groups entrenched in a specific cause, but to allow people, who feel otherwise powerless, to affect public discourse outcomes and come together in matters of public interest.[66] Such *ad hoc* group formation may acquire meaning for individuals who do not belong to established groups, feel disengaged from "politics as usual," but nevertheless crave being able to vent their views in the public sphere.

The internet has been used successfully as a vehicle for networking among people who wish to take part in the public discourse and for whom the traditional means of communication are intimidating or archaic. The internet is increasingly used as a new instrument of protest in societies that are not democratic. In these autocratic societies, opposition forces forbidden to run street protests can now engage in web-based campaigns.[67] One has to note, however, that even these spontaneously organized forms of participation require a threshold of access to modern means of communication and technological sophistication and, therefore, are still far from available to everybody. Furthermore, even though the internet can be used by prodemocracy groups, it can be used equally by groups that promote autocracy and violence.[68]

---

66 One could consider electronic protest as a way to accomplish this. *See Electronic Protest*, The Economist, Feb. 17, 2007. *See also* Beth S. Noveck, *A Democracy of Groups*, New York Law School Public Law and Legal Theory, Research Paper Series 05/06–11, Mar. 2005, available online http://ssrn.com/abstract=838385. *But see also* Neil Weinstock Netanel, *Cyberspace and Self-Governance: A Skeptical View from Liberal Democratic Theory*, 99 California Law Review 395 (2000).

67 *Bloggers May Be the Real Opposition: How the Authorities are Being Nettled*, The Economist, Apr. 14, 2007, at 54 (In Egypt, blogging has become a "shaper of the political agenda." Bloggers, by posting embarrassing video, have opened up issues such as torture or the harassment of women in the streets of Cairo. Bahrain has arrested bloggers for questioning and has requested them to register with the police.).

68 Haskell, *supra* note 52, at 72.

Another way to jolt the democratic process may be through the fusion of functional democracy and representative democracy[69] that has been proposed for the revamping of water boards in the Netherlands as examined below. Another alternative is to infuse functional and representative democracy with elements of direct democracy. Although it is impossible to replicate the original approach, in which the citizens of a *polis* congregated to make decisions, it is possible to use referenda as a way to give each citizen the right to vote on certain issues.[70] Referenda take place on the national scale and, in the period between 1990 and 2000, more than 400 referenda took place in various countries around the world—half of them in Europe.[71] Referenda are susceptible to being manipulated, and they require an informed electorate to be effective.[72] Nevertheless, they are worth experimenting with in river basin management.

Other ideas about how to take advantage of participatory democracy include the introduction of neighborhood assemblies that can address issues of local accountability—for example, a local ombudsman—and interactive television town meetings.[73] Nevertheless, emphasizing direct democracy at the local level reinforces parochialism.[74] Furthermore, local politics address local prerogatives and rarely have an impact on global matters, such as, decisions on war and peace and the proliferation of weapons of mass destruction.

In things that really matter for the long-term prosperity of our societies, such as war and peace, the spread of globalization, and environmental sustainability, what voice is possible for the simple citizen in a participatory process? A blind belief that participatory rulemaking can cure the ills of bureaucratic rulemaking is probably naïve. Democratic politics will continue to be a muddling, cumbersome, and inefficient process. Only procedural safeguards, such as transparency and openness, can ensure some

---

69 *See also* Bruno S. Frey and Alois Stutzer, *The Role of Direct Democracy and Federalism in Local Power*, Working Paper No. 209, Institute for Empirical Research in Economics, University of Zurich, Oct. 2004.

70 *Id.*

71 *Id.* (half of which occurred in Switzerland).

72 For an extensive discussion of referenda, *see* Lars P. Feld and Gebhard Kirchgässner, *The Role of Direct Democracy in the European Union*, GESifo Working Paper No. 1083, Presented at the CESifo Conference "A Constitution for the European Union," Feb. 2003 available on line http://www.ssrn.com/abstract=466584. For a critique of the referendum as an expression of the democratic idea, *see also* Haskell, *supra* note 52, at 113.

73 Barber, *supra* note 53, at 267–307.

74 *Id.* at 309.

transcendence from the pursuit of various private interests to the pursuit of public good.

As analyzed in Chapter 11, states have interpreted the provisions of the water framework directive (WFD) on consultation and participation by creating institutions that are an interesting combination of a public body and a stakeholder advisory board. This is because a number of public institutions, such as municipalities, regions, and provinces, are considered stakeholders in the WFD implementation processes.[75] These institutions need to coordinate their activities with the river basin authorities in order to minimize institutional rivalry and advance the cause of integrated water management. Water users are equally important in the organization of stakeholder bodies. From the perspective of an institution in charge of WFD implementation, it makes sense to involve water users earlier rather than later as it is becoming increasingly difficult to enforce decisions made without stakeholder participation.

Including institutional and political veto players in the process of adopting river basin management plans seems reasonable, at least, for the sake of receiving advance warning about obstacles in the implementation stage. Whether such consultations lead to the adoption of better river basin management plans depends on the circumstances of each state and the spirit of cooperation that exists in a polity. From the viewpoint of public administrators, the crowning moment in the participatory process lies in either effectively amassing public support for their proposed policies or assuaging public opposition—both of which constitute the beginnings of institutional autonomy.[76]

If, in the implementation of the WFD, member states espouse a participatory process that is really an extended version of corporatism, there are two remedies. One addresses the need to maintain openness and transparency. Meetings of stakeholder should be open, the minutes of the meetings should be readily available through a website, and could be

---

75 For the role public authorities have in the participative structures established for the WFD implementation by member states and how such role could constrain other less institutionalized interests, such as e-NGOs, *see* Lucia De Stefano, *Public Participation in the Water Framework Directive, Common Implementation Strategy Pilot River Basin Testing Exercise and the implementation of the Water Framework Directive* (WWF, May 2004) available online http://www.env.cz/AIS/web-pub.nsf/$pid/MZPJMF6RXMZ8/$FILE/OOV_Ucast_verejnosti_dokument_WWF_anglicky_200406.pdf.

76 *See generally* Daniel P. Carpenter, *The Forging of Bureaucratic Autonomy: Reputations, Networks, and Policy Innovation in Executive Agencies* 1862–1928 (2001).

tape-recorded. Too much openness in public meetings can lead to posturing, the adoption of delaying tactics, or even retrenchment (meaning that important discussions move back to the office).[77] Nevertheless, there are rules of procedure that can enhance openness but also allow for decision-making and execution. In principle, the public should have the right to know the rationale behind all decisions that are made in a river basin district, and authorities should avoid concealing information that protects private interests.

The other remedy has to do with the structure of participatory institutions. Institutions embodying the participatory ethic need to be renewed constantly and infused with new societal concerns and interests as they emerge to shape public opinion and challenge established interests. Failure to take into the account new entrants could lead to institutional demise or, even worse, to institutional irrelevance. Established institutions tend to be negatively predisposed toward new entrants bringing new ideas in the public sphere. Such an exclusionary ethic, though sometimes successful in the past, is increasingly self-defeating today. Marginalized groups can instantly publish their views online, and, thus, in the global marketplace of ideas, may find plenty of adherents ready to challenge the authority and legitimacy of established authorities.

[77] Or even to email exchanges. *See* Molly Petrilla, *WW Council Will Set Guidelines for E-mail Use, Princeton Packet*, Jan. 16, 2007. *See also* Chapter 22.

Chapter 15

Public Participation in Practice

Water Boards, the Netherlands

The *waterschap* (water board), as it has evolved in the Netherlands, is examined here because of lessons it offers as a stakeholder-based institution focused on water management. Water boards have been conceived as stakeholder institutions governed by elected bodies. Water boards have evolved since their inception but are based on certain abiding principles, namely, financial independence and the interest-pay-say principle examined below.

Water boards started as spontaneous associations among landowners who, facing an adverse environment, united to fend off their fields from invading waters. Three thousand water boards were established by 1850. Water boards, however, focused on parochial interests and failed to organize collectively to avert flooding disasters. The lack of collective action on the part of water boards led to increasing centralization in water management. A national water authority, the so-called *Rijkswaterstaat* was established[78] and has played a pivotal role in water management. Mergers have gradually reduced the number of water boards without affecting the principles on which they are based.

Water boards are not viewed any longer as water user associations but as public authorities similar to municipalities and provinces. Their role in state administration is guaranteed in the constitution and their functions are delineated in the Water Boards Act of 1992.[79] Water boards are formally under the supervision of provinces. However, because of their ability to collect taxes for the services they provide, they enjoy substantial independence in the pursuit of their duties.[80]

Water boards have clearly defined tasks that include:[81]

- Flood protection including infrastructure maintenance;
- Management of water quantity (drainage and irrigation);
- Management of water quality (improvement of quality of surface waters); and
- Treatment of urban wastewater. [82]

The governance of water boards is comprised of an assembly, an executive assembly, and a chairperson.[83] The assembly is an elected body comprised of representatives of all categories of water users who have an interest in water management in a water board district. The executive assembly consists, on the average, of five members[84] and is appointed by the water board assembly. The chair of water board is appointed by the Dutch monarch, and his or her status is comparable to that of the mayor of a municipality.[85]

---

78 Ine D. Frijters and Jan Leentvaar, *Participatory Planning for Flood Management in the Netherlands,* paper presented at the training workshop held by the (United Nations Economic and Social Commission for Asia and the Pacific) UNESCAP on flood mitigation, Ho Chi Minh City, Vietnam, Mar. 26–29, 2001 available online http://www.unescap.org/esd/water/disaster/2001/netherlands.doc 2001.

79 *Water Governance: the Dutch Water Board Model* (Dutch Association of Water Boards, Herman Havekes *et al.*, eds, 2004) [hereinafter *Dutch Waterboard*].

80 *Id.* at 17 (the tax revenues of water boards were close to two billion euro in 2004).

81 *Id.* at 17–18.

82 Groundwater and soil protection are the responsibility of municipalities and provinces. Drinking water companies are responsible for the management and distribution of drinking water while sewage treatment has been delegated to municipalities. *Id.* at 18–19.

83 *Id.* at 23.

84 The number of members of the executive assembly varies per waterboard. *See id.* at 25.

85 *Id.* at 26.

The assembly is an elected body and the right to vote in the elections of the assembly is linked to the stakeholder categories represented in a water board. For the stakeholder category of residents, all residents of a water board district[86] are entitled to vote to elect representatives.[87] The votes go to individuals who wish to serve in the assembly and not to political parties. The seats of the assembly are preassigned. Therefore, the issue during election time is not which stakeholder interests are going to be represented in the water board assembly, but which people are going to occupy the preassigned seats.[88] The preassignment depends on the area in which a water board is located, and the nature and size of interests that are present in that area. If agriculture is a predominant activity in a water board district, more seats are assigned to agriculture. Overall, the interests that are represented in various combinations in the assemblies of water boards include:

- Owners of real estate consisting of open land (landowners and farmers);
- Owners of real estate consisting of buildings;
- Renters of business buildings;
- Households (residents); and
- Tenants.[89]

That someone needs to have an interest and pay for water management in order to have a say in such management makes the triplet *interest-pay-say* that has been the cornerstone of governance in water boards since their inception. Water boards are unique subnational institutions in that they have their own tax system that guarantees financial independence. Water boards enjoy some democratic legitimacy since the governing assembly is elected rather than appointed. Some water boards are active internationally and advise other institutions how to achieve self-financing in water management.[90]

---

[86] Who are at least eighteen years of age and have not been deprived of the right to vote. *See id.* at 28.

[87] *Id.*

[88] *Id.*

[89] *Id.* at 24.

[90] *See Success Factors in Self Financing Local Water Management: A Contribution to the Third World Water Forum in Japan* (R.W. Uijterlinde *et al.*, eds., 2003).

The water framework directive (WFD), through the institutionalization of public participation, presents interesting challenges for water boards. The directive supports the participation of the public and consultation with stakeholders in water management. Thus, the directive, with its support for public participation, defines interest more broadly than the interest-pay-say model. Member states have interpreted the directive to be a mandate for the creation of governance bodies, based on the inclusion of a wide array of interests, including organizations that are presumed to represent the public interest, such as environmental organizations. In the water boards, such public interest representation is taking place today through the residents category because residents who are elected in water board assemblies often hold environmentally friendly positions.

To be clear, the WFD is addressed to member states and the principles of public participation it establishes do not necessarily apply to local water management associations, such as water boards. As long as the Netherlands can fulfill the requirement of the WFD through other administrative arrangements, the governance of water boards does not need to be amended.[91]

The WFD, though, cannot leave the water boards indifferent if they wish to remain relevant. The WFD has percolated in a period during which water boards are seriously considering reforming their administrative structure. Changes have been proposed to simplify water board governance. Instead of the five categories of interests analyzed above, the creation of two categories of interests has been proposed:

- General task interests (basically all residents who live, work, and recreate in a district managed by a water board);
- Special task interests (i.e., farmers, companies, and managers in the fields of forestry and nature).[92]

This new classification of interests, while it simplifies matters, offers little to address the representation of public interest, and it is more of a gradual

[91] The Netherlands has fulfilled the requirements of public participation through the establishment of "sounding boards" in the various working areas designated to facilitate water management in international river basin districts.

[92] Provinces are to determine how the seats between residents and special interests are to be distributed and how to distribute seats among various special interests. *See Dutch Waterboard*, *supra* note 79, at 29.

Under this renewed structure, environmental interests could be represented either through the residents category or as special interests through the ownership of protected land or other real estate.

reform rather than an overhaul of the water board governance system. An issue that has preoccupied water boards is the disappointing turnout in elections (a mere 25 percent of those entitled to vote).[93] Although the low turnout may be explained on the grounds that successful water management dissipates the urge for public involvement, the issue of democratic legitimacy has preoccupied water boards. From 2008, all water board elections will be held simultaneously in the hope of increasing their overall visibility.[94] It is proposed that the "person voting system" should be replaced with the "list voting system" so that groups that represent a specific interest and vision for water management can submit a list of candidates for water board elections.[95]

Water boards have strengths that, if genuinely explored and explained, can assist them in repositioning themselves as institutions that represent the public instead of stakeholder-based institutions. The resident or household stakeholder category is represented in the water board assembly based on interest-pay-say since households pay taxes for water management. The residents' category is simultaneously the closest manifestation of "the public" in water management. Water board reform can be accomplished, it is argued, by anchoring water board governance to the residents of a water board district; the tenet of "no-choice-but-to-live-here" thus becomes the centerpiece of reform. Other special groups, such as environmentalists and farmers, could be allowed some representation that provides them with an opportunity to iron out their differences in the water board assembly. Industries do not need representation in the water board assembly since they are already able to negotiate their fees and taxes with water boards or establish their own wastewater treatment systems.[96]

The proposal to use the tenet of "no-choice-but-to-live-here" as the lever of reform in water boards expresses the general concern that pure models of functional democracy are neither inclusive enough nor adaptable to social change. Functional democratic systems quickly ossify as they persistently speak for those already represented and rarely make room for new entrants. As a result, old and established interests are represented, but new and more amorphous interests remain outside the

93 *Id.* at 28.
94 *Id.* at 30.
95 *Id.* at 29–30.
96 I am indebted here to discussions with Mr. Roelof Kruize, Chairman of Amsterdam Water board, December 2006.

decisionmaking process. Injecting elements of representative democracy into functional democracy could infuse water management with innovation and some unpredictability—since new entrants are less likely to follow well-trodden paths.

Maybe the future of democracy does not rest on a pure functional or a representative system but on hybrid systems in which functional democracy is challenged by representative democracy, and representative democracy is renewed by functional democratic norms. The injection of representative democracy controls into functional democratic systems may render such systems more transparent but would also make them more unpredictable and may increase the transaction costs of decisionmaking. The pursuit of democracy is not obviously the most efficient pursuit because time is consumed in attaining a majority consensus and ensuring that such a consensus is at least tolerable to those who do not agree with the majority view. However, the democratic process is the only process that, given the opportunity, has a realistic chance of legitimizing decisions and minimizing discord if the time is ripe for implementation. On the other hand, decisions adopted expediently, absent democratic processes, may have an aura of efficiency but lack the force of legitimacy that drives implementation on the ground.

The Ribble Pilot Project, United Kingdom

The guidance document issued by the European Commission (the Commission) to facilitate the implementation of participative processes in member states[97] was tested in a pilot, the Ribble catchment. The Ribble catchment is located in the North West River Basin District of England. For the purposes of the WFD implementation, England and Wales have been divided into eleven river basin districts.[98] These river basin districts are the basic units used in the UK for reporting to the Commission.

---

97 *See supra* note 35.

98 Two of these districts are shared by England and Wales and one of these districts spans the Scotland Wales border. For information on the implementation of the WFD by the UK Environment Agency, *see* www.environment-agency.gov.uk/wfd/. For information on the Ribble Pilot, *see* http://www.environment.gov.uk/regions/northwest/501317/1127771/574439/?lang=_e.

Each district is divided into catchments. The competent authority for the implementation of the WFD is the Environment Agency. The Environment Agency has succeeded in developing a reputation as an agency mindful of the importance of participative process for the success of public policies.[99]

In socioeconomic terms, the Ribble catchment area is characterized by low-skilled, ethnically diverse urban communities.[100] A number of regional authorities are active in the catchment, including the North West Regional Assembly, the Lancashire County Council, and various districts whose territory overlaps with the Ribble basin.[101] The challenge for the UK, in terms of application of the WFD, is the consolidation of the various disconnected and overlapping planning instruments issued by a number of local and regional authorities into an integrated river basin plan.[102]

The Ribble catchment pilot proceeded methodically to test public participation by experimenting with various forms of participation and identifying the lessons learned and usability in the WFD context. A communications strategy was developed to guide the work of the UK

---

99 *See Building trust with communities: a toolkit for staff* (UK Environment Agency, No date).

100 Peter Fox, *Water Framework Directive Programme: Ribble Pilot River Basin Project: Experience of Testing the CIS Guidance*, Mar. 2003–May 2004 (Draft EC Report, UK Environment Agency).

101 *Id.*

102 In the Ribble catchment alone, there is a plethora of plans under the supervision of the Environment Agency:

- The Ribble Catchment Flood Management Plan;
- The Flood Defense Medium and Long-term Plan;
- The Flood Defense Asset Management Plan;
- The Water Level Management Plans;
- The Ribble Estuary Study;
- The Shoreline Management Plan;
- The Douglas Catchment Abstraction Management Strategy; and
- The North West Water Resources Strategy.

There is further planning that takes place outside the Environment Agency:

- The Yorkshire Water Business Plan (2005-2010);
- United Utilities Water Business Plan (2005-2010);
- Yorkshire and Humberside Biodiversity Action Plan;
- North West Biodiversity Audit;
- Yorkshire Dales Biodiversity Action Plan;
- Lancashire Biodiversity Action Plan;
- Regional Planning Guidance;
- Regional Sustainability Plan;
- Local Authority Plans; and
- County Authority Plans. *Id.*

Environment Agency. An Environment Agency project team and a team leader were established to coordinate the pilot. During the pilot, various means of public participation were tested including:

- A stakeholder forum (a group of key stakeholders who are brought together to advise the agency on a regular basis);
- Meetings in person;
- Presentations;
- Scenarios-vision building (meeting with a small number of participants to deepen insights and to devise possible solutions);
- Expert meetings;
- Websites as communicative devices;
- Electronic newsletter; and
- Perception studies and surveys (about 1,000 households were surveyed to identify citizens values, perceptions, and interests in getting involved in river basin planning).[103]

The agency identified four types of stakeholder groups that must be involved directly in the management of a catchment. The groups are those who create direct impacts (industry), contribute indirectly to causing impacts (water users), are responsible for reducing impacts (local government), and have an interest in water protection (environmental NGOs).[104]

Based on the above, a questionnaire was developed that was sent to all stakeholders to identify their interests and desired level of involvement in the river basin. Contrary to what may have been expected given the emphasis on public participation most stakeholders were interested in getting information and being consulted about water management. The perception that water management is in good shape and, that public intervention holds no additional benefits may explain why fewer stakeholders favored active participation instead of consultation.

The stakeholder forum was one method of participation experimented with at the Ribble catchment. Key stakeholders (codeliverers) were invited to participate in the forum. The forum was comprised of twenty-five representatives of different stakeholders. The idea behind the forum was to streamline the work of the agency since many groups that

[103] *Id.*
[104] *Id.*

were interested in different aspects of the WFD had been involved in different consultation meetings and activities, resulting in duplication of effort. The forum became the device that would organize under one roof the various groups, consultations, and meetings that used to run in parallel.

The forum and the way it was run have been considered innovative and an effective means of involving stakeholders in the decisionmaking process. An issue that initially marred the forum was the lack of participation by agricultural interests, a deficiency that was rectified later.[105] The lack of participation by minority groups has been more difficult to address and could undermine the legitimacy of the stakeholder forum, given that the Ribble catchment is located in an area where many minority groups reside. The dilemma for the Environment Agency was whether to undertake what could be viewed as social engineering in cultivating and supporting the formation of groups that would participate in the process. Such an undertaking would contradict the idea of public participation as a grass-roots, bottom-up initiation process. The agency decided not to play the role of social engineer and, although it provided information, chose not to get actively involved in the organization of potentially interested parties.

The stakeholder forum was divided further into issue groups. The decision to break up the work of the forum and establish two issue groups had to do with the number and variety of issues that have to be addressed under the WFD. The agency is well aware of what has been called *participation fatigue*, which is prevalent among stakeholders who attend meetings irrelevant to them and to which they cannot contribute. Because the agency is mindful that meetings have to be considered relevant to encourage and maintain stakeholder involvement, it runs practice sessions before the first stakeholder forum. In these practice sessions, the agency deliberates on what has to be accomplished at the stakeholder forum.

Based on the observation of an issue group's deliberations in 2006, issue groups seem to work reasonably well given the amount of information that is disseminated, absorbed, and commented on during their meetings.[106]

---

105 M. Davis and Y. Rees, *Public Participation in the Ribble River Basin,* Case study report produced under Workpackage 5 of the HarmoniCOP project, Nov. 2004. The HarmoniCOP project was prepared under a contract with the European Commission, Contract No. EVK1-CT-2002-00120. More information on the HarmoniCOP project is available online http://www.harmonicop.uos.de/index.php.

106 The following discussion is based on the author's observation of the deliberations of the Water Resources Group that occurred on February 15, 2006.

The work format of these issue groups seems to be as follows: The agency makes a short presentation on the issues for which a stakeholder consultation is requested. Then, the issue group breaks into discussion subgroups. The presentations made by the agency during the 2006 meeting seemed to focus on the issues, and avoid the use of overly technical jargon. The discussion in the subgroups, however, was much less focused and more like a brainstorming session on the various issues arising from the implementation of the WFD. This is probably true for most stakeholder meetings, and the challenge for the agency is to keep stakeholders focused on the issues at hand without making the process too stifling.

Most of stakeholders who attended the Water Resources Issue Group in February 2006 were satisfied with how the meeting was run. They were pleased that the meeting started on time, the agency did not waste their time, and the presentation of the issues by the agency was clear and concise. Most stakeholders did not have specific expectations of what they would get out of the meeting. They viewed the meeting, instead, as a part of a continuing process of consultation and dialogue with the agency. On the other hand, according to some stakeholders, the agency wanted the meeting to provide confirmation that it was on the right track and guidelines for how to proceed in the future.

It is unclear whether the specific meeting provided the agency with guidelines for how to proceed in the future. Nevertheless, the meeting allowed stakeholders to express their appreciation for the agency's work, confirming that it was on the right track. Thus, in terms of stakeholder satisfaction, the meeting was a success because stakeholders were appreciative that they were involved in the process and their opinions were heard. Whether the stakeholder consultation will contribute to better decisionmaking by the agency is unclear and cannot be possibly deciphered from a single meeting. As most stakeholders mentioned, this is a continuing process of dialogue and consultation; impact must be assessed based on the entire process, not a single meeting.

It must be underlined at this juncture that most stakeholders who participated in the February 2006 meeting had a long-term involvement in the public sector in various capacities. Sometimes, there was a feeling that the agency was preaching to the converted and that more outreach efforts should be initiated to involve, for instance, the mayors of municipalities who, as elected officials, can be disinclined to consult with others on the soundness of their decisions.

Another outcome of the Ribble Pilot project that is considered important in building the stakeholder base is the development of a vision for the river basin. The Vision for the Ribble Basin was adopted through a process of broad consultation with a variety of stakeholders. Many stakeholders have endorsed the vision because of its inclusive language. The vision addresses the issues arising from the Ribble catchment that emanate from various water uses and attempts to place such uses in a coherent framework based on environmental protection.[107]

The cover page of the vision includes the logo of the United Kingdom Environment Agency and the World Wildlife Fund (WWF). The inclusion of the WWF panda logo is somewhat startling and raises a question about why the WWF logo, rather than that of other stakeholders, was used. The inclusion of the WWF logo may solidify perceptions that the agency, because of its function to protect the environment, is a captive of environmental NGOs. On the other hand, the agency, by announcing its affinity with environmental interests, is forced to adopt a more evenhanded approach toward all interests and avoid the uncritical endorsement of positions proposed by environmental groups. Probably, many groups[108] endorsed the vision because there is little risk in a vague statement that nevertheless establishes one as an actor in the water management of the catchment area. The compilation of the vision may have assisted stakeholders in understanding the plurality and complexity of interests involved in the basin and the tradeoffs that are necessary to effectuate water management.

In accordance with the timetable provided by the WFD, the Ribble Integrated Management Plan has been issued for consultation. The plan contains proposals on how the agency plans to address various issues in the Ribble catchment. After the consultation period is over, and taking into account its process, the agency plans to issue the final Ribble Integrated Catchment Management Plan. This integrated plan eliminates the need to develop separate Catchment Abstraction Management Strategies (CAMS), Catchment Flood Management Plans (CFMPs), and Fisheries Action Plans (FAPs).

The experience with the Ribble Pilot has been used by the environment agency to build a framework for stakeholder engagement. Some of

---

[107] *A Vision for the Ribble Basin* (UK Environment Agency, no date).

[108] Including United Utilities, the Westinghouse UK Fuel Business (BNFL) and the National Farmers Union.

the principles that the agency applies in its interaction with stakeholders include:

- Early engagement;
- Provision of clear information;
- Transparency of its work so that others can contribute;
- Listening to others and understanding their needs; and
- Provision of opportunities for involvement so as to make efficient use of the time and resources of stakeholders allowing them to have an effective input.

A number of the principles of active stakeholder involvement that have been developed were the result of a conference held in Bolton (UK) in 2004. These Bolton principles, as they have been called, are ambitious and underline broadly the elements of active involvement. Their operationalization on the ground, however, will not be easy.[109]

In terms of providing information, the environment agency's website is quite informative about what is transpiring in river basin management all across the country. Through the website, the agency is to provide detailed information on specific water bodies based on postcodes through the agency's "What's in my Backyard" pages. Although the internet is a prominent feature in the agency's strategies, more formal tools are also used, including brochures and newsletters that are available in local libraries, local government bodies, and other locations in a river basin district.[110]

---

[109] The Bolton Principles are the following: Good investment takes time, start early!; Develop and share a sense of ownership of the river basin; Work to build and maintain trust with your partners; Undertake "mapping" of stakeholders to find out more about them and their interests; Learning from mistakes is as important as sharing successes; Listening is as important as talking; Be passionate about your cause, passion persuades; Work with each other and build a common vision for your basin, to put the management plan into context; Nobody can do it alone. True partnership leads to shared responsibility and decisionmaking for shared actions; Where cultures and traditions vary, agree on key messages and adapt to their needs. *See Principles of Active Involvement in River Basin Management agreed at the Ripple Effect Conference*, Bolton, Oct. 14, 2004.

[110] *See* para. 46, *Water for Life and Livelihoods: A Strategy for River Basin Planning—A Framework for Stakeholder Engagement* (U.K. Environment Agency, Jan. 2005) [hereinafter *Water for Life*]. This was a draft strategy that was published on the UK Environment Agency website in order to elicit responses from stakeholders. The consultation website of the agency attracted 7,000 visits and the agency received a total of 127 responses. The consultation process lasted three months starting from January 31, 2005 to April 29, 2005. *See also Water for Life and Livelihoods—A Framework for River Basin Planning in England and Wales*, Feb. 2006, http://publications.environment-agency.gov.uk/pdf/GEHO0506BKVX-e-e.pdf.

As mentioned above, easily accessible information is as important as the right to participation in river basin management.

The agency has established four scales for participation in river basin management: The National Scale, the River Basin Scale (the EU reporting unit), the Catchment Scale and the water body.[111] Given these different scales of stakeholder involvement, the following approaches are proposed:

- At the National Level the (Department for Environment, Food and Rural Affairs) DEFRA Stakeholder Group should continue to function.
- At the River Basin District Level, Liaison Panels are envisioned comprised of various organized interests at that level.
- At the Catchment Level, existing formal and informal networks could be used.
- At the Water Body Level, existing activities and networks should be allowed to function.[112]

What is interesting in this proposed model of public participation is the combination of formal and informal channels. At the national and river basin district levels, public participation is formal, but becomes less so at the catchment and water body levels. It is essential to allow for some level of informality so that public participation is tailored to concerns and issues as they are encountered in specific catchments and water bodies. Another interesting element is the interventionist role that the agency designates for itself. The environment agency may bring groups and organizations together to help them with elements of river basin planning. It is prescribed further that the environment agency should build upon the various dynamic but often fragmented processes that exist at the local level.[113]

At Catchment and water body level, there are existing networks that provide an effective mechanism for involving many stakeholders in river basin management. The Environment Agency should where possible build on these dynamic but sometimes fragmented processes, to increase understanding and develop capacities to manage water environments.

---

111 Para. 20, *Water for Life*, *id.*

112 Paras. 23–24, *id.*

113 Para. 23, *id.*

The Environment Agency should take a risk-based approach to involving local communities and individuals, matching our action to the degree of concern in different locations about particular problems.[114]

The liaison panels at the river basin level are considered codeliverers in the implementation of the WFD. A liaison panel should not exceed fifteen members and should include various government authorities, water users, and other interests. Authorities included in a liaison panel could be drawn from a number of authorities responsible for water management in a district—including regional authorities, forestry commissions, highway agencies, harbors and port authorities, and water companies. Nine of the fifteen seats on a liaison panel are to be distributed among statutory bodies—that is, bodies that have the authority and resources to effectuate public policy in water management. The remaining six seats could be occupied by various water users, including environmental NGOs. An indicative composition of a panel includes a representative of the following institutions: the environment agency, the regional government office, the regional assembly, the regional development agency, and the water company. Other representatives include a representative from agriculture, a representative from industry, a representative of Natural England, a representative of an environmental NGO, and a representative of the consumer council of water.[115]

Environmental groups are concerned about the structure of liaison panels. Their concern is the composition of panels in which environmental groups hold but one seat. Environmental groups fear that their contributions will be overwhelmed by water users and the statutory authorities that participate in the panels.[116] Environmental NGOs would have preferred a more spontaneous mode of participation in which voluntary and community sectors are guaranteed meaningful participation, for instance, by making decisions on how resources in water management are to be allocated.

---

[114] *Id.*

[115] Daniel Bond, *Developing a River Basin Plan for the Ribble Catchment: Lessons Learnt and Future Direction* 107, in Proceedings of International Conference Implementing the European Union Water Framework Directive: Towards Integrated Water Management in Europe, May 12, 2006, Athens (DG Environment, European Commission, Technical Report-2007-021, Elli Louka, ed., 2007).

[116] Tom Le Quesne and Colin Green, *Can we afford not to? The costs and benefits of a partnership approach to the Water Framework Directive,* at 9 (Aug. 2005) available online http://www.wwf.org.uk/filelibrary/pdf/canweaffordnotto.pdf.

Environmental groups seem to be more in favor developing a forum or a committee in which different interests are openly played out, rather than a consultation model in which the agency listens to the concerns of interested parties and then goes behind closed doors to form its decisions. Open stakeholder fora are preferable to consultation panels not only because of the relationships they foster between the agency and stakeholders but also because of the potential dialogue they could propel among various stakeholders. Stakeholders who are involved in a forum in which decisions on water management are made through repeated cycles of policy making are more likely to make concessions in one cycle in order to obtain advantages in others.[117]

For participation at the catchment level, the agency mentions the possibility of working with River Trusts and Coastal Fora and establishing stakeholder fora similar to the forum developed in the Ribble Pilot.[118] At the local level, as mentioned above, the agency may assume a more interventionist role. For instance, if local networks do not exist or groups disagree with each other, the agency proposes the provision of supportive mechanisms, especially for organizations that do not have much expertise in river basin management.[119]

It is not sufficient to establish different levels of water management and public participation mechanisms to serve each level. It is equally important to provide linkages and feedback loops between the different scales of water management. Concerns at the local or catchment level should feed back to the river basin district and the national levels. The agency has prescribed that the river basin management plans designed at the river basin district level will be strategic in nature and will be supported by catchment frameworks. The development of catchment frameworks and river basin management plans is not viewed as a sequential process in which the catchment frameworks are developed first and feed into the river basin management plan. On the contrary, the whole process is envisioned as a parallel, iterative process.[120] The agency must ensure that a bottom-up and a top-down approach is applied so that the strategic

117 *See generally* Robert Axelrod, *The Evolution of Cooperation* (1984).
118 Para. 24, *Water for Life, supra* note 110.
119 *Id.*
120 Para. 32, *id.*

guidance provided in the river basin management plan and the knowledge generated at the catchment level feed one another.[121] This can be accomplished partially by having the liaison panels attend some meetings of stakeholders at the catchment level and getting, thus, a direct view of the issues that preoccupy stakeholders.[122] Catchment frameworks are expected to be the "basic building block" for river basin planning, and most planning for water management is to be executed at the catchment level.[123]

In developing an iterative, parallel process of river basin management, the question is how such a process can be applied in practice and the level of coordination required to effectuate it. River basin management can be attuned to a parallel process as catchment plans are developed, providing feedback for the river basin management plans. At the same time, however, river basin management plans provide strategic direction for the compilation of catchment plans. A parallel process would require constant feedback between the strategic level (river basin management plan) and the operational level (catchment plan). The management of this constant feedback loop could be a challenge.

Another challenge that faces the implementation of the WFD in the UK is the integration of a high number of issue-specific plans into the river basin management plan. It is estimated at this point that there are more than fifty issue-specific plans (in some cases, over a hundred plans) that are done at different levels and are based on different geographic boundaries.[124]

Participatory rulemaking is here to stay. A number of participative processes focus on involving the general public through a hybrid model of

---

121 Para. 33, *id.*

122 *Id.*

123 Para. 34, *id.*

124 *See Water for Life and Livelihoods: A Strategy for River Basin Planning—A Consultation* (UK Environment Agency, 2005).
Such plans include:

- Catchment Abstraction Management Strategies (licensing water abstraction to balance the needs of water users);
- Fisheries Action Plans (developed in partnership between the Environment Agency and local angling and fisheries groups);
- Local Development Frameworks and Plans;
- Rural Development Programs;
- Water Level Management Plans (such plans provide a means by which water requirements for a range of activities including agriculture, flood defense and conservation can be balanced and integrated).

functional and representative democracy or through more spontaneous and direct methods of participation. Other participatory processes maintain their role as extended forms of corporatism with little innovation. A participatory process may increase the legitimacy of decisionmaking if the river basin institutions remain evenhanded towards various stakeholders involved in river basin management. Open and transparent conditions could guarantee such evenhandedness. The provision of information is important since information can be used beyond regulatory proceedings to effectuate change through new communication channels in the broader sociopolitical reality.

Part Four

International Institutions for Water Management

Chapter 16

Instruments for Transboundary Water Management

Setting the Foundations of Water Management in Europe

Integrated water management at the trans-European level consists in essence of the implementation of the water framework directive (WFD). The directive, however, is not an isolated regional development. It is, instead, the culmination of processes of European Union (EU) initiatives, international agreements, and evolving regimes whose ultimate ambition is to establish a system for the management and protection of water resources in Europe.

Internationally, this process has been put into motion with the adoption of the 1992 UNECE Helsinki Convention on the Protection and Use of Transboundary Watercourses and International Lakes (the Helsinki Convention). The purpose of the Helsinki Convention is to address water quality as it affects shared watercourses of states.[1] In the region covered by

1 *Convention on the Protection and Use of Transboundary Watercourses and International Lakes*, Mar. 17, 1992 available online http://www.unece.org/env/water/text/text.htm [hereinafter Helsinki Convention]. *See also* Protocol on Water and Health to the 1992 Convention on the Protection and Use of Transboundary Watercourses and International Lakes, June 17, 1999 available online http://www.unece.org/env/water/text/text_protocol.htm.

the convention (the UNECE region), more than a hundred and fifty major rivers and fifty lakes are transboundary.[2] The convention encourages states to cooperate and establish joint bodies, monitoring systems, and information and consultation mechanisms to address the transboundary aspects of watercourse management.[3] The Helsinki Convention focuses primarily on issues of water quality since issues of water quantity appear to be tractable in the UNECE region. The convention, however, sporadically refers to the basic premises of reasonable and equitable sharing of transboundary waters. The convention provides that state parties shall take the appropriate measures to ensure that transboundary waters are used in a reasonable and equitable way especially in the case of activities that are likely to have transboundary impacts.[4] Furthermore, states are to take appropriate measures to:

- Prevent, control, and reduce water pollution that is likely to have transboundary impacts;
- Ensure that transboundary waters are used with the goal of ecologically sound and rational water management, conservation of water resources, and environmental protection;
- Ensure conservation and restoration of ecosystems.[5]

In the course of their actions on transboundary waters, states must adopt the precautionary principle that dictates that action to avoid the potentially transboundary impacts of the release of hazardous substances is not to be postponed on the ground that scientific research has not fully established a causal link between the hazardous substances and the potential transboundary impact.[6]

The precautionary approach was adopted at the Rio Conference on Environment and Development[7] as a milder version of the precautionary

---

2 *See* website United Nations Economic Commission for Europe (UNECE) http://www.unece.org/env/water/text/text.htm.

3 *See* arts. 9, 10, 11 & 13, Helsinki Convention, *supra* note 1.

4 Art. 2(2)(c), *id.*

5 Art. 2(2), *id.*

6 Art. 2(5)(a), *id.*

7 *United Nations Conference on Environment and Development (Earth Summit)*, June 3–June 14, 1992. During the Rio Conference, the Rio Declaration on Environment and Development was adopted. Principle 15 of the Rio Declaration articulates the precautionary approach according to which when there are threats of serious or irreversible damage, lack of full scientific certainty should not be used as a reason for postponing cost-effective action to prevent

principle. The precautionary principle could be characterized as the backlash to an attitude that exploited the absence of scientific certainty to postpone taking action on environmental matters. Environmental issues are scientific issues and scientists often disagree on the effects of a polluting substance on the environment. One good example is climate change, which has generated acrimony in international circles about whether greenhouse gases generated by human activities could potentially have adverse effects on climate. Although scientific certainty is firmer now, action is still lagging behind as countries are weighing the costs of mitigation.[8] Chemical substances often present problems for scientists who try to determine whether their release into the environment will affect public health and the ecosystems. In the past, the lack of scientific certainty, in combination with a belief in the absorbing capacity of the environment, allowed for the discharge of many hazardous substances into the environment. The idea behind the precautionary principle is to reverse the burden of proof and ensure that action is taken even though there is no "fully proven link" between a hazardous substance and a potentially transboundary impact.

The Helsinki Convention adopts the polluter-pays principle that mandates that the costs of pollution prevention, control, and reduction are borne by the polluter.[9] This principle seems to vindicate those who view themselves as victims of pollution. Nevertheless, how much any given polluter pays for pollution control depends on its ability to pass the costs on the consumer. A number of industries, for instance, the oil industry, are monopolistic, and, therefore, can pass many of the costs of pollution reduction to the consumer.

To address pollution state parties are to take specific measures including:

- Reduction of pollution at the source through the application of low- and no-waste technology;

environmental degradation. *See Rio Declaration on Environment and Development*, June 13, 1992, reprinted 13 ILM 876 (1992).

8 *See*, e.g., *Intergovernmental Panel on Climate Change (IPCC), Climate Change 2001: The Scientific Basis* (2001). *See also* IPCC, *Climate Change 2007: The Physical Science Basis—Summary for Policymakers*, Feb. 2007 available online http://www.ipcc.ch/SPM2feb07.pdf. *But see also* Joseph J. Romm, *Hell and High Water: Global Warming—the Solution and the Politics—and What We Should Do* (2006).

9 Art. 2(5)(b), *Helsinki Convention, supra* note 1.

- Measures to address pollution from point sources through licensing of wastewater discharges and through monitoring and controlling authorized discharges;
- Best available technology to determine the limits on wastewater discharges;
- Stricter requirements when a receiving water or ecosystem makes necessary such requirements;
- Biological treatment or an equivalent treatment for municipal wastewater, in a step-by-step approach;
- Best available technology in order to reduce nutrient inputs from industrial and municipal sources;
- Best environmental practices to reduce inputs of nutrients and hazardous substances from diffuse sources of pollution and, especially, agriculture;
- Environmental impact assessment;
- Sustainable water management including the ecosystems approach;
- Contingency planning;
- Measures to prevent the pollution of groundwater;
- Measures to ensure that the risk of accidental pollution is minimized.[10]

In order to realize these specific pollution control measures, parties are to establish programs that would monitor the conditions of transboundary waters,[11] are to engage in research[12] and development, and the exchange of information.[13]

The Helsinki Convention requests that state parties enter into bilateral and multilateral agreements or arrangements on the basis of equality and reciprocity specifying the catchment area of cooperation.[14] These agreements or arrangements must provide for the establishment of joint bodies. Joint bodies are to address all issues covered by the convention, including the collection of data on the sources of pollution, the elaboration of joint monitoring programs, environmental standards for the discharges

---

10 Art. 3(1), *id.*
11 Art. 4, *id.*
12 Art. 5, *id.*
13 Art. 6, *id.*
14 Art. 9(1), *id*

of hazardous substances, and the establishment of warning and alarm procedures.[15]

The convention, echoing the spirit of its time, requires for the provision of information to the public on the conditions of transboundary waters, the measures taken to control pollution, and the effectiveness of such measures. According to the convention, the contracting parties must ensure that information is made available to the public on:

- Water quality objectives;
- Permits issued to allow discharges and conditions that must be met for issuing permits; and
- The results of monitoring and assessment of water quality.[16]

State parties must ensure that information is available to the public at all reasonable times, free of charge, and they must provide the public with reasonable facilities for obtaining copies of information on the payment of reasonable charges.[17] There are caveats to the provision of information since providing information to the public shall not affect the obligations of state parties to protect information related to industrial and commercial secrecy, including intellectual property and national security.[18] This is a wide exception to the provision of information but such exceptions are common if national and international instruments require the provision of information to the public. How frequently these exceptions are used is a test of how democratic a state or a polity really is.

Basic Premises of Global Water Management

Although the Helsinki Convention primarily addresses issues of water quality, the Convention on the Non-Navigational Uses of International Watercourses adopted under the auspices of the United Nations (UN) addresses issues of water quantity and quality.[19] Although water quality has preoccupied European countries, many countries of the developing

15 Art. 9(2), *id.*
16 Art. 16(1), *id.*
17 Art. 16(2), *id.*
18 Art. 8, *id.*
19 *Convention on the Law of the Non-navigational Uses of International Watercourses*, May 21, 1997, reprinted in 36 ILM 700 (1997) [hereinafter *Watercourse Convention*]. For an analysis of the convention, *see* Elli Louka, *International Environmental Law: Fairness, Effectiveness and*

world struggle with issues of water quantity—that is, how to share water that crosses national frontiers in an equitable manner.

Four doctrines have been proposed for the sharing of transboundary water resources:

(1) Absolute territorial sovereignty–An upstream state can manipulate water resources within its frontiers without regard to the concerns of downstream states.
(2) Absolute territory integrity–An upstream state can do nothing to affect the natural flow of water resources downstream.
(3) Limited territorial sovereignty (or obligation not to cause significant harm)–States can use transboundary water resources provided that no significant harm is caused downstream.
(4) Community of interests and equitable use–Concepts developed in some of the early decisions of international courts[20] are now incorporated in the 1997 Watercourse Convention. These concepts derive from the hydrological unity of a watercourse and point to a variety of factors that must be taken into account, given the community of coriparians, when deciding on a fair allocation of water resources.[21]

The 1997 Watercourse Convention is a framework convention that is to be used by states to guide regional and bilateral arrangements and agreements for the sharing and protection of water resources. Article 6 of the convention provides that state parties must take the following nonexhaustive considerations into account when deciding on the reasonable and equitable use of water resources:

- The geographic, hydrographic, hydrological, climatic, ecological and other factors of natural character;
- The social and economic needs of states concerned;

World Order 188 (2006). *See also* Stephen C. McCaffrey, *The Law of International Watercourses: Non-Navigational Uses* (2001).

20 *Territorial Jurisdiction of the International Commission of the River Oder,* (Denmark, Czechoslovakia, France, Germany, the UK and Sweden v. Poland), Sept. 10, 1929, (1929) PCIJ Series A, No. 23. *See also* Diversion of Water from the Meuse, (*Netherlands v. Belgium*), June 28, 1937, (1937) PCIJ Series A/B, No. 70.

21 Louka, *supra* note 19, at 173 (and annotated bibliography).

- The population dependent on the watercourse in each watercourse state;
- Effects of use of a watercourse by one state on other states;
- The existing and potential uses of a watercourse;
- Conservation, protection, development, and economy of the use of waters and the costs of measures taken;
- Availability of alternatives, of comparable value, to a particular planned and existing use.[22]

According to the convention, the weight given to each of these factors must be determined by its importance in comparison with the other factors. To determine what constitutes equitable use, all relevant factors must be taken into account, and a conclusion must be reached on the basis of the whole.[23]

In addition to the requirement of reasonable and equitable use of water resources, the convention provides for the obligation not to cause significant harm. States, when utilizing a watercourse located in their territories, must take all appropriate measures to "prevent the causing of significant harm to other watercourse States."[24] If significant harm is caused to other watercourse states, the state whose use caused such harm, in the absence of an agreement on such use, must take all appropriate measures in consultation with the affected states to eliminate or mitigate such harm and to discuss issues of compensation.[25]

The number of factors to be taken into account for the equitable use of watercourses and the fact that the convention does not attach weights to these factors have frustrated policymakers who are trying to apply the convention in various regional contexts. The obligation not to cause significant harm adds another layer of complexity because it is difficult to determine the threshold of significant harm is such that a victim state is entitled to the elimination or mitigation of harm or even compensation. Despite the conceptual complexity, the requirement not to cause significant harm and the principle of equitable use are repeated in many regional agreements addressing the apportionment of water resources.

22 Art. 6(1), *UN Watercourse Convention, supra* note 19.
23 Art. 6(3), *id.*
24 Art. 7(1), *id.*
25 Art. 7(2), *id.*

The distribution of water resources has been governed by heavy-handed politics, according to which might often makes right. The Nile River basin is a case in point because Egypt is using its historical entitlement to the river to prevent any additional use upstream. The situation has crippled the development of many upstream states that often engage in clandestine diversions of water.[26] By proposing the equitable use of a watercourse, the convention is aspiring to put forward considerations of justice in the international context, a context in which justice has found often self-serving interpretations.

The rest of the convention focuses on the provision of information, notification, and consultation if a state plans a measure on a watercourse (i.e., a dam) that may have possible adverse effects on other states.[27] The mechanics of the notification procedure are analyzed in detail in the convention. The state that notifies must provide all available technical data and information, including the results of an environmental impact assessment, in order to enable notified states to understand the possible effects of planned measures on the river.[28] The watercourse state that provides notification must allow the notified state a period of six months within which the notified state must evaluate the possible effects of planned measures.[29] The notifying state must provide additional information if the notified state so requires and shall not implement the planned measures without the consent of the notified state.[30] The notified state must reply to the notifying state and if it finds that the planned measures are inconsistent with the principles of no harm or equitable use, it must attach a documented explanation to its reply providing the reasons for that finding.[31] The convention provides what to do in the absence of notification[32] or in the absence of reply to a notification.[33] The convention provides for consultations and negotiations on the planned measures[34] and what to do in case there is an urgent need to implement planned measures.[35]

---

[26] For the Nile river basin agreements, *see Louka, supra* note 19, at 193 (and annotated bibliography).

[27] Art. 12, *UN Watercourse Convention, supra* note 19.

[28] *Id.*

[29] Art. 13, *id.*

[30] Art. 14, *id.*

[31] Art. 15, *id.*

[32] Art. 18, *id.*

[33] Art. 16, *id.*

[34] Art. 17, *id.*

[35] Art. 19, *id.*

To a third-party observer, not used to the world of international politics, the notification provisions seem reasonable. It makes sense that a state should notify other states if its use of a watercourse could have adverse effects on them. In practice, though, states are hesitant to notify other states because such notification may launch time-consuming consultations with other states. Consultations with other states often tend to be expensive and are likely to eventually avert unilateral development of a watercourse. States often claim that the threshold of significant adverse effects on other watercourse states has not been met[36] in order to avoid notifying and consulting with other states.

The convention provides further for the protection and preservation of ecosystems of watercourses[37] through the prevention, reduction, and control of pollution[38] and the protection and preservation of marine environment.[39] The convention also addresses emergency situations.[40]

Given pragmatics of international politics, one has to remain somber about the possibilities of equitable use in regions of the world where equity simply means the propping up of national interest. On the other hand, it is encouraging that many countries have entered into cooperative arrangements to share transboundary waters[41] and are finding it increasingly difficult to impose unilateral solutions on transboundary water use. It seems that states are realizing that being a rampaging hegemon has its benefits–but also its costs.

Multilateral and Bilateral Developments

A number of programs and initiatives have propelled developments in the field of integrated water management, such as intergovernmental conferences,[42] the UNESCO hydrological program,[43] and the World Bank's pursuit of integrated river basin management.[44] A plethora of regional

36 *See*, e.g., *Case Concerning Pulp Mills on the River Uruguay, (Argentina v. Uruguay)*, Provisional Measures, Jan. 23, 2007 available online http://www.icj-cij.org/docket/files/135/13615.pdf.

37 Art. 20, *Watercourse Convention, supra* note 19.

38 Arts. 21–25, *id.*

39 Art. 23, *id.*

40 Art. 28, *id.*

41 For a sample of international agreements, *see* Louka, *supra* note 19, at 192–239.

42 *See* Chapter 1, notes 66–69.

43 For more information about the program, *see* http://www.unesco.org/water/.

44 The World Bank has a number of publications on integrated water management and has engaged in projects and partnerships on IWRM, *see* http://go.worldbank.org/4ZEUZDAID0.

agreements establish management regimes for shared waters, usually through joint international commissions charged with regulating transboundary waters.[45] Agreements comprehensively addressing a river basin district as a hydrological entity, though, have not been very frequent.[46] Agreements that attempt to regulate the upstream/downstream relationship rarely refer to the principles of integrated water resources management (IWRM).[47] Most agreements repeat the principles of equitable and reasonable use of shared resources and the obligation not to cause significant harm to other coriparians through a state's planned development of a watercourse. The 1997 United Nations Watercourse Convention,[48] in its final draft, shied away from the notion of IWRM as countries were apprehensive that even mentioning such a term—that mandates the integrated of management of water and land use resources—could authorize an unacceptable interference with land-use management, a matter strictly under national sovereignty.

The sophistication of water management regimes and the level of development in a region are usually highly correlated. The WFD requires the establishment of international river basin districts and provides an extra motivating factor for the evolution of already established international regimes for water management in Europe. The Rhine River regime is a multilateral regime considered one of the most advanced river basin regimes in Europe. The regime owes its success to an active international commission. The Danube River regime, and the Scheldt and Meuse River regimes are relatively recent, but they have been quite accomplished in the amount of effort put into finding accommodations to common problems. Southeastern Europe, on the other hand, is not characterized by strong multilateral development. Even bilateral agreements are not adhered to, and some of them are becoming obsolete. There is a need to seriously rethink water management in the region in terms of collaboration of regional authorities that are becoming responsible for water management. Mutual wariness and a sense of déjà vu are still marring relationships in the region. Bilateral developments should move along because of the

[45] There are over 400 international freshwater agreements. For more information, *see* Transboundary Freshwater Dispute Database by Oregon State University, http://www.transboundarywaters.orst.edu.

[46] *See* Louka, *supra* note 19, at 185.

[47] *Id.*

[48] *See supra* note 19.

adoption of the WFD that renders cooperation mandatory, at least, among member states of the European Union (EU).

Multilateral developments in transboundary water management are often preceded by bilateral accords. These bilateral deals address the logistical issues of establishing a borderline, regulating floods, controlling localized pollution, and apportioning water resources. As multilateral agreements are acquiring a central role in regional settings, one may question the future of bilateralism. It could be claimed that the elaboration of comprehensive multilateral conventions will eventually render bilateral agreements obsolete as most issues can be addressed through the multilateral construct. But the invigoration of multilateralism could very well fuel more bilateralism. This is what is happening today as multilateralism and bilateralism are cross-pollinating each other. Although multilateral agreements address issues that affect all international partners, bilateral agreements zero in on the duo of states that wish to strengthen their relationship. Provided that there is coordination across the multilateral and the bilateral scale, multilateral and bilateral developments will be complementary.

Bilateral cooperation often takes place among similarly authorized government bodies—ministry-to-ministry, water agency-to-water agency, water directorate-to-water directorate, and even between similarly authorized municipalities. This type of trans-governmental cooperation is not a phenomenon witnessed only in the water sector. Cooperation among public institutions at the subnational level is frequently encountered in many international[49] and EU developments. The need to implement the WFD is strengthening transgovernment cooperation in Europe, as local authorities in charge of the operationalization of water management have to identify their counterparts in neighboring member states and work with them for joint implementation.

In addition to the multilateral/bilateral distinction, many parallel international developments have to be scoped out to make sense of multilateral regimes as they are evolving. The creation of an institution is often a matter of convergence of a number of historical and political imperatives. A new institution allows diverging actors to coordinate their activities in a number of domains to achieve common goals. Institutional

49 *See, e.g.*, Robert O. Keohane and Joseph S. Nye, *Transgovernmental Relations and International Organizations*, 27(1) World Politics 39 (1974); *See also* Anne-Marie Slaughter, *A New World Order* (2004).

evolution is somewhat unpredictable at the moment of institutional inception. Although an institutional mandate is provided, how this mandate will be shaped by future circumstances and the actions and reactions of various players is often a matter of conjecture for the initial crafters. Therefore, it is not unusual for countries to create a number of parallel institutions—institutions with slightly different configurations that address more or less similar matters. The more such parallel configurations are put in place, the more it is likely that goals spurned in one forum will find hospitable environment in another. Although parallel institutional development provides safeguards that goals will not be ignored, it could also lead to duplication of efforts with undesirable effects. Lean institutional development prevents duplication of effort but could be ineffective as certain institutions may falter or may be underused. Corpulent institutional development certainly leads to duplication but simultaneously increases the chances of goal fulfillment.[50]

Networking defines the internet. Networks are built as individuals or groups come up simultaneously with similar ideas. As these ideas are put on a network, they are picked up by a smart search engine and eventually "meet," creating further possibilities through a cross-fertilization unforeseeable to their originators. Those who support institutional networking assume that various parallel institutional developments eventually meet at some point in the future, stimulating further institutional evolution through their fusion. Networks certainly account for some of the reality of global institutional development. Parallelism, though, is also an enduring phenomenon either by design or serendipity.[51]

Although parallel institutional development is not a disadvantage at the international scale, it may be an impediment in regions that desire closer integration, such as the European region. In particular, parallel institutional development could undermine the purposes of IWRM, simply because of the number of institutions engaging in parallel activities who are either oblivious of each other or competing with each other. A large number of institutions addressing the same water resources could generate institutional veto players that may be reluctant to coordinate their activities under a lead institution charged with the mandate to coordinate IWRM. The case in point involves the international commissions

50 Louka, *supra* note 19, at 63–65.
51 *Id.*

that have been created for the protection of rivers and that have been designated platforms for the coordination of activities of the WFD implementation. For these commissions to assume a substantive coordinating role, they need to regulate the activities of other commissions and international bodies established for the management of waters in a river basin. Navigation commissions, older international bodies than river basin protection commissions, may be unwilling to be coordinated by a river basin protection commission. Similarly, other technical commissions, research bodies, or more locally based committees may be reluctant to go along with the prescriptions of IWRM. At this point, activities that take place at various international river basins do seem fragmented because there are no concrete coordination mechanisms between the commissions established for the protection of rivers and other bodies. In some cases, there are no concrete coordinating mechanisms between the multilateral river basin protection commission and more localized river basin committees addressing various issues of water quality and quantity at the transboundary level. Such concrete coordinating mechanisms need to be established to begin to envision IWRM in the European region.

Another characteristic of multilateral developments analyzed in this chapter is their consensual character. In a world where multilateral agreements are increasingly infused with compliance mechanisms,[52] the regimes examined in this chapter do not rely much on compliance procedures. The consensual character of the regimes, however, should not blind us to the implications the WFD could have for the evolution of the regimes, especially as infringement proceedings could be trigged for bad implementation by the European Commission. The threat of infringement proceedings can have serious reputation effects for member states considered leaders in EU environmental regulation. The challenge for these leaders, as they proceed with the WFD implementation, is not only to present a more than satisfactory national record of implementation, but also to be able to pull along the so-called laggards so as to ensure international river basin district cooperation. Success in implementation is still a matter of national compliance. But national compliance cannot be complete without multilateral engagement. Such affinity may become costly in regions characterized by different speeds of development, where those who lag behind have to be motivated to move forward.

---

[52] *Id.* at 114.

Chapter 17

Nineteen Countries One River: Trade-offs in the Management of the Danube River

Multiple Uses for a Shared River

The Danube River basin district is frequently referred to as one of the most international river basin districts. Many countries share the river district that covers a large part of the territory of central and southeastern Europe. Most countries in the district are members of the European Union (EU) (Austria, Czech Republic, Germany, Hungary, Slovakia, Slovenia, Bulgaria, and Romania), including accession countries (Croatia). Countries that do not belong to the EU (Moldova, Ukraine, Bosnia and Herzegovina, Serbia, and Montenegro) are involved in many treaties and initiatives that have taken place in the region. Certain countries have small parts of their territory within the district, such as Switzerland, Italy, Albania, the former Yugoslav Republic of Macedonia, and Poland.

The Danube has been used extensively since the sixteenth century for navigation and hydropower production. With the fall of the iron curtain, the improvement of navigation across the Danube River has been taken up with a new sense of urgency. Europe's choice for transportation is the road. The overuse of road transportation has created congested motorways and pollution. The European Commission (the Commission) has made it clear that inland navigation, a more benign and environmentally sound alternative to road transportation, should be sought after.[53] The Commission has developed Trans-European Transport Networks (TEN-T) and has plans to establish Pan-European road, rail, air and waterway transportation corridors. The TEN-T guidelines issued for 2003–2004 designated the Danube River as Pan-European Transport Corridor VII.[54] The idea is to administer a network of rivers that are to proffer a seamless connection between the North Sea and the Black Sea.[55] Navigation is more sustainable in terms of socioeconomic costs, such as accidents, air and noise pollution, climate change, and the effects on the countryside.[56] The EC is further funding river information services (RIS) to create a one-stop-shop for all information needs of cargo ships.[57]

Approximately 30 percent of the length of Danube River is used for hydropower generation. The total energy generation from all the hydropower facilities in the Danube River is 30,000 megawatts.[58] Future hydropower production is likely to have environmental impacts unless measures are undertaken to minimize them.[59] Plans to build more dams on the Danube River include dams on the Sava tributary and on the Drava tributary along the Croatian-Hungarian border. Dyke systems for the prevention of floods were constructed on the river quite early. Today more than four-fifths of the Danube River is regulated for flood protection.[60]

Navigation, hydropower generation, and flood prevention have caused a number of hydromorphological alterations along the Danube. Although some of these changes cannot be undone, there is potential of rehabilitation, especially with regard to reconnecting some of the tributary rivers to their floodplains. Because of the extent of hydromorphological

---

53 *See* Chapter 6 on DG Transport.

54 *See id.*

55 If one takes into consideration that an inland navigation vessel can move 127 tons of goods over one kilometer using one liter of fuel while rail can only transport 97 tons and road can transport 50 tons. *See Striking the Balance-Ships and the River, Danube Watch*, The Magazine of the Danube River/WWW.ICPDR.ORG, at 18, Issue 3/2005 [hereinafter *Danube Watch*].

56 *Id.*

57 *Id.*

58 Available online at the ICPDR website, http://www.icpdr.org/icpdr-pages/dams_structures htm#hydropower.

59 *The Danube River Basin District, Part A – Basin-wide overview, Danube Basin Analysis* (WFD Roof Report 2004), at 170 [hereinafter *Danube Roof Report*].

60 *See* ICPDR website, http://www.icpdr.org/icpdr-pages/dams_structures.htm.

alterations, large parts of the Danube River and various tributaries have been provisionally identified as heavily modified water bodies.

The Danube is subject to multiple pressures from diffuse sources of pollution, such as agriculture, and point sources of pollution, including industrial plants. Discharges of untreated wastewater from municipal plants undermine water quality. Municipalities generate around 60 percent of wastewater discharged into the Danube, most of which is not sufficiently treated.[61] As a result of various polluting discharges, the load of organic pollutants in the Danube is still high while some decrease has been recorded. The modernization and intensification of agriculture in the new member states of the EU may increase pollution that affects the Danube and the Black Sea, unless best agricultural practices are adopted.[62]

In addition to the nutrient pollution, the Danube is affected by a number of hazardous substances. Heavy metals (such as cadmium and lead) exceed their target values in many locations of the lower Danube. Pesticides are at high levels in some tributaries of the Danube River.[63] The chemical, food, pulp, and paper industries are among the worst polluting industries of the Danube River. Industry (including energy generation) and mining are important economic activities, but are simultaneously water-intensive. Many industries are undergoing major restructuring, however, and this is bound to reduce some of discharges into the Danube. Groundwater is overabstracted in many areas of the Danube River basin district, and nutrients and hazardous substances seep from the land into the groundwater undermining, thus, its quality.[64]

It is often claimed that a remedy for environmental problems is to make the polluter pay by introducing water pricing based on water use. Water pricing policies have been introduced, but they are not consistent across the countries that share the Danube River basin. Best practices for the economic use of water need to be further explored by the coriparians.[65]

61 *See* ICPDR website, http://www.icpdr.org/icpdr-pages/municipalities.htm.

62 *Danube Roof Report, supra* note 59,169.

63 *Id.* at 170.

64 *Id.* at 171.

65 *Id.*

Institutional Proliferation

Overall, the European policy for the Danube River is characterized by a number of initiatives that run parallel to each other. The Danube Cooperation Process, examined below, addresses several economic sectors including navigation. Other organizations that address navigation include the UNECE Inland Transport Committee,[66] and the European Commission (DG Transport) with its ambition to transform the Danube into Corridor VII for inland navigation.[67] The International Commission for the Protection of the Danube River (ICPDR) has to be the body geared to protect the Danube River from various pressures and impacts including navigation. A question worth asking is how to make a coherent policy out of ambitions to transform the Danube into a seamless waterway, given the implementation of the water framework directive (WFD) that puts a priority on restoring waters to good status. Navigation interests and environmental interests have yet to find a common ground in many countries of the Danube.[68] Although inland navigation is indisputably a more environmentally friendly means for the transfer of goods in Europe than road transport, how to regulate navigation in the Danube River has still to be ironed out. The riparian states of the Danube River have expressed unrequited support for the ICPDR. However, at the same time, they are strong supporters of uninhibited navigation all through the Danube that should improve their economic condition.

The coriparian countries of the Danube (as well as France, the Netherlands, and Turkey) issued a joint communiqué on July 3, 2006 on the 150th anniversary of the Danube Navigation Commission based on the adoption of 1856 Paris Peace Treaty and the establishment of the European Danube Commission, the first to regulate and oversee free international navigation on the lower Danube. The joint communiqué reiterated the support of coriparian states for the Pan-European Corridor VII and the

---

66 Information on the UNECE Inland Transport Committee available online http://www.unece.org/trans/main/itc/itc.html.

67 *See* Chapter 6 on DG Transport.

68 At a conference that took place in Galati Romania between June 27 and June 29, 2006, navigation specialists and environmental experts spent a lot of time discussing among themselves in separate halls. A joint session was held, however, under Philip Weller, Executive Secretary of the ICPDR. *See Conference on Past and Future in Establishing Institutions on Danube Cooperation*, Galati, Romania, June 27–29, 2006 available online http://www.ramsar.org/mtg/mtg_romania_galati_june2006.htm.

further development of inland navigation in Europe. The countries stressed that more emphasis should be placed on environmental aspects, including the protection of the fragile ecosystem of the Danube Delta. However, how protection and free navigation should proceed in the future still remains to be clarified as further cooperation is necessary between the Ministries of Transport and the Ministries of Environment of the respective countries as well as among pan-European associations that represent environmental and transport interests. Closer communication will also be required between the DG Transport and the DG Environment of the European Commission.

The 1948 Belgrade Convention that established the Danube (Navigation) Commission in its current form is to be amended in the future to reflect new realities and circumstances. It would be useful if such amendments provide more guidance on the conciliation between navigation and environmental restoration. It would be useful, also, if the ICPDR and the Danube (Navigation) Commission, in addition to acquiring observer status on each other's working groups, establish some practical modalities of interaction with each other, such as common policymaking meeting fora. A common policymaking process was initiated on April 25, 2007, with the goal to reach guiding principles and criteria for a Joint Statement on the Development of Inland Navigation and Environmental Sustainability in the Danube River Basin. The joint initiative was organized under the auspices of the ICPDR, the Danube (Navigation) Commission, and the International Commission for the Protection of the Sava River. The purpose of the initiative is to ensure that planned infrastructure projects related to navigation on the Danube are developed in an environmentally friendly manner, especially projects executed within the framework of the EU's Trans-European Transport Networks (TEN-T) program that are aimed to develop Danube into a major transportation corridor for cargo.[69] Over fifty stakeholders participate in the process including governments, the navigation sector, river basin managers, environmental nongovernmental organizations (NGOs), and the European Commission. On March 11, 2008 the first ever "Joint Statement on Guiding Principles for the Development of Inland Navigation and Environmental Protection in the Danube River Basin" was issued establishing the collaboration

[69] ICPDR Press Release, Apr. 25, 2007 available online http://www.icpdr.org/icpdr-pages/pr20070425_navigation_process.htm.

among the International Commission for the Protection of the Danube River (ICPDR,) the Danube Commission on Navigation and the International Sava River Basin Commission. These integrated planning principles include:

- the establishment of interdisciplinary planning teams involving key stakeholders;
- a transparent planning process;
- the completion of Strategic Environmental Assessment (SEA); and Environmental Impact Assessments (EIAs);
- respect for the Danube River Basin Management Plan which is to be ready in 2009;
- the use of best practice to improve navigation including assurances there is no technically viable, environmentally better and not disproportional costly alternative to achieve the required objective; and
- criteria for river engineering.

The Joint Statement offers specific examples on what an integrated planning philosophy to improve inland navigation and river system protection means by referring to the River Engineering Project on the Danube to the East of Vienna. As a follow up event the Danube (Navigation) Commission is to organize before the end of 2008 a special workshop on environmentally friendly river development and maintenance techniques for waterway administrations and navigation authorities in the Danube River basin.[70]

Danube Commission

One of the first multilateral conventions to regulate the Danube River was a navigation convention.[71] According to article 1 of that convention, "Navigation on the Danube shall be free and open" for the nationals, vessels of commerce, and goods of all states. Danubian states undertake the obligation to maintain their sections of the Danube in navigable condition, to perform the works necessary for the maintenance and improvement of

70 *Joint Statement on Guiding Principles for the Development of Inland Navigation and Environmental Protection in the Danube River Basin*, Mar. 11, 2008.

71 *Convention Regarding the Regime of Navigation on the Danube* (often referred to as Belgrade Convention*)*, Aug. 18, 1948 available online at the Transboundary Freshwater Dispute Database, http://ocid.nacse.org/tfdd/.

navigation conditions and not to obstruct navigation on the navigable channels of the Danube.[72] If a Danubian state is unable to undertake works on the Danube that are necessary for the maintenance of normal navigation, it is "bound to allow the Danube Commission" to perform these works "under the conditions determined by the Commission."[73] In that case, the commission must not entrust the execution of such works to another state unless the section of the waterway on which the works are to be performed forms the frontier with that state.[74] The Danubian states agree to afford the commission or the state that executes the works all the necessary assistance.[75]

The convention establishes the Danube Commission for the regulation and further development of navigation on the Danube River. The commission is comprised of one representative from each Danubian state.[76] The commission can prepare a general plan of principal works needed on the river for the facilitation of navigation. Such general plan is based on proposals and projects presented by state parties.[77] The commission is to draft the general budget for the completion of works on the Danube River.[78] The commission, in addition to its role as a supervisory body for the implementation of the convention,[79] is entrusted with the establishment of a uniform system of traffic regulations,[80] with the consolidation of regulations governing river inspections and the coordination of various hydrometeorological services.[81] The commission drafts its own budget that is approved by the majority vote of all states.[82] The commission is financed by equal contributions of all states paid annually.[83]

The commission does not have decisionmaking authority and its resolutions are recommendations not binding on states. Within the spirit of fostering the uninhibited navigation of the Danube, states are requested to enforce sanitary and police regulations without discriminating based

72 Art. 3, *id.*
73 Art. 4, *id.*
74 *Id.*
75 *Id.*
76 Art. 5, *id.*
77 Art. 8(b), *id.*
78 *Id.*
79 Art. 8(a), *id.*
80 Art. 8(f), *id.*
81 Art. 8(g)–(h), *id.*
82 Art. 10, *id.*
83 *Id.*

on the nationality of vessels, points of departure, or destination or any other matter. States are to inform the commission of regulations they issue so that the commission could promote the unification of customs and sanitary regulations as well as the rules governing ship inspection.[84]

The purpose of the Danube (Navigation) Convention is to establish a commission that would facilitate shipping and commerce in the Danube region. The convention, however, does not go far enough in providing the Danube Commission with exclusive jurisdiction in the promulgation of rules governing navigation. The convention provides explicitly that the regulation of navigation must be carried out in accordance with regulations established by respective Danubian states. In establishing these regulations, states "shall have regard" to the basic provisions on navigation issued by the Danube Commission, but they are not mandated to follow such provisions.[85] Furthermore, environmental regulations are not included in the convention because it was adopted in 1948 when environmental concerns were not prominent and because of the history that led to the adoption of the convention. The commission was established without the participation of Germany and Austria.[86] It was comprised of the rest of the riparian states that were, at that point, state-satellites of the Soviet Union, and of Soviet Union itself, and a nonriparian state. Although the commission was supposed to aid in free navigation, in reality what was established was a rather restrictive navigation regime. Through the 1955 so-called Bratislava agreements, concluded between the state-controlled eastern European national shipping companies, transport volume was divided between state parties and fixed tariffs were established.

Today, despite the political changes in the region, Russia still retains its seat on the Danube Commission even though it is not a riparian state. Furthermore, navigation on the Danube River was hampered in the 1990s due to regional conflict. Sanctions by the United Nations Security Council against the former Federal Republic of Yugoslavia and the bombing of some of the bridges of the river by the NATO allied forces led to a dramatic decrease in the volume of inland transport on the Danube River.

Today, there is a renewed interest in inland navigation, but in order to transform the Danube into a seamless corridor between the North Sea

84 Art. 26, *id.*
85 Art. 23, *id.*
86 Austria became a member of the Danube Commission in 1960. Germany became a full member in 1998 along with Croatia and Moldova.

and the Black Sea several so-called bottlenecks need to be removed. Removing bottlenecks entails digging at shallow locations of the river. In 1998, the Danube Commission adopted a minimum depth recommendation for the Danube River at 2.5 meters.[87] This is a nonobligatory recommendation, agreed to by the signatory states of the Danube Navigation Convention.[88] Because inland transport is being favored as an environmental friendly means for the transport of goods in Europe, countries are putting forward proposals to increase the minimum depth requirement so as to facilitate further navigation on the Danube River.[89]

According to a reported statement of the Consular for Public Relations at the Danube Commission, the Danube Commission is always in favor of having the Danube as deep as possible as long as no major problem is caused. This statement has been received unfavorably in environmental circles where it is maintained that the shallow portions of the Danube River are better off if they remain preserved as natural areas[90] and that further works on the river, on which is already heavy construction, should be undertaken with caution. It remains to be seen whether the new process that has been established between the ICPDR, the Danube Commission, and the Sava Commission will resolve the issue of environmental protection of the Danube and the promotion of navigation.[91]

It was mentioned in Chapter 6 that the European Commission is concerned with the institutional fragmentation of inland navigation since three regimes are *de facto,* in effect, for inland waterway transport in central and northern Europe. The Danube River regime is under the auspices of the Danube Commission, the Rhine Regime under the Central Commission for Navigation on the Rhine (CCNR), and the European Community system since the European Commission issues regulations for the integration of transport policy among member states. The fact that two commissions, namely, the Danube Commission and the CCNR, are regulating European waterways is particularly troubling because the Danube and the Rhine are now connected through the Rhine-Maine-Danube canal. The existence of two commissions could mean in practice that ships, as they

87 *Danube Watch, supra* note 55, at 19.
88 *Id.*
89 *Id.*
90 *Id.*
91 *See supra* note 69.

are crossing from the Danube to the Rhine may be subject to different regulations.

The Danube Commission and the CCNR have tried to coordinate their practices through the establishment of joint committees, but significant problems remain. One of them has to do with the fact that the decisions of the Danube (Navigation) Commission are not biding on state parties to the Danube Navigation Convention, while the decisions of the CCNR have a binding character. The fact that the decisions of the Danube Commission are not binding on Danubian states means that each state can issue its own mix of regulatory measures, further fragmenting the navigation regime of the Danube. Although it may be assumed that member states of the European Community (EC), that are simultaneously states parties to the Danube Navigation Convention, may be willing to streamline regulations along EU prerogatives, the same assumption does not necessary hold for Russia, Ukraine, and Moldova, who are not member states of the EU. At the point of writing, there are discussions to amend the Danube Navigation Convention. Amendments discussed include the creation of a council as the governing body of the Danube (Navigation) Commission and the possibility for that council to adopt binding decisions and recommendations. It addition, it has been proposed that a regional economic integration organization that has the competence to adopt its own legislation, with binding effects on its members, (i.e., the EU) could accede to the convention based on a decision of the council.[92] This will allow the EU to take actively part in shaping the regulatory framework in the region.

International Commission for the Protection of the Danube River

Countries sharing the Danube River have entered into bilateral agreements so as to regulate water quantity or address boundary issues. Bilateral agreements, though, often cannot, by their nature, address effectively issues of water quality, unless such issues are localized. Danube is a shared river among many countries and, therefore, it presents the collective action

92 *See* presentation of Dinescu Cosmin, *The Process of Revision of the 1948 Belgrade Convention regarding the Regime of Navigation on the Danube*, 5th IVR-Colloquium, Vienna, Jan. 27–28, 2005. The IVR is an international association representing the mutual interests of inland shipping and insurance and keeps the register of inland vessels in Europe. More information on IVR is available online http://www.ivr.nl.

problems associated with the sharing of common pool resources.[93] Even though some countries engage in efforts to clean up the Danube by limiting their discharges, their efforts could be frustrated by other countries that continue to pollute. A multilateral framework that will engage all states in the basin has been necessary to build a shared understanding and common expectations for the future management of the river.

The Danube River Protection Convention (DRPC)[94] was adopted in 1994 and entered into force in 1998. The objectives of the convention are quite broad and address not only water quality but also water quantity since floods are affecting the Danube region. According to the DRPC, state parties are to strive to achieve sustainable and equitable water management. Such management includes conservation, improvement, and the rational use of surface waters and groundwater. Parties must further engage in efforts to control accidents that involve hazardous substances, floods, and ice hazards.[95] Parties must try to reduce pollution loads in the Black Sea.[96] Article 3 further details the activities likely to have transboundary impacts, such as wastewater discharges, the construction of waterworks, the operation of hydrotechnical constructions, and the handling of hazardous substances.[97]

The convention applies to fisheries and inland navigation only regarding the protection of water against pollution caused by these activities[98]—leaving the general management of these activities to other bodies. In the case of navigation, such a body is the Danube Navigation Commission. The adoption of the WFD, though, establishes as a parameter of good water status, the extent of hydromorphological alterations of a water body. This, in combination with the fact that the ICPDR has been

---

93 *See generally* Louka, *supra* note 19, at 78–81. *See also The Drama of the Commons* (Elinor Ostrom *et al.*, eds., 2003).

94 *Convention on Cooperation for the Protection and Sustainable Use of the Danube River (Danube River Protection Convention* [hereinafter *DRPC*]), June 29, 1994 available online at http://www.icpdr.org/icpdr-pages/drpc.htm.

95 Art. 2(1), *id.*

96 *Id.*

97 Art. 3(2), *id.*

98 Art. 3(3), *id.* However, given the doctrine of *implied powers* of international organizations and the role granted to international commissions due to the implementation of the WFD, the role of international river commissions cannot be restricted to pollution matters and should be extended to all activities that have adverse impacts on the ecology of rivers. On the implied powers doctrine, *see* Certain Expenses of the United Nations, Advisory Opinion, July 20, 1962, (1962) I.C.J. Reports 151. *See generally* José E. Alvarez, International Organizations As Law-makers (2006).

established as an international platform for the WFD implementation, challenges an interpretation of the convention according to which the regulatory ambit of the ICPDR is restricted to pollution and does not extend to hydromorphological alterations of the river. One would expect, therefore, to witness shoulder-to-shoulder cooperation, not only coordination, between the Danube Navigation Commission and the ICPDR in deciding on alterations that are necessary to transform Danube into Corridor VII. Cooperation, however, may be frustrated as some state parties to the Danube Navigation Convention are not members of the ICPDR and because the conciliation of growth and ecological restoration is not an easy task.

The best available technique and best environmental practice[99] as well as the "polluter pays" and precautionary principles are endorsed in the DRPC.[100] The DRPC further includes the sectors of the economy and a guiding list of hazardous substances that adversely affect water quality in the Danube River.[101] The convention provides for specific actions states must undertake to reduce pollution,[102] the compilation of emission inventories,[103] and the establishment of monitoring programs.[104] State parties have an obligation to report to the ICPDR on various matters, including the means they use to implement the commission's decisions.[105] Parties can exchange information and engage in consultations for activities likely to have transboundary impact.[106] The convention provides for the confidentiality of information provided by the parties especially in terms of commercial and industrial secrets, and the procedures that should apply for the release of such information.[107] Information on the state of quality

99 Annex I, *id.*
100 Art. 2(4), *id.*
101 Annex II, *id.*
102 Arts. 5–7, *id.*
103 Art. 8, *id.*
104 Art. 9, *id.*
105 Art. 10, *id.* Reporting includes reports and documents provided for in the convention or requested by the commission; information on relevant bilateral and multilateral agreements in the region; information on relevant national legislation; communication on the way, the timeframe and the financial expenses for implementing decisions, recommendations, programs and measures issued by the commission; designation of competent authorities responsible for the implementation of the convention; and communication on planned activities likely to have transboundary impacts.
106 Arts. 12 and 11, *id.*
107 Art. 13, *id.*

of the environment, though, can be provided to any natural or legal person without that person having to prove an interest.[108]

The DRPC established the ICPDR. The ICPDR elaborates proposals and recommendations for the parties.[109] The Conference of the Parties (COP)[110] is the decisionmaking body and can adopt decisions or recommendations provided that at least three-quarters of the contracting parties are present.[111] The COP must engage in every effort to reach consensus. However, if consensus is not attainable the COP can declare that all efforts in reaching agreement by consensus have been exhausted and, after such an announcement, decisions can be adopted by a four-fifths majority of contracting parties present and voting.[112] Decisions or recommendations, though, which have financial implications can only be adopted by consensus.[113] Decisions become binding on the eleventh month, following the date of their adoption for the parties that voted for the decision unless they otherwise notify the executive secretary of the commission.[114] Parties must send to the commission communication on the way, timeframe, and financial expenses required to implement decisions of the commission.[115]

The commission has engaged in a number of activities to ensure the strengthening of measures to combat pollution in the Danube. The Joint Action Program adopted in 2001 details the ICPDR policy for the protection of the Danube River from 2001 all through 2005.[116] The ICPDR has initiated contacts with various authorities responsible for Danube shipping in order to establish an understanding that navigation should not harm extensively the environment and the natural flow of the river. The ICPDR has an observer status in the Danube Navigation Commission and the Danube Navigation Commission holds an observer status in the ICPDR. The commissions are working together to develop a shared approach to navigation. The ICPDR is developing an inventory of point

108 Art. 14, *id.*
109 Art. 18(1), *id.*
110 Art. 22, *id.*
111 Art. 22(4), *id.*
112 *Id.*
113 Art. 22(6), *id.*
114 Art. 22(5), *id.*
115 Art. 10(d), *id.*
116 *Annual Report on the Activities of the ICPDR in 2004*, at 25 [hereinafter *Annual ICPDR Report*].

discharges of agriculture that could be used by decisionmakers and by local environmental and agricultural authorities.

Since 1996 the ICPDR has put formally in place a Trans-National Monitoring Network (TNMN) Database.[117] Although TNMN was formally launched in 1996, monitoring by various national authorities existed much before 1996. An Accident Emergency Warning System has been updated in 2004 with the support of the UNDP/GEF.[118] The ICPDR has further developed inventories of potential Accident Risk Spots (ARS) in the Danube River basin and the implementation of safety measures that minimize risk potential.[119] The ICPDR has addressed the reduction of impacts of floods in its five-year action program. It has finalized an Action Program for Sustainable Flood Protection and has established an Expert Group on Flood Protection. The ICPDR has deepened its involvement in the transnational efforts for flood management with its support of the Budapest Initiative on Sustainable Flood Management.

The ICPDR is working closely with the Black Sea Commission. Within this framework, the Danube-Black Sea Joint Technical Working Group (JTWG) and the Danube Black Sea (DABLAS) task force have been established.[120]

With the adoption of the WFD, the ICPDR has been nominated the platform for the adoption of the River Basin Management Plan for the Danube River basin district. The ICPDR has decided to produce an umbrella, roof report that identifies the pressures and impacts on the whole Danube River basin. The roof report that came out in 2004 contains an analysis of pressures and impacts on the Danube basin. The roof report could be characterized as a preparatory report the purpose of which is to establish the basics for the elaboration of an international river basin management plan for the Danube River Basin District. The roof report deals with all rivers and catchment areas of more than 4,000 square kilometers and all lakes with an area larger than 100 square kilometers. The roof report provides an overview of transitional and coastal waters, the main navigation canals, and all large transboundary groundwater bodies. The idea behind the production of a roof report is to provide an outlook of the basin having, as a goal, the identification of the economic sectors that

117 *Id.* at 37.
118 *Id.* at 32.
119 *Id.*
120 *Id.* at 41–43.

need to be regulated and the areas of the river most vulnerable or mostly affected by pollution. The report, therefore, serves as the foundation for the elaboration of program of measures to abate pollution. In the context of the WFD, the roof report is the outcome of the completion of stage two out of the four stages that are necessary for the development of a complete river basin management plan.[121]

The roof report was sent to the European Commission in March of 2005. The preparation of the roof report was intensive and was managed by the Technical Expert in River Basin Management at the ICPDR. That expert coordinated the various activities and provided the interface between the ICPDR expert groups, the national experts, and the international consultants. About two hundred national experts from thirteen countries participated in the preparation of the roof report. The effort was financed by the UNDP/GEF Danube Regional Project.[122]

In addition to the roof report (called otherwise Part A report) that provides an overview of the whole Danube River basin district, countries in the region prepared a Part B report. Part B reports are the national reports that provide more detailed information on the water conditions in individual countries. The Part A report and Part B reports were prepared in parallel. Thus, data were collected for the roof report while countries were still developing and analyzing data necessary for the Part B national report. The ICPDR had agreed on common criteria for data analysis, and this facilitated the parallel compilation of roof report and part B reports. The Rhine Commission that prepared similar reports for the European Commission proceeded in a different way than the ICPDR. In the case of the Rhine Commission, the Part B (national) reports were prepared first

121
- The first stage has to do with the identification of river basin districts and institutions that will be in charge of such districts (deadline 2003);
- The second stage has to do with the analysis of river basin characteristics, the identification of pressures and impacts, the economic analysis of water use and the establishment of a register of protected areas (deadline 2004);
- The third stage is concerned with the development of monitoring networks and programs (deadline 2006);
- The fourth stage involves the development of Danube River Basin Management Plan including the program of measures and public participation (deadline 2009).

122 Ursula Schmedtje, *Development of the Danube River Basin District Management Plan – Strategy for coordination in a large international river basin*, at 22–23 (Nov. 23, 2005) [hereinafter *Danube Strategy*].

and then the Rhine Commission extracted data from the Part B reports to prepare the Part A (roof report).[123]

The compilation of the roof report was not simple. A persistent problem with data availability and comparability undermined the quantitative strength of the report. The chronological starting point and the availability of data were vastly different in the countries that make the Danube River basin district. Therefore, it was exigent to develop:

- An improved emission inventory that would lead to the development of a Pollutant Release and Transfer Register (PRTR) for the Danube River basin;
- An inventory of hydromorphological alterations;
- Improved transboundary monitoring including surveillance monitoring of the ecological and chemical status; and
- An inventory of transboundary water bodies and their status.[124]

The methodology of elaboration of river basin management for a large river basin, such as that of the Danube River, is not quite obvious and it is not dictated by the WFD. Adopting a river basin management plan for a large basin can be approached in three different ways. One option is to view the Danube basin as the combination of large subbasins. This way, the overall plan for the Danube will be a combination of the subbasin plans. Another idea is to develop national plans taking into account the existing national boundaries and attempt to forge coordination among the national plans through bilateral treaties. In this case the national plans will be used to draft the overall Danube Basin Management Plan. Yet another alternative is to view the Danube as the amalgam of smaller subbasins. In this case, the overall Danube Plan will be a patchwork of the subbasin plans coordinated by bilateral arrangements.[125]

The method of reporting on river basin planning could be based on two approaches: a strict river basin management approach or a combined approach. A strict river basin management approach is based on the hydrographic borders all the way from the articulation of the river basin management plan for the whole river to the subbasin level and then to the

[123] *Id.* at 23.
[124] *Danube Roof Report, supra* note 59, at 171.
[125] *See Danube Strategy, supra* note 122, at 19.

subsubbasin level. A combined approach would have to take into account the reality of national borders. According to a combined approach, the overall plan for the Danube is executed at the river basin level and national plans are formulated within national borders. The subbasins within the national borders have to be addressed in national river basin management plans.[126]

After the completion of the roof report, the ICPDR is proceeding with the adoption of river management plan for the Danube basin. For this purpose, the ICPDR has adopted a road map for the development of the Danube River basin management plan (2005–2010)[127] and a strategy.[128] Because the Danube River basin district is a large district, the strategy emphasizes the various levels of coordination. Three levels of coordination are envisioned: the Danube River basin level, the bilateral/multilateral level, and the national level. Part A will be at the roof level—the Danube River basin level. Part A is put together at the international level and is coordinated by state parties to the DRPC. The strategy specifies that the amount of coordination at the international level should be limited to what it is absolutely necessary to be accomplished at that level—that is, issues of international nature. Part B could be conceived as river basin management planning at the national level or at the subbasin level and could be based on hydrographic boundaries and/or national borders. If trilateral or subbasin agreements exist, coordination at that level must be included in the national plans. States may include a Part C that has to do with subbasins. The strategy leaves it up to the state parties to decide which approach they would like to incorporate.[129] At this point four subbasins have been identified in the Danube basin:

- The Tisza River subbasin, comprised of the coriparians of Slovakia, Ukraine, Romania, Hungary, Serbia, and Montenegro.
- The Sava River subbasin managed by the Sava River Commission, comprised of the states of Slovenia, Croatia, Bosnia and Herzegovina, Serbia, and Montenegro.

---

126 *Id.* at 22.

127 *Road Map for the Development of the Danube River Basin Management Plan (including a Work Plan and an Operational Plan for Public Participation)* 2005–2010 [hereinafter *Danube Road Map*].

128 *Danube Strategy, supra* note 122.

129 *Id.* at 6.

- The Prut River basin, the management of which requires the trilateral cooperation among Romania, Moldova, and Ukraine.
- The Danube Delta subbasin in which close cooperation between Romania and Ukraine must be established.[130]

The ICPDR strategy provides a view of the Danube River basin district as a district combined by four major subdistricts. River basin management plans developed at the subdistrict level will be taken into account when drafting the overall Danube River Basin Management Plan. Given the reality of the WFD implementation that requires each state to report to the European Commission at the national level, states, in addition to multilateral collaboration, have to adopt national plans based on national and not hydrographic borders.[131]

In addition to the subbasins included in the formal ICPDR river basin planning, other subbasins have been identified in the Danube and further attempts at developing subbasin river management plans have been undertaken. The reason why the ICPDR has chosen to focus on these particular subbasins in lieu of others has probably to do with the emphasis that needs to be placed on strengthening cooperation with countries that have yet to become part of the European Union accession process. Cooperation with these countries will be vital if a river basin management plan for the whole Danube River is to be prepared.

Although the strategy sets the overall guidance and parameters for the preparation of the river basin management plan, the road map deals with the specific details of how such plan will be compiled.[132] The road map breaks down the preparation of the river basin management plan into:

- Issues that have to do with the implementation of the WFD.
- Operational tasks that have to be accomplished in order to address the WFD issues.
- The timeframe within which operational tasks have to be completed.

---

[130] *Id.* at 19.

[131] *Id.* at 20.

[132] *See Danube Road Map, supra* note 127.

- The body responsible within the ICPDR to complete the identified tasks as well as the bodies that are to cooperate with the responsible body.

The ICPDR's decisionmaking body is the Conference of the Parties. The everyday affairs of the commission are coordinated by the Standing Working Group. The standing working group prepares the meetings of the international commission and provides guidance for the work of various expert groups.[133] The ICPDR has reorganized its expert groups in order to align its work with the WFD requirements. The River Basin Management Expert Group coordinates the work of other groups, receives reports produced by these groups, which it further uses to compile the river basin management plan. The Monitoring and Assessment Expert Group, the Pressures and Measures Expert Group, and the Flood Protection Expert Group are key to the work of the River Basin Management Expert Group. Other ICPDR expert groups that perform supportive role include groups on Public Participation, on Information Management and on Geographic Information Systems.[134] The commission's work is facilitated by a secretariat whose purpose is to support the work programs and coordinate the activities of the various expert groups.

The expert groups could form, if needed, task groups. These groups could include members of the expert group and additional experts. Task groups have a specifically designated mandate and their duration is limited. Other coordinating groups include the Danube-Black Sea Joint

[133] Rules of Procedure of the ICPDR, rev2–FINAL, IC/002, Nov. 28, 2002.

[134] The expert groups at the ICPDR are:

- River Basin Management Expert Group (RBM EG)—coordinates all activities that have to do with river basin management within the framework of the WFD;
- Pressures and Measures Expert Group (PM EG)—examines the causes of pressures in the river basin and proposes measures to address them;
- Monitoring and Assessment Expert Group (MA EG)—is concerned with the operation of the Trans-National Monitoring Network and Analytical Quality Control. The group operates also the Accident Emergency Warning System and it is responsible for the communication of alarm/warning messages in case of accidents;
- Expert Group on Flood Protection (Flood EG)—develops the Action Plan for Sustainable Flood Protection and supervises its implementation at the national level;
- Information Management and Geographical Information System (GIS) (*ad hoc* I +GIS EG)—has produced a number of maps for the Danube River Basin;
- Public Participation Expert Group (*ad hoc* PP EG)—provides support regarding information and participation issues;
- Strategic Expert Group (*ad hoc* SEG)—addresses administrative and legal matters that have to do with the implementation of the convention.

Technical Working Group, which coordinates the work of the ICPDR and that of the International Commission for the Protection of the Black Sea. Other such coordinating groups may become necessary in the future. To facilitate the establishment of a continuous and a consistent relationship between the ICPDR and the Danube Commission, a Joint ICPDR-Danube Commission technical working group may become necessary in the future.

The ICPDR has been considered a successful institution, especially in the light that it has to coordinate the efforts of countries with disparate levels of development and aspiration. The metric for the success of the commission, as it is now the platform for the WFD implementation, is whether it is evolving into an honest broker in a region where development and environmental protection would need to be constantly rebalanced. The question is whether the ICPDR will acquire the legitimacy to establish constraints on various activities that generate pressures and impacts on the river, and especially navigation, given the ambition to transform the Danube into Corridor VII for inland transport. The success of the ICPDR depends certainly on the political will of states that make the commission. It is equally dependent on the ability of its executive organs in establishing the middle ground among the various positions and counterpositions. To achieve that middle ground, a high dose of pragmatism will be needed to renegotiate positions if circumstances change.

International Sava Commission

The Sava River[135] Basin Initiative was launched in 2001 by the Stability Pact for South Eastern Europe.[136] The initiative was supported by the EU, the USAID,[137] the Dutch partners for Water Program,[138] and the ICPDR.

---

135 The Sava River is 861 kilometers long. The Sava River is the Danube's second largest subcatchment (95 719 square meters) after the Tisza River. *See Enhancing Integrated Transboundary River Basin Management of the Sava River: Executive Summary of the Partners for Water Project*, at 7, (International Agricultural Center) IAC, Wageningen University and Research, the Netherlands (H. L. Zingstra, ed., 2005) [hereinafter *IRBM Sava*].

136 *The Stability Pact for South Eastern Europe* was adopted on June 10, 1999 by the EU and all countries in the region with the goal to strengthen peace, democracy, human rights and the economies of south east Europe, *see* http:// www.stabiltypact.org.

137 United States Agency for International Development.

138 The Dutch Partners for Water Program aims to strength the Dutch international activities in the field of water management, *see* http:// www.partnersvoorwater.nl.

The Regional Environmental Center (REC)[139] provided secretariat support for the Interim Sava Commission. A series of cooperative efforts eventually culminated into a fully-fledged international commission based on an agreement that was ratified in June 2005 on the Sava River basin. This was the first negotiated agreement in the region, after the conclusion of the Dayton Accords.[140] The agreement is an attempt to use the river basin principle to organize efforts that target both development and environmental protection in the beleaguered region. Bosnia and Herzegovina, Croatia, Slovenia, Serbia, and Montenegro are state parties to the treaty that created the Sava Commission.

The adoption of the framework agreement and the establishment of the Sava Commission was a far from facile process. The framework agreement was signed in 2002, and it was expected that it would be ratified in 2003. Ratification, though, did not occur until 2005. Complex legal and financial issues had to be resolved before the agreement was ratified. Some of the problems involved the lack of communication between the water sector and the environmental sector in each of the countries. For instance, the nature protection sector in each of the countries was not up-to-date with regard to the establishment of the Sava Commission. Other issues that parties had to resolve included various procedural issues such as the seat of the International Sava River Commission (that was eventually established in Zagreb).[141]

The Sava Commission, contrary to the ICPDR, is not concerned solely with environmental protection but has, as an explicit goal, the promotion of navigation. Thus, although for the whole district of the Danube, the function of the promotion of navigation and the function of the protection of the environment are executed by different bodies, in the case of

---

139 The Regional Environmental Center (REC) for Central and Eastern Europe is an environmental non-governmental organization aspiring to function by building partnerships among stakeholders, by transferring "lessons learned" and best practices all across Europe and by establishing centers of excellence on various environmental topics. Various government agencies such as the Swiss Agency for Development and Cooperation and the Ministry of Foreign Affairs of the Netherlands are providing funding for the REC. *See* REC Annual Report 2003.

140 *The General Framework Agreement for Peace in Bosnia and Herzegovina*, also known as the Dayton Agreement or Dayton Accords, is the peace agreement reached at the Wright-Patterson Air Force Base near Dayton, Ohio in November 1995. The Accords were formally signed in Paris on December 14, 1995. These accords ended the war in Bosnia, one of the armed conflicts that broke up the Socialist Republic of Yugoslavia.

141 *IRBM Sava, supra* note 135, at 7–8.

the Sava Commission, the same body is to accomplish both the functions. The question, thus, from an institutional viewpoint, is whether the concentration of the functions of navigation and environment protection under a single body is a preferable arrangement or whether the division of functions assigned to different bodies is bound to bring a more balanced approach to development. This question is examined later in this section.

The objectives of the Sava Agreement are to:[142]

- Establish an international regime of navigation on the Sava River and its tributaries;
- Promote sustainable water management; and
- Undertake measures to prevent or limit hazards, and to reduce and eliminate the adverse consequences of floods, ice hazards, droughts and hazardous substances.[143]

The agreement is based on the principle of reasonable and equitable use and the principle[144] of no significant harm[145] propagated by the United Nations (UN) Watercourse Convention (the Watercourse Convention).[146] Although equitable use is not defined, the agreement refers to the reasonable and equitable share of *beneficial uses* of water resources rather than of water resources *per se*.[147] The adoption of the principle of equitable share of water uses is hoped to generate win-win innovative solutions for state parties.[148] This is because state parties do not have to nitpick water allocations, as they are frozen at a specific point in time, but could afford a more long-term view on the planned use of the river and the sharing of benefits that derive from such use. Furthermore, the equitable use principle is to be based on relevant factors in accordance with international law.[149] This provision alludes to the Watercourse Convention and the factors of equitable use established in that convention.[150] The Sava Agreement

142 *Framework Agreement on the Sava River Basin*, Dec. 3, 2002 available online http://www.savacommission.org [hereinafter *Sava Agreement*].
143 Art. 2, *id.*
144 Art. 7, *id.*
145 Art. 9, *id.*
146 *See supra* note 19.
147 Art. 7(1), *Sava Agreement, supra* note 142.
148 *See also McCaffrey, supra* note 19, at 331.
149 Art. 7(2), *Sava Agreement, supra* note 142.
150 *See Watercourse Convention, supra* note 19.

emphasizes further the no harm principle that is the prevention of significant harm to other coriparian countries because of a state's utilization of the river.[151]

The agreement states specifically that state parties need to cooperate in accordance with the WFD[152] and that state parties are to work in a cooperative fashion with the ICPDR, the Danube Navigation Commission, the United Nations Economic Commission for Europe (UNECE) and the institutions of the European Union.[153] The agreement establishes a regime on navigation by putting forward as a basic principle that navigation on the Sava River will be open to merchant vessels of any state.[154] Merchant vessels are free to enter ports of state parties provided that they observe the national regulations of that state party and the rules promulgated by the International Sava Commission.[155] The agreement does not include the precautionary principle or the polluter pays principle probably because it is not an environmental agreement *per se*. Furthermore, although state parties undertake the obligation to exchange information,[156] they do not have a formal obligation to report to the commission.

Article 11 exemplifies sustainable water management that includes the integrated management of surface waters and groundwater resources. Sustainable water management means the provision of water of sufficient quantity and appropriate quality to allow for the preservation, protection, and improvement of aquatic ecosystems. Water of sufficient quantity and appropriate quality must be made available for navigation and other uses, and the conflict of interests that may be caused by different uses of water should be resolved in a cooperative manner.[157] Sustainable water management means protection from the detrimental effects of water, such as flooding, and ice hazards, and the prevention of groundwater depletion. To achieve sustainable water management, state parties commit to develop an integrated Sava River Basin Management Plan and to establish coordination with the ICPDR.[158] Parties further agree to establish a joint system of measures, warnings, and alarms to confront extraordinary impacts on

---

151 Art. 9, *Sava Agreement, supra* note 142.
152 Art. 3(2), *id.*
153 Art. 5, *id.*
154 Art. 10(1), *id.*
155 Art. 10(3), *id.*
156 *See* arts. 3 and 4 on cooperation and the exchange of information, *id.*
157 Art. 11, *id.*
158 Art. 12, *id.*

the water regime, such as sudden and accidental pollution, floods, water shortages, or obstruction to navigation.[159]

The Sava Commission can make decisions on conditions that are safe for navigation. The commission can also make decisions on financing the construction of navigable waterways and the maintenance of such waterways.[160] The commission can make recommendations with regard to other issues, for instance, recommendations[161] with respect to the improvement of environmental quality. All decisions and recommendations of the Sava Commission are adopted by unanimous vote.[162] Decisions of the commission are binding unless a state party withdraws its vote within thirty days after a decision is made or informs the commission that the decision is subject to approval by the relevant authority within that state. Recommendations, as their name suggests, are not binding but certainly are bound to have authoritative value for state parties. Decisions that affect the regulation of navigation are ensured a binding character explicitly in the convention. The legal nature of recommendations that regulate any other matter is left vague. Although this distinction may lose its relevance in the future, it demonstrates the emphasis placed by state parties on the revitalization of navigation. The decisionmaking body of the Sava Agreement is the Meeting of the Parties that makes decisions by consensus.[163] The convention, further, establishes a secretariat that facilitates the everyday work of the commission.

The provision of information to stakeholders has found a place in the Sava Agreement despite the fact that the agreement is not solely an environmental agreement. The provision of information has to do with the establishment of a monitoring methodology.[164] The implementation of monitoring methodology includes timely provision of information to stakeholders and the general public by the authorities responsible for the implementation of the agreement.[165] Furthermore, while the sessions of

---

159 Art. 13, *id.*

160 Art. 16 (1)(a) and (b), *id.*

161 Art. 16(1)(d), *id.*

162 Art. 5(3), Statute of the International Sava River Basin Commission, *Annex I, Sava Agreement, supra* note 142.

163 Art. 14, *Sava Agreement, supra* note 142.

164 Art. 21(1), *id.*

165 Art. 21(2), *id.*

the Sava Commission are held in private, the commission may invite observers to its sessions.[166]

The agreement provides for a fact-finding expert committee[167] that is to assist in the resolution of disputes among state parties. The committee is to be comprised of three members, two of which are appointed by the disputing sides and a neutral expert[168] who is to chair the committee. At the request of the fact-finding expert committee, the concerned parties are to provide the committee with all information on the disputing matter. Disputing states are to permit the committee to enter their territories, inspect locations, installations, and equipment, as is necessary for the committee to complete its work, and in accordance with national legislation.[169] State parties and experts are to protect the confidentiality of any information they obtain in confidence during the work of the committee.[170] The committee adopts a report on its findings by a majority vote and if there is a dissenting opinion, that opinion is stated in the report produced by the committee.[171] The committee must work fast as it has to report its findings to the concerned parties within two months after it is established.[172] The provision for a fact-finding committee in the Sava Agreement is not unique and has to do with the increasing inclusion of compliance and dispute resolution mechanisms in international agreements. Such fact-finding mechanisms, however, have not been included in many other agreements that address shared watercourses in Europe, especially when most state parties to these agreements are EU member states. Not all countries that are making the Sava Commission are, at this point, members of the EU and, in a climate that is still marred by some mutual suspicion, a fact-finding committee was deemed necessary.

The tasks and competencies of the Sava Commission are expounded in the Statute of the International Sava River Commission (For the structure of the commission, see Figure 17.1).[173] The tasks of the commission are wide-ranging and include the development of the Sava River Basin Management

[166] Art. 3(4), Statute of the International Sava River Basin Commission, *Annex I of Sava Agreement, supra* note 142.
[167] Art. 23, *Sava Agreement, id.*
[168] For the election of the neutral member, *see* art. 23(3), *id.*
[169] Art. 24(2), *id.*
[170] Art. 24(3), *id.*
[171] Art. 24(4), *id.*
[172] Art. 24(5), *id.*
[173] Statute of the International Sava Commission, *Annex I, Sava Agreement, supra* note 142.

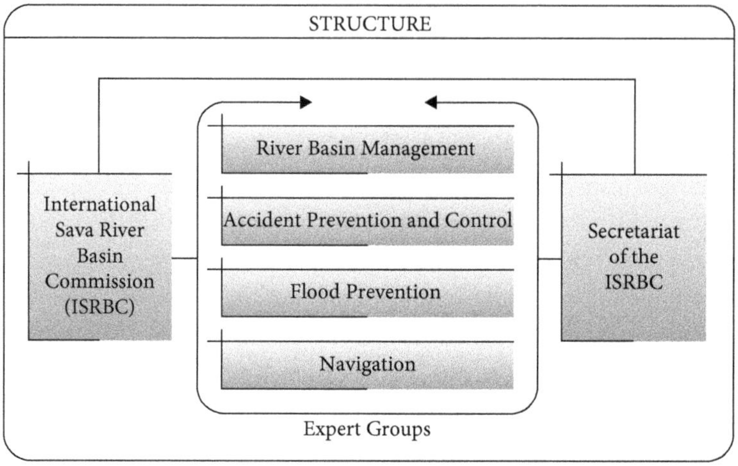

Figure 17.1 Sava Commission

Plan, the regulation of waters in the Sava basin for all purposes, the adoption of decisions that provide conditions for the safe navigation of the river (including the maintenance and development of navigable waterways, unified rules for navigation, and the establishment of a River Information System).[174] The structure of the secretariat of the Sava Commission reflects the multiple functions of the commission. Under the secretary, who is responsible for supervising all of the functions of the commission there are three deputy secretaries, namely, a deputy secretary for navigation; a deputy secretary for integrated river basin management and water planning; and a deputy secretary for protection of waters and aquatic ecosystems.[175]

The commission has experienced some financing problems in its initial startup. There were not enough resources to hire the special advisor on information systems. Also, the seats for the deputy secretary for integrated river basin management and deputy secretary for the protection of waters and aquatic ecosystems remained initially vacant. This had to do with the lack of expertise in the region in terms of the fulfillment of requirements of job description. Members of the commission were also

[174] Art. 4, *id.*

[175] *See Main Functions, Structure of the Secretariat and Job Description*, adopted during the first session of the International Sava River Basin Commission, June 27–29, 2005. Deputy Secretaries are assisted by advisors who specialize in specific issues—such as an advisor on navigation safety and an advisor for protection against the detrimental effects from waters.

disappointed that some of the financing that was promised by donors had not been forthcoming. The Statute of the Commission provides that parties must contribute to the financing of the commission on an equal basis,[176] but it is unclear whether state parties are always ready to put forward the resources to make the commission operational.

The importance paid to navigation in the Sava region is underlined by the Protocol on Navigation[177] that was adopted simultaneously with the framework agreement on the Sava River Basin. The purpose of the protocol is to define the conditions for navigation in the Sava River and the role of the commission in the regulation of navigation. Other protocols may be adopted in the future, such as a protocol on transboundary impacts (related to article 8 of the agreement); on protection against floods and other extreme water circumstances; on water use and gravel exploitation; on protection and improvement of water quantity and quality; and on prevention of pollution caused by navigation and emergency situations.[178]

The concept of the Sava River Basin Management Plan was prepared in 2004 and was supported by the UNDP/GEF Danube Regional Project.[179] The concept concentrates on the development of a "pragmatic RBM plan" that should address not only the main WFD issues but also include other water issues such as flood management and the economic use of water (irrigation, navigation, and hydropower production). The proposed plan would include a public participation strategy for the Sava River basin.

Tisza Basin Initiatives

The Tisza is the largest subbasin (157 186 square kilometers) of the Danube River basin (801 463 square kilometers).[180] The countries that share the Tisza River include Romania, Slovakia, Ukraine, Hungary, Serbia, and Montenegro.

176 Art. 17, *Sava Agreement, supra* note 142. *See also* art. 6, Statute of the International Sava River Basin Commission, *Annex I of Sava Agreement, id.*

177 *Protocol on the Navigation Regime to the Framework Agreement on Sava River Basin*, Dec. 3, 2002 available online www.savacommission.org.

178 Art. 30, *Sava Agreement, supra* note 142.

179 *See Concept for the Preparation of the Sava River Basin Management Plan 2004–2006*, May 2004 (Prepared by Zinke Environment Consulting for Central and Eastern Europe under the UNDP/GEF Danube Regional Project).

180 Karin Burnod-Requia, *Rapid Environmental Assessment of the Tisza River Basin*, at 1 (UNEP, 2004) [hereinafter *Rapid Tisza Assessment*].

The nineteenth and early twentieth centuries witnessed major structural works on the Tisza River and 84 percent loss of its floodplain.[181] The Tisza has been affected by various sources of pollution including agriculture and mining.[182] Although the economic decline that followed the collapse of communism has reduced some of these pressures, they are bound to resume as economic activities in the region are being revitalized.

Since the Tisza basin is part of the Danube basin it falls under the jurisdiction of the ICPDR. In addition to the initiatives undertaken by the ICPDR, the countries of the region signed in 2004 a Memorandum of Understanding for integrated Tisza Basin cooperation and agreed to collaborate to produce the Tisza River basin management plan by 2009.[183] Such a plan would have to conform to the requirements of the WFD and the ICPDR flood action program. The memorandum mentions various initiatives that have been undertaken in the region and the need for more coordination in order to avoid duplication of efforts. The Tisza cooperation, as emphasized in the memorandum, is to make use of the existing structures (namely the ICPDR) avoiding, thus, the proliferation of international bodies. State parties, however, have not excluded the possibility of developing in the future the appropriate legal framework for the Tisza initiative that would take into account the specifics of the Tisza region and the complexity of tasks with which Tisza countries are faced.

The risks of duplication of efforts in the region cannot be stressed enough. Under the auspices of the Council of Europe, countries signed in 2003 the Declaration of Cooperation concerning the Tisza River Basin and the Initiative on the Sustainable Spatial Development of the Tisza River Basin.[184] Other initiatives include the Tisza Environmental Forum that was formed in 2001. The forum was more of a focal point for the coordination of various working groups and did not lead to the establishment of a Tisza Commission. Other programs executed in the region include a program spearheaded by the United Nations Development Program (UNDP), the Commonwealth of Independent States and the REC. The purpose of this program is to strengthen environmental governance

---

[181] *Id.* at 3.

[182] For an extensive analysis of pressures and impacts on the Tisza basin, *see generally Rapid Tisza Assessment, id.*

[183] Memorandum of Understanding: Towards a River Basin Management Plan for the Tisza River Supporting Sustainable Development of the Region, Dec. 13, 2004 available online http://www.icpdr.org/icpdr-pages/tisza_basin.htm.

[184] *Rapid Tisza Assessment, supra* note 180, at 6.

based on sustainable development principles.[185] Various other projects as well as bilateral agreements have been initiated in the region. The World Bank and the Global Environment Facility (GEF) have supported various programs that concentrate on the improvement of socioeconomic and environmental conditions in the Tisza River basin.

A concern that needs to be addressed is whether all these programs and initiatives generate unnecessary duplication or whether they merely act as substitutes for one another, as donors and funding preferences change. Proposing the Tisza as a unique subbasin probably helps channeling funding to the region. The water framework directive (WFD) should bring more coherence to the various Tisza initiatives as efforts need to be directed to the drafting of the subbasin management plan. The production of that plan will provide a more concrete focal point for coordination. In addition, the creation of a Tisza institution has not been excluded for the future.

Black Sea Commission

The Black Sea is one of the most isolated seas in the world given that is connected to other seas and oceans only through the Mediterranean Sea. Because the Black Sea is an isolated sea, pollution has severely affected its ecosystem. The Black Sea is excessively burdened by inputs of polluting substances and nutrients. One of the largest rivers that end up in the Black Sea is the Danube River.

In 1992 countries in the region—Bulgaria, Georgia, Romania, Russia, Turkey, and Ukraine—attempted to address pollution in the Black Sea by adopting the Convention on the Protection of the Black Sea Against Pollution.[186] The convention establishes the International Commission for the Protection of the Black Sea (ICPBS). In addition to this umbrella convention, states have signed a number of protocols that address specific problems of the Black Sea.[187]

---

185 *Id.* at 48.

186 *Convention on the Protection of the Black Sea against Pollution*, Apr. 21, 1992 available online http://www.blacksea-commission.org/main.htm.

187 *Protocol on Protection of the Black Sea Marine Environment against Pollution from Land Based Sources*, Apr. 21, 1992, *id.*
Protocol on Cooperation in Combating Pollution of the Black Sea Marine Environment by Oil and other Harmful Substances in Emergency Situations, Apr. 21, 1992, *id.*
Protocol on the Protection of the Black Sea Marine Environment against Pollution by Dumping, Apr. 21, 1992, *id.*

Cooperation between the ICPDR and the Black Sea Commission started in 1997. In 2001, the two commissions had already signed a memorandum of understanding.[188] The memorandum of understanding underlines the limitations of international conventions. The Black Sea Convention, as is correctly pointed out in the memorandum, is a *shoreline convention*. In other words, it is not drafted in a way that would grant jurisdictional control over watercourses and the land sources of pollution responsible for discharges into the Black Sea.[189] The memorandum takes note that the pollution in the Black Sea seems to be decreasing but emphasizes that more efforts need to be undertaken for pollution reduction. Although it is speculated that many polluting discharges enter the Black Sea, the magnitude of the problem is not entirely clear, because the comparability of available data is not always possible.[190]

The ICPDR and the Black Sea Commission have initiated jointly various initiatives including the establishment of a Joint Technical Working Group. The purpose of this working group is to draft guidelines for the achievement of good environmental status in the coastal waters of Black Sea in accordance with the requirements of the WFD. The DABLAS Task Force was established in 2001 as a platform for cooperation among international financial institutions, the EU, various donors, and other global and regional organizations, including the Black Sea Commission and the ICPDR. The DABLAS Task Force proposed an inventory of priority investment projects that would be eligible for financing by international donors so as to reduce as much as possible the gap between project inception and project financing. A Black Sea Strategic Action Plan (BSSAP) was adopted in 1996 and was endorsed by state parties to the Black Sea Protection Convention. The implementation of the plan, though, requires strong administrative structures and financing to succeed.

The institutional weakness of the Black Sea regime derives from the institutional shortcomings of the countries that are responsible for the administration of the regime. Given current geopolitical circumstances, the evolution of the regime is likely to suffer because of tensions between

Black Sea Biodiversity and Landscape Conservation Protocol to the Convention on the Protection of the Black Sea Against Pollution, June 14, 2002, *id.*

188 Memorandum of Understanding between the International Commission for the Protection of Black Sea (ICPBS) and the International Commission for the Protection of the Danube River (ICPDR) on common strategic goals, Nov. 26, 2001.

189 *Id.*

190 *Id.*

Georgia and Russia. For countries like Georgia and Russia, the WFD presents, under a best-case scenario, a distant idea. Turkey could be considered a developing economy likely to put more emphasis on growth than environmental protection and for which EU membership is attractive but not alluring enough to induce the reformation of some of its policies. Under such circumstances, it is hard to envision the Black Sea Commission operating as a unitary body. It is up to Romania and Bulgaria, member states of the EU, to drive the Black Sea process and to ensure that it becomes aligned with the WFD since they have a formal obligation to implement the directive.

A number of projects have been undertaken to assist Black Sea countries in the implementation of the convention. The European Commission has supported the secretariat of the Black Sea Commission by investing in the information infrastructure and technical capacity of that secretariat. The Black Sea Information System has been modified to reflect the reporting requirements under the WFD. The activity centers and advisory groups of the Black Sea secretariat receive substantial financial support from the European Commission. Turkey has received financing for the Implementation of the Integrated Pollution Prevention and Control Directive. The World Bank and the GEF have provided financing for the Anatolia Watershed Rehabilitation Project, the purpose of which is to support sustainable resources management and the reduction of poverty in the region. A EuropeAid Project called Technical Assistance to the Black Sea Environmental Programme in Russia, Georgia and Ukraine has been finalized. In Russia, the project provided support for a Regional Activity Center on Development of Common Methodologies for the Integrated Coastal Zone Management.[191] Overall, without the support of donors, such as the EU and the GEF, not much in terms of environmental improvement or commitment to such improvement would have happened in the region.

Other Initiatives and Projects

The Danube Cooperation Process (DCP) was launched through a Ministerial Declaration in Vienna on May 27, 2002, and adopted by the

[191] For more details on programs and activities executed in the region, *see* Saving the Black Sea, Official Newsletter of the Commission on the Protection of the Black Sea against Pollution and the GEF Black Sea Ecosystem Recovery Project, May 2005.

ministers of foreign affairs of Austria, Bosnia and Herzegovina, Bulgaria, the Czech Republic, Croatia, Germany, Hungary, Moldova, Romania, Slovakia, Slovenia, Ukraine, Serbia, and Montenegro as well as the European Commission and the Special Coordinator of the Stability Pact for South-Eastern Europe.[192]

The DCP is a political process, the goal of which is to promote solidarity among the countries in the region and to forge a European identity. The focus of the process is to broaden and deepen Danube cooperation using structures already in place and promoting further existing initiatives.[193] The DCP supports the efforts that are underway to amend the 1948 Danube Navigation Convention and the idea of trade liberalization among the Danube countries through the promulgation of uniform regulations and the development of trans-European transport networks. In the same vein, the process is supportive of the ICPDR and the development of river basin planning, both at the regional and national scale, as well as of efforts to improve wastewater treatment infrastructure and prevent and control the damaging effects of flooding. The further development of tourism is supported via the Danube Tourist Commission as well as various cultural initiatives.[194]

The Carpathian Convention provides another opportunity for cooperation for the countries that share the Carpathian mountains. The Carpathian Convention is a framework convention the purpose of which is to develop an encompassing framework for the protection of Carpathian mountains. The countries in the region, namely, the Czech Republic, Hungary, Poland, Romania, Slovakia, Ukraine, Serbia, and Montenegro agreed to adopt the convention.[195] The Convention for the Protection of the Alps adopted in 1991 provides a successful model for the protection of environment and sustainable development of mountain regions expected

---

192 *See Final Document of the Second Ministerial Conference of the Danube Cooperation Process*, July 14, 2004.

193 *Id.*

194 Participants of the Danube Cooperation Process are supportive, *inter alia*, of the efforts of the Working Community of Danubian Regions (ARGE-Donauländer). The working community of Danubian regions is comprised of over thirty regions from ten Danubian countries. The purpose of the working community is to promote sustainable development in the Danube basin. In this context the working community of Danubian regions has undertaken a number of initiatives including the development of digital maps inclusive of cultural data, a declaration on soil protection, and a study on transport and shipping.

195 *Framework Convention on the Protection and Sustainable Development of the Carpathians*, May 22, 2003 available online http://www.carpathianconvention.org/index.htm.

to be emulated by state parties to the Carpathian Convention.[196] The Carpathian Convention includes the precautionary and prevention principles, the polluter pays principle, public participation, and the integrated planning and management of land and water resources.[197] The convention endorses an integrated approach to the management of natural resources.[198]

The Carpathian Convention addresses various sectors of the economy such as sustainable agriculture and forestry,[199] sustainable transport,[200] industry and energy.[201] Further articles are included regarding cultural heritage,[202] the promotion of environmental assessment, and information systems including monitoring and early warning.[203] Since the Carpathian Convention covers a wide array of issues, including integrated water management,[204] it remains to be seen how it would be applied in practice. The question is whether the convention will develop a focused level of activity and whether it will play a critical role in the sustainable development of the region.

The Körös and Crisuri River basin district is a subdistrict of the Danube shared between Hungary and Romania and for which a partial river basin management is being prepared through French financing. The ICPDR is acting as the managing authority for this project.[205] The development of a partial river basin management plan for the Hornad and Hernád subdistrict—shared between Hungary and Slovakia—is financed by the Netherlands.[206]

---

196 Preamble, *id.*

197 Art. 2(2), *id.*

198 An integrated approach to the management of natural resources includes:
- An integrated approach to land resources management (art. 3), *id;*
- Conservation and sustainable use of biological and landscape diversity (art. 4), *id;*
- Spatial planning (art. 5), *id;* and
- Sustainable and integrated water/river basin management (art. 6), *id.*

199 Art. 7, *id.*

200 Art. 8, *id.*

201 Art. 10, *id.*

202 Art. 11, *id.*

203 Art. 12, *id.*

204 Art. 6, *id.*

205 *ICPDR Annual Report, supra* note 116, at 43.

206 Petur Farkas, *Implementation of the Water Framework Directive in a Transboundary Context: Partial River Basin Management Plan for the Hornad/Hernád River* 97, in Proceedings of International Conference "Implementing the European Union Water Framework Directive: Towards Integrated Water Management in Europe", May 12, 2006, Athens (DG Environment, European Commission, Technical Report-2007-021, Elli Louka, ed., 2007).

The UNDP/GEF has provided generous financing for the support of activities of the ICPDR. The UNDP has been active in the Danube region since 1992. The UNDP/GEF Strategic Partnership for Nutrient Reduction in the Danube/Black Sea had a budget of $95 million and it was probably the most ambitious project related to water management undertaken by the GEF anywhere in the world.[207] A large amount of the resources was dedicated to fostering public participation in river basin management promoted as a harbinger of democratic reforms.[208] The public participation component was focused on building the capacity of the Danube Environment Forum (DEF). The DEF is a Danube River Basin-wide platform for the coordination of environmental NGOs in the Danube region. The DEF network is comprised of about 175 member organizations from thirteen different countries.

Bilateral Arrangements

Agreements dealing with bilateral issues of water management usually precede multilateral developments in many regions. The purpose of bilateral agreements is to settle issues in border areas, arrange for the distribution of water resources, and provide mechanisms of cooperation for constructing and maintaining joint technological devices, such as dams or flood prevention mechanisms. In the Danube region, bilateral agreements coexist with multilateral arrangements.

The Czech Republic and Germany share a long international border. Joint management of common waters, therefore, was established early on. More details on the bilateral cooperation between the Czech Republic and Germany are provided in the section devoted to the Elbe River regime. An agreement between the Czech Republic and Poland was adopted in 1958[209] and has resulted in the creation of joint working groups on issues of flood, irrigation, and water quality. The working groups established under the agreement involve experts from water management institutions of both countries.[210] Cooperative relationships with Austria have been in place

---

[207] *See UNDP/GEF Danube Regional Project* available online http://www.undp-drp.org/drp/index.html. The final seminar of the project took place on Feb. 21–22, 2007 in Bucharest.

[208] *Id.*

[209] *Agreement between Governments of the Czechoslovak Republic and the Polish People's Republic on management of transboundary waters*, Mar. 21, 1958 entered into force Aug. 7, 1958.

[210] The working groups that have been established include:

- Water management planning of transboundary waters;

since 1928.[211] The convention between Czechoslovakia and Austria on the settlement of water management issues concerning transboundary waters was adopted in 1967.[212] The treaty focuses on a number of issues such as the erection of high-water embankments, the protection against flooding and ice, land reclamation, and the improvement of navigation.[213] The treaty refers to the no-harm principle as it specifically provides that each state must refrain from carrying out, without the consent of the other state, measures relating to frontier waters that would adversely affect water conditions in the other contracting party. However, the consent of a state party with regard to the execution of works in shared waters may be refused "only on serious grounds."[214] The treaty touches on issues of transfrontier pollution since it provides that, in order to prevent the pollution of frontier waters, state parties must arrange for the purification of wastewater discharged from new sources.[215] The treaty requires the reimbursement of costs for services rendered by one state party that have benefited the other state party,[216] and includes provisions on how to adjudicate water rights.[217] In this respect, it is stated that the water management authorities of contracting states may communicate with each other directly on matters relating to water rights.[218] The same holds true with gravel extraction that is subject to a prior agreement between the competent river engineering

- Hydrology, hydrogeology, and flood protection—interestingly, this working group coordinates the cooperation between the Czech Hydrometeorological Institute and the Polish Institute of Meteorology and Water Management;
- River training of transboundary watercourses, water supply, irrigation, and drainage concentrates on a number of issues including reparation of damages done by flooding;
- Protection of transboundary waters against pollution has been conducting for thirty years regular analysis at nine sites located on transboundary watercourses. *See* The Czech Republic Submission to the Notification No. 21–Application of Water Frameworks—policy intervention to sustainably use inland waters (prepared by the Ministry of Environment of the Czech Republic, Department for the International Conservation of Biodiversity, Apr. 27, 2005).

211 *International Cooperation of the Czech Republic in Water Protection*, at 27 (Ministry of Environment of the Czech Republic, no date, ISBN 80-7212-120-0) [hereinafter *Czech Republic International*].

212 *Treaty between the Republic of Austria and the Czechoslovak Socialist Republic concerning the Regulation of Water Management Questions Relating to Frontier Waters*, Dec. 7, 1967, entered into force Mar. 18, 1970.

213 Art. 2, *id.*

214 Art. 3(1), *id.*

215 Art. 3(4), *id.*

216 Art. 9, *id.*

217 Art. 10, *id.*

218 Art. 10(5), *id.*

authorities of contracting parties.[219] This encouragement of cooperation at the subnational scale is an early example of the emerging transnational governance in water management. The Austrian-Czech Frontier Water Commission has extensive responsibilities but the decisions of the commission can have legal effect upon the approval of governments of contracting parties.[220] Today, the commission concentrates on measures that address transboundary pollution from localized sources[221] and the reconstruction of transboundary water structures.[222]

The management of boundary waters between the Czech Republic and Slovakia has been spearheaded by a general agreement on cooperation in the area of the environment.[223] Some initial conditions for the management of common waters were set also in the Agreement between the Czech Republic and the Slovak Republic on a common state border.[224] An agreement that specifically addressed transnational waters was signed in 1999.[225] The agreement deals, *inter alia*, with environmental matters. The agreement established the Czech-Slovak Commission for Transboundary Waters charged with the implementation of the agreement.[226]

Slovakia, as a new independent state, had to conclude agreements with neighboring countries on various water management issues. A number of agreements have been signed in this regard with Ukraine,[227]

---

219 Art. 12, *id.*

220 Art. 14(2), *id. See also* art. 2, Statute of the Austrian-Czechoslovak Frontier Water Commission. The statute of the commission is Annex 1 to the Treaty between the Republic of Austria and the Czechoslovak Socialist Republic concerning the Regulation of Water Management Questions relating to Frontier Waters, Dec. 7, 1967. The commission can be consulted on a variety of matters including practical solutions for the execution of hydraulic works, the planning of such works and the determination of methods of execution of such works, verification of implementation of decisions, execution of works and measures and questions regarding the cleaning of frontier waters as well as various other disputed matters.

221 For instance, in the 1970s, the Danube and Dyje Rivers were heavily polluted by discharges coming from sugar factories. In 1990s, the reduction of the number of such as factories and the construction of wastewater treatment plants contributed to the improvement of water quality. *See Czech Republic International, supra* note 211, at 27.

222 *Id.*

223 *Agreement between Governments of the Czech Republic and the Slovak Republic on Cooperation in the area of Protection of the Environment*, Oct. 29, 1992 entered into force Jan. 1, 1993.

224 Signed on Jan. 4, 1996, entered into force July 25, 1997.

225 *Agreement between the Government of the Slovak Republic and the Government of the Czech Republic on Transboundary Water Cooperation*, Dec. 16, 1999.

226 *Czech Republic International, supra* note 211, at 28.

227 *Agreement between the Government of the Slovak Republic and the Government of Ukraine on Water Management Issues on Transboundary Waters*, June 14, 1994, entered into force, Dec. 15, 1995.

Hungary,[228] Austria,[229] and Poland.[230] The agreement with Hungary is quite elaborate. This agreement establishes cooperation on a variety of matters, including general environmental policy, the assessment of information on environment, climate protection, environment and energy, waste management, and the formulation of integrated regional environmental policy. A Hungarian-Slovak Joint Commission on Environment and Nature Conservation has been established. In addition to the Ministry of Environment, other relevant ministries are represented in this commission. On the Hungarian side, the Ministry of Economy and Transport, the Ministry of Interior through its National Emergency Protection Directorate General, the Ministry of Health, Social and Family Affairs, through the National Center of Environment and Health, and the Hungarian Spatial and Regional Development Authority send representatives to the meetings of the commission.[231]

Hungary, given that 95 percent of its territory is within the Danube River basin, has placed emphasis on multilateral and bilateral cooperation. Hungary has concluded bilateral treaties with Austria, Slovenia, Ukraine,[232] the former Yugoslavia,[233] Slovakia, and Romania. The agreement

---

228 *Agreement between the Government of the Republic of Hungary and the Government of the Republic of Slovakia on Cooperation in the field of Environmental Protection and Nature Conservation*, Feb. 12, 1999, entered into force, May 27, 1999.

229 *Treaty between the Slovak Republic and the Austrian Republic on Water Management Cooperation on Boundary Waters*, Dec. 2001.

230 *Agreement between the Government of the Slovak Republic and the Government of the Polish Republic on Transboundary Water Management*, May 14, 1997, entered into force Dec. 6, 1999. This is a treaty that addresses principally the Vistula River shared between the Slovakia and Poland.

231 The following working groups have been formed:

- Protection of the environmental elements and informatics;
- Environmental impact assessment;
- Environmental safety;
- Nature conservation and landscape protection;
- Spatial planning/integrated regional environmental policy;
- Waste management;
- Environmental health;
- Meteorology;
- Geology; and
- Consultative forum on environmental education and awareness raising.

232 A Hungarian-Ukrainian agreement was signed in 1999. It is speculated, however, that it would be hard for Ukraine to execute its side of the agreement without additional financial resources.

233 *Agreement between the Governments of the Hungarian People's Republic and the Yugoslav Federal Socialist Republic on Water Management Issues*, Aug. 8, 1955.

with Austria was adopted as early as in 1956[234] and lately the parties have decided to strengthen their cooperation. The treaty addresses a number of matters that affect frontier waters, such as the construction and maintenance of hydraulic works,[235] water rights,[236]warning requirements, in case of floods and ice hazards,[237] and pollution issues.[238] The treaty was remarkable in its time since it provides for measures against pollution. In order to prevent the pollution of frontier waters, the parties must ensure that factories, mines, industrial plants, and similar installations, as well as residential communities discharge wastewater only after suitable purification. This applies especially to new installations that must take measures to purify their wastewater.[239] The treaty establishes a commission, the Hungarian-Austrian Water Commission, in order to promote cooperation among the parties.[240] The commission is comprised of experts in water management. In addition to the official members of the commission, water managers at the regional level participate in the work of the commission—the water manager from the Federal State Office of Burgenland in Austria and the water manager from the North Transdanubian District Water Authority of Hungary, demonstrating the importance of subgovernmental contacts for the management of bilateral issues of transnational significance. A number of subcommissions and working groups assist the commission. A number of these working groups are permanent, such as the working group on flood control. Other working groups are formed *ad hoc* as needs emerge. The commission meets officially once a year but before the official meeting, various preparatory meetings take place through the various subcommissions and working groups. The commission makes decisions based on unanimity and the

[234] *Treaty between the Hungarian People's Republic and the Republic of Austria concerning the Regulation of Water Economy Questions in the Frontier Region*, Apr. 9, 1956.

[235] Art. 2(2), *id.*

[236] Art. 2(4), *id.*

[237] Art. 11, *id.*

[238] Art. 2(7), *id.*

[239] *Id.*

[240] Art. 12, *id.* The tasks of the commission are enumerated and include:
decisionmaking on finding practical solutions for technical and economic water management problems; the planning of hydraulic works and the approval of methods for their maintenance; the supervision of jointly executed works and preparation of studies in connection with hydraulic construction. *See* art. 13, *id.*

commission's decisions are incorporated into the respective legal order of state parties.[241]

The Hungarian-Austrian Commission is not an information gathering body. The commission, instead, facilitates the exchange of data between the parties. Since the two countries measure different water parameters and use different analytical techniques, the results of monitoring exercises are difficult to compare.[242] The commission holds a press conference on an annual basis in which interested groups are welcomed to participate. The commission has been producing a brochure that provides updates on its work every ten years.[243] In general, most of the communication with interested groups and the public is not executed by the commission but by the regional authorities involved in its work. In the future, the implementation of the WFD should influence the work of the commission and it is anticipated that the monitoring system used by the commission will be coordinated with the monitoring system for the whole Danube River basin. Communication with the public should be cultivated further to fulfill the requirements of the WFD.[244] Overall, cooperation between the parties has worked well. This is mostly because the commission is perceived as an expert commission rather than as a political body. A shared cultural and historical affinity has certainly helped in the achievement of the goals of the commission.[245]

The Permanent Hungarian-Slovene Commission on Water Management is the result of the cooperation between Hungary and Slovenia.[246] Subsidiary bodies of the commission include a joint body on water management and a joint body on water quality. The work program of the commission includes flood protection, water quality, maintenance works, and planning.

---

241 *Environmental Information in Transboundary River Basin Policy-Making and Management* 42, in Selected European Case Studies (Sindre Langaas, ed., Oct. 2002). This is a study executed under the EU research project *Integrated Strategies for the Management of Transboundary Waters on the Eastern European Fringe (MANTRA-East)*, EU Fifth Framework Programme.

242 *Id.* at 46.

243 *Id.*

244 *Id.* at 47.

245 *Id.* at 43.

246 *Agreement between the Government of the Republic of Slovenia and the Government of the Republic of Hungary on Issues of Water Management*, Oct. 21, 1994.

In 2003, an updated agreement was adopted between Romania and Hungary.[247] The agreement recognizes the fact that state parties, in the course of their cooperation, have produced detailed regulations especially in the field of flood and inland water protection that can be used in the future.[248] The agreement summarizes the rules and obligations of international cooperation and establishes the structural, economic, and institutional conditions upon which state parties can further their cooperation.[249] The scope of the agreement is quite large as it addresses issues of water abstraction, floods, pollution from point and diffuse sources, and accidental pollution.[250] The agreement contains extensive provisions on the protection and sustainable use of waters and provides that dangerous substances must be identified in accordance with the WFD.[251] New installations or the renovation of installations must take into account the use of "economically reachable best technology."[252] Article 9 is devoted to flood protection and the prevention of ice hazards. State parties should not undertake unilaterally works that may cause flood, salinization, and swampification on the territory of the other party.[253] In the event of failure of a dam, both parties must take measures to protect their territory and must cooperate with each other to the maximum extent possible.[254]

The Hungarian-Romanian Joint Committee, established under the 2003 agreement, consists of five representatives from each contracting party.[255] The function of the committee is regulatory. The committee has issued new regulations and has updated already adopted resolutions.[256] The regulations endorsed by the committee have to be in accordance with the WFD and regulations adopted by the ICPDR.[257] The committee adopts its resolutions by consensus and holds an ordinary session each

---

247 *Agreement between the Government of the Republic of Hungary and the Government of Romania on Cooperation in the Field of Protection and Sustainable Exploitation of Water Resources*, Sept. 15, 2003. The agreement follows in the footsteps of an agreement adopted on June 25, 1986 between the parties.
248 Preamble, *id.*
249 Art. 1, *id.*
250 Art. 5, *id.*
251 Art. 7, *id.*
252 Art. 7(5) *id.*
253 Art. 9(5), *id.*
254 Art. 9(8), *id.*
255 *See* art. 10, *id.*
256 Art. 6(3), *id.*
257 Art. 6(2), *id.*

year alternating between the territories of the two state parties.[258] Representatives of the EU, the ICPDR, and representatives of water authorities of state parties can attend the committee's meetings. State parties are requested to ensure the representation of the central government and local authorities responsible for executing the resolutions of the committee in the sessions of the committee.[259] The committee does not only oversee the execution of the agreement, but also evaluates such execution so as to ensure that implementation is in accordance with the provisions of the agreement. The committee determines insufficiencies in the cooperation between the parties and proposes measures to correct such insufficiencies.[260] It further examines the water supply needs through the potential construction of canals in border areas and evaluates the effectiveness of measures for flood protection.[261] The committee is involved in the application of the WFD and the establishment of goals that have to do with the achievement of good status for surface water and groundwater.[262]

Other agreements that have been signed by Romania include an agreement with Ukraine that was adopted in 1997[263] and an agreement with Bulgaria.[264] A 2004 Agreement between the Ministry of Environment and Water Management of Romania and the Ministry of Environment and Water of Bulgaria[265] is less detailed than the agreement concluded between Romania and Hungary. The areas of cooperation under the agreement are water management, in particular the provisions of the WFD, integrated coastal zone management, and impact assessment of socioeconomic activities on water resources, and the use of economic instruments.[266]

---

258 Art. 10(7), *id.*
259 Art. 10(10), *id.*
260 Art. 11(1), *id.*
261 Art. 11(6), *id.*
262 Art. 11(4), *id.*
263 *Agreement between the Government of Romania and the Government of Ukraine on Cooperation in the field of Transboundary Water Management*, Sept. 30, 1997. The agreement mentions both the 1992 Helsinki Convention and the Convention for the Protection of the Danube River. Cooperation between the two countries concentrates on the improvement of water quality, the promotion of rational water use, flood control, control of ice hazards, the construction and operation of hydrotechnical works and the exchange of data and information.
264 *Agreement between the Government of Romania and the Government of the Republic of Bulgaria on Cooperation for the Protection of the Environment*, Dec. 9, 1991.
265 *Agreement between the Ministry of Environment and Water of the Republic of Bulgaria and the Ministry of Environment and Water Management of Romania on Cooperation in the Field of Water Management*, Nov. 12, 2004 (entered into force Mar. 15, 2005).
266 Art. 2, *id.*

A Joint Commission on Water Management is established composed of representatives of the two parties.[267] Interestingly, English was established as the working language of the commission[268] under an agreement executed between the ministries responsible for water management in the two countries.

A Memorandum of Understanding was adopted between the Apele Romane (the central water agency of Romania) and the Moldavian Waters (the central water agency of Moldova) in 1995 demonstrating that cooperation between specialized agencies is important for launching transnational water management.[269] Cooperation with Serbia[270] and Ukraine has been more challenging for Romania, and there are further efforts to establish cooperation with Moldova and Ukraine on the Prut River. The bilateral agreements to which Romania is a party present characteristics that are common to all the bilateral agreements examined here. As in most bilateral agreements, a joint commission is established. The secretariat functions for the agreement are provided by the Water Department of the Ministry of Environment and Water. The Apele Romane, the central water agency of Romania, is in charge of implementation. Bilateral agreements usually have to do with the transmission of meteorological and hydrological data between the parties, the mutual assessment of water quality and quantity, building consensus on the future of hydrotechnical works, and procedures to follow in case of accidental pollution and floods.

Slovenia inherited a number of bilateral agreements signed in the 1950s and 1970s when the multilateral framework was just emerging. Updating these international agreements has not been undertaken yet since the operational structure of the agreements remains functional. Working groups have been established to further cooperation under the agreements.

---

267 Art. 5, *id.*

268 Art. 5(8), *id.*

269 A further agreement between the Ministry of Water and Environmental Protection of Romania and the Environmental Protection Department of the Republic of Moldova in the field of environmental protection and sustainable development was signed in 1996.

270 *Agreement between the Government of Romania and the Government of FPR of Yugoslavia concerning Water Engineering Issues related to Boundary and Transboundary Systems and Watercourses*, Apr. 7, 1955.

An agreement between Italy and Yugoslavia for the Protection of the Adriatic Sea was adopted in the 1970s[271] when Yugoslavia was a unitary state. Now Slovenia and Croatia are considered the successor state parties to the agreement. The agreement provides for cooperation on the protection of the Adriatic Sea and coastal waters against pollution. The Joint Slovene-Italian-Croatian Commission is the body in charge of the execution of the agreement.[272]

Slovenia is the successor state of Yugoslavia with regard to the Agreement on the Permanent Yugoslav-Italian Commission on Water Management.[273] The Permanent Slovene-Italian Commission is comprised of the Sub-Commission for Hydrology and the Sub-commission on Water Dams and Early Warning System.[274] Another agreement concluded with Austria is managed by the Permanent Slovene-Austrian Commission for the Drava River[275] and is assisted by a Joint Body for Water Management, a Joint Body on Hydroelectric issues and a Joint Body on Water Resources of the Karst and the Karavanke area.[276] An agreement on the frontier waters of the Mura River was adopted between Yugoslavia and Austria in 1954.[277] Today the Slovenian-Austrian Commission for the Mura River is active in the area and deals with diverse matters, such as hydropower production, the management of waterworks, the management of pollution from sewage plants, and accidental pollution.[278] Since both the Mura and

---

271 *Agreement between the Republic of Italy and the Government of the Socialist Federal Republic of Yugoslavia on the Protection of the Adriatic Sea and the Coastal Area from Pollution*, Feb. 14, 1974.

272 The commission is comprised of two sub-commissions and an *ad hoc* joint body for integrated coastal management. The work program of the commission includes:

- A master plan for the Adriatic Sea;
- Integrated coastal water management;
- Research on water quality of the Adriatic Sea;
- Environmental safety of marine traffic; and
- Exchange of information. *See International Obligations of the Republic of Slovenia in the Field of Water Management* (Ministry of Environment and Physical Planning of the Republic of Slovenia, Oct. 2000) [hereinafter *Slovenia International*].

273 Mar. 30, 1978.

274 *Slovenia International, supra* note 272.

275 *Agreement on Water Management Issues of the Drava River*, May 25, 1954 (the agreement was initially signed between Yugoslavia and Austria).

276 *Slovenia International, supra* note 272.

277 *Agreement on Water Management of the Frontier Sector and the Frontier Waters of the Mura River*, Dec. 16, 1954.

278 *Slovenia International, supra* note 272.

the Drava Rivers are shared between Austria and Slovenia, it would probably make sense to establish a joint commission for both rivers.

An agreement between Slovenia and Hungary was signed in 1994[279] establishing the Permanent Slovene-Hungarian Commission on water management. An extensive agreement was signed further with Croatia.[280] The body that manages the agreement is the Slovene-Croat Commission for Water Management. The agreement does not only cover the river basin areas but also the common coastal waters of the Adriatic.[281]

Since the bilateral agreements analyzed here are now executed within established multilateral frameworks the question that emerges is whether such agreements will continue to be useful or whether bilateral cooperation will be incorporated into the execution of multilateral treaties. This could be so as parties to multilateral agreements meet formally or informally under a number of permanent or *ad hoc* working groups in multilateral settings.

Although it is possible for bilateral exchanges to take place in multilateral fora, bilateral agreements on which transboundary coordination is based should flourish in the future. There is abundant evidence that many bilateral agreements will operate at the level of national water agency with local or regional involvement. For instance, the 2003 Hungarian-Romanian agreement explicitly mentions the involvement of local authorities. Also, some agreements have been executed at the level of the implementing agency, for instance, the agreement between Apele Romane and Moldovian Waters. Many bilateral agreements have fostered cooperation between like-minded research institutions in the contracting parties and have allowed for the exchange of expertise among state parties.

Overall, bilateral agreements in a multilateral framework could be viewed as a way to address the technicalities and specifics of international cooperation that are too issue-specific or region-specific to be addressed

279 *Agreement between the Governments of the Republic of Slovenia and the Republic of Hungary on Issues of Water Management*, Oct. 21, 1994.

280 *Treaty between the Government of the Republic of Slovenia and the Government of the Republic of Croatia on Water Management Relations*, Oct. 25, 1996.

281 The subcommissions that have been created under this agreement include those addressing the:

- Drava and the Mura Rivers;
- Sotla, Sava and Kolpa Rivers;
- Sea and the Karst area;
- Water quality. *See Slovenia International, supra* note 272.

at the multilateral level. For instance, bilateral efforts focus on the repair of certain works that have been damaged due to flooding, on sources of pollution that characterize a specific subregion and on the maintenance and development of hydropower plants. Despite the specialized character of bilateral arrangements, for the purposes of WFD execution, bilateral and multilateral initiatives cannot afford to remain disjointed and they need inform each other. It will be helpful to see bilateral and multilateral arrangements as a network of institutions that constantly feed each other information on their activities and initiatives. As many multilateral and bilateral developments run in parallel, the WFD should help forge the missing bond that consolidates national, bilateral, and multilateral efforts, at least, for the countries that are member states of the EU.

Chapter 18

Institutional Congestion in the Management of the Rhine River

The work of the International Commission for the Protection of the Rhine (ICPR) is a rare success in the reality of international relations, where many ambitious conventions are adopted but then languish because there is no political will to implement them. The success of Rhine regime has been mostly attributed to the countries of the region, all which had achieved significant economic development before taking decisive action to clean up the river. The Rhine is a small river but it is well known in Europe because of its extensive use. The length of the Rhine is 1,320 kilometers, of which 880 kilometers are navigable.[282] The countries that make the Rhine River basin include primarily France, Germany, and the Netherlands. Switzerland, Italy, Austria, Liechtenstein, Luxembourg, and Belgium have small parts of their territory in the Rhine River basin. The Rhine has been polluted by the discharges of cities and industries surrounding the basin. Major flood works were constructed as early as in 1900s. The Rhine has been used intensively for shipping, agriculture,

[282] Ine D. Frijters and Jan Leentvaar, *Rhine Case Study*, at 2, Joint UNESCO-Green Cross International Project, "From Potential Conflict to Cooperation Potential (PCCP): Water for Peace," 2003 [hereinafter *Rhine Case Study*].

energy generation, and recreation as well as for providing drinking water to twenty million inhabitants.[283]

Central Commission for Navigation on the Rhine

As is the case with the Danube River, one of the first commissions to be established in the Rhine was a navigation commission. The freedom of navigation on the Rhine was first established by the final act of the 1815 Congress of Vienna and further institutionalized by the 1868 Act of Mannheim that established the Central Commission for Navigation on the Rhine (CCNR).[284] State parties to the commission are Belgium, Germany, France, the Netherlands, and Switzerland (the only member of the commission that is not a member state of the EU), and the European Commission participates in the meetings of the CCNR as an observer. The commission operates based on the principle of free navigation.[285] The convention that establishes the commission advances freedom of navigation, the equal treatment of ships of all nations, and the absence of physical or administrative obstacles to navigation. One of the goals of the commission is to unify the navigation regulations, such as police regulations, inspection regulations, and regulations for the transport of dangerous goods. The CCNR is one of the oldest institutions in Europe dedicated to European integration through its efforts to unify regulations facilitating inland navigation.[286]

As the commission has evolved, it has inevitably addressed environmental matters. Under the auspices of the commission, a committee for waste disposal and environmental questions and a working group on the transport of dangerous goods have been established.[287] The commission has broad responsibility as it examines all complaints that have to do with the application of the convention, the enforcement of regulations adopted

---

283 *Id.* at 2–4.

284 *See Convention for Rhine Navigation* first adopted on October 17, 1868 and amended on November 20, 1963 [hereinafter *Rhine Navigation Convention*]. The history of commission and other relevant information on the current activities of the commission are available on line http://www.ccr-zkr.org/.

285 *See* Art. 1, *id. Rhine Navigation Convention.*

286 *Rhine Case Study, supra* note 282, at 5. *See also* Objectives and Orientation of the Work of the CCNR, Resolution of CCNR, 2001-I-3.

287 *Rhine Case Study, id.* at 5–6.

by governments, and the measures adopted with common government agreement.[288] The right of complaint in front of the commission is open to any individual, organization, or government. The commission is to further deliberate on proposals made by riparian states on the advancement of navigation and the amendment of the convention or regulations already in force.[289] The commission has further some semijudicial functions.[290] The CCNR administers an agreement on the social security of boatmen in Rhine navigation and the working conditions of boatmen. It regulates the technical requirements for vessels that navigate the Rhine. The CCNR competence is considered exclusive, and the decisions of the CCNR are binding on state parties.[291]

The extensive jurisdictional competence of the CCNR, though, seems to conflict with the desire of the European Community (EC) to establish a more integrated regime for the realization of a common transport policy. A common transport policy requires common rules for access to market via inland waterway, for the improvement of safety of transport and regulation of working conditions of those employed in inland navigation. Up to this point, jurisdictional conflict between the CCNR and the EU has been averted either by excluding the Rhine area from the applicability of secondary EC law or by the adoption by the CCNR of measures similar to those adopted by the EU. The European Commission (the Commission) and the CCNR signed on March 3, 2003, an agreement the purpose of which is to strengthen cooperation between the EU and the CCNR, especially through an information exchange procedure.[292] On November 28, 2002, member states of the CCNR signed the seventh protocol to the Mannheim Treaty that makes it possible to recognize certificates and licenses issued based on regulations that are comparable with the regulations issued by the CCNR. In addition, and in order to enhance cooperation with the Danube Commission, joint committees have existed

288 Art. 45(a), *Rhine Navigation Convention, supra* note 3.

289 Art. 45(b), *id.*

290 Arts. 45(3) and 34, *id.* The functions of the Chamber of Appeal of the Central Commission for Navigation on the Rhine are available online http://www.ccr-zkr.org.

291 *The Integration of European Waterways, European Strategies to Promote Inland Navigation* (SPIN-TN), Working Paper, at 16 (Project GTC2-2000-33036), Sept. 10, 2004 [hereinafter *Integration of European Waterways*]. The thematic network SPIN-TN has been funded by the Directorate General on Energy and Transport of the European Commission under the 5th Framework Programme for Research and Technological Development.

292 *Id.* at 30.

for years between the CCNR and the Danube Commission. This is necessary since the Danube has been connected to the Rhine through the Maine waterway and an integrated river engineering project on the Rhine-Meuse-Maine-Danube waterways is bound to facilitate further inland navigation. It is estimated that freight traffic in the joint waters will double by 2020.[293]

International Commission for the Protection of the Rhine

The International Commission for the Protection of the Rhine was one of the first international commissions to address pollution. The commission was established in the 1950s when awareness of environmental issues was largely dormant.[294] The commission became active in the 1970s. The adoption of a new convention for the protection of the Rhine became imperative in the late 1990s to address new developments in international environmental law. Indeed, the 1999 Convention on the Protection of the Rhine (the Rhine Convention)[295] incorporates some of the terminology widely popularized by the Rio Conference on Environment and Development[296] such as the polluter pays principle and the precautionary principle. The parties to the Rhine Convention are Switzerland, France, Luxembourg, Germany, the Netherlands, and the European Union. The aims of the ICPR include:

- Pursuit of sustainable development through maintenance and improvement of quality of the Rhine ecosystem. The protection of the Rhine ecosystem involves, *inter alia*, the control of pollution caused by noxious substances and nutrients;[297] the protection

293 On the projects that have been planned on the waterways, *see* http://www.inlandnavigation.org/en/transport/tip/rhine_main_danube.html.

294 The Commission was first established through the exchange of diplomatic notes among riparian countries and eventually found solid legal basis under the 1963 agreement. *See Agreement on the International Commission for the Protection of the Rhine against Pollution*, Apr. 29, 1963.

295 *Convention on the Protection of the Rhine*, Apr. 12, 1999 [hereinafter *Rhine Protection Convention*] available online www.iksr.org.

296 *UN Conference on Environment and Development (Earth Summit)*, Rio de Janeiro, Brazil, June 3-June 14, 1992.

297 Art. 3(1)(a), *Rhine Protection Convention, supra* note 295.

of populations of organisms and species;[298] and the maintenance, improvement, and restoration of natural functions of water.[299] The sustainable development of the Rhine ecosystem involves taking into account ecological requirements when implementing technical measures to develop the waterway. Such technical measures may concern:

- Hydropower, flood protection, and shipping;[300]
- Production of drinking water;[301]
- Improvement of sediment quality;[302]
- Flood prevention and protection taking into account ecological requirements;[303] and
- Restoration of the North Sea.[304]

Based on the principles[305] and goals of the convention, state parties undertake certain obligations delineated in article 5. Article 5, entitled "Undertakings by the Contracting Parties," provides that states undertake to implement in their territory the international measuring programs and studies of the Rhine ecosystem and to inform the commission about the results.[306] Parties undertake measures to limit pollution in their territories and to implement decisions taken by the commission.[307] Information regarding flooding and accidents that affect water quality should be disseminated promptly in accordance with the warning and alerting plans initiated by the commission.[308]

---

298 Art. 3(1)(b), *id.*
299 Art. 3(1)(c), *id.*
300 Art. 3(1)(f), *id.*
301 Art. 3(2), *id.*
302 Art. 3(3), *id.*
303 Art. 3(4), *id.*
304 Art. 3(5), *id.*
305 The principles adopted under the convention include: the precautionary principle; the polluter pays principle; the principle of preventive action; the principle of rectification as a priority at the source of polluting action; the principle of not increasing damage; the principle of compensation in the event of major technical measures; the principle of sustainable development; the application and development of state of the art and best environmental practice; and the principle of not transferring environmental pollution from one environment to another. *See* art. 4, *id.*
306 Art. 5(2), *id.*
307 Art. 5 (4)–(5), *id.*
308 Art. 5(6), *id.*

The tasks of the commission, as defined in the convention, are quite extensive. The commission must:

- Prepare international measuring programs and studies of the Rhine ecosystem and make use of their results;
- Make proposals on programs of measures to be undertaken including economic instruments; and
- Coordinate the warning and alert systems for the Rhine.[309]

Most important, the commission must evaluate the effectiveness of actions taken, not only based on the reports provided by state parties but also based on the measuring programs and studies of the Rhine ecosystem.[310] The commission's role is strengthened since it is granted decisionmaking authority. In article 10, entitled "Decision-making in the Commission," it is mentioned that decisions of the commission are taken by unanimity.[311] After a decision is adopted in the form of a recommendation, it is expected that implementation will follow. Article 11 of the convention, entitled "Implementation of Commission's Decisions," does not allow for any conjecture with regard to the authoritative role of decisions adopted by the commission. The convention provides extensively on the follow-up required after a recommendation is adopted and the means at the disposal of state parties who cannot implement the recommendations of the commission. Contracting parties are to report to the commission on:

- The legislative, regulatory, and other measures they have undertaken to implement the provisions of the convention on the basis of commission's decisions;
- The results of legislative, regulatory, and other measures they have undertaken; and
- Problems they have encountered in implementing the legislative, regulatory, and other measures.[312]

If a contracting party cannot implement the decisions of the commission, it has to report this to the commission within the timeframe specified by

[309] Art. 8 (1)(a)–(c), *id.*
[310] Art. 8(1)(d), *id.*
[311] Art. 10(1), *id.*
[312] Art. 11(3), *id.*

the commission. The report of nonimplementation is not by itself sufficient. The party must provide, additionally, the reasons for nonimplementation and must submit a request for consultation to which a response by the commission must be given within two months.[313] On the basis of reports provided by states parties and consultations conducted with state parties, the commission may decide on measures to be undertaken to assist in the implementation of decisions by state parties.[314] The commission keeps a list of decisions addressed to state parties. The contracting parties are to provide updates for this list on the progress they have made in implementing the decisions of the commission, at least two months before each plenary session of the commission.[315] It could be said that the Rhine Convention provides in its founding text one of the most extensive follow-up provisions on the state of implementation of the convention by state parties.

Expenses for the functioning of the commission are shared proportionally by state parties based on their share of the Rhine.[316] The plenary assembly is the decisionmaking organ of the commission while the coordination group addresses the everyday affairs of the ICPR and prepares the decisions to be adopted by the plenary assembly.[317] The coordination group coordinates the everyday tasks, prepares the decisions of the plenary assembly, and decides on the structure and composition of various working groups.[318]

Since the Rhine Convention is a framework convention, further treaties have been adopted to address specific problems of pollution. The Convention on Chemical Pollution was adopted in 1976 and provides the limit values for the discharge of toxic substances into the environment.[319] The Rhine Action Plan and the promotion of adoption of best available technology (BAT) have assisted in the reduction of pollution in the Rhine.[320] Another acute problem has been the pollution by chlorides (salt).

---

313 Art. 11 (4), *id.*

314 *Id.*

315 Art. 11(5), *id.*

316 The Netherlands, France and Germany contribute 32.5 percent each to the annual budget, while Switzerland contributes 12 percent, and the EU and Luxembourg contribute each 2.5 percent. Para. 9, Rules of procedure and financial regulations of the ICPR, Decision of the 70th plenary assembly of the ICPR, Bern, July 8/9, 2004.

317 Para. 1, *id.*

318 Para. 4, *id.*

319 *Agreement on the Protection of the Rhine against Chemical Pollution*, Dec. 3, 1976.

320 *Rhine Case Study, supra* note 282, at 25.

In 1976, the Convention for the Protection of the Rhine against Chloride Pollution was adopted.[321] The treaty has not been successful, though, in resolving the dispute between France and the Netherlands on the acute pollution caused by the French potassium mines. The issue was finally resolved through the Permanent Court of Arbitration.[322] Other issues that have preoccupied the ICPR include floods and other extreme weather phenomena. The ICPR adopted the Action Plan on Flood Defense in 1998 and has worked cooperatively with the Meuse Commission on the reduction of damages and effects of floods.[323]

The adoption of the water framework directive (WFD) has contributed to the evolution of the ICPR. Since the requirements of the WFD apply to the entire river basin district, in addition to the contracting states to the Convention on the Protection of the Rhine (namely, Switzerland, France, Luxembourg, Germany, the Netherlands, and the European Union), other countries whose territories are but a small part of the Rhine River basin have to be included in the WFD coordination efforts taking place at the ICPR. Thus, Italy, Austria, Liechtenstein, and Belgium, member states of the EU but not state parties to the Rhine Protection Convention have no other option but to be actively involved in the development of a RBMP for the Rhine. Switzerland is an idiosyncratic case as it is a contracting party to the Rhine Convention, but it is not a member state of the EU. Being in that position, Switzerland does not have a legal obligation to implement the WFD.

The WFD implementation process emphasizes coordination at the level of water director. Therefore, most coordination for WFD in the Rhine was initially taking place during the water director meetings rather than through the ICPR. It seemed that ICPR was sidelined initially with regard to the preparation of a river basin management plan for the Rhine.[324] The ICPR still meets annually as a plenary assembly consisting of the highest

---

321 *Convention on the Protection of the Rhine against Pollution by Chlorides*, Dec. 3, 1976. *See also Additional Protocol to the Convention on the Protection of the Rhine against Pollution by Chlorides*, Sept. 25, 1991.

322 *Arbitration in Application of the Convention of December 3, 1976 on the Protection of the Rhine against Pollution by Chlorides and the Additional Protocol of September 25, 1991*, Mar. 12, 2004, available online http://www.pca-cpa.org.

323 *Rhine Case Study, supra* note 1, at 31.

324 Jan Leentvaar, *Integrated Water Management in River Basin Districts*, (Swiss Federal Institute of Aquatic Science and Technology) EAWAG news 51, 2002 available online http://www.eawag.ch/publications/eawagnews/www_en51/en51e_pdf/en51e_leent.pdf.

officials from the contracting parties. The coordination group is still organizing most of planning work at the ICPR and coordinates the tasks of working groups. In addition to the working groups that existed before the adoption of the WFD—such as groups on water quality, emissions, and floods—new working groups have been added that address groundwater, water economy, and geographic information systems (GIS). Working groups are to report to both the coordination group (for the purposes of the ICPR) and the preparatory group (for the purpose of coordination with the WFD).

This double reporting is necessary because, in addition to the existing ICPR structure (See Figure 18.1), another coordinating structure called a Coordinating Committee of Rhine and WFD functions in parallel with the Plenary Assembly of the ICPR and a Preparatory Group functions alongside the Coordination Group of the ICPR. The Coordinating Committee of Rhine and the WFD (the CC) was put into effect during a conference of the Rhine ministers that was held on January 29, 2001. Germany, France, the Netherlands, Austria, Switzerland, Belgium, Luxembourg, Liechtenstein, and Italy participate in the CC at the level of water director. The CC includees representatives of federal *länder* of Germany and representatives from the region of Wallonia of Belgium. The number of competent authorities involved in the CC, especially because of the federal structure of Germany, will certainly increase the complexity of decisionmaking. Eight *länder* of Germany have been designated competent of authorities for the implementation of the WFD in the Rhine

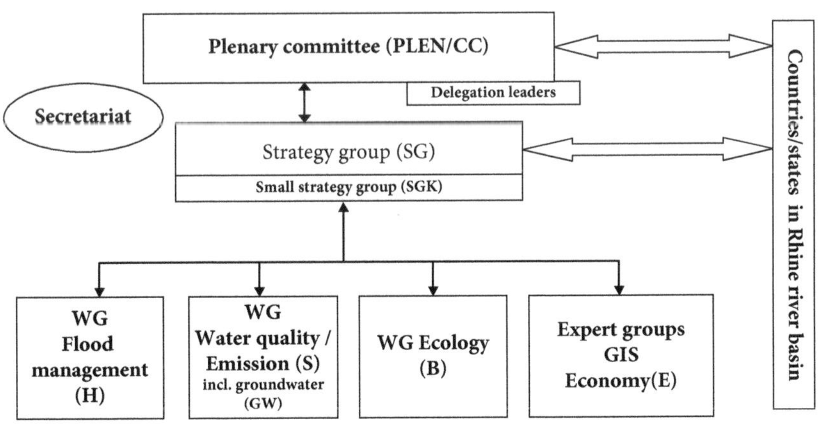

Figure 18.1 Organizational Structure of the ICPR

River basin.[325] The number of authorities that these *länder* need to coordinate to ensure the effectiveness of the WFD at the local level is equally large. In the case of Baden-Würtemberg, forty-seven local authorities have to coordinate their efforts to ensure the WFD implementation (four regional presidents and forty-three local collectivities).[326] Furthermore, certain states, such as France and Belgium, have designated regional authorities for the implementation of the WFD. Belgium has designated the General Direction of the Natural Resources and of the Environment of the Ministry of Wallonia and France has designated the préfet (prefect) for the coordination of the Meuse and Rhine River basins. The Netherlands, Austria, and Luxembourg have designated a central institution to be primarily in charge of the WFD implementation in the Rhine while Switzerland, not being an EU state, does not have to designate a competent authority.[327] Coordinating these national, regional and länder authorities is obviously not an easy task and the secretariat of the ICPR assists the CC in the execution of its tasks.[328]

To enable the implementation of the WFD, the Rhine River basin district has been divided into nine subbasin working areas. These working areas of the Rhine are international working areas. The final river basin management plan will be comprised of a part A that would provide an overview of the Rhine River basin district and nine parts B for each of the nine working areas.[329]

Part A and part B reports produced for the Rhine River basin district should be seen as an integral document. The completion of part A requires the coordination of all states including the *länder* and regions of the Rhine district. The completion of part B reports require coordination among the states, *länder*, and regions that constitute the working areas for which the part B report is prepared. The reports prepared for the working areas follow a uniform structure that is adjusted by the coordination committee.

---

325 These *länder* are Baden-Würtemberg, Bavaria, Hesse, Rhineland-Palatinate, Saarland, North Rhine-Westphalia, Lower Saxony, and Thuringia.

326 *International Hydrographic District of Rhine, Characteristics, study of the effects of human activity on the environment and economic analysis of the water use, Part A of Report submitted to the European Commission*, at 14, Mar. 18, 2005 [hereinafter *Rhine Roof Report*].

327 *Id.* at 14.

328 *Id.* at 3.

329 The nine working areas that have been designated for the Rhine River Basin District are Alp Rhine/Lake Constance; High Rhine; Upper Rhine; Neckar; Main; Middle Rhine; Moselle and Sarre; Lower Rhine and; Delta Rhine. *Id.* at 4.

Both part A and part B reports are calibrated to ensure the coherence of the final report.

Other International Commissions and Initiatives

International Regulatory Commission of the Alpine Rhine

The International Regulatory Commission of the Alpine Rhine was established in 1995 with the participation of the Swiss cantons of St. Gallen and Graubunden, the Principality of Liechtenstein, and the state of Vorarlberg in Austria. The purpose of the commission is to coordinate river basin management in the region.[330]

Coordination in Lake Constance

Lake Constance is shared among Germany, Austria, and Switzerland. The lake provides drinking water for more than four million people and it is at the center of multiple activities taking place in the region including tourism, agriculture, and intensive industry. The upper Lake Constance is one of the rare areas in Europe where the border between Switzerland and Germany remains undefined. This upper Lake Constance is considered common property between the two countries and it is called *condominium*.[331]

The first regulatory efforts in the lake targeted fishing.[332] The International Conference of Deputies for Fishery in Lake Constance (IBKF) was the only regulatory body in the region until 1959 when the International Commission for the Protection of Lake Constance (IGKB) was established.[333] Two German *länder*, Baden-Württemberg and Bavaria, and Austria and Switzerland adopted an agreement for the protection of

330 *See Public Participation in River Basin Management in Switzerland: "Fighting against Floods,"* Report produced as part of the Workpackage 4 of HarmoniCOP Project (Colenco Power Engineering, Dec. 15, 2003). The HarmoniCOP project, which run from 2002 to 2005, had as a goal to promote the understanding of participatory river basin management in Europe. The HarmoniCOP project was sponsored by the European Commission. For information about the project *see* http://www.harmonicop.uos.de/index.php.

331 H. Gerd Schröder, *Transboundary Water Management in Lake Constance: from tradition to co-operation* presented at the International Workshop Value of Water–Different Approaches in Transboundary Water Management, Koblenz, Germany, Mar. 10–11, 2005.

332 *Id.*

333 *Id.*

the lake.[334] The main duties of the IGKB consist of monitoring pollution in the lake and recommending measures to be undertaken for the protection of the lake.[335] The commission adopts resolutions by unanimity.

Other organizations involved in the region include the Syndicate of the Waterworks in the Lake Constance-Rhine Region (AWBR) that was founded in 1968 as an international nongovernmental organization (NGO). The association is responsible for the water supply of ten million people.[336] The International Conference of Heads of Governments (IBK) started as an informal process in 1972. The process was formalized in 1995 when the conference adopted its operating statute and a budget. The IBK has political importance as it is comprised of government leaders in the region.[337] The International Navigation Commission for the Lake Constance (ISKB) was established in 1973 by Austria, Switzerland and Germany. Since navigation is a federal issue in Germany, the federal government, and not the *länder*, participates in the works of the ISKB. [338]

The role of the ICPR and the CC is to integrate the work of these different, stand-alone bodies, the data that they have collected and their contribution to water management in the region. The coordination of these divergent bodies is essential in order to develop a coherent river basin management plan for the Rhine. An issue pertinent here is whether the WFD will change or reorient the agenda of some of these regional bodies.

At the time of this writing, there are not many indices that the International Commission for the Protection of Lake Constance is ready to align its agenda with that of the WFD, at least in terms of organization of its work. For instance, the expert groups of the IGKB, as of June 2007, consist of expert groups on catchment area, damage defense, the lake, and public works.[339] The organizational structure of the IGKB does not yet reflect the work that has to be performed under the WFD. Switzerland,

---

334 *Id.*

335 *Id.* The commission publishes green reports that include monitoring data and blue reports that are studies on specific topics. The IGKB has established an information system called "Lake Constance Water Information System 'BOWIS'" that provides data about the lake. The IGKB has concentrated its efforts on the reduction of eutrophication and four billion euros have been invested in sewage treatment plants that have improved water quality. *Id.*

336 *Id.*

337 *Id.*

338 *Id.*

339 Information on the commission is available at its website www.igkb.de.

one of the members of the commission, does not have a plan to implement the WFD,[340] although it has legislation and regulations to achieve results tantamount to those pursued by the directive. Switzerland, a European Free Trade Association (EFTA) country,[341] cooperates with neighboring countries for the WFD implementation by providing the necessary data. It also takes part in the EU meetings of water directors. But the restructuring of the IGKB cannot take place as long as Switzerland is reluctant to proceed with it. Whether the WFD will be implemented smoothly in the Lake Constance region depends on the cooperation of Switzerland and the cantons that manage the lake. Since Switzerland has programs similar to those promoted by the WFD, one can claim that the basis for cooperation is already established.[342]

One of the challenges in the region is to create more coherence among the plethora of international institutions that compete for legitimacy. Many decisions on the use of the lake are made at the local level and transboundary cooperation among local authorities needs to be pursued. Intersectoral coordination between the protection of the environment and the pursuit of navigation is still at its infancy.

International Commissions for the Protection of the Moselle and Sarre against Pollution

The International Commissions for the Protection of the Moselle and Sarre against Pollution (CIPMS or Commissions Internationales pour la

340 S. Nilsson *et al.*, *International River Basin Districts under the EU Water Framework Directive, European Water Management Online*, at 5 (2004).

341 The European Free Trade Association (EFTA) is comprised of Iceland, Liechtenstein, Norway, and Switzerland. The EU and its member states have entered into an agreement in 1992 with Iceland, Liechtenstein and Norway on the creation of a European Economic Area. More information on EFTA is available online http://www.efta.int.

342 *See also Environmental Information in Transboundary River Basin Policy-Making and Management 32*, in Selected European Case Studies, Working Paper (Sindre Langaas, ed., Oct. 2002) available online http://www.lwr.kth.se/Personal/personer/nilsson_susanna/info_report.pdf. This is a study executed under the EU research project "Integrated Strategies for the *Ma*nagement of *Tra*nsboundary Waters on the *East*ern European Fringe (MANTRA-East), EU Fifth Framework Programme. *See also* Adeline Kroll *et al.*, *Integrated Water Resource Management for Important Deep European Lakes and their Catchment Areas, First Analysis of Legislation*, at 39, Feb. 21, 2003 available online http://www.hydromod.de/Eurolakes/results/D32.pdf. Eurolakes is a project funded by the European Commission's Fifth Framework Program under the Key Action Sustainable Management and Quality of Water. Information about the project is available online www.eurolakes.com.

Protection de la Moselle and de la Sarre-CIPMS) play an important role in the working area of the Moselle/Sarre of the Rhine River basin. As early as in 1956, the Convention for the Canalization of Moselle provided that state parties must undertake measures to ensure the protection of waters of the Moselle River.[343] The cooperation of state parties was institutionalized on December 20, 1961, when Germany, France, and Luxembourg signed an agreement that established the International Commission for the Protection of the Moselle against Pollution.[344] The International Commission for the Protection of the Sarre, which is one of the tributaries of Moselle, was established simultaneously with the Moselle Commission under an agreement between Germany and France.[345] The conventions that established the two commissions entered into force in 1962.

To avoid duplication of work, states decided to join the Moselle Commission and the Sarre Commission and to establish a common secretariat to be shared by both commissions. The commissions merged into a single institutional structure through a protocol that was adopted on March 22, 1990,[346] to form CIPMS.

The purpose of the commissions is to determine the sources and nature of pollution affecting the Moselle/Sarre and to recommend measures to protect the rivers. A permanent secretariat for the commissions was established in 1991, and the commissions have been involved in various activities including the establishment of a working group on ecology and recommendations on measures to control flooding.

The adoption of the WFD has affected both the structure of the CIPMS and the work executed by them. In 2001, France, Luxembourg,

---

343 *Convention for the Canalisation of Moselle*, Oct. 27, 1956 with signatory states Luxembourg, France and Germany. The Moselle Commission established under the convention has extensive administrative powers including the levying of tolls, the supervision and execution of works of the canalization of the Moselle and the establishment of special navigation courts. *See Integration of European Waterways*, *supra* note 291, at 20.

344 *Protocol between the Governments of the Federal Republic of Germany, the French Republic and the Grand Duchy of Luxembourg concerning the Constitution of an International Commission for the Protection of the Moselle against Pollution*, Dec. 20, 1961 available online http://www.iksms-cimps.org.

345 *Protocol between the Federal Republic of Germany and the French Republic concerning the Constitution of an International Commission for the Protection of the Sarre against Pollution*, Dec. 20, 1961 available online http://www.iksms-cimps.org.

346 *Complementary Protocol between the Governments of Federal of Germany, the French Republic and the Grand Duchy of Luxembourg*, Mar. 22, 1990 available online http://www.iksms-cimps.org.

and Germany, the latter through the *länder* of North Rhine-Westphalia, Rhineland-Palatinate, and Saarland that are responsible for water management in the Moselle/Sarre, decided to coordinate their efforts for the implementation of the directive. Furthermore, the Wallonia Region of Belgium—that is affected by water management in the region—has been invited to participate in the works of the CIPMS. The CIPMS are to provide the platform for the coordination of processes that would lead to the effectuation of the WFD, including coordination on groundwater management.

The CIPMS went through a reorganization in 2002 with the goal to adapt their process to the requirements of the WFD and produced by 2005 a report on the state of waters in the Moselle/Sarre basin. After the finalization of the 2005 report, that was presented to the public in June 2005, the commissions restructured again in order to implement the monitoring program and to elaborate the river basin management plan that is mandated by the WFD. The new reorganization of the Moselle/Sarre basin involves the plenary assembly that is the official decisionmaking body and a coordination group (Organizational Chart of Moselle-Sarre, Figure 18.2).

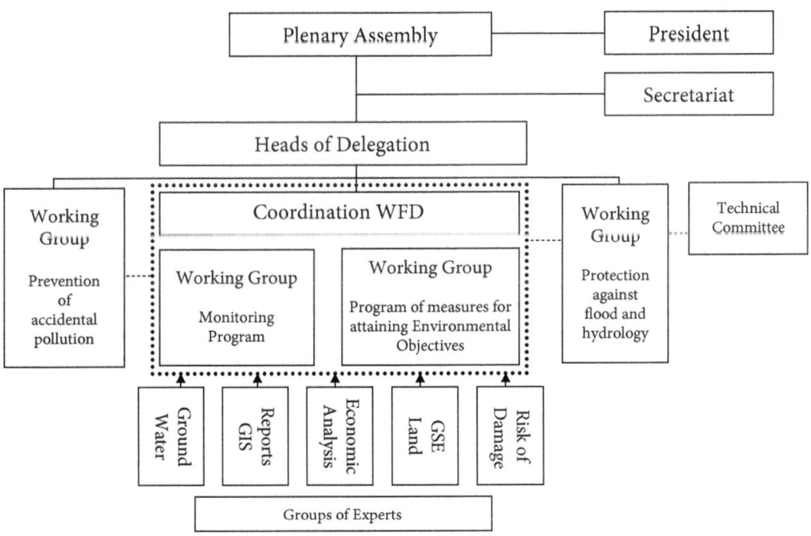

Figure 18.2 Organizational Chart of CIPMS

Since the Moselle/Sarre is one of the working areas of the Rhine, it must produce the part B report that details the impacts and pressures on the basin. The 2005 Part B report of the Moselle/Sarre has been prepared under the coordination of two regional authorities, two *länder*, and one central national authority.[347]

The CIPMS have identified the problems that affect the Moselle/ Sarre working area. In addition to pollution, that is to be expected in an industrialized region, the lack of continuity of rivers, and the impact of various uses (navigation, energy production, and flood control) have been mentioned.

International Commission for the Hydrology of the Rhine Basin

The International Commission for the Hydrology of the Rhine Basin (CHR) was established in 1970 and its member states include Austria, Germany, France, Luxembourg, Switzerland, and the Netherlands. The CHR operates within the framework of the International Hydrological Program (IHP) of UNESCO and the Hydrology and Water Resources Programme (HWRP) of WMO (World Meteorological Organization). The CHR is a permanent, autonomous international commission that has the status of a foundation registered in the Netherlands. Members of the commission are the scientific and water management organizations of the Rhine River basin.[348]

347
- The Coordinating Prefect of the Rhine-Meuse Basin (France);
- The Ministry of Environment of Saarland (Germany);
- The Ministry of Environment and Forest of Rhineland-Palatinate (Germany);
- The Ministry of Wallonia Region (Belgium);
- The Ministry of Interior (Luxembourg). *See* District Hydrographique International Rhin, Secteur de travail international "Moselle Sarre," Partie B: Etat des lieux, at 22 (translation: *International Hydrographic District of Rhine, Working Area "Moselle-Sarre," Part B: a Status Assessment*) (Commissions Internationales pour la Protection de la Moselle and de la Sarre, June 2005)[hereinafter *Moselle-Sarre, Part B*].

348 These organizations include: the Federal Office for Water and Geology in Switzerland, the Federal Institute of Hydrology in Germany, the Regional Office for the Environment, Lorraine, France, the Rhine-Meuse Water Agency in France, the Directorate-General for Public Works and Water Management (RIZA) in the Netherlands, the Water Management Authority of Luxembourg, the Government Office of the State Vorarlberg—Water Management Department, Austria, the Federal Ministry for Agriculture, Forestry, Environment and Water Management, Dept. VII/3, Austria, and the EAWAG, Switzerland.

The CHR consists of permanent representatives of member states, who are the coordinators of the commission, and a secretariat. The permanent representatives are responsible for encouraging the involvement of public and private sector research organizations in the work of the CHR. The commission defines its strategy and program of activities and decides on projects that are to be pursued. The CHR coordinates its activities with other international bodies, such as the ICPR. The secretary of the ICPR attends the CHR meetings and the CHR members take part in ICPR working groups.[349]

The mission of the CHR is the expansion of knowledge on hydrology of the Rhine River basin through joint research. The CHR hopes to contribute to the solution of cross-border problems through the formulation and management of information systems.[350] The CHR is conducting research on water economy and flood control, sediment management, hydrological forecasts and models, and climatic changes and their possible effects on the river.

The ICPR and the CHR have worked cooperatively for the development of the Rhine Alarm Model since the early 1990s. The model predicts the status of pollution following an accidental discharge of harmful substances. When water becomes polluted, it is essential for users, such as water supply companies and water boards, to be appraised of the nature and extent of pollution so that they can take necessary measures.

Specific Agreements

In addition to the multilateral initiatives, a number of agreements deal with specific issues of the countries that border the Rhine. Specialized agreements address a variety of matters, including the frontier between two states or two regions,[351] hydrological works,[352] various issues of water quantity,[353] the

---

349 However, the ICPR coordination group rejected the application of CHR for the acquisition of an observer status within that group based on the rationale that the written goals of the CHR compete with the goals of the ICPR. *See Rhine Case Study, supra* note 282, at 23.

350 *See* website of CHR, http:// www.chr-khr.org.

351 *Treaty of Limits between France and the Netherlands Concluded at Courtray*, Jan. 22, 1998.

352 *State Treaty between Luxembourg and West Germany concerning the Construction of Hydroelectric Power-installation on the Our*, Apr. 25, 1950.

353
- *Agreement between Belgium and the Netherlands for Withdrawal of Water from the Lake Constance*, Feb. 24, 1961.
- *Convention between the Delegates of the Riparian States of Lake Constance: Bade, Bavaria, Austria, Switzerland and Wurtemberg concerning the Flow of Water of the Lake Constance near Constance*, Oct. 27, 1956.

further development of the river[354] environmental protection,[355] and flood management.[356]

The evolution of the Rhine regime depends on the collaboration of the three commissions, namely, the International Commission for the Hydrology of the Rhine Basin, which is more research oriented, the ICPR, and the Central Commission for Navigation of the Rhine. The coordination among these centralized international bodies and the various other subregional commissions regulating the management of working areas could provide the key for a more consistent and integrated approach to water management based on the requirements of the WFD.

Coordination with the aim to reduce some of the inevitable duplication of effort is the operative goal here.[357] Eventually, good cooperation in the Rhine would involve the recognition of one of these commissions as the lead commission for the protection and further development of the Rhine. The ICPR, because of its function and jurisdictional reach, could assume a leading role in the region. Whether the other commissions would be ready to recognize such a role for the ICPR remains to be seen.

354
- *Convention between the French Republic and the Federal Republic of Germany concerning the Development of the Rhine between Strasbourg/Kehl and Lauterbourg/Neuburgweier*, Apr. 30, 1966.
- *Agreement between the Government of the Federal Republic of Germany and the Government of the Grand Duchy of Luxembourg concerning the Maintenance, Restoration and Operation of the Section of the Moselle Common to the two States*, Mar. 28, 1820.
- *Treaty between the Swiss Confederation and the Republic of Austria for the Regulation of the Rhine from the Mouth of Ill to Lake Constance*, Sept. 14, 1976.
- *Convention between the Federal Republic of Germany and the French Republic on the Management of the Upper Course of the Rhine between Basel and Strasbourg and Protocol Annexed to the Convention*, Dec. 3, 1976.

355
- *Convention concerning the Collection, Storage, and Discharge of Waste from Ships Navigating along the Rhine and other Inland Waters*, Nov. 19, 1924.
- *Convention concerning the Protection of Italo-Swiss Waters against Pollution*, Sept. 9, 1996.
- *Agreement between the Government of the Land Badenwurttemberg and the Swiss Federal Council concerning the Joint Construction and Operation of a Monitoring and Control Station Downstream of Basel to Monitor the Water Quality of the Rhine River*, Sept. 25, 1991.

356 *Agreement between the Government of the French Republic, the Government of the Federal Republic of Germany and the Government of the Grand Duchy of Luxembourg on Flood Warning for the Catchment Basin of the Moselle*, Mar. 12, 1986.

357 *See also Rhine Case Study, supra* note 1, at 32.

Chapter 19

Institution Building in the Scheldt and Meuse Rivers

Scheldt Regime

Early Institutional Development

The Scheldt River is shared between France (31 percent), Belgium (61 percent),[358] and the Netherlands (8 percent). France is the upstream riparian while Belgium and the Netherlands are downstream of the river.[359] The Scheldt River, because of its strategic position for navigation, has been a source of conflict between the Netherlands and Belgium. The Western Scheldt is located on the Dutch territory and Belgium, particularly the Flemish region of Belgium, depends on the Netherlands for the maintenance and improvement of the navigation channel.[360] The thorny issue in

---

358 Flemish Region, 43 percent; Walloon Region, 17 percent; and Brussels Region, 1 percent.

359 André Wehrli and Peter Kienzler, *Case Study Schelde/Scheldt/Escaut,* Swiss Federal Institute for Environmental Science and Technology and Swiss Federal Institute of Technology Zurich, Nov. 2003[hereinafter *Scheldt Case Study*]. For a comprehensive study on the international developments on the Scheldt, *see* Sander V. Meijerink, *Conflict and Cooperation on the Scheldt River Basin: A Case Study of Decision Making on International Scheldt Issues between 1967 and 1997* (1999).

360 *Scheldt Case Study, id.* at 6.

the Scheldt River basin is that the Netherlands, as a downstream state, depends on France and Belgium to safeguard water quality by preventing the discharge of pollutants that end up downstream while Belgium (the Flemish region) depends on the Netherlands for the maintenance of the navigation channel in the Western Scheldt that allows for access to the port of Antwerp.

The institutional development in the Scheldt River basin goes back to the 1839 Separation Treaty concluded between Belgium and the Netherlands which provided that on the Scheldt River, freedom of navigation is established for all nations. The treaty guarantees the freedom of navigation between the Scheldt and the Rhine.[361] The 1839 Separation Treaty established the Permanent Commission for Supervision of Scheldt Navigation (Belgisch-Nederlandse Permanente Commissie van Toezicht op de Scheldevaart) which held its first meeting in 1840.[362] The Permanent Commission (PC) was established to guarantee Belgium access to the port of Antwerp since the Western Scheldt was under the jurisdiction of the Netherlands. The PC is comprised today of four commissioners: two from the Netherlands and two from the region of Flanders of Belgium. The Netherlands is represented to the commission by the Director General for the Transport of Goods of the Ministry of Transport, Public Works and Water Management and the Chief-Engineer-Manager of the province of Zeeland.[363] On February 5, 2001, the PC held its 600th meeting. The PC has been considered the highest body for the management of navigation on the Scheldt, and it meets every quarter alternating between Vlissingen and Antwerp. Today, the purpose of the PC has shifted from the supervision of navigation to the development of a common nautical policy given the specific characteristics and traffic volumes on the Scheldt River.[364]

Cooperation between Belgium and the Netherlands has not been smooth always because of the reality of circumstances that placed the navigational Scheldt under the jurisdiction of the Netherlands, a jurisdiction that the Netherlands had to willy-nilly share with Belgium through the PC. Overall, though, the PC has worked in a satisfactory manner given the tensions and the potential for conflict in the region.

---

361 *Integration of European Waterways, supra* note 291, at 21.
362 *Scheldt Case Study, supra* note 359, at 10.
363 Information on the PC is available online http://www.vts-scheldt.net/.
364 *Id.*

Another commission that has played an important role in the development of the Scheldt is Technical Scheldt Commission (Technische Sheldecommissie or TSC).[365] The Technical Scheldt Commission was established in 1948 with the objective to advise Belgium and the Netherlands on the technical problems of navigation in the Western Scheldt including the deepening of the Western Scheldt. The TSC is comprised of officials of both the countries and functions through several subcommissions that are assisted by various working groups.

A 1995 treaty has been adopted between the Netherlands and the Flanders region on the deepening of the Scheldt[366] followed by a 2005 agreement on the further deepening of the river.[367] In 2002, the Dutch and the Flemish governments adopted the memorandum of the Vlissingen that establishes a long-term plan (until 2030)[368] for the Scheldt as a healthy and multifunctional water system that supports human needs in a sustainable way.[369] To ensure the sustainability of projects undertaken on the Scheldt, the Netherlands and the region of Flanders have commissioned an environmental impact report and a social cost-benefit report. The reports have not found any significant environmental deterioration or impacts on flood protection due to the deepening of the Scheldt.

What is interesting about these early institutional developments, that are still enduring, is how they are disconnected from the institutional framework, analyzed below, on the protection of the Scheldt. The overall separation of the works on the Scheldt from the work of the International Scheldt Commission point out to the segmentation of the regime of the Scheldt. The question is whether such segmentation is still acceptable given the new regime established under the water framework directive (WFD).

---

365 *Scheldt Case Study, supra* note 359, at 14.

366 January 17, 1995. Under the terms of the agreement, the Flemish region is charged with taking care of dredging operations while the Netherlands is responsible for cleaning up the shipwrecks and restoring the natural environment. The bulk of the costs of the operation were undertaken by the Flemish government. The Belgian Audit Office and the Netherlands Court of Audit found that the parties should have conducted a cost-benefit analysis before deciding on the deepening of the river.

367 March 11, 2005. The further deepening of the Scheldt has not been excluded. The deepening of the Scheldt is considered necessary in order to maintain the competitiveness of Antwerp as ships that enter the port are becoming larger to accommodate the increase in the transport of goods worldwide.

368 The Scheldt Estuary Development Plan 2010.

369 *Scheldt Case Study, supra* note 359, at 16.

International Scheldt Commission

Unlike the Rhine, where multilateral cooperation has been an early institutional development, comprehensive cooperative arrangements for the protection of the Scheldt River were not established till 1994. The Charlesville-Mézières Treaty that took its name from the place of its signing was the first treaty to address the protection of the river.[370] State parties to the treaty were France, the Netherlands, the Walloon Region, the Flemish Region, and the Brussels Capital Region of Belgium. Although parties to international treaties are rarely regions of states, this became necessary here because of the federal structure of Belgium and the important role played by regions in the development of water policy.[371]

The treaty defines the fluvial basin of the Scheldt and the basin that surrounds the Scheldt.[372] The convention was adopted under the auspices of 1992 Helsinki Convention. Countries undertake to cooperate, in the spirit of good neighborliness, to preserve and improve the quality of the Scheldt.[373] Some of the principles on which this convention is based are principles of international environmental law that were amplified in the 1992 Rio Conference on Environment and Development.[374] These are the principle of precaution, the principle of prevention, the principle of reduction of pollution at the source and the polluter pays principle.[375] The parties undertake to put in place measures of integrated management of waters of the basin.[376]

The 1994 treaty established the International Commission for the Protection of the Scheldt against Pollution. The goals of the commission include identification of sources of pollution, coordination of monitoring programs with the aim to achieve a network of homogenous measures, development of inventories and promotion of exchange of information

370 *Treaty for the Protection of the Scheldt*, Apr. 26, 1994 [hereinafter *1994 Scheldt Treaty*] available online http://www.isc-cie.com/members/docs/documents/2288.pdf.

371 After Belgium became a federal state, most of the competencies with regard to the management of water and the protection of the environment became exclusively the competencies of the three regions. Coastal waters, remained, however, under the competence of the federal government. *See Scheldt International River Basin District: Roof Report*, Feb. 2005, at 1, note 1 [hereinafter *Scheldt Roof Report*].

372 Art. 1, *1994 Scheldt Treaty, supra* note 370.

373 Art. 2, *id.*

374 *UN Conference on Environment and Development (Earth Summit)*, Rio de Janeiro, Brazil, June 3-June 14, 1992.

375 Art. 3(2), *1994 Scheldt Treaty, supra* note 370.

376 Art. 3(4), *id.*

regarding the sources of pollution.[377] The commission must put into effect programs of action and it must, at regular intervals, evaluate programs of action it has put in place.[378] The 1994 Scheldt Agreement already addresses, therefore, some of the activities that need to be undertaken to effectuate integrated water resources management. A homogenous monitoring network has been put in place since 1998 and the commission has been issuing annual reports on the progress of cooperation in the Scheldt.

The adoption of the WFD precipitated further developments in the Scheldt River basin and state parties resolved to adopt a new treaty in 2002.[379] This new treaty that was signed by Belgium, in addition to its regions, established the international hydrographic district of the Scheldt. This international hydrographic region includes, in addition to the water-course of the Scheldt, the terrestrial and maritime zone, and the ground-water that is connected to the river.[380] The treaty was adopted to serve the goals of the WFD.[381] The International Commission for the Protection of the Scheldt has been renamed International Scheldt Commission denoting, thus, the more extensive duties of the new commission in accordance with the WFD.[382]

The goals of the commission are redefined to fulfill the obligations of state parties under the WFD. The treaty now clearly provides that the commission must issue opinions or recommendations to ensure the implementation of the agreement[383] and ensure the coordination of activities that have to do with the implementation of the WFD.[384] The functions of the commission are now broader and include flood management, taking into account ecological and spatial matters,[385] the designation of alarm and warning systems and the control of accidental pollution,[386] and the

377 Art. 5(a)-(c), *id.*
378 Art. 5(d)-(e), *id.*
379 *International Treaty for the Scheldt,* Dec. 3, 2002 [hereinafter *2002 Scheldt Treaty*] available online http://www.isc-cie.com/members/docs/documents/4653.pdf.
380 Art. 1(d), *id.*
381 *See*, e.g., preamble and art. 1(a), *id.*
382 Art. 1(e), *id.*
383 Art. 4(2), *id.*
384 Art. 4(3), *id.* Such activities include the analysis of characteristics of the international river basin district, the economic analysis of water, the monitoring programs, the programs of measures and the production of a river basin management plan for the hydrographic district of the Scheldt.
385 Art. 4(4)(a), *id.*
386 *Id. See also* art. 4(4)(c).

improvement of fisheries.[387] The commission must ensure coordination among subbasins and among basins situated entirely within a state party.[388] The jurisdictional reach of the commission can be further extended as long as state parties agree to do so.[389] The protection of the river from the impacts of navigation is not mentioned as an explicit goal in the treaty. Such a goal is important as the improvement of Seine-Scheldt connection is becoming one of the Trans-European Transport Networks (TEN-T) priority goals for the advancement of inland navigation in Europe and given that the International Scheldt Commission has to become an effective organization in administrating the WFD in the river basin.

The commission adopts its recommendations and opinions by unanimity.[390] The treaty does not provide details about the legal ramifications of the nonimplementation of opinions and recommendations issued by the commission and under what circumstances these recommendations are binding. The treaty does not provide for an obligation of states to report back to the commission on the state of implementation of recommendations that have been issued. The inclusion of provisions in the treaty that identify the legal nature of recommendations and that provide for some method of accountability for lack of compliance are usually helpful to move treaties forward and could prong reluctant parties to compliance.

The decisionmaking organ of the commission is the plenary assembly of the parties.[391] The heads of delegations coordinate the work of the commission in between the meetings of the plenary assembly.[392] The heads of delegations can establish working groups that may be restructured to fulfill the requirements of the WFD.[393] The commission's activities are financed by state parties.[394]

---

387 Art. 4(4)(d), *id.*

388 Art. 4(5)–(6), *id.*

389 Art. 4(7), *id.*

390 Art. 5(4), *id.*

391 Art. 5, International Scheldt Commission, *Internal and Financial Rules of Procedure*, adopted Dec. 2, 2003 [hereinafter *Rules of Procedure Scheld Commission*].

392 Art. 7, *id.*

393 Art. 8, *id.*

394 Art. 7, 2002 *Scheldt Treaty, supra* note 379. France and the Flemish Region of Belgium provide the majority of funding for the operation of the commission (France provides 40 percent, the Flemish Region provides 37.5 percent). Wallonia and the Netherlands together provide 17 percent while the rest of funding comes from the Brussels Capital Region and the federal state of Belgium.

State of Waters and River Basin Management Plan

The manipulation of waters to accommodate human purposes has had a long history in the Scheldt River basin. Polders are found all over the river. Canals link the Scheldt River basin with neighboring river basins resulting in water transfers[395] rendering cooperation necessary beyond the district level. The Scheldt River basin district is densely populated and highly urbanized. Industrialization, agricultural development and an advanced transportation infrastructure characterize the area.[396] Antwerp, one of the many ports defining the landscape, is the second largest petrochemical complex in the world after Houston.[397]

Putting together the roof report for the Scheldt River basin district was quite challenging. Because of the heavy industrialization of the area, it is difficult to find areas where water bodies have remained undisturbed. The lack of such areas has impaired the process of establishing reference conditions for the characterization of waters. Over the years, parties have used different criteria and methodologies to identify water bodies, thus undermining the development of a comprehensive and consistent system of typification of such bodies. The monitoring network that has been developed since 1998 has enabled the parties to develop more accurate assessment of water quality. Based on monitoring, it has been concluded that the quality of most waters of the Scheldt ranges from moderate to bad, although there has been some improvement.[398]

The data for the year 2000 for the whole district demonstrate that about half of the domestic wastewater produced by the 12.8 million inhabitants in the Scheldt district is discharged untreated.[399] The distribution of this percentage, however, varies from 3 percent to 80 percent among state parties. Most wastewater is discharged from Lille, Brussels, and Antwerp, major cities located within the basin. Based on the data collected for industrial discharges, the chemical industry, metallurgy, and food industries are heavy polluters in the region.[400]

It is difficult to quantify the impacts from agriculture as methods used by state parties to identify the releases of nutrients into surface water

395 *Scheldt Roof Report, supra* note 371, at 7.
396 *Id.* at 9.
397 *Id.* at 11.
398 *Id.* at 43.
399 *Id.* at 45.
400 *Id.*

and groundwater differ. The results of a partial analysis have demonstrated that the Scheldt River basin is impacted by agriculture as a result of historic pollution.[401] It is expected that wastewater discharges will be reduced in the future. It has been more challenging to determine the evolution of polluting impacts of agriculture as the application of best agricultural practices has yet to become widespread. Discharges from industry are expected to be reduced but at a more gradual pace.[402] Overall, most transboundary watercourses and more than 80 percent of groundwater bodies are estimated to be at risk of not achieving the "good status" prescribed by the WFD.[403] The economic instruments for cost recovery of water services differ from region to region and it has not been possible to construct a comparative overview of the economic analysis of water use.[404]

The compilation of the roof report for the Scheldt River basin district was supported financially by the Interreg III B North-West Europe.[405] Interreg III B is program of the European Community with the aim to promote cooperation among national, regional, and local government actors in the European Union (EU) arena. The idea is to strive to achieve sustainable development and greater territorial coherence.[406] The Interreg III B funded a project called *Scaldit* that took place between January 1, 2003, and December 2006.[407] The focus of the project for the first two years was the compilation of the roof report for the Scheldt River basin that was published and submitted to the European Community in 2005.[408] During 2005 and 2006, Scaldit contributed to the process of developing a river

401 *Id.*

402 *Id.* at 46.

403 *Id.* at 46–47.

404 *Id.* at 46.

405 For more information on this project, *see* Significant Water Management Issues of General Interest in the International Scheldt River Basin District, D/2006/6871/007 available online www.scaldit.org.

406 "The objective of Interreg III B is to promote transnational co-operation between national, regional and local government in order to integrate large groups of European regions more closely in spatial terms, with a view to achieving sustainable, harmonious and balanced development in the Community and greater territorial coherence with Candidate Member States and other neighbouring countries." For more information on Interreg as it relates to the Scaldit project, *see* http://www.scaldit.org. For more information on Interreg North-West Europe, *see* http://www.nweurope.org.

407 The final event of the Scaldit project occurred on October 24, 2006 in Mechelen, Belgium entitled "Boundaries to Water—Water Across Borders: Looking back on the Scaldit Project —Offering an Answer to the International Water Management Issues for the river Scheldt." The Scaldit project was extended till 2008.

408 *See Scheldt Roof Report*, *supra* note 371.

basin management plan for the Scheldt. A number of national and regional bodies of coriparian states have been actively involved in the Scaldit project.[409] The Scaldit project was not run by the International Scheldt Commission and was not coordinated by its secretariat. The Scaldit project had its own Secretariat in the Flemish Environmental Agency.

Participants in the Scaldit project have underlined the role of the International Scheldt Commission as the backbone of cooperation.[410] This has been politically necessary since the commission provides the connection with the political authorities through each contracting party's head of delegation. The support of political authorities is necessary so that documentation produced through the Scaldit project becomes a reference source for all future actions that have to do with integrated river basin management. The coordination between the Scheldt Commission and the Scaldit project notwithstanding, the rationale of not employing the Scheldt Commission for the production of the roof report and the need for a separately financed project is somewhat enigmatic. It seems that certain contracting parties wanted to move the WFD process at a faster pace and that a team dedicated to the project was likely to make that happen.

The Scaldit project had positive effects on the cooperation among state parties. This is because of various factors including:

- A strict calendar under deadlines the meeting of which was necessary for the continuation of funding;
- The provision of a work plan that facilitated collaboration and served as a reminder, when the project was slowed down for reasons of political expediency, that work had to be completed; and

[409] The authorities involved in the Scaldit project include:
- the Flemish Environment Agency (VMM) (Belgium/Flemish Region),
- the Brussels Institute for the Management of the Environment (IBGE) (Belgium/Brussels Capital Region),
- the Direction General of Natural Resources and the Environment (DGRNE) (Belgium/Walloon Region),
- the Coordinating Prefect of the Artois-Picardie Basin (DIREN) (France),
- the Ministry of Transport, Public Works and Water Management (Netherlands); and
- the Province of Zeeland in the Netherlands.

Information on the authorities involved in the Scaldit project is available online http://www.scaldit.org.

[410] *The International Scheldt Commission—the backbone of cooperation*, available online http://www.scaldit.org/scstart_en.cgi?id_boom=21.

- Increasing recognition in international circles of the Scheldt River basin district and its work.

Scaldit has had a positive influence on the cooperation in the Meuse River basin since state parties to Scheldt treaty are also active in the Meuse River basin district. Working under deadlines produced results in the Scheldt basin but simultaneously contributed to a tense environment. This was especially true when some state parties demanded the swift production of data that other parties were not ready to provide. Thus, one could claim that the Scaldit experience was somewhat taxing for some states and regions under continuous pressure to produce results so that the resources provided for by the Scaldit project were not wasted.

The Scaldit project proposed the restructuring of the International Scheldt Commission to facilitate the readiness of that commission to implement the WFD. The decisionmaking organ of the Scheldt Commission is the plenary assembly. The heads of delegation coordinate the work of the commission. As the commission has been restructured to fulfill the requirements of the WFD, the following working groups have been established (See Figure 19.1):

- Communication and public participation;
- Cartography;
- Coastal and transitional waters;
- Fresh surface water;
- Monitoring;
- Groundwater;
- Cost-effectiveness analysis; and
- Floods.

The role of the International Scheldt Commission in the future of water management in the region is unclear, given the number of projects planned for the improvement of navigation on the Scheldt. It was mentioned above that a number of memoranda have been executed between the Netherlands and the Flemish region of Belgium on the deepening of the Scheldt. Other projects currently under way include the connection between the Seine River and the Scheldt River. It is expected that when the Seine-Scheldt connection is realized, one of the major bottlenecks for the further development of the navigation in the region will be removed. The project is already under way and, according to its proponents, it has been planned in

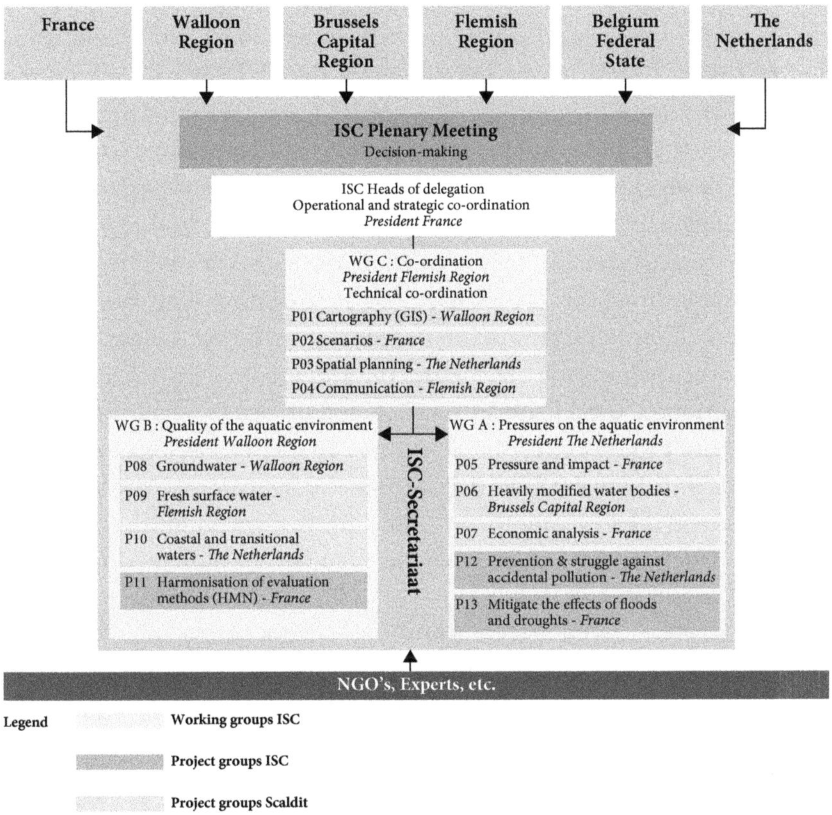

Figure 19.1 Scheldt Commission

a way that would avoid interference with Natura 2000 sites and the conservation of water quality.[411] If the Scheldt Commission is to play the role of the coordinating platform for the implementation of WFD, it is should be given increasing authority to address issues of protection of the environment, as it may be affected by the further development of navigation and other development activities in the region.

Meuse Regime

The Meuse River basin regime has been characterized by an evolution similar to that of the Scheldt regime. The Meuse River basin district is

[411] For more information on the connection Scheldt-Seine project, *see* http://www.inlandnavigation.org/en/transport/tip/seine_scheldt.html.

shared by five countries: France, Belgium, Luxembourg, the Netherlands and Germany. The Brussels capital region, the Flemish region, and the Wallonia region of Belgium are also parties to international agreements that provide the legal basis for cooperation in the Meuse River. The Meuse has been viewed historically as a shipping road and countries in the region have attempted to create a connection between the Scheldt, the Meuse and the Rhine through canals the construction of which dates as early as 1825. The canalization of the Meuse gave rise to a dispute that was brought before the Permanent Court of International Justice.[412] Multilateral efforts to protect the river were not successful until 1994 when the Agreement for the Protection of the Meuse was signed simultaneously with the agreement for the protection of the Scheldt.[413] The agreement was part of a package deal that involved the two treaties, the treaty for the protection of the Meuse and the treaty for the Scheldt, a convention on the deepening of Western Scheldt, and a convention to regulate the flow of the Meuse River.[414]

The 1994 agreement for the protection of the Meuse is similar to the agreement for the protection of the Scheldt adopted on the same date. The agreement was updated in 2002 in order to ensure that cooperation in the Meuse River basin incorporates the requirements of the WFD.[415] The agreement establishes the international hydrographic district of the Meuse.[416] The functions of the commission, which has been renamed the International Commission of the Meuse, are broadened to include the implementation of the WFD,[417] protection against floods,[418] and any other matter that state parties deem necessary for the commission to undertake.[419] The commission's financing is based on contributions by state parties.[420]

---

412 The Diversion of Water from the Meuse, June 28, 1937, (1937) PCIJ, Series A/B, No.70.

413 *Agreement for the Protection of the Meuse*, Apr. 26, 1994 available online http://www.cipm-icbm.be/files/files/FR2.pdf.

414 *See* Erik Mostert, *International Cooperation in the Scheldt and Meuse River Basins, Case Study for the Toolbox Integrated Water Management*, Global Water Partnership, 2001 available online http://www.gwptoolbox.org.

415 *International Meuse Agreement*, Dec. 3, 2002 available online http://www.cipm-icbm.be/files/files/FR1.pdf.

416 Art. 1(d), *id.*

417 Art. 4(3), *id.*

418 Art. 4(4), *id.*

419 Art. 4(6), *id.*

420 Art. 7, *id.* Sixty percent of the funding is divided equally between the Netherlands and the Wallonia region of Belgium. France and Germany provide about the rest 30 percent while the other countries and regions provide the remainder of funding.

The roof report for the Meuse River basin district was ready in 2005.[421] The states and regions of the Meuse River basin district decided on November 28, 2003 that:

- Each state would compile national and/or regional reports in accordance with the WFD.
- State parties would produce a common roof report for the International River Basin of the Meuse in order to complement the national and regional reports. This roof report would include an overview of characteristics of the river basin and of pressures and impacts that affect the river basin at the scale of the district as well as a summary of coordination activities undertaken internationally.[422]

As it was the case with the Scheldt River basin, methodological differences among state parties jeopardized the development of a comprehensive roof report.[423] The roof report for the Meuse River basin, like those of most international river basins, provides an overview of pressures and impacts, and it is based mostly on qualitative rather than quantitative data. Industrialization, agriculture, urbanization, and navigation are the major driving forces of the declining quality of waters of the Meuse. About 50 percent of the natural surface waters of the Meuse are at risk of not meeting environmental objectives by 2015. Almost all artificial and heavily modified water bodies are at risk.[424] Ten percent of groundwater bodies are at risk because of overabstraction, and more than 60 percent of groundwater bodies are at risk because of deteriorating quality.[425] State parties have established methodologies that would allow them to comparatively examine their cost-recovery systems and the economic analysis of water use.

421 *International River Basin District of Meuse, Characteristics, Review of the Environmental Impact of Human Activity, Economic Analysis of Water Use, Roof Report on the International Coordination pursuant to Article 3(4) of the analysis required by Article 5 of Directive 2000/60/EC establishing a framework for Community action in the field of water policy*, Mar. 23, 2005 [*Meuse Roof Report*] available online http://www.cipm-icbm.be/files/files/Rapport_20final_20MEUSE_angl_def_4Mb.pdf.

422 *Id.* at 5.

423 *Id.*

424 *Id.* at 56.

425 *Id.*

Cost recovery varies not only among countries but also among regions of the same country.[426]

The Meuse roof report contains extensive information on the authorities in charge of the WFD implementation. The report gives the impression that regional authorities are to play a vital role in the implementation of the directive. The Coordinating Prefect of Artois Picardie Basin and the Coordinating Prefect of the Rhine-Meuse Basin are the competent authorities for the WFD implementation in the Meuse district in France. In Belgium, it is the regions that are at the driving seat of the WFD implementation. The Flemish region (through the Coordinating Commission on Integral Water Management), the Wallonia region and the Brussels-Capital region have a decisive role to play in the implementation process. In the Netherlands, in addition to the Ministry of Transport, Public Works and Water Management and cooperating ministries, the provinces and water boards that are entirely or partially located within the district have been designated as the competent authorities for the WFD implementation. This includes four provinces, eleven water boards, and the Association of Netherlands Municipalities. Because of the federal structure of Germany, the state of North-Rhine Westphalia[427] has been designated the competent authority for the WFD implementation in the Meuse.[428] The participation of regional and local authorities in international fora makes it imperative to develop policies of participation in international bodies that are coordinated with the national policies. The coordination between national and regional authorities will be vital especially in states where local authorities claim exceptionalism allowing for deviation from national polices.

The restructuring of the Meuse Commission, like that of the Scheldt Commission, was necessary because of the WFD implementation. The plenary assembly is the decisionmaking organ of the commission and the

[426] *Annex 26, Meuse Roof Report, id.* For instance, in France cost-recovery rates are between 59 and 89 percent. In Wallonia, cost recovery with regard to the production of drinking water is 84 percent but with regard to wastewater treatment is only 31 percent. Flanders has declared 100 percent cost recovery for drinking water while in the Netherlands cost-recovery rates vary between 80 and 100 percent. In Germany, cost recovery varies between 88 and 118 percent for drinking water and is about 94 to 126 percent for wastewater.

[427] Through its Ministry for Environment and Nature Protection, Agriculture and Consumer Protection.

[428] For a list of all the competent authorities involved in the management of the Meuse, *see Annex I, Meuse Roof Report, supra* note 421.

heads of delegation, along with the president of the commission and the secretariat, coordinate the operations of the commission. Working groups (on coordination, hydrology and floods, monitoring and programs of measures and objectives) and project groups (on ecology, chemistry, and groundwater) execute the technical work at the commission (See Figure 19.2).

In addition to the multilateral treaty that focuses primarily on water quality, state parties have attempted to resolve issues of water quantity bilaterally. The Meuse Discharge Treaty was adopted in 1995 between Flanders and the Netherlands.[429] The treaty provides for an equal division of water during periods of low water flow as well as for the regulation of specific canals. The treaty focuses on the apportionment of water because of the variability of water availability at different periods of time. Water quantity is expected to continue to be an issue in the region since water demand is estimated to increase in the future.[430]

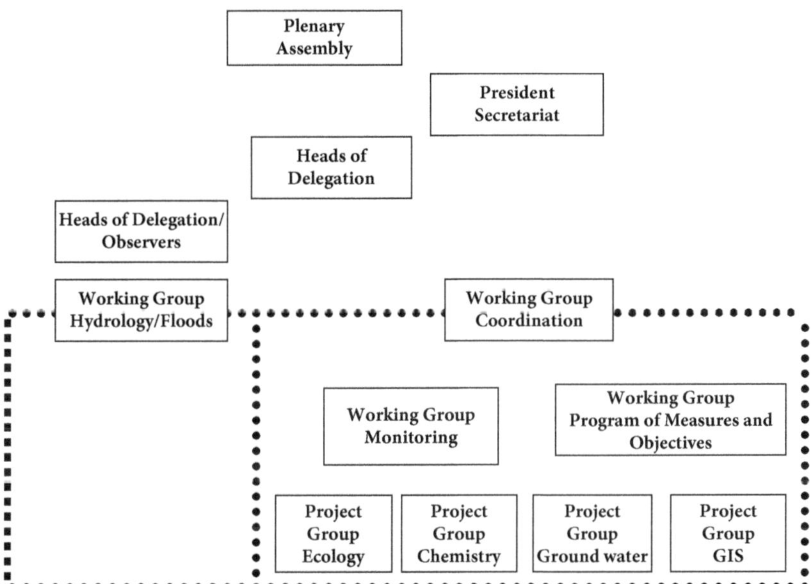

Figure 19.2 Meuse Commission

[429] The treaty was adopted on January 17, 1995 as part of a package deal, *see supra* note 414.

[430] A. Jaskula-Joustra, *River Management and Low Flows in the River Meuse in the Netherlands*, in Proceedings of First International Scientific Symposium on the River Meuse, Maastrich, the Netherlands, Nov. 27–28, 2002.

Chapter 20

The Future of the Elbe River Regime

The Elbe River is shared primarily between the Czech Republic and Germany.[431] Austria and Poland share small portions of the river basin. The Elbe River has been navigable since 1842 and provides a shipping route between Prague and the North Sea. The Elbe River has been considered an excessively polluted river. Today, some of the pollution has been abated due to the closure of factories in the former East Germany and the construction of wastewater treatment plants. Pollution from diffuse sources, though, is still not under control. Nutrients generated from agricultural use[432] negatively affect water quality in the basin. Future pressures may be eminent due to a Danube-Oder-Elbe canal plan that has been proposed.

431 About two-thirds of the Elbe River basin is located in Germany and the rest is located in the Czech Republic. *See Baseline Assessment of the Elbe Basin*, at 4 (NeWater Report Series No. 17, Valentina Krysanova *et al.*, eds., Nov. 2005) (The baseline assessment was prepared by the Potsdam Institute for Climate Impact Research, Germany, the T.G. Masaryk Water Research Institute, Czech Republic and the Institute of Hydrodynamics, Czech Republic.) [hereinafter *Elbe Baseline Assessment*].

432 *Id.* at 4–6.

Some of the first conventions concluded in the region had to do with navigation.[433] After World War II, though, these treaties were not revitalized and as a result the German *länder* undertook the function of regulation of shipping.[434]

The Convention on the International Commission for the Protection of the Elbe (the Elbe Commission) was adopted between the major coriparians in 1990 just after the fall of the iron curtain.[435] The convention is the first international instrument for the protection of the Elbe against pollution. In addition to the state parties to the treaty, Austria and Poland regularly attend the meetings of the commission as observers. As the preamble of the convention explicitly states, state parties are concerned with keeping the Elbe free of pollution and recognize the need to make a sustained contribution to the reduction of pollution in the North Sea.[436] Although the convention does not regulate fishing and shipping, it does cover matters that have to do with the protection of waters against pollution caused by these activities.[437] The commission's role consists of documenting the effects of pollution on the Elbe and of proposing measures to prevent pollution. The commission prepares surveys that show the major sources of pollution, that describe the hydrological conditions in the Elbe area and that

433 *See Convention Instituting the Statute of Navigation of the Elbe*, Feb. 22, 1922 (adopted by Italy, France, Belgium, Germany, Great Britain. and Czechoslovakia). *See also Convention Supplementary to the Statute of Navigation of the Elbe*, Jan. 27, 1923.
A number of bilateral agreements have been executed in the region between Germany and Poland:

- Treaty between Germany and Poland for the Settlement of Frontier Questions, Jan. 27, 1926;
- Agreement between the Government of the Polish Republic and the Government of the German Democratic Republic concerning Navigation in the Frontier Waters and the Use and Maintenance of Frontier Waters, Feb. 6, 1952;
- Agreement between the Federal Republic of Germany and the Republic of Poland on the Cooperation in the Field of Water Management at Border Waters, May 19, 1992.

434 *See Environmental Information in Transboundary River Basin Policy-Making and Management* 52, in Selected European Case Studies (Sindre Langaas, ed., Oct. 2002). This is a study executed under the EU research project "Integrated Strategies for the *Man*agement of *Tra*nsboundary Waters on the *East*ern European Fringe (MANTRA-East), EU Fifth Framework Program.

435 *Convention on the International Commission for the Protection of the Elbe*, Oct. 8, 1990 [hereinafter *Elbe Convention*] (Germany, the Czech Republic, and the European Community). The convention was supplemented by a Protocol, *see Protocol to the Convention of 8 October 1990 between the Governments of the Federal Public of Germany and the Czech and Slovak Federal Republic and the European Economic Community on the International Commission for the Protection of the Elbe*, Dec. 9, 1991.

436 Preamble, *Elbe Convention, id.*

437 Art. 1(4), *id.*

provide documentary evidence regarding the ecological importance of various biotope elements of waters.[438] The commission makes proposals regarding the improvement of conditions of aquatic and coastal communities, proposes limit values for pollutants and the achievement of specific quality objectives, and coordinates the implementation of joint programs of measures.[439] The commission could acquire responsibility for any other matter that state parties assign to it.[440]

State parties need to inform the commission about measures they have undertaken and the commission may, in turn, submit proposals to state parties regarding improvements on those measures.[441] The Elbe Commission can issue decisions and make proposals adopted by unanimity.[442] Given the record of the commission, which has been credited for the improvement of water quality, one could conclude that the compliance of state parties is high. The success of the commission was initially driven by Germany that provides 65 percent of the funding of the commission.[443] Given that the Czech Republic is active in organizing and further developing its water sector, however, it is bound to assume an increasing role in the affairs of the commission and internationally.

The commission has adopted many initiatives in order to abate pollution in the region. The commission adopted an action program (1992-1995) for the Elbe[444]and produced the article 5 report that was submitted to the European Commission. The report addresses, *inter alia*, the economic analysis of water use.[445] The commission has adjusted its structure to fit in with the requirements of the WFD.[446] In addition to the commission that is comprised of representatives of Czech Republic and Germany, a parallel

---

438 Art. 2 (a), (i) and (j), *id.*

439 Art. 2(j), (b), (c), and (d), *id.*

440 Art. 2(2), *id.*

441 Art. 4, *id.*

442 Art. 8, *id.*

443 Art. 14, *id.*

444 The program provided for the construction of new wastewater treatment plants and the reduction of fifteen industrial pollutants by at least 30 percent. The second action program that has been put in place for the period between 1996 and 2010 concentrates on wastewater treatment, the reduction of discharges of additional pollutants as well as the abatement of diffuse pollution.

445 The report is available on the commission's website, http://www.ikse.de.

446 Three working groups assist the commission:

- Implementation of the WFD (WFD);
- Flood protection (FP); and
- Accidental pollution (H).

structure, a Coordinating Committee for the implementation of the WFD (ICG-WFD) has been created. The ICG-WFD is comprised of representatives of Germany, the Czech Republic, Austria, and Poland, as well as the president of the International Elbe Commission (See Figure 20.1).

Cooperation in the Elbe basin, on the German side of the border, is the responsibility of the *länder*. Since a number of *länder* share the basin, they have formed consortia that are responsible for water management in the basin. The Consortium for the Prevention of Pollution of the Elbe (ARGE-Elbe) became active in the region even before the establishment of the Elbe Commission. The ARGE-Elbe was established in 1964 by an agreement of three German *länder* namely Hamburg, Low Saxony, and Schleswig-Holstein. The 1964 agreement was amended in 1977 to give the

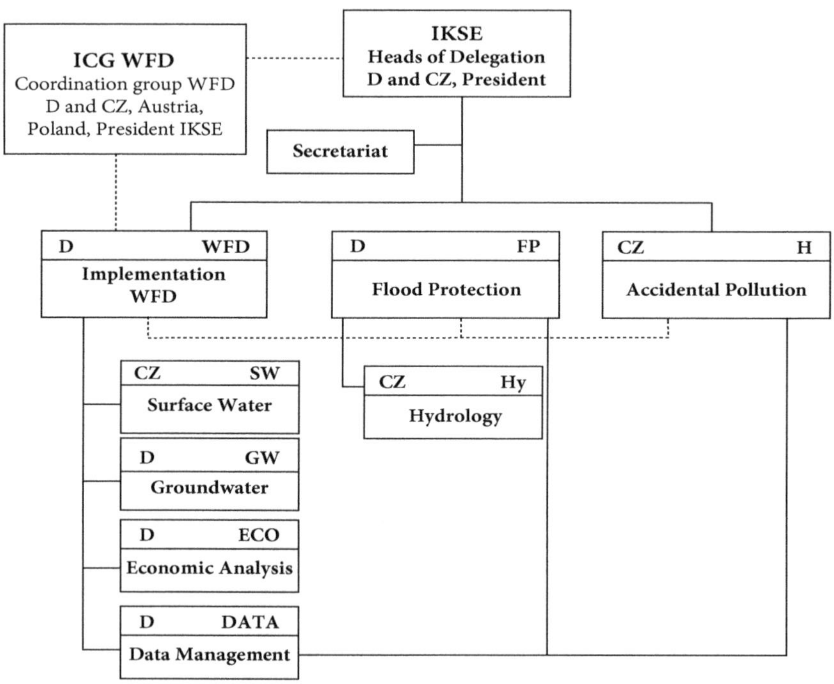

Figure 20.1 Elbe Commission

The working group on the implementation of the WFD is supported by teams of experts on surface water, groundwater, economic analysis, and data management. The working group on flood protection is supported by a team of experts in hydrology. *See* http://www.ikse.de.

ARGE-Elbe its current form. In 1993, the *länder* of Saxony, Saxony-Anhalt, Mecklenburg-Western Pomerania, and Brandenburg joined the ARGE-Elbe that now includes all states that are riparian states of the Elbe. However, states that share the catchment, but are not necessarily coriparians, do not participate in the ARGE-Elbe.[447] Water quality monitoring and flood protection are the primary responsibilities of the ARGE-Elbe, and two working groups have been formed within the consortium to address these matters. Commentators have noted that there has been some tension between the International Commission for the Protection of the Elbe (ICPE) and the ARGE-Elbe due to the fact that the ARGE-Elbe is a much older institution that claims expertise on many ecological issues affecting the Elbe River.[448] The ARGE-Elbe, however, presents only the German side of cooperation on the Elbe River basin, and, therefore, cannot command the legitimacy of an international organization put together by the common will of cooperating states.

Another consortium dedicated to water management in the Elbe River basin is the River Basin Consortium Elbe (FGG–Elbe). The FGG Elbe is comprised of all the *länder* of the Elbe catchment, that is—Bavaria, Berlin, Brandenburg, Hamburg, Macklenburg-Western Promerania, Lower Saxony, Saxony, Saxony-Anhalt, Schleswig-Holstein and Thuringia, and the federal government. This makes the FGG-Elbe a more inclusive and, thus, more authoritative organization than the ARGE-Elbe. The FGG-Elbe was established on March 4, 2004, having as its purpose to coordinate river basin planning for the WFD implementation. The *länder* that make the FGG-Elbe have recognized that the WFD cannot be implemented based on administrative boundaries and that working areas of the Elbe have to be prescribed based on hydrological boundaries.[449]

---

447 Michelle Stubbs and Sophie Bonjour, *Case Study — Elbe River, ETH Seminar: Science and Politics of International Freshwater Management 2003/04*, Swiss Federal Institute of Technology (ETH) Zurich and Swiss Federal Institute for Environmental Science and Technology (EAWAG), Nov. 2002.

448 *Id.* at 6.

449 The FGG-Elbe consortium is organized at three levels. The supreme body of the consortium is the Elbe-Ministerial Conference that consists of ministers and senators of contracting parties with responsibilities in water management. The Elbe-Council consists of the heads of water management departments of the ministries and the senate departments. The Elbe-Council decides on basic issues that have to do with the WFD implementation and the representation of FGG-Elbe in international panels handling international coordination. The Coordinating Council acts as a specialized panel where all partners are represented by one member each. *See* website of FGG-Elbe, http://fgg-elbe.de.

The International Commission for the Protection of the Elbe has been credited for the success of pollution abatement efforts in the region.[450] The Elbe treaty does not give the ICPE the authority to address shipping matters unless they pertain to pollution.[451] Now given the adoption of the WFD and the evolution of the ICPE into a platform for the implementation of the directive, an expansive role of the commission to address all aspects of WFD implementation (including hydromorphological alterations) has to be recognized.

It has been claimed that the ICPE does not exert as much influence as the ICPR. This can be attributed to many factors. The ICPR regime is an older regime (established first in 1950s) that had time to evolve and become ingrained in the Rhine region. The cohesion among the contracting states in the ICPR regime is higher since all countries involved have enjoyed economic stability for a number of years. The same cannot be said for the ICPE regime where the economic disparity between Germany and the Czech Republic is still obvious. One must note that Germany shares a large portion of the financial burden for the functioning of the ICPE and, thus, would probably expect to have more say in its decisions.[452] The treaty that established the ICPE is not an instrument for integrated water management as it predominantly addresses issues of water quality. Germany and the Czech Republic have signed further agreements to address issues of water works and water allocation across the borders.

The Czech Republic shares a border with Saxony that is 454 kilometers long where most of watercourses from the territory of the Czech Republic flow into Germany, the Elbe River, and then into the North Sea. The Bavarian boundary between the Czech Republic and Germany is 357 kilometers long and at many areas it crosses the divide between the Elbe River and the Danube River.[453]

Cooperation between the Czech Republic and Saxony on the management of transboundary waters was initiated as early as in 1955. In 1970

---

450 *See* Susanna Nilsson, *The Role and Use of Information in Transboundary Water Management*, at 15 (Department of Land and Water Resources Engineering, Royal Institute of Technology (KTH), Stockholm, Apr. 2003).

451 *See* art. 1(4), *Elbe Convention*, *supra* note 435. *See also* Stubbs, *supra* note 447.

452 Stubbs, *id.* at 15.

453 *International Cooperation of the Czech Republic in Water Protection*, at 19 (Ministry of Environment of the Czech Republic, no date, ISBN 80-7212-120-0) [hereinafter *Czech Republic International*].

transboundary water cooperation was launched with Bavaria.[454] It is worth noting here that the level of cooperation is between the Czech Republic and the *länder* of Germany because of the federal structure of Germany. A 1995 treaty[455] between the Czech Republic and Germany has created the Commission for the Joint Management of Transboundary Watercourses that is to work closely with the Commission for the Protection of the Oder River and the Commission for the Protection of the Elbe River, the other two rivers shared by the two countries. The commission has established a Permanent Committee-Bavaria[456] and a Permanent Committee-Saxony[457] involved in the every day matters of treaty implementation—from the discharges of local municipalities to the provision of information in cases of emergency. The organization of the commission on the *länder* basis is demonstrative of the importance of the subnational level in the execution of bilateral agreements. The commission is basically continuing the work that has been undertaken in boundary areas since 1955 (with Saxony) and since 1970 (with Bavaria).

Overall, the adoption of international treaties dealing with river protection has not led to the abandonment of older structures based on bilateral arrangements that regulate water use at the border. These structures have persisted and work in parallel with the newer umbrella treaties that focus on environmental protection. One has to wonder why the 1995

---

454 *Id.* at 19.

455 *Regulation for the Treaty of 12 December 1995 between the Federal Republic of Germany and the Czech Republic concerning the Common Work for the Water Economy at Border Waters*, Dec. 12, 1995. The treaty replaces a 1974 treaty adopted between Germany and Czechoslovakia. The treaty entered into force on October 25, 1997 available online at the transboundary freshwater dispute database http://www.transboundarywaters.orst.edu/.

456 The Permanent Committee-Bavaria is involved in a variety of matters including the maintenance of transboundary watercourses, the elimination of flood damages, the protection and maintenance of water resources for local drinking water supply, the collection and exchange of hydrometeorological data and the measuring of flows of watercourses. The committee discusses problems associated with boundary passages, wastewater discharges from local municipalities, which can affect the quality of transboundary waters, and mutual results of quality analysis of transboundary rivers. The secretariats of the committee located in Pilsen and Regensburg coordinate the work of the committee. *See Czech Republic International, supra* note 453, at 19.

457 The Permanent Committee-Saxony has established secretariats in Pilsen and in Dresden and four expert groups. The committee focuses on the collection of information on water management plans and the determination of minimum flows in transboundary watercourses which are used for energy generation, protection of water resources and further decisions about the use of water resources. Working groups have been established to deal with a variety of matters including elimination of failures during joint inspections of transboundary watercourses and the provision of information when accidents occur. *See id.* at 20.

treaty was necessary and why the parties did not opt, instead, for an integrated international treaty to address all issues of water quality, quantity, and waterworks. In that case, the Committees of Saxony and Bavaria could have become subcommittees of the ICPE. Maybe one of the problems with such an arrangement has to do with the fact that at international borders, there are may be instances of river conflation. For instance, the Committee-Bavaria addresses international waters that are at the divide of the Danube and Elbe Rivers and, thus, could potentially fall under the jurisdiction of the ICPDR as well. Given the potential jurisdictional overlap, it is essential for these committees to establish communication channels with the international commissions so that networks of integrated water management are established.

The Elbe River basin district is an exemplification of the coordination that is required among various levels and authorities for the implementation of the WFD. Three hydrological levels of cooperation have been established—the international river basin district of the Elbe, working areas of the international district, and the FGG-Elbe that is organized based on hydrographic working areas. There are four administrative levels that must be coordinated on the German side, namely, the international level, the federal state, the *länder*, and the local level. And there are five administrative levels that must be coordinated on the Czech side, namely, the international level, the national government, the water boards, the regions, and the municipalities. How these different levels on each side of the border will identify their counterparts on the other side and work closely with them, especially given that certain administrative levels in the Czech Republic have been recently established, remains to be seen.

Chapter 21

Tepid Institutional Development in Southeast Europe

In the southeast European region, the level of multilateral cooperation is low and the framework of international cooperation is still led by bilateral agreements.

One of the bilateral agreements that have been adopted in the region concerns the Mesta/Nestos River shared between Bulgaria (53.63 percent) and Greece (46.36 percent). Bulgaria is the upstream country and, therefore, is in physical control of the flow of the river. Both countries' economies are dependent on the river as the river is used for irrigation and energy production. The delta of the river is protected under the RAMSAR treaty on wetlands.[458]

Negotiations for the apportionment of water resources shared by the two countries started in 1964 and joint meetings were held both in the 1970s and the 1980s.[459] An agreement between the parties was eventually signed in 1995 with regard to the use of waters of the Nestos River.[460]

---

458 Eleni Kampragou *et al.*, *Implementing Equitable Water Allocation in Transboundary Catchments: The Case of River Nestos/Mesta*, 21(5)Water Resources Management 909, May 2007.

459 *Id.*

460 *Agreement between the Government of the Hellenic Republic and the Government of the Republic of Bulgaria for the use of the Mesta/ Nestos River Waters*, Dec. 22, 1995 available online http://faolex.fao.org/waterlex/.

The agreement sets Greece's rights to the water at 29 percent, but it is unclear to what the 29 percent is referring.[461] Parties are to further exchange information concerning the water status and the development of plans that are to affect the flow of the river.[462] The agreement touches upon issues of water quality and refers to the "preservation of the balance of the ecosystem of the river."[463] Water quality is to be assessed based on EU suggestions. A Permanent Commission on Hydro-economy is to be established that would be involved in the implementation of the agreement.[464]

Despite what seems to be an ambitious effort to solve their differences, the Mesta/Nestos agreement has yet to take effect. There are many ambiguities in the agreement that could jeopardize even the allocation of resources as provided for in the agreement. It is not specified in the agreement whether the 29 percent of water volume that is allocated to Greece refers to monthly or yearly flows.[465] No provision is made about the apportionment of water resources in case of drought. The exchange of data between the parties has been scant with the Greek side complaining of receiving too much pollution from the upstream activities of Bulgaria. To make matters worse the Greek-Bulgarian Hydro-economy Committee has not been constituted.

As it is expected for an agreement signed before the adoption of the WFD, the concept of water management at river basin and the development of a joint river basin management plan are not foreseen in the agreement. The agreement was signed without the participation of any concerned stakeholder.

An attempt at integrated water management was undertaken in 2005 under the framework of INTERREG IIIA/PHARE Cross Border Cooperation Bulgaria/Greece.[466] The purpose of that project was to apply a common approach to water quality and quantity objectives and establish a common approach to methodology. Cooperation between the two

---

461 Art. 1, *id.*
462 Art. 3, *id.*
463 Art. 4, *id.*
464 Art. 5, *id.*
465 Though it seems that the 29 percent refers to the sum of the average natural flow based on the available data between 1935 and 1970 estimated to be one and a half billion cubic meters (1,500,000,000 cubic meters). This average natural flow is to be updated by the Commission on Hydro-economy established under the agreement.
466 The Operational Programme Interreg III A / PHARE CBC Greece Bulgaria 2000-2006 was approved by the European Union on December 27, 2001. Total funding for the Joint Programme amounts to €405.593.332, of which €254.443.332 were allocated to the Greek Programme INTERREG III A and €151.150.000 were allocated to the Bulgarian Programme. For more information about the program *see* http://www.interreg.gr/en/EL_BU/main.asp.

countries may be enhanced further through a 2002 agreement signed between the Greek Ministry for the Environment, Physical Planning and Public Works, and the Ministry of Environment and Water of Bulgaria.[467] The agreement addresses broader environmental issues and refers to the water framework directive (WFD) as well as joint research efforts and monitoring. Another effort to coordinate activities in the region has been pursued through the "Nestos–Mesta" Euroregion.[468]

The Maritsa/Evros River is shared between Bulgaria (66 percent), Turkey (26 percent), and Greece (8 percent).[469] At this point, there is no formal joint agreement between Greece and Bulgaria on the management of the river. There is some informal cooperation between the Prefecture of Evros (Greece) and the Region of Chaskovo (Bulgaria). Through a number of meetings and working groups, some issues have been decided such as water quantity, agrotourism, health issues, and pollution. Cooperation between the parties could be characterized as hesitant.

Bulgaria has been able to reach a joint agreement with Turkey on cooperation in the use of waters of rivers shared between the two countries.[470] The agreement establishes cooperation on hydrotechnical construction.[471] State parties agree to refrain from causing any substantial damage to one another as a result of the construction and use of installations on rivers that flow through their territories.[472] State parties agree to exchange information on floods by "the most expeditious means possible"[473] and agree to exchange hydrological and meteorological data. The agreement does not establish a joint commission. Parties are to exchange the addresses of authorities in charge with the implementation of the agreement.[474] The

467 *Agreement between the Ministry of Environment and Water of the Republic of Bulgaria and the Ministry for the Environment, Physical Planning and Public Works of the Hellenic Republic on Cooperation in the field of Environment Protection*, Nov. 1, 2002 (entry into force, July 15, 2005).

468 Veselka Ivanova, *Mechanisms of Planning and Monitoring Structures for Co-ordination at Regional and National Level in Bulgaria*, at 18, in the INTERREG Model: Practical Experiences in Cross Border Co-operation (Friedrich Ebert Stiftung, Zagreb Office, 2001).

469 Available online at transboundary freshwater dispute database http://www.transboundary-waters.orst.edu/.

470 *Agreement between the People's Republic of Bulgaria and the Republic of Turkey Concerning Co-operation in the Use of the Waters of Rivers Flowing through the Territory of both Countries*, Oct. 23, 1968 available online at transboundary freshwater dispute database http://www.transboundarywaters.orst.edu/.

471 Art. 1, *id.*

472 Art. 2, *id.*

473 Art. 3, *id.*

474 Art. 6, *id.*

agreement provides for a dispute settlement mechanism through a Mixed Bulgarian-Turkish Commission consisting of an equal number of experts from each contracting party. If the commission fails to reach agreement disputes will be settled through the diplomatic channel.[475] Overall, the agreement between Bulgaria and Turkey cannot be characterized as an example of robust cooperation. Except for the exchange of information and the establishment of principle of avoiding causing any substantial damage to the other party, the agreement does not provide for an operational mechanism of collaboration. A bilateral expert commission with coordinating and fact-finding functions could have been used if the parties wished for a closer cooperation. A more recent agreement on environmental cooperation adopted in 2004 may provide for that closer cooperation.[476]

Another example of the older generation of bilateral agreements is 1959 Yugoslav-Greek agreement.[477] The agreement established a Permanent Yugoslav-Greek Hydro-economic Commission. The purpose of the commission is to study the hydroeconomic problems and projects submitted jointly by state parties. The treaty affects the regulation of a number of watercourses shared between the two countries, such as the Vardar (Axius) River, the regulation of streams in the border area and the hydroeconomic problems in Lake Doiran, and Lake Prespa.[478] A function of the Permanent Yugoslav-Greek Hydro-economic Commission is to propose the apportionment of the costs of carrying out works and to give effect to measures undertaken in the common interests of the parties or in the interests of one state. The proposals of the commission are to be submitted to the two governments for approval.[479] The agreement is a classic bilateral agreement that addresses the issue of the hydrotechnical construction on shared waters. Issues of water quality and integrated water management are not addressed in the agreement.

475 Art. 8, *id.*

476 *See Agreement between the Government of the Republic of Bulgaria and the Government of the Republic of Turkey on Cooperation in the field of Environmental Protection*, Apr. 19, 2004 (not entered into force as of writing).

477 *Agreement between the Federal People's Republic of Yugoslavia and the Kingdom of Greece Concerning Hydro-economic Questions*, June 18, 1959.

478 Art. 1, *id.*

479 Art. 2, *id.*

A more recent example of cooperation involves the efforts of Albania, former Yugoslav Republic of Macedonia,[480] and Greece to reach an agreement on Lake Prespa. About 88 percent of the basin of Lake Prespa is located in Albania, 9 percent is found in the former Yugoslav Republic of Macedonia, and 3 percent is located in Greece.[481] The lake, that drains into Lake Orchid through porous and Karst Mountains, has declined in the past twenty years while the primary activities in the region are still tourism and fruit production.

An institutional framework for the management of the lake was adopted in 2000 as a Declaration on the Creation of the Prespa Park and the Environmental Protection and Sustainable Development of the Prespa Lakes and Their Surroundings.[482] The 2000 declaration established the first transboundary protected area in south-east Europe. The Prespa Park Coordination Committee (PPCC) composed of nine representatives of the three countries (representing environment ministries, local authorities and nongovernmental organizationss) held its first meeting in Skopje on January 30–31, 2001. Observers from the Convention on Wetlands, donor organizations, and NGOs participated in that meeting.[483] A trilateral secretariat was established, with an NGO member from each of the countries, to develop a strategic action plan for the sustainable development of the Prespa Park.[484]

Furthermore, an agreement was signed in 2005 between Albania and Greece on the establishment of the permanent Greek-Albanian Commission on Transboundary Freshwater Issues (the Greek-Albanian Commission).[485] This agreement affects all transboundary waters shared

---

480 A dispute emerged in the early 1990s between Greece and the breakaway region of Yugoslavia, former Yugoslav Republic of Macedonia, regarding the name of the latter as an independent country. The region, now an independent country, wished to keep the name Macedonia to which Greece objected given the historical connotations of the name and potential confusion with the northern region of Greece called Macedonia. Greece, instead, offered as an alternative the name "Former Yugoslav Republic of Macedonia" (FYROM). Since no country likes to be called "former," "FYROM" has not prevailed in international circles. While the dispute seems to most outsiders like an immaterial Balkan scramble over a name, it is demonstrative of the sensibilities in a region marred by frequent conflict.

481 Available online transboundary freshwater dispute database http://www.transboundarywaters.orst.edu.

482 Feb. 2, 2000 (Albania, Greece, former Yugoslav Republic of Macedonia). The text of the declaration is available online http://www.ramsar.org/wwd/0/wwd2000_rpt_prespa.htm.

483 Information on the first meeting of the PPCC is available online http://www.ramsar.org/wn/w.n.prespa_meeting1.htm.

484 *Id.*

485 *Agreement between the Government of the Hellenic Republic and the Government of the Republic of Albania on the Establishment of the Permanent Greek-Albanian Commission on Transboundary Freshwater Issues*, Apr. 13, 2005 available online http://faolex.fao.org/faolex/.

between the two countries.[486] The tasks that have been assigned to the Greek-Albanian Commission are quite extensive.[487] The commission is to serve, *inter alia*, as a forum for the exchange of information on existing and planned uses of water and related installations that are to have transboundary impacts or to adversely affect the quality of freshwaters.[488]

As the sample of agreements examined in this section demonstrate efforts for transboundary cooperation in the southeast European region are still fragmented with a number of agreements that do not reflect current realities. In the case of coriparian states of the Rhine and the Danube, the presence of an international river basin shared by many riparians has helped to pull countries together and move forward. Such international river basin does not exist in the southeast European region. For the countries of the southeast European region to begin implementing the WFD, they need to strengthen their relationships through bilateral and trilateral commissions that exert authority in the successful management of common resources wielding the technical expert paradigm that is familiar in the management of shared water resources. These commissions, when they are established, must be authorized to streamline the river basin management plans as they are now developing separately at the opposite sides of a border. One of the problems that countries are already facing has to do with the identification of regional authorities that are responsible for river basin management. In some cases, a number of central and regional authorities have cocompetence in the management of waters creating confusion about which subnational government body could be trusted to have the authority to coordinate efforts for the improvement of water management.

[486] Namely, Aoos (Viosa) River, Drinos River and Prespa Lakes, *see* preamble, *id.*

[487] The tasks of the Greek-Albanian Commission include:

- Collection and evaluation of data in order to identify pollution sources;
- Definition of joint water quality objectives;
- Discussion and evaluation of proposals of hydro-technical works and the supervision of such works;
- Promotion of establishment of national networks of monitoring water quality;
- Assistance in the exchange of practical experience and technical knowledge;
- Promotion of collaboration of competent authorities of state parties. *See* art. 2, *id.*

[488] Art. 2(4), *id.*

Part Five

International Governance Mechanisms

Chapter 22

Participation of Stakeholders in International Water Commissions

Becoming an "Observer" in International Water Commissions

International commissions have used various devices to ensure the flow of information to constituencies with a stake in water management and establish consultation with selected stakeholders in their work. International commissions have granted stakeholders an observer status. The observer status provides stakeholders with an opportunity to acquire a consultative role within an international commission. International commissions have organized, additionally, large stakeholder conferences and have designated days dedicated to the celebration of rivers that foster the spirit of cohesion in a region.

The requirements for the participation of observers in the deliberations of international commissions are usually provided for in the rules of procedure of international commissions. The provisions on observers, who can participate in the workings of international commissions, are, in essence, an invitation to intergovernmental organizations and non-governmental organizations (NGOs) to contribute to the work of international commissions. The observer requirements open the door for environmental and business NGOs to participate in international fora and to provide insights that could influence international policymaking.

The International Commission for the Protection of the Danube River (ICPDR) has adopted detailed rules of procedure for "participants with consultative status and for observers to the ICPDR."[1] Proposals for acquiring observer status are examined by the commission on a case-by-case basis, taking into account the readiness of a possible future observer to make "a practical and valuable contribution" to the implementation of the main principles and goals of the convention.[2] The issue of whether an organization would acquire the status of observer is addressed at the earliest possible meeting of the commission and, if the application is accepted, the president of the ICPDR extends a letter of admission to the observer.[3] For candidates to obtain the role of an observer, they must meet certain conditions including:

- Acknowledge the goals and basic principles of the Danube River Protection Convention (DRPC);
- Have specialized technical or scientific competence or other competences as they relate to the goals of the DRPC;
- Have a structured, permanent administration; and
- Have a regional or a basin-wide perspective.[4]

The ICPDR has further defined the rights and duties of observers. Observers have a right to:

- Be informed of the date, place, and agenda of the meetings and activities in which they are entitled to participate;
- Have access to the documents of the international commission and its bodies in accordance with the decisions of the international commission;
- Participate in meetings with the possibility to express their position and views and to have those positions and views reflected in the relevant documents;

1 *Guidelines for Participants with Consultative Status and for Observers to the ICPDR*, FINAL, IC/021, Apr. 26, 2005.

2 *Guideline* 2.2 (a), *id.*

3 *Guideline* 2.2.(b)-(c), *id.*

4 *Guideline* 3.2, *id.*

- Submit relevant documents and proposals to the international commission, which will be distributed by the secretariat and may be discussed at meetings;
- Take part in programs and contribute to projects initiated under the auspices of the convention in which they are invited to participate or make other voluntary contributions.[5]

Observers, however, cannot take part in decisionmaking and cannot cast votes for the adoption of decisions and recommendations because this falls strictly under the competence of state parties.[6] Thus, one could claim that the rules for the admission of observers in the workings of the ICPDR are quite open. At the same time, the ICPDR attempts to ensure that those who are invited as observers share the goals of the commission and have something to contribute to its deliberations.

The rules for the acquisition of an observer status are provided for in the text of the Rhine Convention. The International Commission for the Protection of the Rhine (ICPR) may recognize as observers NGOs as long as their field of interest or activity is pertinent to the work of the commission.[7] The commission must exchange information with observer NGOs and shall consult with them before making decisions likely to have an important impact on them and must inform them as soon as such decisions are made.[8] Observers can submit to the commission reports and any information relevant for the accomplishment of the goals of the convention.[9] Observers may be invited to participate in the commission's meetings without having, though, a right to vote.[10] The conditions for the eligibility of observers and their participation in the workings of the commission are provided for in detail in the rules of procedure.[11] Many of these conditions are similar to the conditions provided for in ICPDR.

[5] *Guideline* 3.1, *id.*
[6] *Guideline* 4.1, *id.*
[7] Art. 14(2)(c), *Convention for the Protection of the Rhine*, Apr. 12, 1999 available online www.iksr.org.
[8] Art. 14(3), *id.*
[9] Art. 14(4), *id.*
[10] *Id.*
[11] Art. 14(6), *id.*
In order for NGOs to obtain an observer status with the ICPR, they must:

- Accept the targets and principles of the ICPR convention;
- Have technical and scientific knowledge or other knowledge that pertains to the targets of the convention;

The Scheldt and Meuse agreements provide similar requirements on the conditions under which NGOs can participate in the work of the international commissions. For such organizations to acquire the status of an observer, they must have common interests and objectives with the commission.[12] Observers can participate in the plenary assemblies of the commission without having a right to vote and can share with the commission any information, any report or any opinion that has to do with the agreement.[13] The commission can exchange information with the observers. In particular, the commission can consult with observers if it decides that such consultation will be important for its decisions. The commission must also inform observers of the opinions or the recommendations it has adopted.[14]

Details for collaboration with observers are provided in the rules of procedure of the Scheldt commission.[15] Observers can participate in regular plenary sessions and working groups but not, as a rule, in the assembly of heads of delegation.[16] Non-governmental organizations can obtain the status of observer provided their mission and interests and their scientific or technical knowledge are related to the work of the commission. Furthermore, they must recognize the principles of the agreement that sets up the commission and accept the internal and financial rules of procedure of the commission.[17] Safeguards are provided that increase the effectiveness of observers. The commission, for example, aims at achieving the equilibrium of different interest groups that become observers.

- Have a well-structured administration of their organization;
- Be accredited by their organization to be that organization's representative.
- An NGO must further provide:
- A description of its organization and its competence and experience to contribute to the commission's work;
- A list of reasons why its contribution is important for the commission's work;
- Confirmation in writing of its conformance with the ICPR rules of procedure.

The commission makes decisions on granting of observer status during its meetings. The coordinating group at the commission decides on the kind of information to be exchanged with NGOs that have an observer status. The coordination group also decides whether NGOs will be invited to attend the plenary sessions of the commission as observers. In that case the "equilibrated participation" of different interest groups must be sought. *See* Section 8, *Rules of procedure and financial regulations of the ICPR*, Decision of the 70th plenary assembly of the ICPR, Bern, July 8/9, 2004.

12 *See*, e.g., art. 6(1)(c), *International Treaty for the Scheldt*, Dec. 3, 2002.

13 *See*, e.g., art. 6(2), *id.*

14 *See*, e.g., art. 6(3), *id.*

15 *Annex I, International Scheldt Commission, Internal and Financial Rules of Procedure*, adopted Dec. 2, 2003.

16 Para. 6, *Annex I, id.*

17 Paras. 1 and 2, *Annex I, id.*

The number of observers are limited to a reasonable number so as allow for effective collaboration.[18]

The Role of Public Consultation in the Work of International Commissions

Danube Basin

The ICPDR has taken the issue of public participation seriously and the commission has executed studies on the different elements of stakeholder consultation. The UNEP/GEF Danube Regional Project has provided funding for the strengthening of public participation mechanisms in the Danube region and in the ICPDR.[19] Twenty-three types of stakeholders[20] have been identified as relevant to the work of the commission. The problem is that not all of these stakeholders have formed Danube-wide or European-wide organizations that could be actively involved in the work of the commission. The ICPDR, in its classification scheme of stakeholders, takes into account various parameters including the legitimacy a stakeholder enjoys in the region, its power (the ability to influence the actions of other stakeholders and bring desired outcomes), and the capacity to capture attention about its needs and interests. Based on the legitimacy, power, and ability to attract attention, stakeholders are placed in categories such as dangerous (high in power, but low in legitimacy), dominant (high in power and legitimacy), and dormant (high in power and legitimacy but low in their ability to get attention). The commission is well aware that many public initiatives fail because of lack of ownership of those initiatives by those who are to implement them. Consequently, many projects falter and regulations languish because of widespread resistance of stakeholders.[21]

---

18 Para. 4, *Annex I, id.*

19 *UNDP/GEF Danube Regional Project, Stakeholder Analysis Workshop,* Baden, Austria, Dec. 10–12, 2003 [hereinafter *Danube Stakeholder Analysis*].

20 Agriculture, fisheries, forestry, recreation, flood protection, transport, water supply, wastewater, industry, energy, consumers, education and research, professional organizations, European level governance (DG Environment, DG Transport, Council of Ministers of Transport, Council of Ministers of Energy, DG Agriculture, Council of Ministers of Agriculture), municipalities, communication and media, environmental organizations, international agreements and organizations, granting institutions, lending institutions and investors, and political parties, *id.*

21 *Id.*

ICPDR has developed a strategy that includes a step-by-step guide to public participation[22] and an operational plan[23] that provides many details of the process of public participation. The ICPDR has tried to broaden its stakeholder base by enlisting stakeholders that represent business and industry interests in the Danube region. The Danube Tourist Commission[24] and Via Donau, an organization that deals with the promotion of inland navigation, are stakeholders in the ICPDR process.[25]

The Danube Stakeholder Conference took place in June of 2005 with the aim to present to stakeholders the activities of the ICPDR including the 2004 Danube Analysis Report, the development of program of measures, the ICPDR Action Program on Sustainable Flood Protection, and the opportunities that exist for stakeholders to be granted an observer status with the ICPDR. About a hundred stakeholders, representing governments at different levels, industry, environmental NGOs, and research institutions attended the conference.[26] Some concerns expressed at the conference were the lack of NGO participation in the compilation of the 2004 Danube Analysis Report. Summarizing the results of the conference, the Executive Secretary of the ICPRD underlined two issues that became all too salient during the two-day conference proceedings, namely:

- The importance of including additional stakeholders particularly from the agricultural and industry sectors;

---

22 *Danube River Basin Strategy for Public Participation in River Basin Management Planning 2003–2009, Elaborated Synthesis Report of the Public Participation Workshop*, Bratislava, Apr. 4–5, 2003 (Oct. 2003).

23 *ICPDR Operational Plan to ensure Public Participation in implementing the EU Water Framework Directive on the basin-wide (roof) level as of September 17, 2004*, IC/WD 168, Final Web, Sept-2005.

24 More information on the Danube Tourist Commission (DIE DONAU) is available online http://www.danube-river.org/en_werbe-werbe.html.

25 More information on Via Donau is available online http://www.via-donau.org/en. Other organizations with observer status in the ICPDR:
Black Sea Commission (BSC); Danube Environmental Forum (DEF); Danube Commission (DC); European Barge Union (EBU); Global Water Partnership (GWP/CEE); International Association for Danube Research (IAD); International Association of Water Supply Companies in the Danube River Catchment Area (IAWD); International Hydrological Programme of the UNESCO (IHP/Danube); International Sava River Basin Commission (ISRBC); RAMSAR Convention on Wetlands; Regional Environmental Center for Central and Eastern Europe (REC); VGB PowerTech e.V. (VGB);World Wide Fund for Nature–Danube-Carpathian Programme (WWF-DCP).

26 *Danube River Basin Stakeholder Conference*, Budapest, Final Conference Report, June 28–29, 2005 (Nicole Krantz et al., eds., 2005).

- The need to address stakeholders from the agricultural and industry sectors in a different format having the Danube Conference as a reference point for future activities.[27]

Some business NGOs were uncertain about the focus of the Danube Stakeholder Conference. Business associations expect concrete results from their participation in international proceedings. For environmental NGOs, because of their nature as organizations whose reputations are based on public opinion and the creation and change of public perceptions, the ability to openly express their views in various multinational fora is, in itself, a reason for participating in such fora. Although business associations are not immune to reputation incentives, they prefer to play a low-key role in international meetings and channel their positions through various informal networks and relationships.

The ICPDR became aware that although large conference meetings may be necessary to reach a wide audience of a specific type of stakeholder, they are not an effective vehicle to reach industry and agriculture—stakeholders that are to play a central role in the implementation of program of measures. The ICPDR espouses the position, which is also expressed by the European Union (EU), that the purpose of stakeholder participation is to create ownership of regulatory outcomes so that these outcomes are implemented on the ground more swiftly. Whether participation decreases the costs of implementation, though, is not entirely clear and depends to a great extent on who is participating. In some cultures, participative proceedings may become just a delaying tactic, in the host of other tactics, to hold back implementation.

In the aftermath of the stakeholder conference, the ICPDR issued a response to the consultation process that addressed issue-by-issue, the points that were raised during the conference demonstrating, thus, that the consultation process was taken into account in the deliberation process.[28]

Some of the NGOs most active in the Danube River basin include the Danube Environmental Forum (DEF) and the Regional Environmental

---

27 *Id.* at 23.

28 *ICPDR Response to the stakeholder consultations process 2005, Final*, IC/WD/235-4, Nov. 2, 2006. The ICPDR asked stakeholders who participated in the 2005 stakeholder conference to fill out a feedback form. About ten percent of these forms were returned to the ICPDR. The quality of the feedback was quite good. Communication with Jasmine Bachmann, expert in Public Participation and Public Relations, at ICPDR, Dec. 21, 2006.

Center for Central and Eastern Europe (REC). The DEF is a network of NGOs dedicated to the protection of the Danube River by strengthening cooperation among governments and stakeholders. The DEF has received financial assistance from the UNDP/GEF Danube regional project channeled to the development of a regional secretariat for the DEF with the goal to fulfill the multicountry activities of the organization. The DEF, today, has a strong secretariat and serves as an umbrella organization of 174 member organizations and thirteen national focal points in thirteen Danubian countries.[29] The DEF is stakeholder in the ICPDR process and an active participant in the Danube Day, a day dedicated to the celebration of the river with a number of activities all through the basin.[30] The REC is another example of a regional environmental organization that receives funding from countries in the region. Other donors include the European Union, Japan, the United States, and the Netherlands.[31]

This top-down creation and organization of environmental NGOs has been promoted in central and eastern Europe after the fall of communism by international organizations and various donors. Supporting environmental NGOs is a means to strengthen environmental protection and, more importantly, a method to encourage democratization in a region. The organization of civil society under umbrella NGOs, inclusive of smaller and more local organizations, is advantageous to governments that they rather address a large consolidated organization rather than a number of disjointed institutions each of which with its own wish list, unable to articulate a common position. Localized NGOs may also gain by channeling their voice through an international grouping and, taking advantage of economies of scale, could acquire more say and more power in international fora.

29 *See* Kari Aina Eik, *International Development of NGOs: Danube Environmental Forum (DEF), International Waters Experience Notes*, 2006 GEF/IW: LEARN (International Waters Learning Exchange and Resource Network) available online http://www.iwlearn.net/publications/experience-note/expnote_danube_ngoforum.pdf/view.

30 Jasmine Bachmann, *Public Participation Strategies and Methods: Perspectives of an International Secretariat* 90, in Proceedings of International Conference "Implementing the European Union Water Framework Directive: Towards Integrated Water Management in Europe," May 12, 2006, Athens (DG Environment, European Commission, Technical Report-2007-021, Elli Louka, ed., 2007).

31 According to the state of contributions for the period between 1990 to 2004, major donations to the REC came from the EU (€20 737 924), Japan (€12 041 923), United States (€11 625 159), and the Netherlands (€9 029 146). The donations are available online http://www.rec.org/REC/Introduction/Donations.html.

Sava Basin

The statute of the International Sava Commission provides that the sessions of the Sava Commission shall be held in private unless the Sava Commission decides otherwise.[32] It is, therefore, upon the discretion of the Sava Commission to determine whether it would include observers in its sessions.[33] The Sava Commission has a bifurcated mandate. It has to protect the Sava River and to facilitate navigation and the development of the river.

The commission intends to adopt an open policy and allow observers in its meetings. For this reason, the formalization of consultation with stakeholders needs to be elaborated. The double role of the commission—river development and river protection—is likely to make stakeholder consultation acrimonious. It is likely that ministries of transportation, ministries of development, and ministries of environment will become quite involved in the work of the commission. Many stakeholders would like to see themselves play an influential role in the decisions of the commission.

Black Sea

A number of steps have been taken to strengthen public participation in the Black Sea region. A network of environmental organizations concerned with environmental quality in the Black Sea region called the Black Sea NGO Network (BSNN) has been established for that purpose. The BSNN exceeds sixty members, brought together because of the decreasing environmental quality of the Black Sea and the importance of the transmission of democratic values and practices to the Black Sea countries.[34] The BSNN has been funded to address environmental degradation based on an ambition to promote democratization in the region.[35] In other words, the BSNN, like the DEF and the REC, is a case in which the development of an NGO has been supported for propagating the democratic ideal in a region. Some of the priorities of the BSNN are to lobby Black Sea countries to invest in the protection of the Black Sea environment, and in the application of the convention; raise environmental awareness; facilitate

32 Art. 3(4), *Statute of the International Sava Commission, Annex I of Framework Agreement on the Sava River Basin*, Dec. 3, 2002 available online www.savacommission.org.

33 Art. 3(5), *id.*

34 *See* Black Sea NGO Network Website available online http://www.bseanetwork.org/About.htm.

35 *Id.*

public participation in decisionmaking; and build the capacity and self-sustainability of NGOs in the region.[36] The BSNN is the only organization representing the interests of the broader civil society that holds an observer status with the Black Sea Commission.

The NGOs involved in the BSNN have organized the International Black Sea Day, infobus campaigns, seminars, and public debates. Black Sea Environment, Information, Education, and Resource Centers have been established in Bulgaria and Romania. Black Sea countries have organized national NGO fora. Training in public participation and environmental management for Black Sea NGOs has taken place in certain countries. In general, there are many activities in the region and a lot of information is disseminated through newsletters, leaflets, seminars, exhibitions, and libraries.

Rhine Basin

The ICPR is most active in matters of information dissemination and stakeholder consultation. The ICPR has for years published and distributed reports on its activities. A number of selected stakeholder groups were involved in the drafting of the 1999 Convention on the Protection of the Rhine.[37] Other international commissions have acquired observer status in the ICPR, such as the Rhine Navigation Commission, the Moselle and the Sarre Commissions, the Lake Constance Commission, the Elbe Commission, and the Scheldt Commission. Although the meetings of the plenary assembly are generally open to various NGOs, the coordination group itself is closed to them. Since 2001, NGOs have been allowed to participate in the meeting of working groups.[38]

Since its establishment, the Coordinating Committee of the Rhine (CC), which functions in parallel with plenary assembly of the ICPR, has been inviting for consultations environmental NGOs and water users. These consultations occur simultaneously with the annual reunions of the CC.

---

[36] *Id.*

[37] Eleftheria Kampa *et al.*, *Public Participation in River Basin Management in Germany: "From borders to natural boundaries,"*at 33, Dec. 2003 (report produced as a part of the workpackage 4 of the HarmoniCOP Project). The HarmoniCOP project was sponsored by the European Commission. For information about the project *see* http://www.harmonicop.uos.de/index.php.

[38] Ine D. Frijters and Jan Leentvaar, *Rhine Case Study*, at 23, Joint UNESCO-Green Cross International Project, "From Potential Conflict to Cooperation Potential (PCCP): Water for Peace" (2003)[hereinafter *Rhine Case Study*].

Consultations take place with representatives of environmental groups, industry federations, distributors of water, and scientific associations.[39] In addition, coriparian states and the *länder* of Germany have engaged in efforts to include the public through a number of consultative committees, fora, and internet sites.[40]

Stakeholder participation in the multigovernance regime of Lake Constance is still rudimentary. This is because the provision of information has been treated more as technical and administrative matter rather than as an opportunity to establish consultation with various stakeholders. Simultaneously, though, the federal structure of certain state parties to international agreements has assisted in the development of other channels for the provision of information and consultation. The cantons of Switzerland and the *länder* of Germany have tried to bring the work of various regional bodies closer to the local population. Representatives of *länder* and cantons usually outnumber the representatives of the federal government in the different regional institutions that have been established.[41] Switzerland, especially, with its direct democracy system, is perceived as a country quite receptive to participatory processes in both national and international settings.

Another subbasin of the Rhine, the Moselle/Sarre subbasin, has been the focus of public participation initiatives. The Moselle/Sarre Commission conducted a public outreach meeting in 2005 to share the findings of the 2005 roof report.[42] The roof report itself provides examples of how national and regional authorities have tried to involve the public. In France, for the purposes of informing the public, an internet site has been put in place (www.eau2015-rhin-meuse.fr) coordinated by both the Rhine-Meuse Basin Committee and the Coordinating Prefect of the Rhine-Meuse Basin in France. Studies executed on the basin can be accessed through the website. The site provides links to the roof reports of

39 International Hydrographic District of Rhine, *Characteristics, Study of the Effects of Human Activity on the Environment and Economic Analysis of the Water Use*, at 80, Part A of Report submitted to the European Commission, Mar. 18, 2005.

40 *Id.* at 80.

41 H. Gerd Schröder, *Transboundary Water Management in Lake Constance: from Tradition to Cooperation* presented in International Workshop "Value of Water–Different Approaches in Transboundary Water Management" Koblenz, Germany, Mar. 10–11, 2005.

42 International Hydrographic District of Rhine, *Working Area "Moselle-Sarre," Part B: a Status Assessment*, at 149–53 (Commissions Internationales pour la Protection de la Moselle and de la Sarre, June 2005)[hereinafter *Moselle-Sarre, Part B*].

the Scheldt River basin, Meuse River basin, Rhine River basin and Moselle/ Sarre River basin, all of which are river basins in which France has a stake. The website includes the detailed results of consultations with stakeholders.

In France, commissions have been established to facilitate consultations with various stakeholders.[43] Representatives of the International Commissions for the Protection of the Moselle and the Sarre (Commissions Internationales pour la Protection de la Moselle and de la Sarre or the CIPMS) and other coriparians have been invited to participate in the commissions established in France. The assessment of water status produced by the CIPMS is to be distributed electronically through a CD-ROM and the internet. Furthermore, a questionnaire was sent to two million households.[44] This was a major effort, the results of which may not provide the sought-after enlightenment.[45] Grand-scale surveys in the form of questionnaires filled out self-selectively by those interested in water matters may serve more as a validation tool for the authorities that conduct them rather than a means to discover genuine public attitudes.

A website (www.waasser.lu) accessed by the public provides all information on the process of implementation of the WFD in Luxembourg. Although no specific initiatives have been undertaken to engage the general public in consultations, efforts have been made to establish contacts with users and local authorities that deal with water management, for instance, through the Intercommunal Syndicate of Towns and Communes (Syndicat Intercommunal des Villes et Communes du Luxembourg (SYVICOL)). The syndicate—comprised of 118 local communes—allows for discussion with elected local representatives who are concerned with issues of cost recovery of water services.[46]

In Germany, almost all states involved in the water framework directive (WFD) implementation have created websites that provide information

---

43 *Id.* at 149.

44 *Id.* at 150.

45 Out of the 1.8 million questionnaires distributed, about 770,000 were returned to the water agency. In addition to the questionnaires, about 40,000 free opinions were expressed. The water agency understood these free opinions to mean that the public was interested in water issues, viewed water management as an important issue, and was in agreement with the general purposes of the directive and French law. However, questionnaires left some issues unanswered, for instance one-third of the respondents opposed the idea that the consumer should pay for the provision of water. The results of the questionnaire are found online, *see* http://www.eau2015-rhin-meuse.fr.

46 *Moselle-Sarre, Part B, supra* note 42, at 151.

on the process of WFD implementation. Practices of consultation and participation are not consistent, though, all across the *länder*.[47]

Elbe Basin

The International Commission for the Protection of the Elbe (ICPE) has been open to various stakeholders since its inception. Since 1991, the ICPE has organized annual international information meetings with various NGOs from both Germany and the Czech Republic. The meetings are usually organized a month before the annual meeting of the ICPE. The meetings tend to have different themes each year such as flood protection or the impact of wastewater treatment plants on the improvement of water quality.[48] Stakeholders are invited to participate in the working groups of the ICPE.[49] The problem is that many local NGOs are reluctant to devote the resources required to participate in the international meetings of the ICPE, while some international NGOs are more active.[50] In 2007, the ICPE organized an international Elbe forum in which more than 160 people participated representing nongovernmental associations, including environmental NGOs and water users. The subjects covered during the forum included monitoring programs and the focus of the future work program of the commission.[51]

The organization of a network of NGOs in the context of the ICPE modeled after the BSNN or the DEF has not been that successful. Although various German and Czech NGOs[52] are active in the basin,

---

47 *Id.* at 151–52.

48 Kampa, *supra* note 37, at 37.

49 *Baseline Assessment of the Elbe Basin*, at 18 (NeWater Report Series No. 17, Valentina Krysanova *et al.*, eds., Nov. 2005) (The baseline assessment was prepared by the Potsdam Institute for Climate Impact Research, Germany, the T.G. Masaryk Water Research Institute, Czech Republic and the Institute of Hydrodynamics, Czech Republic.) [hereinafter *Elbe Baseline Assessment*].

50 Michelle Stubbs and Sophie Bonjour, *Case Study—Elbe River*, at 11, *ETH Seminar: Science and Politics of International Freshwater Management 2003/04*, Swiss Federal Institute of Technology (ETH) Zurich and Swiss Federal Institute for Environmental Science and Technology (EAWAG), Nov. 2002.

51 Information available online http://www.ikse-mkol.org.

52 ARNIKA has been mentioned as a local environmental NGO with involvement in the Elbe. Other possible relevant stakeholders in the Czech Republic include the:

- Association of Water Supply and Sewage Services (SOVAK) that has been established as a voluntary non-governmental, non-profit organization that supports the drinking water sector;
- Czech Agrarian Chamber, the Agricultural Association of the Czech Republic and the Association of Private Farming represent the interest of the agricultural sector;

cooperation among them is tenuous. Furthermore, the ten *länder* that share the basin have established different procedures for public participation and not all *länder* accord to public participation the same level of salience.[53]

Scheldt Basin and Meuse Basin

The Scaldit project used to jump-start the process of WFD implementation in the Scheldt River basin addressed issues of public participation and communication. All through the project, seminars were organized to inform stakeholders about the status of the project. Certain NGOs were invited to participate in the International Scheldt Commission's project group meetings. Information about the project was available at the Scaldit website and through brochures and newsletters.

In the first public participation meetings of the Scaldit project that took place in 2003, many NGOs were invited to participate[54] but only a handful of them did show up. In subsequent meetings, the number of participants increased. Despite what seems to be an open door policy of the

- Association of Chemical Industry of the Czech Republic (founded in 1990 as a voluntary association);
- the Czech Union of Shipowners provides representation for the shipping interests and it is now a member of the European Barge Union (EBU). *See* Elbe Baseline Assessment, *supra* note 49, at 16–17.

53 Kampa, *supra* note 37, at 51.

54 With regard to NGOs active at the international level, the following NGOs were invited to participate:
- Escaut Sans Frontières
- European Chemical Industry Council (CEFIC)
- Vereniging van Rivierwaterbedrijven (RIWA)
- Comité des Organisations Professionelles Agricoles de l'Union Européenne (COPA)
- Fédération de la Batellerie

With regard to NGOs involved at the national/regional revel, the following NGOs were invited:
- Escaut Vivant
- Nord Nature
- Bond Beter Leefmilieu (BBL)
- Inter-Environnement Bruxelles (IEB)
- Union Wallonne des Entreprises (UWE)
- Inter-Environnement Wallonie (IEW)
- Zeeuwse Milieufederatie
- WWF.

See Veronique Van Den Langenbergh and Ilke Dieltjens, *Progress Report for Pilot River Basin Testing: Scaldit – Scheldt International River Basin District*, Oct. 31, 2003 available online http://www.scaldit.org/uploads/38Scaldit_progress_report3_Oct_2003.pdf.

International Scheldt Commission, NGO participation could still be characterized as tepid. Most NGOs expect the commission to fund the cost of traveling to participate in the works of the commission. The fact that some organizations have obtained observer status does not necessarily mean that they are actively involved in the work of the commission.

The participation of NGOs in the Meuse Commission has been subject to lengthy deliberations. Wallonia was initially reluctant to grant observer status to NGOs. This is because some NGOs have been combative regarding Wallonia's lack of investment in wastewater treatment plans. Eventually, though, the Meuse Commission following in the steps of other international commissions, started to investigate the possibility of NGO participation in its deliberations. Five options were put on the table for the participation of NGOs in the work of the commission:

- NGOs' participation in the preparatory meetings of delegations;
- Consultation with NGOs prior to meetings;
- NGOs' participation as members of a delegation;
- NGOs' participation as observers; and
- NGOs' participation as full members.

It was finally agreed that NGOs could participate as observers in the meetings of the commission.[55]

The Meuse Commission hosted in May 2006 the second international symposium of the Meuse.[56] The symposium was attended by a large number of stakeholders, but also what could be considered the general public including a number of high schools and colleges. The two-day symposium was filled with presentations and discussions initiated by various associations that have an interest (commercial or research) in the future of the Meuse. Those who participated in the symposium took cognizance of the different approaches to the river: a more natural approach on the side of France and an integrated economic/ecological approach on the side of Germany. The forging of a culture of common identity of people who live around the Meuse was one of the goals of

55 ECE/UNEP Network of Experts on Public Participation and Compliance, *Water Management: Guidance on public participation and compliance with agreements*, Mar. 2000, at 20 (under the guidance and assistance of W. Kakebeeke, P. Wouters and N. Bouman).

56 Second International Symposium of the Meuse: La Meuse, Un Avenir Partagé, Sedan, France, May 18–19, 2006.

the symposium.[57] Given the number of presentations and posters prepared for the symposium, one could characterize it a success. The fact that the symposium reached beyond the traditional categories of stakeholders and involved members of the public and local schools sets it apart from strict stakeholder meetings usually held by international water commissions.

The success of the Meuse symposium should be evaluated based on the development of public awareness about the river and networking that took place among various organizations and interest groups that focus on the river. The Meuse symposium has its place among the various tools that authorities can use to create shared perceptions of affinity and belonging around a river.

Public Consultation and the Direction of International Policymaking

Information

Most international commissions are equipped with websites that provide information about the treaties that govern them, the projects, activities and programs they are involved with as well as the progress of the WFD implementation. Commissions provide information on their website in their official languages—often the languages of signatories of the treaty that established the commission. Some commissions have opted to provide information in a third language (usually English) in order to make their proceedings more transparent to third-party observers. Providing information in more languages than the official languages of a commission, in addition to furthering transparency, helps the commission publicize its role in the region and increases the potential for the commission's practices to be disseminated and be considered best practices in other regions of the world. As the WFD is deepening the integration process in the European region, and it is the first extensive application of the concept of integrated water management on a transfrontier scale, the lessons learned in Europe could provide the impetus for action in other regions of the world. Such an opportunity should not be lost to the commissions.

Commissions rarely provide in their websites the minutes of meetings of working groups or plenary sessions. Some have argued that the publication of minutes of meetings would hamper the free exchange of

---

57 *Id.* at 13.

opinions and data during the meetings of international commissions. Participants in meetings the minutes of which are expected to be published may decide to "to play to the future readership" of those minutes rather than to concentrate on the task of deliberation. On the other hand, supporting a position that will render minutes of meetings inaccessible to the public would seem suspect. Keeping the minutes off websites but available upon request may cover the middle ground between online accessibility and no access.

International commissions have been active in providing newsletters, brochures, and other communication material to the general public. How actively these newsletters and brochures are distributed is not entirely clear. There is a residual concern that these materials may not have a wide outreach. Having said that, mailing materials indiscriminately to all possibly conceived stakeholders may intensify information overload. Many stakeholders, especially those representing business interests, often prefer customized information, tailored to their needs with instructions for their contribution rather than general information material. As it was underlined in Chapter 12, the provision of information means the provision of customized and tailored information. Documents full of acronyms and jargon familiar to an international institution—and its general court of stakeholders—may be intimidating to newer stakeholder entrants and commissions must engage in efforts to demystify some of their technical proceedings.

Commissions have attempted to reach a large number of stakeholders through conferences. The ICPDR organized in 2005 a conference that involved a number of stakeholders. Although some participants viewed the conference as an effective means to express their concerns and network, other participants were unclear about the benefits of a large-scale international event in terms of a meaningful contribution they could make or the feedback they would receive. Divergent expectations of different types of NGOs suggest a more tailored approach to public participation. On the other hand, celebration of river basins (like the Danube Day) is a good opportunity not only to share information about the activities of international commissions but also to advance a spirit of cohesion around a river.

Consultation

Most commissions have invited selected stakeholders to become observers in working groups or during plenary meetings. Working groups perform all the groundwork for the commissions. The plenary meetings or the conference of the parties is where final decisionmaking occurs. But the meetings of heads of delegation that coordinate the everyday affairs of commissions and stage the plenary meetings are, as a rule, not open to observers.

The meetings of working groups are technical in nature and expertise is necessary for a meaningful contribution to their deliberations. Unless a stakeholder has, at its disposal, experts with knowledge of the subject matter deliberated in a working group, it is highly likely that any sort participation will be cosmetic rather than substantive. As commentators have noted, all international water commissions have been conceived as expert/technical commissions. This is the technical/scientific paradigm of international river basin management[58] conceptualized as an attempt to inject objectivity and reason in environments expected to be political and often opportunistic. The strict application of the so-called technical/scientific paradigm has been essential in order to establish a presumption of objectivity in the work of commissions where no party, no matter how overbearing, can prevail unless it has the scientific data to convince its partners that it is right. Commissions need to maintain and cultivate their image as objective bodies that take into account scientific judgment rather than interested discourse to solve differences among the parties.[59]

The implementation of the WFD presents a challenge to this assumed scientific/technical paradigm. Although the WFD does not provide that the international commissions themselves should be open to stakeholders and the public, it would probably be an oxymoron to have national river basin districts open to consultative and participative processes while international river basin commissions remain closed to participation. This is especially so since many major decisions in river basin management would be forged through bilateral and multilateral relationships. Because of the importance of inclusion of participative process, international commissions have been urged to abandon or to temper, at least, the technical paradigm and to develop strategies to strengthen their communication

58 Susanna Nilsson, *The Role and Use of Information in Transboundary Water Management* (Department of Land and Water Resources Engineering, Royal Institute of Technology (KTH), Stockholm, Apr. 2003).

59 Many postmodernists could claim that no discourse is objective. This may be true but an attempt to be objective and an awareness of one's biases is probably a more useful approach to international policymaking rather than an approach that everything is politics and, therefore, anything goes.

with the public. Most international commissions are interested in exploring the potential of consultation with stakeholders.

For the most part, the websites of international commissions examined in this study are informative but not consultative. Interactive websites are rare in terms of providing the possibility of sending to international commissions electronic comments on matters that the commissions are deliberating on. The Baltic Marine Environment Protection Commission, known also as the HELCOM Commission,[60] has provided for the possibility of conducting e-meetings with all stakeholders, the general public, and professional stakeholders (state parties, observer organizations, and other professionals).[61] It remains to be seen how successful these meetings will be. The development of interactive websites may be considered, at this point, premature for many commissions especially if the expectation is that comments received through this method may be not well educated or may be repetitions of positions already iterated in other meetings. Interactive websites could, however, provide groups that do not have the resources to participate in international meetings with an opportunity to give some feedback on the work of a commission. As such, they could be encouraged as a complement to the observer status already provided for in some commissions. Receiving electronic comments, however, will increase the work of the commissions since they will have to provide feedback on comments they receive.

Questionnaires are another method of consultation that could help a commission get informed about the attitudes and beliefs of stakeholders on matters of interest to the commission. Some international commissions have already used such questionnaires to gauge stakeholder positions. At the Danube Stakeholder conference, the ICPDR handed out feedback forms in order to elicit evaluations from stakeholders about its processes. Questionnaires may provide a useful consultative tool if a water authority has to make a decision on a specific topic and would like to measure the popularity of that decision or the degree of resistance, it is likely to attract from those that the decision will affect. Sending out questionnaires of general

---

60 The HELCOM Commission supervises the implementation of the Convention on the Protection of the Marine Environment of the Baltic Sea Area, Apr. 9, 1992, entered into force, Jan. 17, 2000. More information on the commission is available online http://www.helcom.fi/home/en_GB/welcome. Contracting parties to the convention are Denmark, Estonia, the European Community, Finland, Germany, Latvia, Lithuania, Poland, Russia, and Sweden.

61 To access the e-meetings, *see* http://sea.helcom.fi/discussion.

nature, however, could hardly provide guidance for authorities on the actual matters of water management. Questionnaires could be designed in a manner that elicits canned responses to expected questions. Questionnaires could be used as a way to validate actions already taken by authorities or as yet another item to check off a to-do-list so that authorities confirm their images as participatory bodies. Questionnaires functioning as confirmation devices are of dubious value for the pursuit of integrated water management.

It is still quite early to confer final conclusions on the role of the observer status that some NGOs have acquired and how the attainment of such a status has influenced the work of international commissions. No reports are available on how stakeholder consultation has altered the course of decisionmaking in a commission or on how it has complemented already developed decisionmaking. Unless some formal reports are issued on the role of stakeholders in the deliberations of international commissions and how that role has influenced the workings of commissions, the contributions made by stakeholders will remain unclear to a third-party observer.

Another metric that could be used to gauge the success of consultation has to do with inclusiveness—that is, the diversity of the stakeholder pool that a commission calls upon for consultation. A safe presumption could be made that an understanding of an international commission as a decisionmaking body will increase the general interest in the work of the commission. On the other hand, if commissions were seen as purely coordinating bodies of decisions already taken at the national or EU levels then stakeholders would be better off to concentrate their efforts on those levels. Environmental NGOs were some of the first organizations to show interest and join in the work of international commissions. The interest of industry and agriculture is still quite tepid. Some EU-wide business associations have acquired observer status in some commissions, but they are not involved in active consultation. Agricultural organizations are almost absent in the deliberations of international commissions.

The lack of diversity in participation has less to do with the efforts of commissions to attract diverse actors and more to do with the agendas of such actors. Many EU-wide associations view the international commissions as merely coordinating bodies with the real power residing in the hands of the EU and member states. Such associations believe that it is more helpful to be involved in consultations at the EU level and leave it to their member organizations to engage national governments. In most cases, lack of participation has to do with a lack of appreciation for the decisions taken at the international level and how these decisions can affect local matters.

Whether stakeholder consultation will evolve into participation in terms of codecision could be debated. At this point, most international commissions have focused on processes that strengthen the provision of information and the execution of effective consultation. Making stakeholders formal codeciders in international processes is tantamount to the emergence of power-sharing between the nation-state and various NGOs. This power-sharing paradigm has yet to be attempted and for good reasons. These reasons have to do with the legitimacy of various groups that claim to represent various strands of public interest.[62] The issue of NGO accountability can present problems under international law as NGOs are usually funded by private donors and are frequently not subject to extensive disclosure requirements that are applicable to public institutions.

The participation of the general public is not actively pursued by international commissions. This is because of the nature of the work of the commissions and the mechanisms of accountability that are present in the work of international bodies. International commissions have not been voted into office by democratic election processes, as such processes apply to the election of national governments. They are, instead, examples of delegated forms of authority. National governments—democratically elected in Europe make a conscious choice to delegate some of their assigned authority to international commissions for the management of shared waters. Therefore, international commissions are not accountable to the public, but to the states that have established them. Each of these states, in turn, is accountable to its own public for the authority it has delegated to international institutions.

There is not a democratic system in the world that does not function through some form of delegation of authority.[63] Accountability in a delegation model means that those who delegate authority can evaluate whether that authority has been used properly and can impose sanctions if there is an abuse of authority. Under a representative democracy system,

62 Ruth W. Grant and Robert O. Keohane, *Accountability and Abuses of Power in World Politics*, 99(1) American Political Science Review 1, Feb. 2005.

63 *Id.*

government officials are accountable to the electorate and sanctions are realized by voting them out of office. In delegation models of international institution-making, sanctions are imposed by states in the form of withdrawal of funding, demands for top officials to resign, and pressures that may lead to a final loss of legitimacy of an international organization.

Despite the fact that international institutions are conceived under a delegation model of accountability, they have often been reproved for not being democratic enough because of lack of participatory processes. The World Bank and the World Trade Organization have been derided frequently as closed organizations that do not allow for participative policymaking by various NGOs that conceive themselves as stakeholders in the outcomes of international organizations. The fact that international organizations derive their power from the delegation of authority executed by states has not altered a general conviction that the participatory process is the appropriate means for democratizing the international sphere.

In addition to stressing their character as institutions of delegated power granted by the nation state, international institutions have attempted to enshrine participative processes into their decisionmaking structure. The World Bank often speaks of the need to empower people who experience poverty[64] and the international water commissions, examined in this study, have been struggling with the development of methods for the inclusion of stakeholders in their processes.

Most international commissions provide adequate information, have established a consultative process and, in general, are encouraging participation of stakeholders in their deliberations. Creating conditions for participation, though, is not an easy task. Good will on the part of the commissions is not always sufficient. The question is whether all efforts—stakeholder conferences, symposia and observer opportunities—generate perceptions that the relevant information is indeed shared, that the consultation process is meaningful and has some impact on decisionmaking.

Another problem with participation is that international policymaking rarely does occur in open and formal fora but, instead, is often shaped in the "corridors" of international meetings. There is a fear, in other words, that the quest for transparency in international fora will move actual deliberation further into the corridors or even into harder to penetrate internal discussion fora that are today available through electronic mail.

64 *Id.*

To take an example from the local experience: The state of New Jersey in the United States has enacted the Open Public Meetings Act, called the Sunshine law, that mandates that all meetings of public institutions should be open to the public. The public in the West Windsor Township of New Jersey has complained that the council of West Windsor has been using the email to discuss important matters, which could be construed as a closed-door deliberation in violation of the Sunshine law. As a result of the public's complaints, the West Windsor council has decided to set guidelines for email use.[65]

Language Politics

The choice of working language is not always presented as an issue in international institutional development. Language, however, has to do with communication, and communication is the essence of international cooperation. Most international agreements provide that the official languages to be used in the execution of the agreements are the languages of state parties. This has been the prevailing practice in the European Union, an organization based on international treaties in which twenty-three languages are the official languages. However, since negotiations and bargaining do not necessarily happen at official conference meetings that provide with the possibility of simultaneous translation, a common language is *de facto* established. This language is increasingly English.

Most international treaties examined in this chapter have established, as official languages, the languages of state parties except for the DRPC that has established as official languages English and German.[66] The Sava Agreement provides diplomatically for the use of state parties' language but also for the use of other languages if necessary.[67] The website of the Sava Commission provides information in the languages of state parties and in English. The official languages used at the Scheldt and the Meuse Commission's websites are the languages of the contracting parties. The Scaldit project, however, that was financed by the INTERREG and had to do with the first phase of implementation of the WFD used English

65 Molly Petrilla, *WW Council will Set Guidelines for E-mail Use*, Princeton Packet, Jan. 16, 2007.

66 Art. 13, *Statute of the International Commission for the Protection of the Danube River, Annex IV, Convention on Cooperation for the Protection and Sustainable Use of the Danube River (Danube River Protection Convention)*, June 29, 1994 available online at http://www.icpdr.org/icpdr-pages/drpc.htm.

67 Art. 8, *Statute of the International Sava River Basin Commission, Annex I* of the *Framework Agreement on the Sava River Basin, supra* note 32.

(in addition to French and Dutch) at its website. The ICPR has used English as an alternative language on its website, despite the fact that English is not an official language of the ICPR. Other commissions have followed the path of providing information in English in addition to the official languages.

If, indeed, English is the language mostly learned as second language and the language that is mostly used in international institutions the question is why it is not made the official "international language," and instead, a huge amount of resources is spent on translation services.[68] The answer has as much to do with the realities of institutional development as with politics. In terms of politics, it would have helped if English were not the mother tongue of certain nations. The division of speakers of English into those with an advantage of being native speakers and into those with, consequently, a disadvantage of being nonnative speakers creates a fundamental inequity in international discourse.[69] This fundamental inequity is witnessed by anyone who has attended an international conference where, in the absence of translation services, speakers who speak English with foreign accents are often inaudible. It would have helped if some native English speakers were not rodomont that their native tongue is the language of choice in international fora.[70] The endorsement of English as the official language at the ICPDR has been viewed by some as a cultural victory. The pragmatics of communication in a multilateral forum where most parties speak a different national language militate, though, for the use of a common "neutral" language.

English is usually advanced as the language of choice in international fora, based on a belief that most people, especially those who work for ministries and government agencies, have a working knowledge of English. This may be a correct assumption for civil servants who are selected to attend international meetings. It is not always true, though, for all the people who staff the national administrative apparatus holding key positions. Most people who work in national administrations have a knowledge of English that may be superficial and not detailed enough to assist in understanding a technical document written in English. If international negotiators go back to their national administration with a

68 For some interesting insights on language policy in Europe, *see* Robert Phillipson, *English-Only Europe? Challenging Language Policy* (2003).

69 *Id.* at 40.

70 *Id.* at 41, 70–96.

technical proposal drafted in a foreign language, the swift adoption of that proposal cannot be realistically expected. This is because of the additional transaction costs of translation that are necessary before application.

The use of English in transnational fora will not banish the costs of translation. It is just that translation will be executed at the national level rather than at the international level. A case in point is the EU in which, with successive enlargements, the number of official languages has grown significantly. Thus, although all official documents are translated in all languages, many of the unofficial documents—not published in the official journal—are often issued in a couple of languages. The guidance documents issued for the implementation of the WFD were drafted only in English causing consternation in some circles that the documents will not reach local water managers. Another case involves the European Court of Justice. Many have argued persuasively that the court would not have had the influence that it has today on national juridical fora, if its decisions were not translated into the national languages of all member states.

Chapter 23

International Water Authorities and the Role of Secretariats

International Water Commissions: From Coordinating Bodies to Water Authorities?

In evaluating the work of international commissions, the question is whether the international commissions will evolve into institutions akin to international water agencies or will remain platforms of coordination for the implementation of the water framework directive (WFD). In other words, will the commissions remain frameworks through which member states pursue their goals and disparate interests or will they develop an independent capacity to shape transnational policy?

The implementation of the WFD has strengthened the role of international commissions. The implementation of the WFD at the river basin cannot be achieved just by having state parties coordinating decisions that they have already made unilaterally. This would create duplication of effort or, even worse, lapses, and lacunae in implementation. The codecision of state parties with regard to what must get accomplished in a basin will be a prerequisite for action.

It could be argued that this is what the commissions have been doing all along since they have been issuing decisions and recommendations by consensus of state parties. And this is true to some extent. However, the decisions and recommendations addressed issues in a somewhat fragmented manner—one polluting sector at time. Decisions and recommendations concentrated on pollution and did not extent to hydromorphological alterations of a river that can be created through the construction of dams, flood protection devices, or hydropower facilities. Hydromorphological alterations are caused by development projects that require financing and investment. Putting such projects under the preview of the international water commissions can be accomplished through the WFD. The treaties that have established some of these international commissions provide that the commissions could regulate only the polluting aspects of navigation. Since the commissions are now officially the coordinating platforms for the WFD implementation, placing hydromorphological alterations under the regulatory ambit of the commissions cannot be avoided forever.

Navigation and environmental protection are, in principle, antithetical goals. It is probably unrealistic to maintain that both can be executed simultaneously with the same fervor. Opening up more routes for navigation in the Danube River would mean the deepening of the river with some environmental repercussions that are undesirable. One could conceive the ICPDR as a regulatory body that puts some constraints on navigation in order to serve the goal of environmental protection. Such constraints currently do not exist but the ICPDR is certainly willing to pursue them in the future. Already the ICPDR has engaged with the Danube Commission to find common modes of operation.[71] It would be interesting to see whether the much-discussed amendments of the 1948 Danube Navigation Convention would include requirements that set some environmental parameters on navigation.

Having two institutions, namely, the Danube Commission and the International Commission for the Protection of the Danube River,

[71] *See* ICPDR Press Release, Apr. 25, 2007 on a common policymaking process with the goal to reach guiding principles and criteria for a *Joint Statement on the Development of Inland, Navigation and Environmental Sustainability in the Danube River Basin*, available online http://www.icpdr.org/icpdr-pages/pr20070425_navigation_process.htm. The Joint Statement on Guiding Principles for Development of Inland Navigation and Environmental Protection in the Danube River Basin was adopted on March 11, 2008.

simultaneously involved in the evolution of the Danube regime may eventually be beneficial. The give and take between the commissions, provided they find a common *modus operandi*, could facilitate the development of a regime for sustainable navigation. It seems that the Danubian countries are set on the liberalization of trade and the development of inland navigation. The development of seamless waterways connecting the North Sea with the Black Sea certainly promotes the concept of European integration. On the other hand, the adoption of the WFD and the transformation of the ICPDR into a coordinating body of the WFD provide the ICPDR with some authority to set the parameters of navigation. Having said that, one cannot sideline the fact that the two commissions are separate institutional developments—not subordinate to each other. As such the navigation commission is not legally bound by the recommendations of the ICPDR. Ignoring them, on the other hand, is not an option as it would just demonstrate plain incoherence in the policies of states most of which are members of both commissions.

For those who believe that international organizations are fictions through which state politics are played, international commissions are nothing more than their constitutive parts, namely, the states, the members of the commissions. These state parties often send their ministries of environment to ICPDR and their ministries of transport and finance to the Danube Commission. Cooperation then at the national level between the Ministries of Transport and the Ministries of Environment is becoming essential to avoid looking incoherent at the international scale. Whether such cooperation will be forthcoming is not clear at present. One must not overlook that for most countries in the region, development is a priority.

The bifurcated functions of the Sava Commission, which are navigation and environmental protection, are bound to generate some institutional confusion. What motivated the establishment of the Sava Commission was the restoration of inland navigation for the whole Sava River, that was disrupted during the war. The protocol on the inland navigation regime was adopted simultaneously with the agreement that established the Sava Commission, underlining that development is a priority for the countries in the region.

The traditional separation of navigation from environmental protection—a paradigm that has been followed in the Danube and the Rhine—was not adopted for the Sava River. This paradigm of division of functions between two commissions—one devoted to environmental protection and the other focused on navigation—is due to historical evolution rather than deliberate decisionmaking. Whether the Sava paradigm will prove more successful than the "division of functions" model remains to be seen.

Needless to say, a lot of what will happen in various regions examined in this section depends on political will. This political will is expressed by the annual gatherings of state parties (COPs) the purpose of which is to define the future of international water commissions. The political will is translated further in the day-to-day work of commissions through the various coordinating and working groups that have been established. Political will can be transmitted through the mandates given to secretariats and how secretariats are to use these mandates to further the mission of the convention they have been entrusted to serve.

International Secretariats: Setting the Agenda of International Policymaking

The role of secretariats in the evolution of international law has remained obscure to the point that some have called international secretariats the invisible governance.[72] Secretariats are viewed as bodies that have to deal with the logistics of running an international treaty—setting the agenda of the meetings, providing the necessary documentation to all parties, and facilitating communication among state parties. Secretariats are not conceived as decisionmaking bodies and, under a best-case scenario, they assume and execute competently the role of administrators maintaining their impartiality as they deal with various international actors.

Conceiving secretariats, though, solely as administrators would do injustice to the role that some secretariats have played in the furtherance of mission of many conventions, especially international environmental conventions. There is a misconception about the role of an administrator that she or he is usually conceived as the operator of mandates received from above. As experienced negotiators know, those who are able to set the agenda of a meeting are often those that define the direction of that meeting. Administration and policymaking are not diametrically disconnected roles in that it requires an experienced policymaker to conduct

[72] John Mathiason, *Invisible Governance: International Secretariats in Global Politics* (2007).

effective administration. Secretariats are after all the bodies that know all state actors and provide the first point of contact with various NGOs.

For a secretariat to become more than a logistical operator, it needs to acquire legitimacy, in other words, respect for its impartiality and objectivity by state parties and to slowly establish a track record that would demonstrate its accomplishments. In this respect, the leadership qualities of the secretary-general are central. The secretary general (or executive secretary) has to be resourceful and build networks among the various actors without ceding to any interest (of a state or an NGO). The executive secretary protects the mission of the convention from being captured by a coalition of states or stakeholders. The executive secretary needs strong administrative skills to assist in the development of a network organization that will move forward the international regime based on a convention.

For a convention to work, there must be a partnership between the plenary assembly (or conference of the parties) and the secretariat. For this to be achieved, the secretariat must demonstrate consistently competence and impartiality. The plenary assembly, on its part, must take measures to support state party capacity, to mediate issues among parties and to nudge those with no will or no way along the way.

The secretariats of the international water commissions examined here have been given modest roles if one takes into account the agreements *per se* and the rules of procedure that have followed the adoption of international agreements.[73] The secretariats of international commissions operate with small staffs[74] and limited budgets. It is good news, though, that the international regimes provide for a secretary general (or executive

[73] According to the rules of procedure of the ICPDR, the executive secretary is the executive official for the international commission. He is responsible to the commission for the administration of the secretariat and he is responsible for the compilation of the annual budget, *see* Section 9, *Rules of Procedure of the ICPDR*, rev2–FINAL, IC/002, Nov. 28, 2002.
Article 18 of the Framework Agreement on the Sava River Basin refers to the establishment of a secretariat run by a secretary and three deputies, *see Framework Agreement on the Sava River Basin*, Dec. 3, 2002 available online http://www.savacommission.org.
According to Section 7 of Rules of Procedure and Financial Regulations of the ICPR, the secretariat carries out tasks with which the commission entrusts it and preserves neutrality, *see Rules of Procedure and Financial Regulations of the ICPR*, Decision of the 70th plenary assembly of the ICPR, Bern, July 8/9, 2004.

[74] For instance, the ICPDR Secretariat has eleven staff members. The ICPR Secretariat has thirteen staff members. The Sava Secretariat has been provided with fifteen members, *see Decision of the Sava River Basin Commission on its First Session on the Main Functions, Structure of the Secretariat and Job Description*, June 27–29, 2005. The Secretariat for the International Scheldt Commission has four members.

secretary) who has a long enough mandate that could allow for the building of a legacy for both the secretariat and the commission that it serves. Secretaries-general of international commissions are preoccupied with the question of how to add value to the work of state parties and are keen on demonstrating how a multilateral forum is preferable to *ad hoc* diplomacy. The "how we add value" question[75] is a pivotal question to ask if secretariats and the commissions they serve are to find innovative ways to go beyond conflict and to devise solutions that would be acceptable to all parties. It is similarly important for a secretariat not to antagonize state parties, especially state parties that are rediscovering statehood, by underlining that a commission is, after all, the sum of wills of state parties, while knowing fully well that the sum of wills has often a will of its own.

International water commissions should acquire significant authority in water management simply because it is at the international scale where tradeoffs are to be made for the future development and protection of a transboundary river basin. How the international commissions will be structured is, therefore, important. Most commissions have been restructured and their new structure coincides with the structure that is necessary for the implementation of the WFD. Most commissions have established a planning group in charge of preparation of an international river basin management plan exemplifying that the commissions' function will not any longer consist of *ad hoc* decisions and recommendations but of river basin planning. River basin management plans for international river basin districts cannot be the aggregation of national plans or subdistrict plans as they are put together unilaterally or bilaterally. An international plan cannot be the accumulation of national plans because such plans may be conflicting or simply incongruent with each other. This is the reason why a parallel process through which there is constant cross-checking between the national and the international level is becoming increasingly necessary. The development of parallel planning processes at the national and international levels with feedback loops and crosschecking points at critical junctures may achieve the goals of integrated water resources management as mandated by the WFD.

75 I owe this insight to Mr. Lefébure, Secretary-General of the International Scheldt Commission.

Part Six

Anticipating the Future

Chapter 24

Sketches from National and Transnational Experience

Learning from the Veterans: the Australian Experience

Can lessons learned from practicing integrated water resources management (IWRM) be transferred from country to country (or even from region to region)? Or is integrated water management tailored to the circumstances of each country and not much can be learned by comparing experiences?

To answer the question, I will transgress a bit and use the Australian experience as a benchmark for measuring European Union (EU) performance. The Murray-Darling Commission (MDC) in Australia has been projected as a good illustration of IWRM. The Murray-Darling Commission was born out of an agreement of states that make the commonwealth of Australia to establish a common commission to manage their shared rivers—namely, Murray and Darling. Australia has a federal system of government in which, while the commonwealth, the federal government, retains most of the financial resources, many of its decisions could be blocked by the states.[1]

The arrangements to establish a river commission for the Murray-Darling started as early as in 1914 and, by the 1980s, the Murray-Darling River Basin was already managed by a full-blown organizational structure comprised of the Murray-Darling Basin Council, the Murray-Darling Basin Commission, and the Murray-Darling Advisory Committee. The Murray-Darling arrangement is emblematic of the integrated water management organization found in national and transnational river basins, including those of Europe. This organization typically involves a decisionmaking body (council, plenary assembly, conference of parties), an everyday coordinating and executing body (commission), and an advisory forum of stakeholders.[2]

Given that IWRM is implemented through what seems to be a well-organized structure, the question is what went wrong to prompt the federal government to propose in 2007 to invest A$10 billion to reform rural water management and to take control of the Murray-Darling basin?[3] Such federal control, if it happens, will declare the end of river basin management as now executed by the states through the Murray-Darling Commission.

A drought that has gripped southern Australia has become one of the most formidable challenges facing the Murray-Darling Commission. The drought conditions are expected to worsen due to climate change and are undermining the institutional understanding on which the Murray-Darling Commission is based. It is not that the commission was not confronted with challenges before. There have been severe environmental issues, including the increasing salinity of water supplies. The conditions of drought, though, have recast these issues into a new light due to the pressure exerted by water scarcity.

To their credit, the states that make the commission have decided to deal with the drought by placing a limit, a cap, on water withdrawals from the basin. The cap is voluntary, though, and states have not enforced the cap vigorously when under pressure from special interests, especially

---

1 *See* Daniel Connell, *Water Politics in the Murray-Darling Basin* 180 (2007).

2 *Id.* at 16. *See also* William Blomquist *et al.*, *Institutional and Policy Analysis of River Basin Management: The Murray Darling River Basin in Australia*, World Bank Research Working Paper 3527, Feb. 2005 available online http://econ.worldbank.org.

3 *Australia's Water Shortage: The Big Dry*, The Economist, Apr. 26, 2007.

farmers who need water for irrigation. What is even worse is that, because of its voluntary nature, failure to comply with the cap does not trigger enforcement action and recalcitrant states may continue to violate the cap they themselves voluntarily adopted. Overall, the lack of quick institutional response to the drought has been blamed on the voluntary character of compliance with the standards set by the commission including the cap on water withdrawals. Given that these standards are adopted by the consensus of states, one would expect a high degree of compliance. Unfortunately, states readily bow to parochial interests when under pressure from such interests.[4]

States, while they have supported the commission as a coordinating arrangement, have consciously refrained from delegating responsibilities to the commission that would allow it to act as an independent body. When having to choose between the forging of an independent commission and the preservation of state autonomy, states have always opted for the latter. The institutional foundations of the commission are exemplary of a coordinating organization rather than an independent body. The commission is based on the following institutional arrangements:

- Unanimous voting that paralyzes decisionmaking;[5]
- Lack of financial independence;[6]
- Appointment of commissioners as representatives of state interests.[7]

Proposals made to revamp the Murray-Darling Commission as an independent body have put forward institutional devices that have been deployed at the EU-wide level to make the EU the independent institution that it is today, namely:

- Doing away with unanimous voting (as much as possible);
- Having commissioners independent of the states that appoint them;
- Securing some degree of financial independence for the commission.

[4] Connell, *supra* note 1, at 125.
[5] *Id.* at 155.
[6] *Id.* at 193.
[7] *Id.* at 190.

Juxtaposing the EU and the Australian Experience

The European Union, as mentioned before, is better understood as a multilevel governance system. Multilevel governance is obvious in river basin management that takes place in a number of levels.

- The EU (federal) level;
- The international level (through the international river basin commissions that are now coordinating authorities for the WFD implementation, but are simultaneously independent organizations based on international treaties);
- The national level (the level that is to coordinate international and subnational river basin arrangements); and
- The subnational level (regions, municipalities, river basin boards).

The Australian experience is particularly instructive as member states of the EU are to cooperate in international river basin districts to apply the WFD. Although member states of the EU have delegated some of their authority to the EU and other international bodies, they remain sovereign and they have the prerogative to withdraw that delegated authority.

Attempts at integrated river basin management have been undermined in Australia by the states of the Australian commonwealth. These states, while they have consented to organize an intergovernmental commission to deal with transboundary water problems, the MDC, have at the same time refrained from providing that commission with sufficient authority to actually execute river basin management.[8] Therefore, the commission functions more as a coordinating body of various states interests rather than as a river basin authority in charge of a river basin district. Furthermore, the fact that decisionmaking is based on the principle of unanimity and that there no rules of procedure on how to prod recalcitrant states to compliance have undermined decisive action urgently needed today to address water scarcity.

Many European river basin commissions functioning today at the international level have become the coordinating bodies in the WFD implementation. The commissions have coordinating functions and are rarely presented as executive bodies in charge of the WFD implementation. The decisionmaking rule in the commissions is predominantly consensus.

---

8 *Id.* at 147, 156.

Furthermore, there are parallel international developments that are still not completely under the control of the EU, such as navigation commissions that have their own procedures and decisionmaking rules. A decision of a navigation commission to deepen a river to accommodate larger ships cannot today be vetoed by a river basin commission. Both the navigation commission and the river basin protection commission are independent international bodies and are not subject to each other's decisionmaking rules. Coordination between a navigation commission and a river basin protection commission may not present obstacles if all state parties to both commissions are also member states of the EU, assuming that transportation and environmental protection policies are well coordinated. Problems arise if some state parties to river basin commissions or navigation commissions are not member states of the EU and could, in fact, be states for which the WFD implementation is not a matter of great urgency.[9] Today, many important decisions for the development of navigation are taken by member states through other fora, in which river basin commissions, now coordinating platforms for the WFD implementation, do not participate.

The commissions have more control over pollution as they were initially conceived as standard-making bodies for polluting activities and each of the commissions issues its share of recommendations and resolutions for controlling pollution. Now these recommendations are to have an obligatory character as they will have to take their cues from the EU legislation on hazardous substances—provided that states parties to the commissions that are not member states of the EU are willing to go along with the WFD implementation.

Another common experience between the European river basin protection commissions and the MDC is that commissioners are appointed to represent state interests and not basin-wide interests. In the MDC the lack of a basin-wide view of the commissioners is exacerbated by the lack of comity—that is good faith and the will to reach mutually beneficial solutions. A certain lack of comity in the context of the MDC is exhibited by an emphasis on managerialism and the rapid turnover of ministers

9 Russia is a member of the Danube Navigation Commission but not an EU member and not a member of the ICPDR. Because of this position and its role as a regional heavyweight, Russia may be less than cooperative in the efforts made to find common discourse points between the Danube Navigation Commission and the ICPDR.

and commissioners.[10] Such lack of comity is not evident at the European river basin commissions; however, it is too early to claim whether state parties will always work hard to find mutually beneficial arrangements, since by 2007 only the preliminary steps of the WFD implementation had been accomplished and decisions on the implementation of environmental standards had yet to be made.

What the European River Basin Commissions have to their advantage is a more formidable enforcement apparatus. The European Commission could bring member states in front of the Court of Justice for violations of the water framework directive (WFD). Such violations could include violations of rules enacted by international commissions (as the rules that a commission issues will have to be in compliance with the WFD) or involve the failure of a member state to collaborate with international river basin commissions, as it is mandatory for member states to engage in international river basin development. Today, even for states parties to international river basin protection commissions, but not simultaneously member states of the EU, the decisions of the commissions, while not mandatory, are often authoritative and international commissions have established procedures to spot and deal with cases of noncompliance. In the case of the ICPR, a number of procedures are provided through which states parties are to report back to the commission on their compliance and on reasons why implementation may have not been that swift. The Sava Agreement establishes a fact-finding committee that is to act as an arbiter when there is a disagreement between the parties.

In addition to sticks, there are carrots. The EU has demonstrated that is more than willing to provide funding to states that are not member states of the EU but whose compliance is necessary for the meaningful application of EU standards. Funding has been provided for the establishment and functioning of the Black Sea Commission and the Sava Commission. And the ICPDR would not have advanced as a decision-making body if it were not for the generous funding of UNDP/GEF, institutions supported financially by the EU.

In the case of Murray-Darling, shortcomings in river basin management have to do with the fact that financial support for water management has been channeled through the states of the commonwealth, rather than through the MDC, the intergovernmental forum that states have put

10 Connell, *supra* note 1, at 196.

in place for the management of transboundary waters. This has weakened the MDC and has strengthened the independence of states that feel comfortable flouting the rules of MDC as federal funding does not depend on their compliance.

The European River basin commissions are functioning based on funding provided by state parties. While withdrawal of such funding may seem improbable at this point one has to note the difficulties of the Sava Commission to get off the ground after the signing of the Sava Agreement. As the European Commission is to further support the implementation of the WFD through regional development projects, it would be interesting to see if some funding for such projects will go directly to international river basin commissions or to member states which support the commissions. As things stand now, funding received from the EU for the further implementation of the WFD goes to member states since states are the responsible unit for implementation. It would be interesting, however, to examine whether providing funding directly to international river basin commissions may be a way to secure a more independent character for these commissions.

Finally coordination at international, national, and subnational levels will take its cue from the coordination between the various Directo-rates-General (DGs) of the European Commission. The Commission is under a mandate to coordinate its policies and to ensure the compatibility of such policies with environmental protection. At the same time, the various DGs of the European Commission have their prerogatives and usually serve sets of interests not always attuned with each other. The Council of Ministers is in essence a multiforum of various councils that address various EU matters from foreign policy to information policy to agricultural affairs. The question then for the various directorates of the European Commission and the Council of Ministers is whether they will be able to foster coordination of policies adopted by different EU institutions. What will be unfortunate is to present a façade of policy coordination at the EU-wide level, while engaging in proxy fights through the different international commissions, bilateral commissions, and other parallel developments that exist out there.

Chapter 25

Towards a Future Water Policy

A question that has preoccupied evolutionary biologists is whether change takes place by evolutionary steps or in evolutionary jumps. In the case of member states of the European Union (EU), for which the implementation of IWRM has been an imposed rather than an endogenous change, the answer has been: Proceed cautiously. Instead of lessons learned from the European experience, as it has been unfolding by the end of 2007, one can find, instead, techniques of coping. Most member states have recognized that integrated water resources management (IWRM) is a necessity for Europe, a continent characterized by many transboundary river basin districts where the management of water resources has been fragmented. On the other hand, states have been reluctant to institute new administrative arrangements and overhaul engrained administrative structures of water management.

Most member states have attempted to concoct a stratagem for the application of IWRM without spiraling out of control institutional development. Therefore, no new institutions have been developed in most states examined here for the implementation of the water framework directive (WFD). Instead, what has happened has been a reorientation of existing institutions to water management at the river basin. Most countries examined in this study have had some form of river basin institutions in place that they decided to keep for the purposes of implementation of the directive. However, by 2007, no much authority was delegated to these institutions. Instead, water management has remained fairly centralized in all states examined in this study. This persistent centralization is useful as states need to better organize water management especially when such management has been fragmented and conducted by various ministries, departments, national, and subnational institutions in various centralized and decentralized fora.

Member states have demonstrated more innovation in transnational fora where a number of states have made clear that the international river basin district is *the river basin district*. At the same time, states have engaged in multiple parallel bilateral developments to arrange issues of water quantity and to address localized pollution problems. Many bilateral arrangements today coexist with multilateral agreements and, while bilateralism is useful in addressing specific issues at transboundary areas, it is unclear whether there is much coordination between the multilateral enterprise and the bilateral happenings. It would probably make sense to make the river basin commissions the focal points of international activities that are taking place today in too many different fora, not in order to avoid duplication of effort, that may sometimes be desirable, but in order to keep the information flow that would allow for more coherent transgovernmental developments.

With regard to public participation, environmental groups have been disappointed by the stylized structure of public participation bodies, which are inundated with government agencies and water users, and in which environmental NGOs usually do not hold but one seat. For water ministries and water managers, though, overloading river basin bodies with public agencies and other governmental institutions, whose acquiescence is essential for the go ahead of river basin management plans, is an institutional necessity. The on-the-ground success of river basin management is dependent on the number of institutional veto players and the amount of resistance exerted by players for whom the implementation of the WFD is not a priority. Unless government institutions addressing water resources coordinate their action, the institutional congestion in the field of water management could bring such management to a grinding halt.

Advantages of Centralization

Counterintuitively, the European experience with integrated water resources management (IWRM) is that of centralization rather than decentralization. Member states that make an international river basin district have decided to view the international river basin district as *the district* for the purposes of WFD implementation. This international river basin district has then been divided further into bilateral/trilateral/national working areas so as to facilitate coordination.

One of the primary advantages of the WFD implementation is that it has forced states to work within the shared river basin district and, thus, to start to organize water management in a way that takes into account upstream and downstream externalities. On the national level, states examined in this study have been reluctant to release central control over water management. This has to do with the fact that the WFD is a new sweeping legislation, and it is unclear whether river basin bodies or local institutions are able to grapple with the complex oeuvre of implementation. Furthermore, given the amount of coordination required at the international level, including the EU reporting requirements, entrusting implementation to local institutions, not experienced in water management, might have not worked well in states with minimal experience in decentralization. Therefore, water management may have changed hands, since most states assigned water management to ministries of environment, but central control over such management endured all through 2007. A number of states, Greece in this study, created new centralized water agencies the purpose of which is to focus single-handedly on the implementation of the WFD. Other countries have tried to revamp older structures into planning bodies for the WFD implementation.

Emphasis on centralization is justified also because of the number of regional institutions involved in water management. In situations where fragmentation is, in essence, dysfunctional decentralization, a refocused centralization based on the precepts of IWRM may produce the potential for future devolution of authority. For most states examined here, centralization is viewed as a temporary necessary evil, and there is aspiration that future IWRM will be more decentralized. This aspiration is not unfounded, given the number of transgovernmental communications that have been established in some parts of Europe between neighboring river boards and water directorates. Member states have vowed that, after the first planning cycle of RBMPs, they will be more willing to rebalance the benefits and costs of devolution of river basin management to regional river boards and/or appropriate administrative authorities. It remains to be seen whether this will happen, given an ingrained propensity to centralize in Europe.

Multilevel Coordination

Coordination is the devil of implementation of IWRM. As many have noted, though, asking organizations to coordinate is tantamount to an empty request. How to coordinate is, instead, the real question. The centralization and decentralization of water management institutions, furthermore, cannot be seen as a value in itself and has to be viewed within general framework of coordination that involves the interaction between central institutions and decentralized entities, taking into account the international dynamics of coordination. As underlined in Chapter 2, the WFD, as much as it supports decentralization of water management at the river basin district level, also champions centralization of water management at the international river basin scale.

Coordination in water management at the EU has to be understood within the paradigm of multilevel governance and the ensuing complexity of coordination among multilevels. The interaction among these levels—the EU, international, national, regional and local—could make the application of the WFD nothing short of an administrative ordeal as horizontal and vertical linkages among all administrative levels have to be established to produce coherent prescriptions in water management. The understanding of dynamics of functioning of multilevel governance is often missed in studies that concentrate on the development of river basin districts at the national level. Such studies do not stress enough the point that, at least, in the European context, it is not so much the prescription of national river basin districts that would make the directive work but the effective functioning of national coordinating arrangements within the scope of international river basin districts. Since the ultimate river basin district is the international river basin district, one has to focus on the effectiveness of institutional arrangements states put in place that facilitate the functioning of the international river basin district. Whether these arrangements are hydrographic or administrative at the domestic level is not so much the point as whether they are coordinated effectively and have been able to work cooperatively with their counterparts in neighboring states.

The EU is first in the hierarchy of river basin management since the mere fact of the adoption of the WFD at the EU level is fundamentally changing the dynamics of water management in all subsequent sublevels. The international commissions that were in place, before the adoption of the WFD, have been operating in parallel with the EU institutions. International commissions used to adopt decisions and recommendations based on the prerogatives of state parties and not of those of the EU legislation. This obviously created some inconsistencies as different regulations applied at the international level for state parties to a treaty who were simultaneously members of the European Community and had to transpose EU regulations.

With the adoption of the WFD and the transformation of international commissions into platforms for the WFD implementation, the job of the international commissions is transformed to that of application of EU rulemaking. The WFD could, thus, be perceived now as the organizing legislation for the international commissions that are becoming subordinated to the EU prerogative. Although before the adoption of the WFD, the EU level and the international level used to function as parallel processes, today these processes have met in order to fulfill the requirements of the WFD. Not only have they met, but also, for the international water commissions, the EU is now the ultimate umpire of decisions made at the international level. This transformation of international water commissions into water agencies of the EU could not have happened without the acquiescence of states that are nonmember states of the EU, but nevertheless aspire to future membership or of states that would not like to be viewed as spoilers of EU policies.

The state and its centralized authorities have remained important factors in the WFD implementation, especially in the unitary states of Europe. Whether this is a lasting phenomenon probably depends on the state concerned and has to do with a number of considerations including a state's size, its overall governance regime (that may favor or disfavor decentralization) and the quality of governing structures (so that corruption is not a paramount concern). In federal states and states that are more decentralized (such as Germany, France, Spain), decentralized structures already play an important role in the WFD implementation. In the Meuse

River Basin, for instance, the roof report is replete with the regional agencies that are in charge of implementation.

Maintaining central control in water management may make sense for new member states as these states are trying to disentangle newer and older administrative arrangements. In the future, though, more decentralized structures have to be invested with the authority to make decisions that are more appropriate for the catchment and subcatchment levels. The nitty-gritty details of implementation cannot be prescribed at the international and national level. But the quality of on-the-ground implementation lies in these details. River basin boards or catchment directorates can be vested with the authority and resources to address local water management problems, as they emerge, without having to always go through central channels. This can be achieved when all IWRM institutions are familiar with their role in the implementation of the RBMPs as they are articulated at the international, national, and regional levels.

The role of local and regional authorities has been intensifying in many international river basin districts. From the roof reports that are available countries have designated local and regional authorities and river boards as the competent authorities for the WFD implementation, often additionally to central actors. Local and regional involvement in transnational commissions, and especially in the work of bilateral commissions, is not an entirely new development and it is likely to become more prominent in the future. Because of their increasing prominence in international relations, local and regional authorities have to demonstrate more sophistication in international matters and the ability to place local issues within the context of international developments. Water management is to buttress the phenomenon of transgovernmentalism where cooperation is not effectuated only between foreign ministries but extends to other branches of government at the national and subnational levels, for instance, between ministries in charge of water management, between water agencies, between water directorates, and even between neighboring municipalities.

Parallel Coordinating Processes

Coordination is not always a top-down process undertaken if a public institution assumes the role of coordinator while the remainder of institutions is willing to be coordinated. Coordination, instead, could be accomplished when parallel processes are at work through which various institutions plan simultaneously for water management.

Parallel coordination processes have been designated in the Netherlands and the United Kingdom to address the implementation of the WFD. This is because of the tight schedule of implementation of the WFD that makes it difficult for decisions to be made at the central level, first, and then for these decisions to trickle down and to be tailored to the regional and local levels. Instead, all levels must work in a parallel, synchronized fashion since they are working towards the common goal of WFD implementation. In the United Kingdom, this parallel process of implementation takes place between the different levels—the central level, the river basin district level, the catchment level, and the water body level. The idea behind this parallel coordinating system is for central authorities to work for the fulfillment of a strategic direction while catchment authorities are working on the development of catchment plans. The expectation is that concerns at the catchment level will feed into the river district level while the catchment plan will have to follow the general strategic direction of river basin district plan. What facilitates this sort of coordination between the central level and the catchment level is that the United Kingdom Environment Agency is in charge of implementation (through its central and district offices) at all levels.

In the Netherlands, parallel processes that work at different levels (national, provincial, waterboards, municipalities) are brought together through specific coordinating institutions that include representation of all bodies that have a role in river basin management. The Netherlands has a highly structured system of coordination as new river basin authorities have not been prescribed for river basin management and traditional authorities are to coordinate with each other to effectuate the implementation of the WFD.

Parallel coordinating processes have been established between the international and the national level. In the Danube River basin district, the compilation of roof (part *A*) report took place in parallel with the compilation of national (part *B*) reports. As international river basin management plans are now being prepared in various transboundary river basin districts, parallel coordinating processes are the only option. This is because the international plan cannot be just a compilation of national river basin management plans. If states were to independently create RBMPs and then national RBMPs were to be used to make the international river basin management plans (IRBMPs), the outcome will be nothing close to an international planning instrument. Plans developed independently by national authorities are certain to be inconsistent with each other. For instance, although a state may take measures to improve water quality, neighboring states may be less willing to oblige. This is exactly what the WFD is trying to avoid: an inconsistent patchwork of national instruments that are a cause of frustration in river basin management. An international river basin management plan cannot be just a compilation of national plans, and a parallel process with constant feedback between the national level and the international level is becoming increasingly necessary.

Parallel coordinating processes cannot function effectively in the absence of feedback loops that allow for constant information flow between what is happening at the local level and what is transpiring at the central level. Because of its complexity, a parallel process of coordination would require a well-developed administrative structure driven by the pursuit of common goals. Parallel process coordination is, in essence, another term for cooperation in the sense that the institutions involved must have a sense of a common mission and a desire to achieve similar goals in water management.

Complexity is a function of the number of institutions involved in water management and the rivalries that may be developed among these institutions. The WFD has proposed that the river basin district should be the organizing unit of water administration. Most states have interpreted this provision to mean that, in ideal circumstances, each river basin district should be managed by a river basin authority. However, in reality, for various reasons, not all countries have subscribed to the river basin authority model and most states have prescribed for coordination of a number of authorities that are active in a river basin district. Although this may make sense at the national level, it could create havoc in international relations if it is unclear which of the coordinating authorities has the power and legitimacy to make decisions in water management in the international arena.

Today, there is still significant confusion about which authorities should coordinate across borders to help design or implement river basin management plans. The same problem is presented when a central authority is designated as the competent authority of implementation but there is a realization that such authority cannot function effectively at the district or catchment level. Similar issues are presented when regional and local water directorates lack the authority and legitimacy to make decisions on local matters. The lack of correspondence between the mission and authority of institutions involved in water management could generate frustration and friction in transnational matters.

Decentralization through Participation

The implementation of the WFD has meant the centralization of water management for many member states of the EU. No matter the degree of central control, however, water management cannot be executed by a single central institution and often a variety of regional and local institutions and agencies have been involved *de facto* in water management. Sidelining such organizations under the prerogative of centralization is not politically savvy since such organizations have often an important role to play for the application of a system of integrated water resources management.[11]

Member states of the EU have been faced with a double challenge: assuming control over water management, in order to reduce current institutional fragmentation, while at the same time avoiding the alienation of local institutions and agencies involved in water management. Thus, although the centralization of water management has remained, a simultaneous effort has been launched to involve local and regional authorities as stakeholders in the promulgation of river basin management plans through the stakeholder participation procedures prescribed by the WFD and transposed into national legislation.

Based on the provisions of consultation with stakeholders, member states have attempted to include local and regional governance organizations, which are involved or have a potential interest in water management, in the administration of such management. For instance, the stakeholder bodies for water management in Romania, the river basin committees, are comprised of:

(1) Two representatives of the Ministry of Environment and Water Management;

---

[11] *See also* Sergio Graf Montero *et al., Collaborative Governance for Sustainable Water Resources Management: the Experience of the Inter-municipal Initiative for the Integrated Management of the Ayuquila River Basin, Mexico,* 18(2) Environment and Urbanization 297 (2006). Montero analyzes the role that associations of municipalities can play in IWRM provided that they have the necessary technical and management capacity, financial resources, and are inspired by the principles of public service.

(2) A representative of the Ministry of Health;
(3) Two municipality mayors and one town or commune mayor;
(4) One prefect nominated by the Ministry for Public Administration;
(5) One president of the County Council;
(6) Two representatives of National Administration, Apele Romane;
(7) One representative of an NGO;
(8) Three representatives of water users within the relevant basin;
(9) One representative of the National Authority for Consumers Protection.

This river basin committee is, in turn, the institution to initiate wider consultation with the public. A stakeholder body like that envisioned in the Romanian water act is not the type of body that somebody will intuitively have in mind when trying to translate the provisions for stakeholder and public participation in river basin management. From the point of view of a water manager, however, it is important that river basin stakeholder committees include local authorities such as mayors of municipalities or regional governors. Municipalities are, after all, the entities that operate in most member states the water supply and sewage systems. Prefect and county authorities are invited to participate to ensure that they are in tune with decisions made at the river basin so that they do not attempt to derail such decisions for the sheer lack of knowledge. Overall, states have tried to include in their consultative mechanisms institutions that, although they are not the primary coordinating bodies for the WFD implementation, could derail such implementation through their action or inaction.

It is unclear how these river basin stakeholder committees will function in the future and whether they will evolve into rubber-stamping bodies or exert some authority in river basin management. One sure thing is that these committees are the mechanisms though which some decentralization in water management can be achieved in the near future as local and regional organizations are granted, at least, a consultative role in river basin developments.

Organization of Participation

A concern that has emerged in many national and international circles is how to ensure the representation of the wider civil society in river basin management. The experience has been that, in many cases, civil society organizations exist but they are too small and not organized enough to address representation at the national and international organization of IWRM.

In the European context, the development of civil society institutions has been simultaneously a bottom-up and a top-down process. The Danube Environmental Forum (DEF), that is playing an important role in the Danube region, is a network of NGOs that is dedicated to the protection of the Danube River and has prospered through funding provided by the UNDP/GEF. The Regional Environmental Center (REC) is another regional environmental organization that has been established through top-down processes—prominent donors including the EU, Japan, the United States and the Netherlands. The Black Sea NGO Network (BSNN) is comprised of about sixty NGO members from all through the Black Sea region and has been receiving funding from the Global Environment Facility (GEF). In the case of the Ribble catchment, the United Kingdom Environment Agency adopted initially a neutral stance with regard to participation but, in later strategic documents, has vowed to adopt a more interventionist role in organizing in-flux groups at the catchment level.

The generous funding for environmental NGOs in eastern and central Europe has not only to do with the promotion of environmental protection but also with the support for democratization in the region. This top-down streamlining of public participation, though, conflicts with perceptions that civil society organizations are the pure outcome of bottom-up processes born out of opposition to a state or to corporate interests that despoil nature. In the case of eastern Europe, the organization of civil society involved, in some cases, heavily funded top-down processes. In other words, the overarching question is: Can a civil society organization deserve its name as a civil society institution when it has been put together by states and receives funding from them? Although the NGOs examined in this study are exhibiting independence in articulating their views and in challenging the state apparatus, they have a sophisticated understanding of the issues that states are faced with due to lack of revenues or other hapless administrative arrangements. This nuanced understanding of problems that states are faced with in trying to apply legislation is not typically exhibited by organizations formed through bottom-up processes that are not recipients of government funding.

Information, Information, Information

The focus in river basin management has been placed on stakeholder consultation and participation. What is lacking in many countries and international institutions, however, is the provision of useable information that could be acted upon to ensure effective public participation. The provision of information ensures that, even if government organizations are not open to participative proceedings, civil society groups could explore other means to air their grievances such the media, campaigns, or other more direct action tactics.

Information and its provision is tricky today in the information age, in which there are many sources of information and, often, the challenge is not the lack of information but the disentanglement of relevant information from the stream of constant information bombardment. The Aarhus Convention has entrusted states with the duty to streamline information for users in easy to use databases and access formats. Some states have taken the provision of information seriously and are willing to provide information on matters not crucial for national security and on issues not considered government secrets. The United Kingdom Environment Agency has promised to provide a website where, after typing one's zip code, one could find all the environmental issues that are affecting one's own immediate living area ('what is my backyard' website). Other states still pursue a policy of secrecy that serves better their interests.[12]

No matter the information readily available and the information provided by states, the function of civil society is to remain skeptical about the information offered through traditional channels and to execute its own fact-finding. This is to guarantee some independence for civil society groups the ultimate function of which is to challenge the state.

The reason IWRM has been given a chance in Europe has to do with the willingness of member states that make the EU to do away with some of their sovereignty in order to strengthen the whole–Europe–viewed as the only viable means to develop an authoritative voice in international society. Europe is an idea that is still evolving since preconceived geographical boundaries are probably poor indicators of the extent of polity that it may be and the depth of integration that may be achieved.

---

[12] *Nuclear Dumps and Nuclear Secrets*, June 25, 2007 available on line http://www.alphabetics.info/international/?p=177.

Member states that make the EU are not equal in power and resources. The EU, nevertheless, is run under a presumption of sovereign equality if one takes into account the make-up of bodies that make the EU and the decisionmaking procedures that have been put in place to ensure that there are not consistent winners in terms of the clout that resources can bring. In addition, a vast amount of resources are expended on weak regions (not states) under schemas based on the motto "nobody should be left behind."

The jury is still out about whether the concept of IWRM will be applied successfully in Europe. What can be said with certainty, though, is that the WFD has put into motion strategic thinking about how to address water management in an integrated fashion in Europe. For member states that had no water policy, the directive has provided the impetus to develop an integrated water policy. For countries that already had a water policy the directive has provided an incentive to examine how their policies could be coordinated with other states' policies on shared river basins.

The implementation of the WFD has not yet led to the adoption of a uniform administrative arrangement common in all member states of the EU. At the international level, however, states could not afford but to organize water management around the international river basin district. The structure of the commissions that manage these international river basin districts seems to be converging to a single standard. A lot needs to be accomplished, though, in terms of the coordination of various international commissions and many feedback loops need to be established between multilateral and bilateral developments.

The reason why the concept of integrated water management is difficult to apply on a transnational scale has to do with the idea of fairness that is embedded in IWRM. Although this fairness is not some abstract version of equity based on a 50/50 sharing of a water resources, it is fairness based on the commonality of interests of states that share a river basin district and rests on the principle that even regional hegemons should refrain from managing water resources unilaterally and must take into account the whole river basin district and the impacts of their activities on other states. This is a revolutionary version of equity for many regions of the world today.[13]

13 For the role of China in the Mekong River basin and how it has affected the work of the Mekong River Basin Commission, *see*, e.g., Katri Makkonen, *Integrated Water Resources*

It is unclear whether the application of the IWRM in Europe can offer much for replication in other regions of the world, because of the lack of fundamental preconditions that are present in the EU but are absent in other areas. Despite the difficulties involved in applying IWRM, IWRM has been adopted by many countries and by international development agencies in many global arenas at least in rhetoric with half-hearted attempts at implementation. The implementation of the WFD is the largest experiment ever conducted on the application of IRBM at the national and transnational scale anywhere in the world. If there is one phrase that can summarize the lessons learnt from the European experience is the importance of the quality of coordinating structures put in place to implement IWRM, as it is unlikely that one institution will be entrusted with water management at all scales. Good coordination seems like an easy recipe to follow. For many parts of the world, including parts of Europe, coordination is still an interesting utopia, hard to relinquish as it is hard not to aspire to a better future.

Management in China 267, in Integrated Water Resources Management in South and South-East Asia (Asit K. Biswas, *et al.*, eds., 2005). For a general notion of equity in river basin management, *see* Elli Louka, *International Environmental Law: Fairness, Effectiveness and World Order* 179 (2006).

Index

www.ingramcontent.com/pod-product-compliance
Ingram Content Group UK Ltd.
Pitfield, Milton Keynes, MK11 3LW, UK
UKHW020850150926
475595UK00003B/107

9 780195 374131